A World of Its Own

Connect the words in alphabetical order.

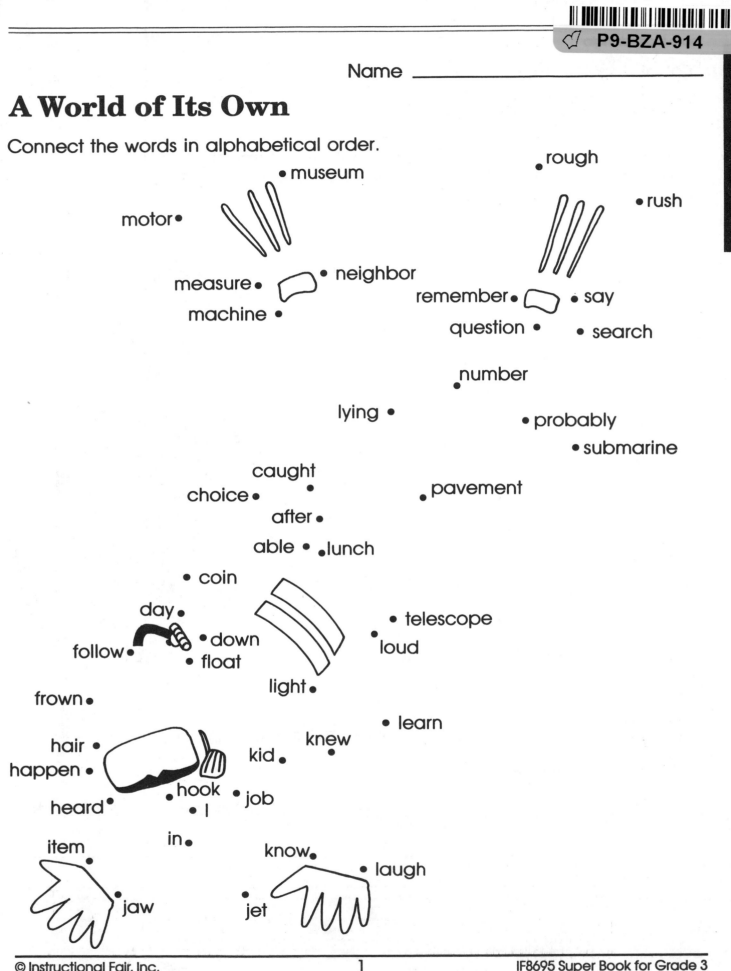

Name _____

What's Your Name?

Column A lists general insect names while **Column B** gives more specific names for the same insects. Number the two columns in ABC order and then answer the questions below.

Column A

___ grasshopper
___ butterfly
___ wasp
___ flea
___ moth
___ fly
___ cricket
___ bee
___ ant
___ beetle

Column B

___ long-horned grasshopper
___ monarch butterfly
___ paper wasp
___ snow flea
___ silk moth
___ housefly
___ tree cricket
___ bumblebee
___ army ant
___ whirligig beetle

1. Does the ABC order change when a more specific insect name is used? _____

2. The insects whose order remained the same in both lists were _____ and _____ .

3. I find _____ insect names more interesting
   (Column A, Column B)

   because _____

   _____ .

Name _____

The Bus Route

This map shows all the stops this bus makes on its route.

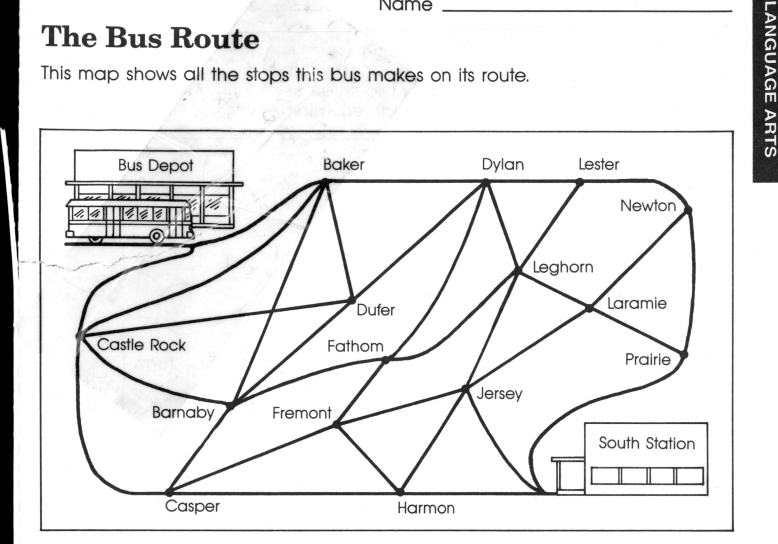

Write the names of the stops in alphabetical order to show the bus route.

1. _____

2. _____

3. _____

4. _____

5. _____

6. _____

7. _____

8. _____

9. _____

10. _____

11. _____

12. _____

13. _____

14. _____

15. _____

• Use a crayon to connect the stops in the order of the bus route.

Name _____

Ouch!

Color the space **orange** if the word has one syllable.
Color the space **blue** if the word has two syllables.
Color the space **black** if the word has three syllables.

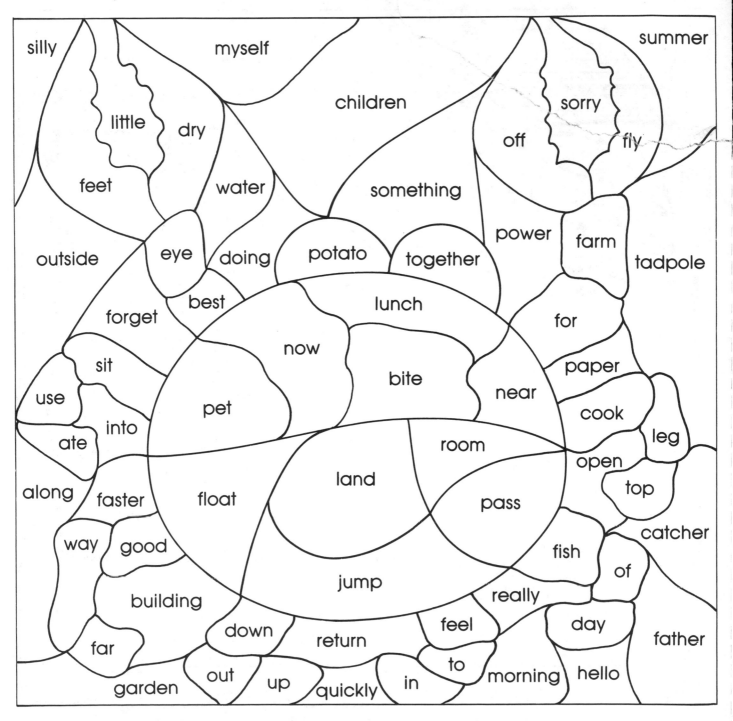

What can make you say ouch? _____

Name _____

Quilting Bee

Ruth and Naomi threaded the needles for the quilters. Follow the code to color the quilt squares.

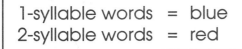

1-syllable words = blue	3-syllable words = green
2-syllable words = red	4-syllable words = yellow

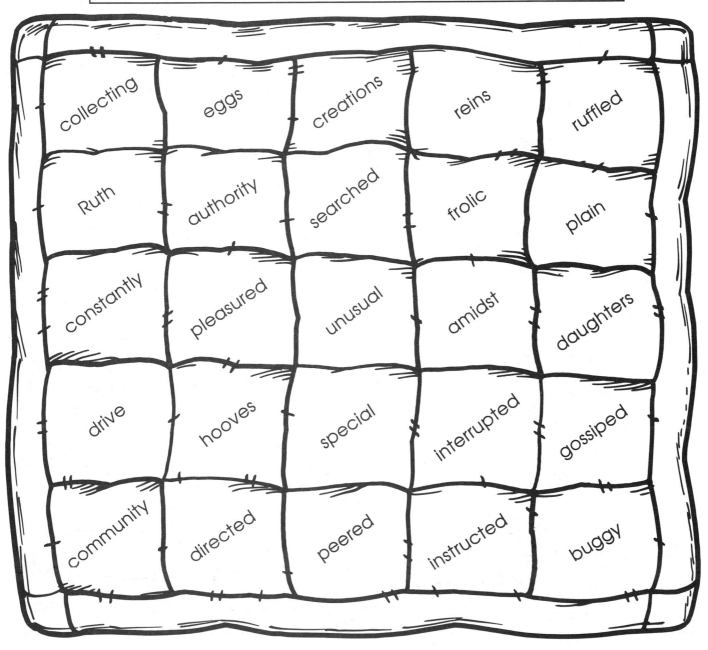

collecting · eggs · creations · reins · ruffled

Ruth · authority · searched · frolic · plain

constantly · pleasured · unusual · amidst · daughters

drive · hooves · special · interrupted · gossiped

community · directed · peered · instructed · buggy

Name _____

Together We Stand

Some insect names are compound words which are made up of two smaller words. Look at each picture and write each insect name. Some words in the Word Bank will be used more than once.

1. _____

2. _____

3. _____

4. _____

5. _____

6. _____

7. _____

8. _____

9. _____

10. _____

Word Bank

bug	worm	butter	honey
fly	bee	hopper	bed
grass	fish	fire	silver
house	lady	glow	dragon

Name _____

Beautiful Butterflies

After the baku devoured Yukio's nightmares, his dreams were pleasant ones of yellow butterflies fanning him on a hot day. If the two words on a butterfly's pair of wings make a compound word, color the butterfly **yellow**. If they do not, put an **X** on the butterfly.

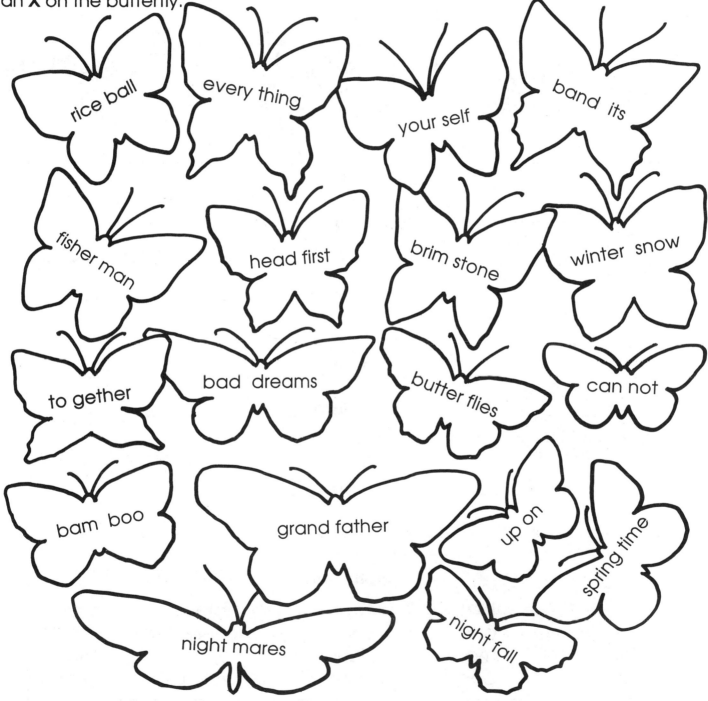

Name _____

Lead or Follow?

Write a word that can be placed in front of the bold-faced word to form a compound word. Then write a word that can follow the bold-faced word to form a second compound word.

Example: __back__   **door**   __knob__

_____ **to** _____

_____ **tree** _____

_____ **path** _____

_____ **line** _____

_____ **noon** _____

_____ **button** _____

_____ **room** _____

_____ **body** _____

_____ **side** _____

_____ **house** _____

Word Bank

up	tow	out	hole	way
swingle	after	on	every	time
clothes	mate	lunch	top	belly
night	boat	doll	walk	guard

Name _____

Brother Eagle, Sister Sky

Eagle has a long **e** sound. **Sky** has a long **i** sound. Cut out and glue the words below the picture with the matching vowel sound.

Brother Eagle

Sister Sky

brief	buy	delay	dessert	drive	style
dye	easy	eye	fright	giant	stream
cry	knees	leaf	lion	private	regal

Name _____

The Money Box

When Xiao Sheng put the pearl in the money box with its one remaining coin, the coin multiplied and the box brimmed over with gold coins.
Cut out and glue the coins that have the same vowel sound as **coin** in and around the money box.

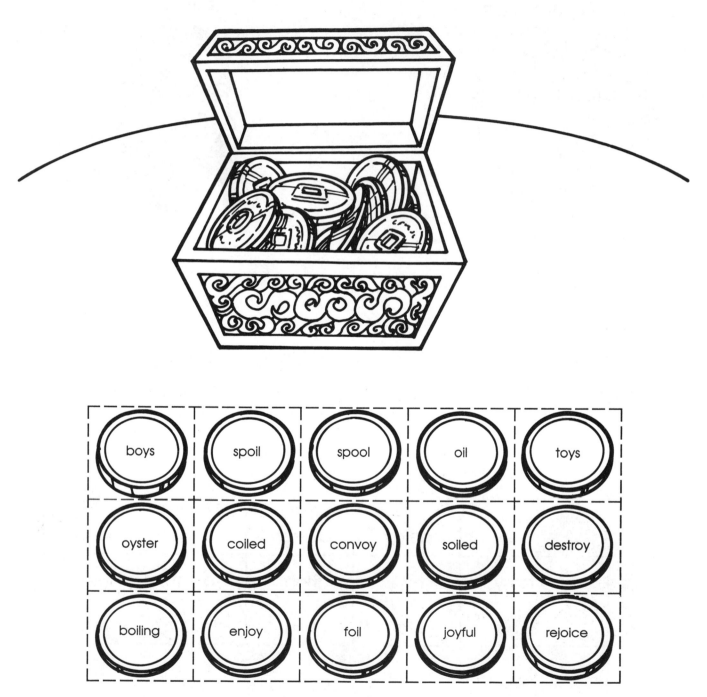

boys	spoil	spool	oil	toys
oyster	coiled	convoy	soiled	destroy
boiling	enjoy	foil	joyful	rejoice

Name _____

Phonics Fun

Help Richard with his phonics by following these directions.

Circle the short a words in black.
Underline the short i words in pink.
Put a red box around the short e words.
Draw an olive green X over the short o words.
Draw a green line over the long e words.
Draw a wavy gray line over the long a words.
Put a white X over the long i words.
Draw a gold circle around the long o words.

Beast	Drake	plane
Holly	Hansel	kids
Kettle	teacher	Noah
Matthew	banner	Mancina
stage	best	
Richard	wished	liar
smell	smile	top
Gretel	fig	piece
Polk	class	stop

Name _____

The Puzzling Printout

Professor Gizmo built his own computer. But sometimes the professor was a little absent-minded, and he would push the wrong buttons. Today he printed some "Funny Food Facts."

Read each silly sentence. Cross out the noun that doesn't make sense. Find a noun in another sentence that fits but still makes a silly sentence. Write it over the crossed-off word. The first one is done for you.

Funny Food Facts

1. Lazy people eat ~~chili~~ meatloaf. (from sentence #7)

2. The Easter Bunny's favorite vegetables are chicken.

3. The best fruit to drink is strawberries.

4. If you're scared, don't eat dough.

5. Jellybeans must be a cold food.

6. Dancing cows make blueberries.

7. Cavemen ate meatloaf.

8. Bread is rich because it has watermelon.

9. Milkshakes are an unhappy fruit.

10. Club sandwiches grow on the floor of a barn.

Name _____

Nouns in the Clouds

Look at the list of words. If a word is a **common noun**, copy it in the cloud titled common nouns. If it is a **proper noun**, change its first letters to capital letters and copy it in the cloud titled proper nouns.

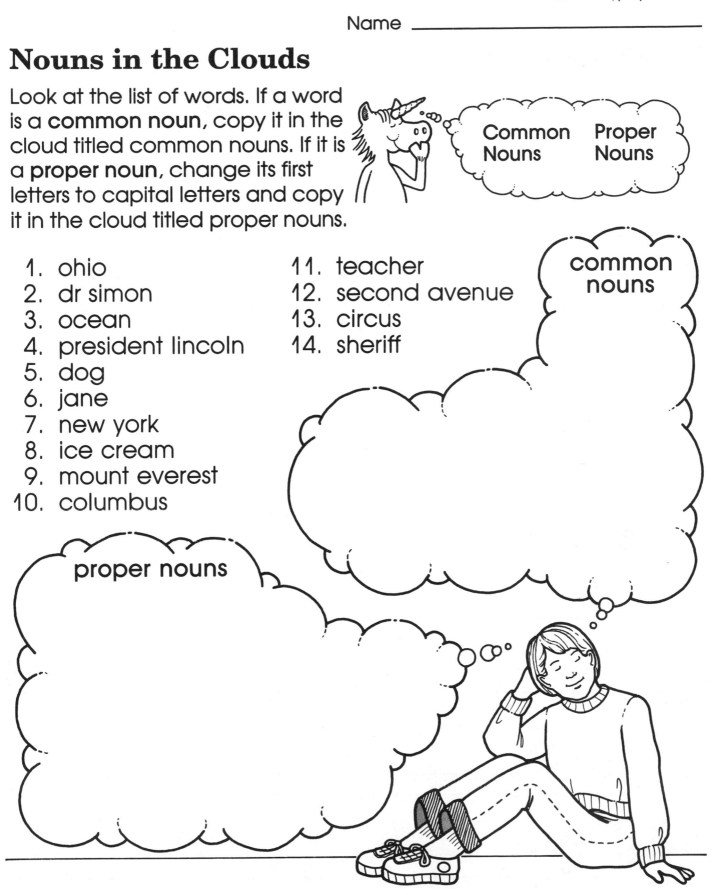

Common   Proper
Nouns   Nouns

common nouns

1. ohio
2. dr simon
3. ocean
4. president lincoln
5. dog
6. jane
7. new york
8. ice cream
9. mount everest
10. columbus

11. teacher
12. second avenue
13. circus
14. sheriff

proper nouns

Name _____

Pencil in the Plural

Write the plural for each of the nouns below.

wish *Example*	hobby	sheep	day
<u>wishes</u>	_____	_____	_____
deer	bluff	child	boss
_____	_____	_____	_____
rash	cookie	match	knife
_____	_____	_____	_____
car	success	pony	foot
_____	_____	_____	_____
kiss	city	couch	mouse
_____	_____	_____	_____
woman	half	mirror	trout
_____	_____	_____	_____
person	tooth	dress	girl
_____	_____	_____	_____

Name _____

Bright and Beautiful

Color the space **yellow** if you have to only add an **s** to make the word plural.

Color the space **orange** if you have to add **es** to make the word plural.

Color the space **blue** if you have to change the last letter and then add **es** to make the word plural.

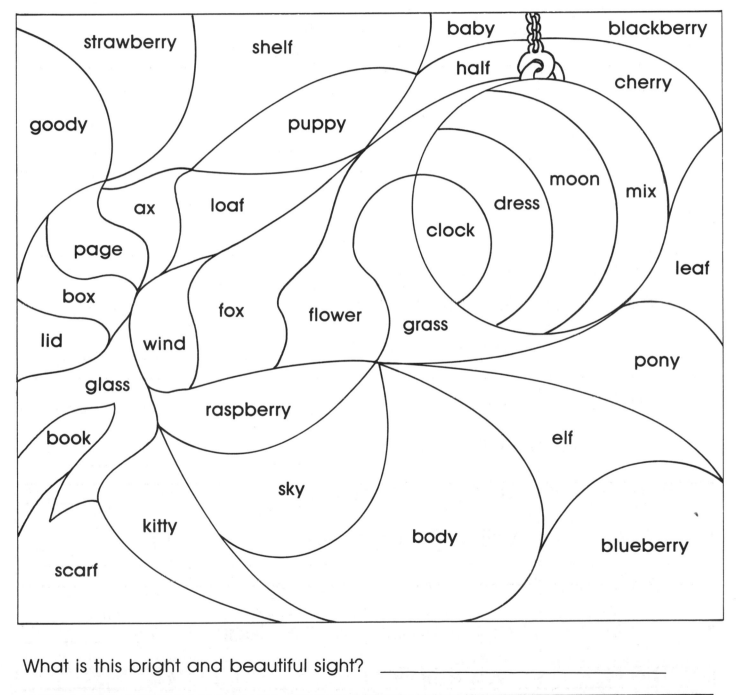

What is this bright and beautiful sight? _____

P.J.'s Cup

Name _____

Change the underlined word to show possession by adding an apostrophe or apostrophe and s. Write the possessive form on the line.

possessive

Example> The <u>balloon</u> string is long.   balloon's

1. The three <u>cats</u> paws were wet.   1. _____

2. <u>Mary</u> pencil was broken.   2. _____

3. Both <u>boys</u> grades were good.   3. _____

4. This house is <u>Cliff</u> house.   4. _____

5. <u>Tony</u> aunt came to visit.   5. _____

6. Some <u>flowers</u> leaves were large.   6. _____

7. We saw two <u>bears</u> tracks.   7. _____

8. The <u>children</u> room was messy.   8. _____

9. My <u>sister</u> birthday is today.   9. _____

10. The <u>clowns</u> acts made us laugh.   10. _____

11. Charlie Brown filled <u>Snoopy</u> dish.   11. _____

12. Mark joined the game with the <u>boys.</u>   12. _____

13. The baseball <u>players</u> uniforms are clean.   13. _____

14. The <u>dog</u> dish was empty.   14. _____

Name _____

Be a Star!

Follow the rules to color each design.

Rule 1: Add **ed** to most verbs to show the past tense. Color these words **blue**.

Rule 2: If the verb ends in **e**, drop the **e** and add **ed**. Color these words **green**.

Rule 3: If the verb has a short vowel followed by a single consonant, double the final consonant and add **ed**. Color these words **white**.

Rule 4: If the verb ends in **y**, change the **y** to **i** and add **ed**. Color these words **yellow**.

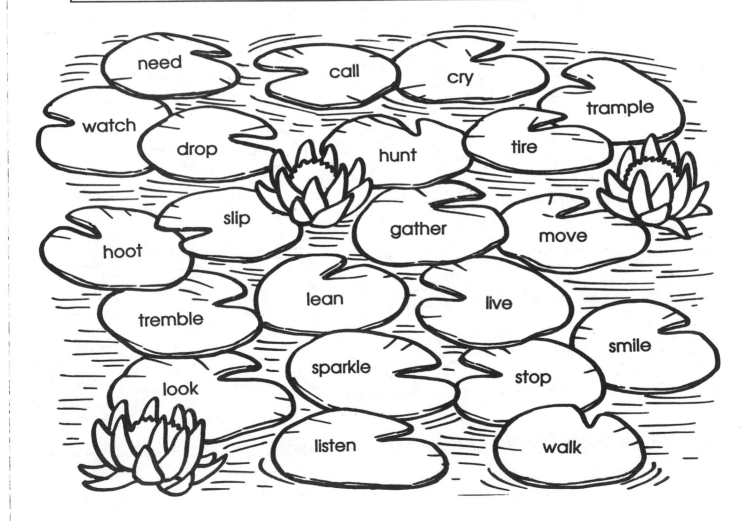

Name _____

Hop – Hopped – Hopping!

Help bouncy Bong hop to his special piece of liver. If you can add an "**ed**" or "**ing**" to a word, color that piece of liver brown. Do not color the other pieces.

Bong is certainly a frog of action. All of the words he hopped on are . . .

_____ .

Name _____

Little Words Mean a Lot

A pronoun is a word that takes the place of a noun. Above each underlined word below, write a pronoun from the Word Box that could replace it.

Word Box									
she	it	her	we	he	his	I	him	they	your

1. Uncle Nick shouted at Mus Mus as Uncle Nick walked to the kitchen.

2. Lucy ran to Lucy's mother in tears.

3. The Littles crowded up to the kitchen door.

4. Granny Little said, "Granny Little wouldn't believe it if Granny Little didn't see it with these old eyes."

5. Lucy said, "Mus Mus is a cute name."

6. Will and Tom have gone to get some leftovers.

7. Uncle Nick kept on writing Uncle Nick's life story.

8. Mrs. Little whispered, "Don't bother Uncle Nick."

9. Granny Little turned Granny Little's back on Uncle Nick.

10. Tom told Uncle Nick, "Lucy and Tom want to read Uncle Nick's book."

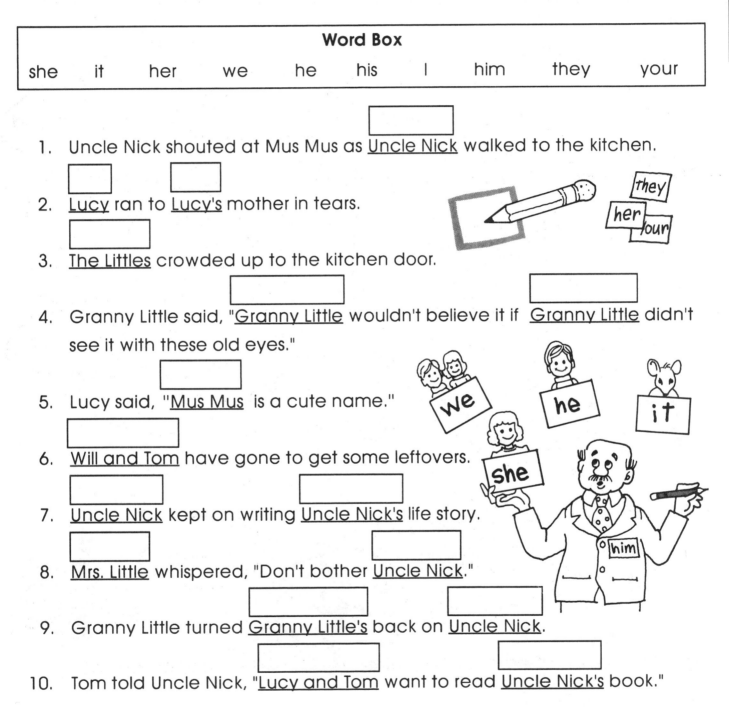

Name _____

Words of Worth

The words below are adjectives. They describe nouns (persons, places or things). Write a noun to go with each adjective. Then draw its picture in each Indian shield.

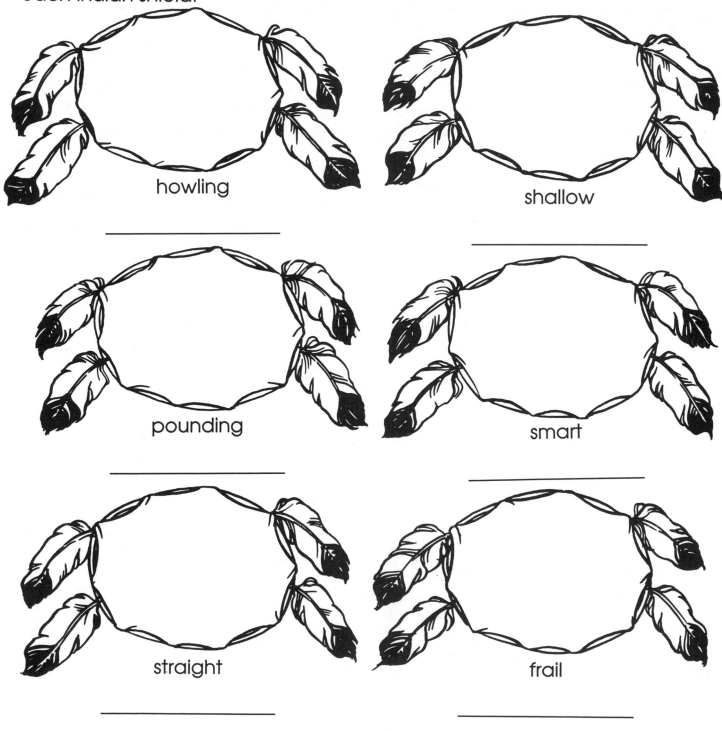

howling

shallow

_____

pounding

_____

smart

_____

straight

frail

_____

_____

Name _____

Marvelous Modifiers

Words that describe are called adjectives.
Circle the adjectives in the sentences below.

1. Lucas stared at the cool white paint in the can.
2. The green grass was marked with bits of white paint.
3. The naughty twins needed a warm soapy bath.
4. The painters worked with large rollers.
5. Lucas thought it was a great joke.

WET PAINT

TOP PAINT

For each noun below, write **two** descriptive adjectives. Then write a sentence using all three words.

1. marshmallows _____ _____

_____

_____

2. airplane _____ _____

_____

_____

3. beach _____ _____

_____

_____

4. summer _____ _____

_____

_____

5. teacher _____ _____

_____

_____

A NOW... D Some adjectives like *good* and *bad, big* and *little, happy* and *sad* are overused. Make a list of more descriptive adjectives that could be used in place of these words. Compare your list with the lists of other classmates.

Name _____

Where's That Monkey?

In the sentences below, write an adverb on the line to complete each sentence. The word in parentheses tells the kind of adverb to write. Do not use an adverb more than once. Answers will vary.

Example> The car is ___here___ . (where)

1. Our team played _____ . (when)
2. Brian writes _____ . (how)
3. The cows move _____ . (how)
4. Melissa will dance _____ . (when)
5. My dog went _____ . (where)
6. We ran _____ . (how)
7. The choir sang _____ . (how)
8. The cat purred _____ . (where)
9. Hilary spoke _____ . (how)
10. We'll go on our vacation _____ . (when)
11. The sign goes _____ . (where)
12. Mother brought the groceries _____ . (where)
13. David read the directions _____ . (how)
14. We'll be leaving _____ . (when)
15. We have three bedrooms _____ . (where)
16. Our family goes on a vacation _____ . (when)
17. Jim ran _____ down the street. (how)
18. They_____ laid the baby in the crib. (how)
19. The man went _____ with his paper. (where)

Name _____

Speech Puzzle

Unscramble each word to name the parts of speech. Write each word in the correct puzzle spaces.

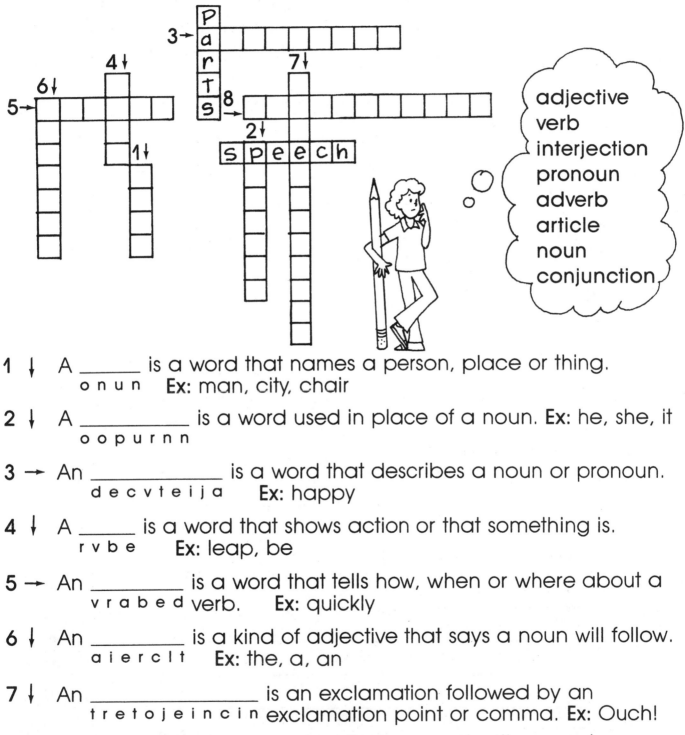

adjective
verb
interjection
pronoun
adverb
article
noun
conjunction

1 ↓   A _____ is a word that names a person, place or thing.
   o n u n   **Ex:** man, city, chair

2 ↓   A _____ is a word used in place of a noun. **Ex:** he, she, it
   o o p u r n n

3 →   An _____ is a word that describes a noun or pronoun.
   d e c v t e i j a   **Ex:** happy

4 ↓   A _____ is a word that shows action or that something is.
   r v b e   **Ex:** leap, be

5 →   An _____ is a word that tells how, when or where about a
   v r a b e d verb.   **Ex:** quickly

6 ↓   An _____ is a kind of adjective that says a noun will follow.
   a i e r c l t   **Ex:** the, a, an

7 ↓   An _____ is an exclamation followed by an
   t r e t o j e i n c i n exclamation point or comma. **Ex:** Ouch!

8 →   A _____ is a word that connects other words.
   o u c n o n i c t n j   **Ex:** and, or

Name _____

Abracadabra

Write a complete sentence using each of the following subjects.

Example> The magician <u>performs difficult tricks</u> .

1. The truck _____ .

2. Mr. and Mrs. Turner _____ .

3. The clowns _____ .

4. Fresh strawberries _____ .

5. Our team _____ .

6. A large crowd _____ .

7. Pancakes _____ .

8. All of the joggers _____ .

9. The skeleton _____ .

Write a complete sentence using each of the following predicates.

Example> _____ The busy street _____ was noisy.

1. _____ was funny.

2. _____ will be ready.

3. _____ went too quickly.

4. _____ is on the corner.

5. _____ were ruined.

6. _____ still exists.

7. _____ was fun.

8. _____ were on my desk.

9. _____ turned to gold.

Capital Review

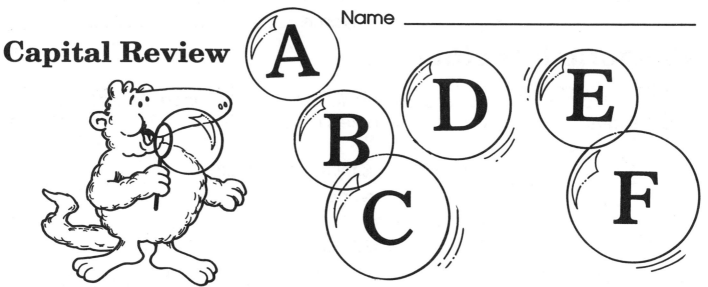

Name _____

In the sentences below, circle the words that should begin with a capital letter.

Example ▷ (is) ("i) (love) (lucy") still on television?

1. "after lunch," said sue, "let's go shopping."

2. i learned a lot from the book, *inside the personal computer*.

3. my class from hudson school went to forest park.

4. carlos speaks spanish, french and english.

5. the carter family lives on terrace drive.

6. "the new kid on the block" is a great story.

7. we saw the movie "ghostbusters" last saturday.

8. christopher columbus discovered america in 1492.

9. i was born june 12, 1965, in denver, colorado.

10. next thursday, mr. and mrs. evans have an anniversary.

11. my brother will attend harvard college in boston.

12. the letter to montie ended, "love from aunt rose."

13. in hawaii, kamehameka day is celebrated each june.

14. mrs. hardy said, "don't be late for the party."

15. stone brothers hardware is on elm street.

Name _____

Patriotic Punctuation

Decide which punctuation mark should follow each sentence. Add it. Then draw its design in the matching numbered area on the flag.

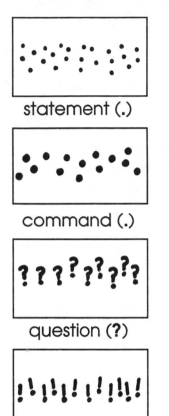

statement (.)

command (.)

question (?)

exclamation (!)

1. Phoebe was thirteen years old
2. Finally, everyone would be free
3. Trust no one
4. Where was Mr. Hickey
5. Should she go back to Queen's Head
6. You must find out who it is
7. Run, get my father
8. Phoebe packed and headed for Mortier House
9. Mr. Green never spoke to Phoebe at all
10. Thomas was "T"
11. Should Phoebe tell Mr. Hickey the secret
12. Go feed the seed to the chickens
13. Did you air and turn Mrs. Washington's quilt
14. Mr. Hickey has put poison in your dinner
15. She placed the peas on the general's plate
16. What jest is this
17. My very favorite, June peas

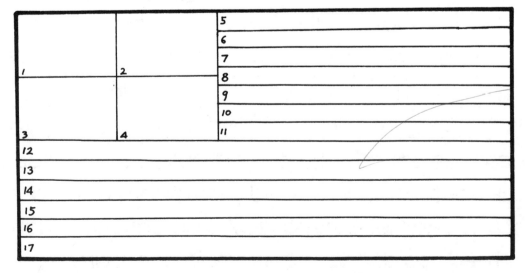

Sealed with a Kiss

Read the letter Ut sent to Vietnam.

> january 20 1993
>
> dearest mother
>
>   i find america to be a beautiful country i even saw many flakes of snow fall on the ground
>
>   father my brother my sisters and i miss you greatly i look at your picture often but sometimes i am so lonely i will try to be your angel child
>
>   love
>   ut

Rewrite the letter correctly with capital letters and punctuation.

_____

_____

_____

_____

_____

_____

_____

_____

_____

Name _____

More Than Two, Do!

Commas are used to separate the items in a series when there are more than two items joined by the word *and*. **Example:** Little Abraham was a happy, calm, and intelligent child.

Add commas, where needed, to the sentences below.

1. Abe's parents paid the teacher with firewood venison and potatoes.

2. Abraham could read and write when he was only six years old.

3. A book Abe had borrowed was rained on and became water-stained.

4. Abe liked to tell jokes stories and tales.

5. Abe's mother got sick and died.

Copy the following sentences, adding capitals and punctuation as needed.

6. abraham lincoln lived in kentucky and indiana as a child

   _____

   _____

7. he loved to read write and talk with people

   _____

   _____

8. mr lincoln guided his country through a period of frustration hardship and war

   _____

   _____

   _____

Rabbit Remarks

Name _____

For each of the quotes below, add a set of quotation marks around exactly what was said.

Is it Spring yet?

Examples: "That's a good sign," said Rahm.
He called, "You can come out now."

1. I think it is time for us to build the nursery, Silla said.
2. When do you think it will happen? asked Rahm.
3. Silla said, When the moon is round again.
4. How many children do you think we'll have? asked Rahm.

Copy these quotes, adding a set of quotation marks, a capital letter at the beginning and a period or question mark at the end.

5. there is no way of telling, she answered

_____

_____

6. let's just wait and see, said Silla

_____

_____

7. well, then, asked Rahm, where do you want your nursery to be

_____

_____

A NOW ... D Predict what Rahm and Silla will say about the new kits when they are born. Write a line of dialogue for each of them. Remember to use quotation marks, capitals and other punctuation as needed.

Name _____

The Root of the Problem

Yukio, his family, and the villagers had a problem. No one was able to sleep well because they kept having nightmares. The baku got to the root of the problem—he gobbled up all the nightmares! Everyone was able to sleep peacefully again.

Help the baku gobble up root words by underlining the root of each word in the list. Then circle the root words in the wordsearch. Words may go →, ←, ↓, ↑, ↗, and ↙

1. planting
2. mending
3. fishing
4. golden
5. swimming
6. certainly
7. suddenly
8. arrows
9. foolish
10. sounds
11. sighing
12. rushing
13. safely
14. asleep
15. longer
16. arms
17. stones
18. bandits

A	P	L	A	N	T	H	S	I	F
R	O	C	E	R	T	A	I	N	O
M	E	N	D	D	N	U	O	S	O
I	A	E	L	P	R	E	K	I	L
W	R	D	O	G	N	O	L	G	E
S	R	D	G	O	R	U	S	H	F
N	O	U	T	S	L	E	E	P	A
V	W	S	T	I	D	N	A	B	S

Name _____

Syncopated Synonyms

Choose a word from the Word Bank that means nearly the same as the clue word. Write it in the crossword puzzle.

Word Bank

crate	section	laugh	nation	academy
distant	plank	rickety	stomp	bandana
pretend	fiddle	fancy	lurch	rhythm

Across

1. country
4. elaborate
5. imagine
7. violin
9. stamp
11. unstable
12. scarf
13. beat
14. box

Down

2. school
3. area
5. board
6. far
8. wobble
10. chuckle

Name _____

Serpent's Synonyms

In some dragon stories the dragon has the tail of a serpent. A synonym for serpent is snake. Choose a word from the Word Bank that means nearly the same as the clue word. Write it in the crossword puzzle.

Word Bank

rich	hut	lunge	ruffian	pleasant
lush	trip	sear	bellow	splendid
look	wail	full	wither	precious

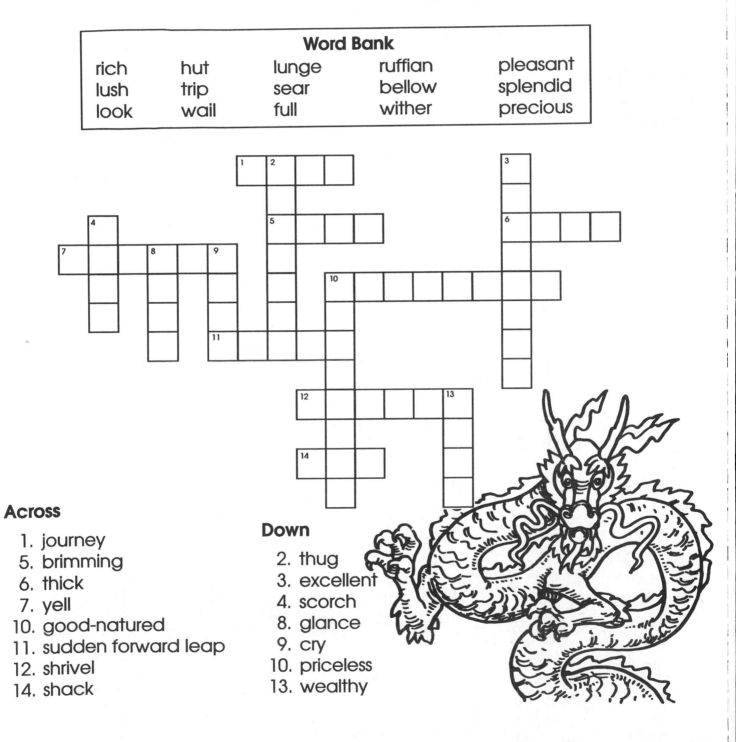

Across

1. journey
5. brimming
6. thick
7. yell
10. good-natured
11. sudden forward leap
12. shrivel
14. shack

Down

2. thug
3. excellent
4. scorch
8. glance
9. cry
10. priceless
13. wealthy

IF8695 Super Book for Grade 3

Name _____

Searching for Opposites

Select an antonym for the underlined words in the sentences below from the words in the Word Bank. Write the antonym on the line following each sentence.

Word Bank

unbolt	strong	purchase	cooked
sharp	evil	ancient	assemble
minor	present	praised	learned
disarray	increase	day	

Example > The salesperson was <u>courteous.</u>   __rude__

1. The old man was <u>feeble.</u> _____
2. The castle was <u>modern</u> inside. _____
3. Caroline likes <u>raw</u> carrots. _____
4. The character in the book was <u>good.</u> _____
5. She <u>taught</u> Spanish every day. _____
6. Doug was <u>absent</u> yesterday. _____
7. The knife was <u>dull</u> and rusty. _____
8. The teacher <u>criticized</u> the student. _____
9. <u>Lock</u> the door, please. _____
10. The meeting will <u>adjourn</u> soon. _____
11. It was a <u>major</u> decision. _____
12. I am going to <u>sell</u> shoes. _____
13. You should <u>decrease</u> your sugar intake. _____
14. We went fishing in the middle of the <u>night</u>. _____
15. The room was in great <u>order.</u> _____

Name _____

Alike or Not Alike?

Choose a word from the Word Box that means just the same or almost the same as each given word. Write your answers on the rungs of the ladder.

Word Box

hoisted	suddenly
admiring	estimate
naughty	surge
departed	propped
examine	cautiously
climb	taunted

1. inspect
2. flow
3. carefully
4. check over
5. supported
6. teased
7. ascend
8. left
9. lifted
10. cherishing
11. disobedient
12. swiftly

Choose words from the Word Box that mean the opposite of each given word.

1. slowly _____
2. arrived _____
3. recklessly _____
4. hating _____
5. descend _____

Name _____

In Other Words

Amelia Bedelia often mixed up her homonyms, such as when she "pared" the vegetables by laying them in "pairs."

Amelia has used the wrong homonyms in these sentences. Can you help her by underlining the wrong homonyms and writing the correct homonyms on the lines below?

1. How much do you think I way?
2. Amelia Bedelia blue the car's horn loudly.
3. She needed to so Mr. Rogers's torn shirt.
4. The son shone through the curtains.
5. Amelia Bedelia baked the cake with flower.
6. Mrs. Rogers went on a plain to visit her aunt.
7. Amelia Bedelia swept the stares.
8. Mr. Rogers's shirt was bright read.
9. Amelia Bedelia was stung by a be.
10. Amelia Bedelia rode a Ferris wheel at the fare.

1. _____
2. _____
3. _____
4. _____
5. _____
6. _____
7. _____
8. _____
9. _____
10. _____

Hairs on Hares

Name _____

Words that sound alike but are spelled differently and have different meanings are called homonyms. On the line before each homonym, write the letter of the phrase that best defines its meaning.

_____ 1. hare   A. any creature hunted for food

_____ 2. hair   B. a mass of unbaked bread

_____ 3. peer   C. a body part used to smell

_____ 4. pier   D. something that is owed

_____ 5. doe   E. the end of an animal's body

_____ 6. dough   F. an animal related to the rabbit

_____ 7. bare   G. a large, furry animal with a short tail

_____ 8. bear   H. to look closely; to gaze

_____ 9. dew   I. to beg for or ask for by prayer

_____ 10. due   J. a female deer, hare or rabbit

_____ 11. nose   K. a platform built out over water

_____ 12. knows   L. a story

_____ 13. prey   M. naked; without any covering

_____ 14. pray   N. growth that covers the scalp of a person or the body of a mammal

_____ 15. tail

_____ 16. tale   O. understands; to be certain of something

    P. water droplets

Name _____

Pairs About Hares . . . and Rabbits

Some words have two or more very different meanings even though the spelling remains the same. For each sentence below, write the correct definition of the underlined word.

blow a. hit
       b. breathe hard

peer a. one of the same age
      b. look at closely

nurse a. give milk
        b. care for

pelt a. strike; attack
     b. skin with fur

sage a. plant
      b. wise

box a. fight
     b. container

cuff a. end part of a sleeve
     b. slap

buck a. dollar (slang)
      b. male

drum a. beat; pound
      b. musical instrument

sharp a. pointed
       b. alert; observant

1. Most <u>bucks</u> leave the digging to the does. ____male____

2. Shortly after the babies were born, Silla <u>nursed</u> them. _____

3. Hares are born with a warm <u>pelt</u>. _____

4. The hawk's <u>sharp</u> eyes searched the ground. _____

5. When he sensed danger, the Old One <u>drummed</u> the ground. _____

6. When the buck tried to come close, the doe gave him a <u>blow</u>.

_____

7. The bucks balanced on their hind legs to <u>box</u>. _____

8. The young hares continued to <u>peer</u> over the tall grass. _____

9. The doe nibbled on a piece of <u>sage</u>. _____

10. The buck gave his opponent one last <u>cuff</u> then ran away. _____

**A
NOW . . .** Write a sentence for each word using the other definition.
D

Name _____

Zoo Loos

Zucchini is a ferret who lives in a zoo. Finish each rhyme to identify the other animals in the zoo. Draw the animals.

1. I'm tiny, not chunky,
   A little brown _____.

2. I'm mostly hair,
   I'm a grizzly _____.

3. My name is Ryan,
   I'm a proud _____.

4. So very teeny,
   I'm Billy's _____.

5. See you later,
   A green _____.

6. My tail can shake,
   I'm a rattle _____.

7. My home is no villa,
   I'm a huge, hairy
   _____.

8. You won't have to hunt,
   for this gray _____.

10. Sharp-toothed and dark,
    A man-eating _____.

9. You'll love to laugh,
   At the tall _____.

lion	elephant	gorilla	giraffe	Zucchini
bear	monkey	alligator	shark	snake

Name _____

What a Recipe!

Read the clues. Write the words that mean the same. Find and circle your answers in the puzzle.

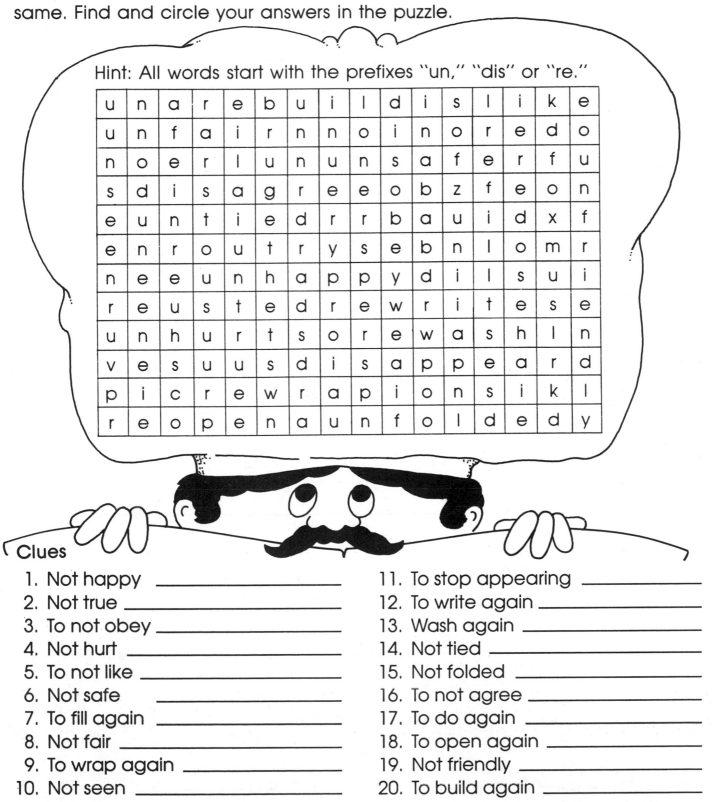

Hint: All words start with the prefixes "un," "dis" or "re."

u	n	a	r	e	b	u	i	l	d	i	s	l	i	k	e
u	n	f	a	i	r	n	n	o	i	n	o	r	e	d	o
n	o	e	r	l	u	n	u	n	s	a	f	e	r	f	u
s	d	i	s	a	g	r	e	e	o	b	z	f	e	o	n
e	u	n	t	i	e	d	r	r	b	a	u	i	d	x	f
e	n	r	o	u	t	r	y	s	e	b	n	l	o	m	r
n	e	e	u	n	h	a	p	p	y	d	i	l	s	u	i
r	e	u	s	t	e	d	r	e	w	r	i	t	e	s	e
u	n	h	u	r	t	s	o	r	e	w	a	s	h	l	n
v	e	s	u	u	s	d	i	s	a	p	p	e	a	r	d
p	i	c	r	e	w	r	a	p	i	o	n	s	i	k	l
r	e	o	p	e	n	a	u	n	f	o	l	d	e	d	y

Clues

1. Not happy _____
2. Not true _____
3. To not obey _____
4. Not hurt _____
5. To not like _____
6. Not safe _____
7. To fill again _____
8. Not fair _____
9. To wrap again _____
10. Not seen _____
11. To stop appearing _____
12. To write again _____
13. Wash again _____
14. Not tied _____
15. Not folded _____
16. To not agree _____
17. To do again _____
18. To open again _____
19. Not friendly _____
20. To build again _____

Name _____

Just Buzzing Around

Find the answers to the clues in the maze.
Write them on the lines.

Prefixes
re = again
un = not

Clues

1. make again _____

2. not opened _____

3. not kind _____

4. fill again _____

5. not used _____

6. write again _____

7. not told _____

8. do again _____

9. build again _____

10. not known _____

11. wrap again _____

Follow a path through the maze in the same order
as your answers to get the bee to the honey pot.

unopened · refill · remake · unkind · unknown · unused · rewrap · rebuild · redo · rewrite · untold

Honey Pot

Name _____

Tasty Morsels

The baku munched away on everyone's nightmares. In this exercise, the baku will only devour words that have the suffix **ed**. Color those cookies brown. Put an **X** on the cookies the baku will not eat.

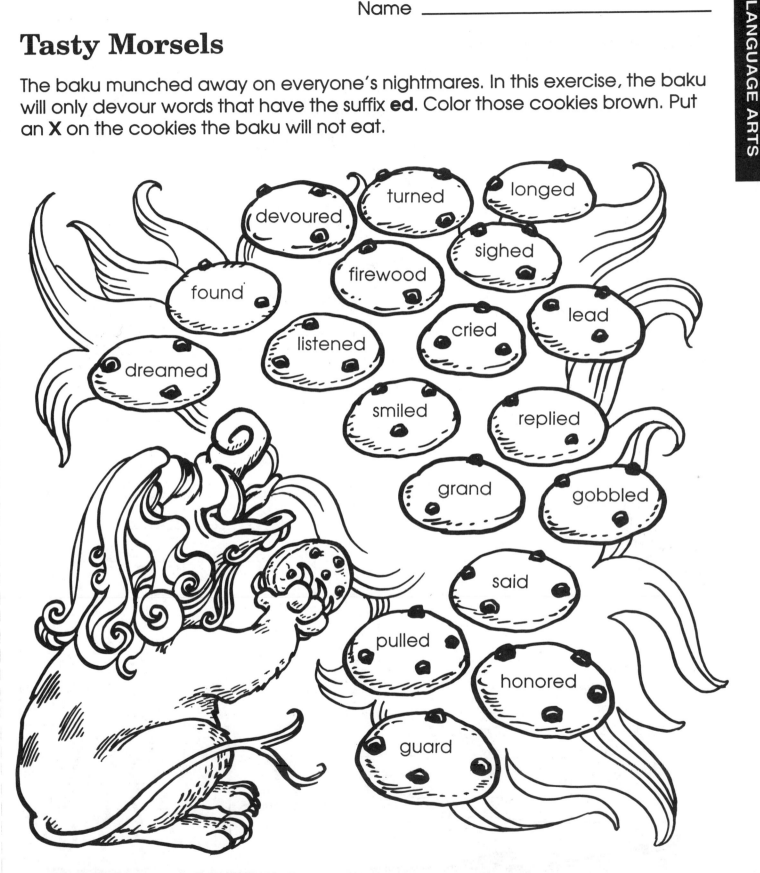

Name _____

Laughable Fellow

Use the Word Bank to work the puzzle.

Across
2. Opposite of darken
4. To make wider
5. Can be sunk
7. To make hard
8. Can be read
11. Can be broken

Down
1. Put in writing
3. To make something not crooked
4. Can be washed
6. A lot of fun
9. To make darker
10. Opposite of harden

Word Bank

breakable
widen
readable
sinkable
harden
lighten
soften
washable
darken
enjoyable
written
straighten

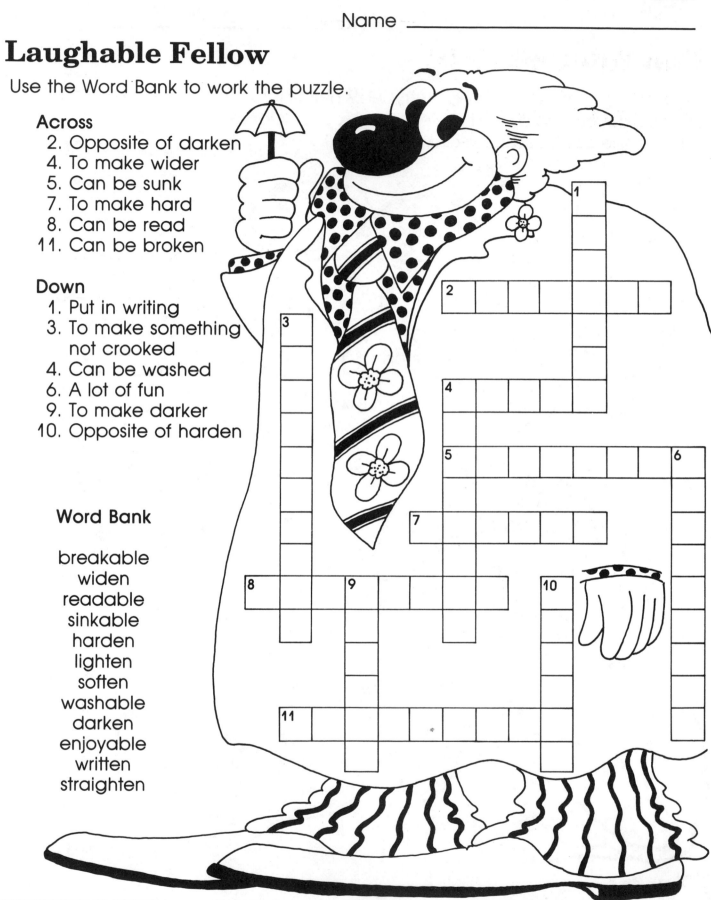

Name _____

Can You Unlock It?

Find the contractions in the puzzle to match
the numbered words. Write them.

1. I am _____

2. we are _____

3. they have _____

4. we will _____

5. she is _____

6. can not _____

7. I have _____

8. he is _____

9. is not _____

10. it is _____

11. you are _____

12. have not _____

13. do not _____

14. that is _____

15. she will _____

16. what is _____

17. did not _____

18. they will _____

Connect the dots. Begin with the answer to
number 1. Draw a line to the answer of
number 2 and keep going until you come
to the last word.

don't

• she'll

• that's

• what's

• I'm

• haven't   isn't •   • he's   • didn't

it's   I've   • they'll
                                        • can't

we're •

you're

they've •   we'll

• she's

Name _____

As Easy As Pie

Cut out and paste a picture to correctly complete each simile.

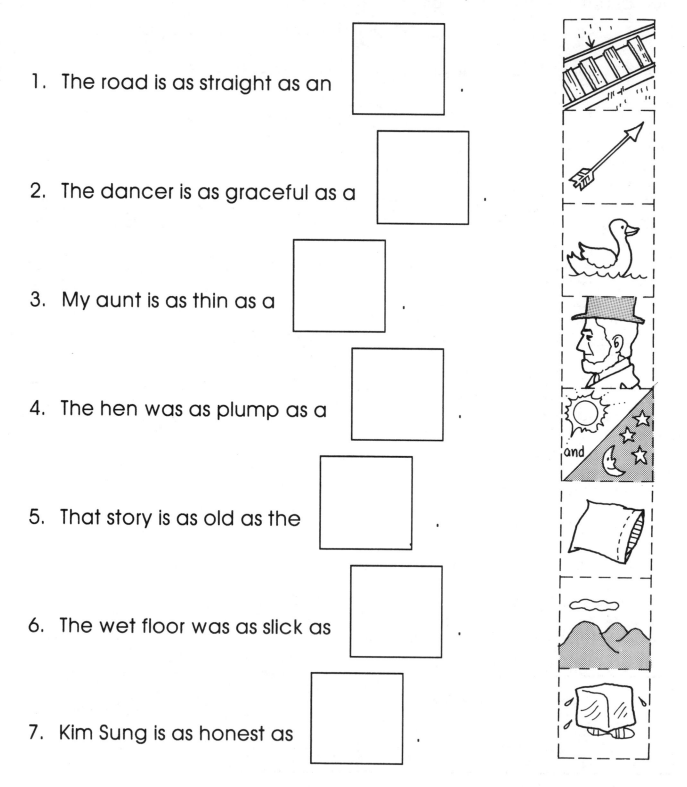

1. The road is as straight as an ⬜ .

2. The dancer is as graceful as a ⬜ .

3. My aunt is as thin as a ⬜ .

4. The hen was as plump as a ⬜ .

5. That story is as old as the ⬜ .

6. The wet floor was as slick as ⬜ .

7. Kim Sung is as honest as ⬜ .

Name _____

Animal Analogies

Animals have distinguishing features and inherited characteristics. These traits can be related in quite interesting and unusual ways by the use of analogies.

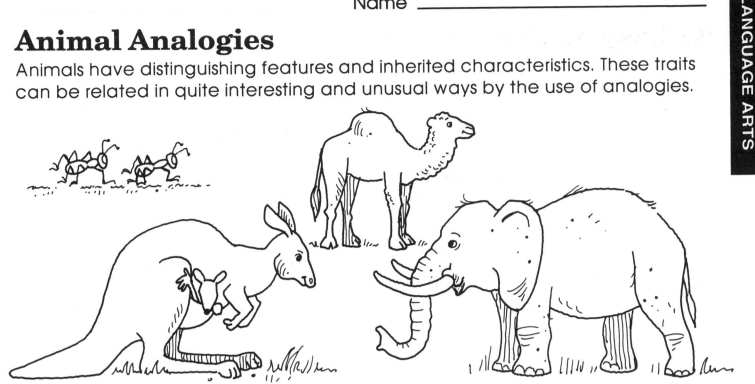

Use the Word Box to complete these analogies. You may need to use an encyclopedia. Be prepared to explain your answer.

1. An awning is to a window as eyebrows are to the eyes of a _____ .

2. A hand fan is to a human as ears are to an _____ .

3. Four quarters are to a dollar as four stomachs are to a _____ .

4. Flypaper is to flies as an anteater's tongue is to _____ .

5. A needle is to a seamstress as a beak is to a _____ .

6. Glass is to a window as skin is to a _____ .

7. A mouth is to a crocodile as a pouch is to a _____ .

8. A chest beat is to a gorilla as a shaking rattle is to a _____ .

Word Box			
kangaroo	cow	glass catfish	camel
tailorbird	ants	rattlesnake	elephant

IF8695 Super Book for Grade 3

Name _____

What's the Connection?

Complete each analogy with a word from the Word Bank.

1. A **tepee** is to some **Indians** as a **cave** is to some _____ .
2. **Hair** is to a **person** as a **mane** is to a _____ .
3. A **bow** is to a **ribbon** as a **knot** is to a _____ .
4. **Galloping** is to a **horse** as **flying** is to an _____ .
5. **Blindness** is to **eyes** as **deafness** is to _____ .
6. **Softness** is to a **feather** as **colorful** is to a _____ .
7. **Shallow** is to **deep** as **beginning** is to _____ .
8. **Mountains** are to **rocks** as **lakes** are to _____ .
9. **Strong** is to **frail** as **brave** is to _____ .
10. **Trot** is to **gallop** as **fly** is to _____ .
11. **Sweet** is to **sweat** as **breed** is to _____ .
12. **Counting** is to **numbers** as **reading** is to _____ .

Word Bank			
ears	afraid	water	horse
end	eagle	bread	soar
rope	bears	words	rainbow

Name _____

Cool As a Cucumber

Sometimes people use funny expressions to say what they mean. Complete each sentence by writing the letter of the word that would best explain what is meant.

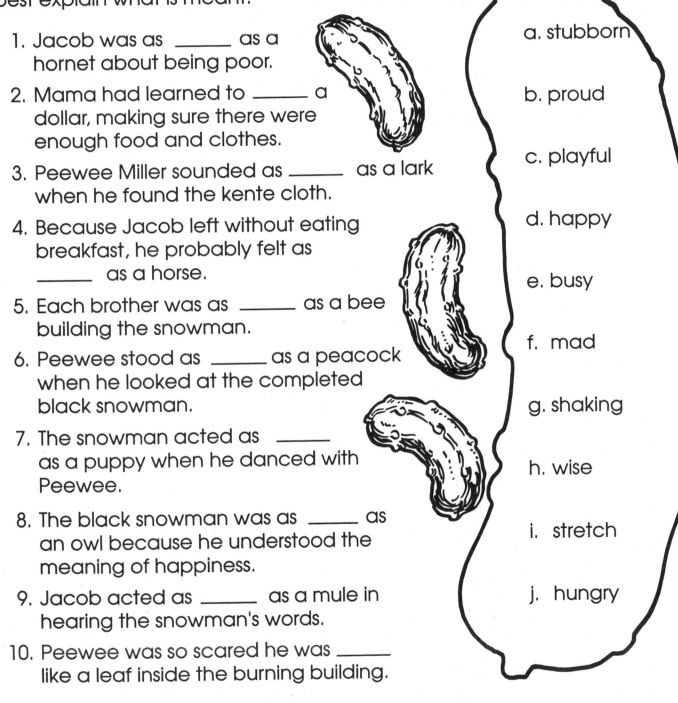

1. Jacob was as _____ as a hornet about being poor.

2. Mama had learned to _____ a dollar, making sure there were enough food and clothes.

3. Peewee Miller sounded as _____ as a lark when he found the kente cloth.

4. Because Jacob left without eating breakfast, he probably felt as _____ as a horse.

5. Each brother was as _____ as a bee building the snowman.

6. Peewee stood as _____ as a peacock when he looked at the completed black snowman.

7. The snowman acted as _____ as a puppy when he danced with Peewee.

8. The black snowman was as _____ as an owl because he understood the meaning of happiness.

9. Jacob acted as _____ as a mule in hearing the snowman's words.

10. Peewee was so scared he was _____ like a leaf inside the burning building.

a. stubborn

b. proud

c. playful

d. happy

e. busy

f. mad

g. shaking

h. wise

i. stretch

j. hungry

Cool Heads

Name _____

Circle sentence "a" or "b" to show which one means the same as the numbered sentence.

1. Eddie Whitestone always had something up his sleeve.
   a. He keeps things up his sleeve.   b. He liked to plan surprises.

2. His room was a pigsty.
   a. It was very messy.   b. He lived with pigs.

3. She would be late if she didn't step on it.
   a. She needs to hurry.   b. She needs to step on something.

4. Sometimes David could be hardheaded.
   a. His head was very hard.   b. He could be stubborn.

5. Roger always tried to keep a cool head.
   a. He tried to be calm.   b. He kept ice on his head.

6. Horseplay was not allowed in the hall.
   a. No horses were allowed in the hall. b. No playing was allowed in the hall.

7. Ali Baba wrapped up another mystery.
   a. He solved the mystery.   b. He wrapped the mystery in paper.

8. Ali Baba kept an eye on Eddie Whitestone.
   a. He drew an eye on Eddie's shirt.   b. He watched him.

9. His neighbors skipped town.
   a. They skipped all over town.   b. They left town.

10. The criminal was in hot water.
    a. He was standing in hot water.   b. He was in trouble.

Name _____

What's the Point?

Harry and Sidney giggled as they started painting the winter mural. Instead of painting a snow picture, they painted themselves in a cemetery "burying the hatchet." This meant that they would forget about their past fighting and be friends.

Read each sentence below. Then write the letter of the phrase that tells what the speaker really means.

He says . . .

____ 1. It's "raining cats and dogs."

____ 2. I remember when you were "knee-high to a grasshopper."

____ 3. You "eat like a bird."

____ 4. He "held up the bank."

____ 5. You "light up my life!"

____ 6. Which way should I turn "at the fork in the road?"

____ 7. The speaker "had a frog in her throat."

What he means is . . .

a. don't eat very much

b. make me very happy

c. robbed the bank

d. very small

e. pouring hard

f. was hoarse

g. where the road splits

Name _____

Which Is Which?

Like twins, words are sometimes hard to tell apart. Can you tell these word pairs apart? Answer each question by writing the correct word in the box.

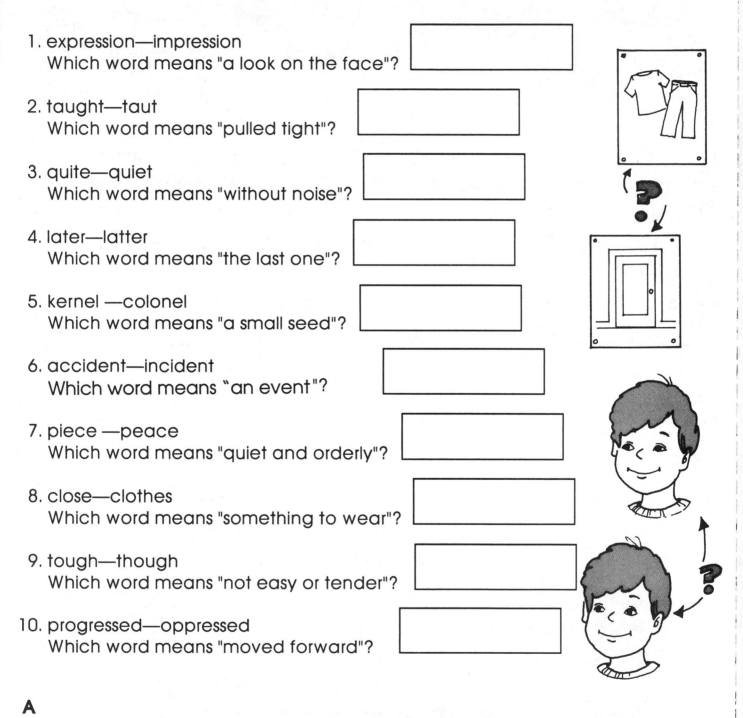

1. expression—impression
   Which word means "a look on the face"?

2. taught—taut
   Which word means "pulled tight"?

3. quite—quiet
   Which word means "without noise"?

4. later—latter
   Which word means "the last one"?

5. kernel —colonel
   Which word means "a small seed"?

6. accident—incident
   Which word means "an event"?

7. piece —peace
   Which word means "quiet and orderly"?

8. close—clothes
   Which word means "something to wear"?

9. tough—though
   Which word means "not easy or tender"?

10. progressed—oppressed
    Which word means "moved forward"?

A NOW . . . D Imagine that you had a twin. What would your names be? Would you dress alike? Would you do and like the same things?

 IF8695 Super Book for Grade 3

Name _____

Candy Store Dilemma

Read the label on each candy jar. Write the words from the Word Bank on the candy jar where they belong.

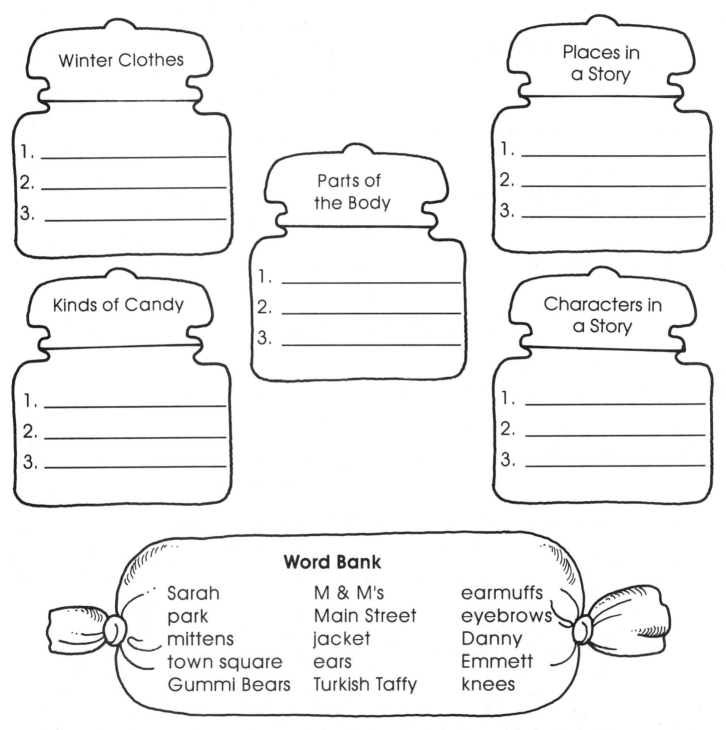

Winter Clothes

1. _____
2. _____
3. _____

Places in a Story

1. _____
2. _____
3. _____

Parts of the Body

1. _____
2. _____
3. _____

Kinds of Candy

1. _____
2. _____
3. _____

Characters in a Story

1. _____
2. _____
3. _____

Word Bank

Sarah	M & M's	earmuffs
park	Main Street	eyebrows
mittens	jacket	Danny
town square	ears	Emmett
Gummi Bears	Turkish Taffy	knees

At the Pet Store

Name _____

Use a dictionary to help you determine in which category each of these words belongs.

malamute	chameleon	mud puppy	mouse
guppy	newt	skink	Pekingese
angelfish	macaw	sheepdog	canary
cockatoo	pointer	rat	tomcat
spaniel	guinea pig	Siamese	goldfish
platy	finch	mutt	hamster
Manx	parrot	Persian	swift
gerbil	swordfish	salamander	setter
parakeet	iguana	mastiff	myna
frog	tabby	cockatiel	

Reptiles & Amphibians	Birds	Dogs
1. _____	1. _____	1. _____
2. _____	2. _____	2. _____
3. _____	3. _____	3. _____
4. _____	4. _____	4. _____
5. _____	5. _____	5. _____
6. _____	6. _____	6. _____
7. _____	7. _____	7. _____
8. _____	8. _____	8. _____

Fish	Rodents	Cats
1. _____	1. _____	1. _____
2. _____	2. _____	2. _____
3. _____	3. _____	3. _____
4. _____	4. _____	4. _____
5. _____	5. _____	5. _____

AND NOW . . . Research the differences between reptiles and amphibians. Separate the "Reptiles & Amphibians" list above into two separate lists. To which list would you add the word *tadpole*? To which list would you add the word *anole*? Find other words to add to these lists.

Name _____

Do We or Don't We?

If the word is a **compound** word, color the space **blue**.
If the word is a **contraction**, color the space **gray**.
If the word is a **verb**, color the space **yellow**.
If the word is an **adjective**, color the space **black**.

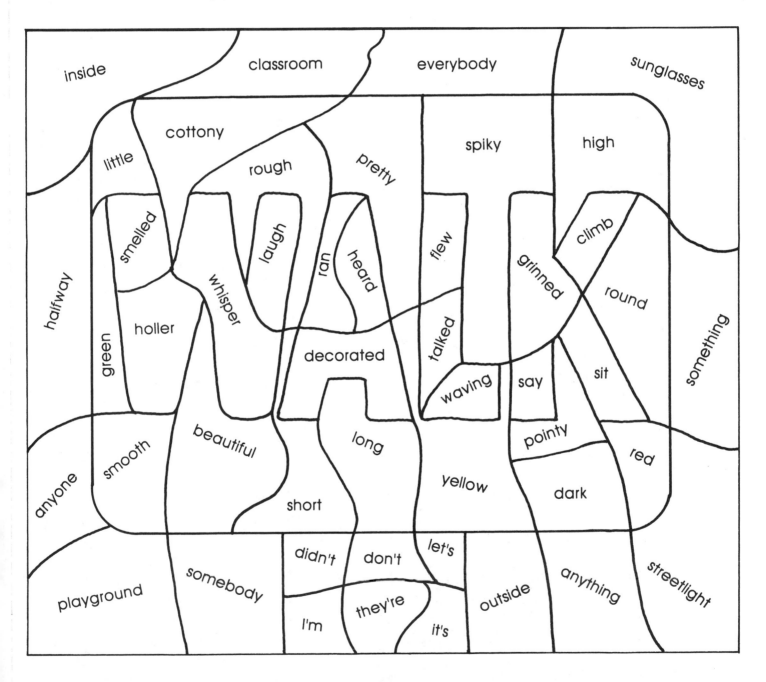

inside classroom everybody sunglasses

cottony

little rough pretty spiky high

smelled laugh ran heard flew grinned climb

halfway whisper round

green holler decorated talked say sit something

waving

beautiful long pointy red

anyone smooth yellow dark

short

didn't don't let's

playground somebody they're outside anything streetlight

I'm it's

Name _____

What a View!

On a separate paper, rewrite the story below, substituting the correct word from the Word Box for each underlined word or phrase.

Space shuttle astronauts <u>view</u> our <u>earth</u> from an <u>altitude</u> of 160 miles. Because the shuttle <u>orbits</u> the earth so <u>rapidly</u>, the astronauts see several sunrises and sunsets in one <u>24-hour period</u>.

They pass over the place where the Mediterranean Sea <u>separates</u> Europe from Africa. It is very <u>easy</u> to <u>locate</u> the Nile River and the Red Sea from that altitude.

The shuttle travels across Asia, the largest <u>landmass</u>. The astronauts <u>film</u> the <u>peaks</u> of the Himalaya Mountains before crossing over the Pacific Ocean. Their <u>journey</u> is <u>incredible</u>.

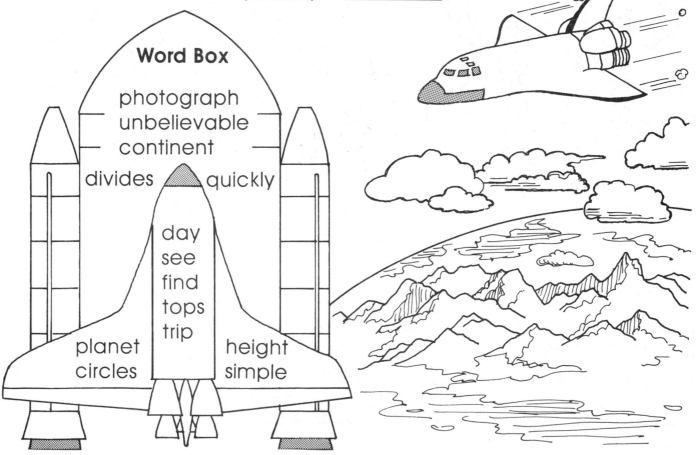

Word Box

photograph
unbelievable
continent
divides   quickly

day
see
find
tops
trip

planet   height
circles   simple

Name _____

I'll Be Switched

A silly sheriff always switched his word parts around when he got excited. Use the Answer Box to write what the sheriff meant to say.

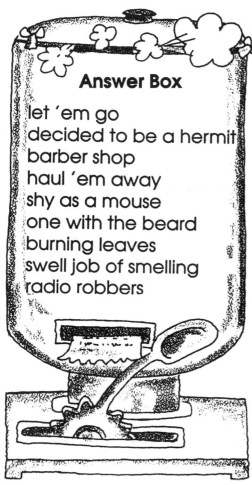

Answer Box

let 'em go
decided to be a hermit
barber shop
haul 'em away
shy as a mouse
one with the beard
burning leaves
swell job of smelling
radio robbers

1. my as a shouse

2. sarber bhop

3. smell job of swelling

4. robbio raiders

5. waul 'em ahay

6. lurning beaves

7. get 'em lo

8. hecided to be a dermit

9. one bith the weard

IF8695 Super Book for Grade 3

Name _____

The Prince and the Dragon

The prince had come to save the princess who was trapped in a cave by a huge, ferocious, fire-breathing dragon. The prince brought only a rope, a rock, and a bucket of sand, but he could also do excellent voice imitations.

Help the prince think of ways to save the princess from the dragon.

1. _____

2. _____

3. _____

4. _____

5. _____

6. _____

7. _____

8. _____

9. _____

10. _____

Name _____

Painting with Words

Ut was from Vietnam and didn't express herself in the same way the other children in her new American school did. However, her expressions were colorful and explained what she meant.

Read each sentence. Then use the Word Bank to rewrite each sentence by changing the underlined words to more common English words. Don't forget capitals and final punctuation!

1. The <u>round-eyed children twittered</u> when Ut answered.

   _____

2. A <u>snowrock</u> stung her chin.

   _____

3. The children <u>screeched like bluejays</u>.

   _____

4. She sat down and hid her angry <u>Dragon</u> face.

   _____

5. <u>The clock needles ticked slowly</u>.

   _____

6. His eyes <u>gleamed like watermelon seeds</u>.

   _____

7. <u>Small feathers floated</u> past the frosty windows.

   _____

8. Her fingers <u>danced on</u> the desk top.

   _____

Word Bank

American children laughed	sparkled	time went slowly	laughed
snow fell	snowball	tapped	scowling

Name _____

What Am I?

Solve each riddle by writing a word from the Word Bank.

1. People usually think I am imaginary, but there is an example of me in the reptile family. I am a _____ .

2. I contain small sticks that can become very hot. I am a _____ .

3. I am very light and cold, although when I am packed in a group, together we become very hard. I am a _____

4. Sometimes I'm fuzzy, and sometimes I'm not. Often I change shape to become something very beautiful. I am a _____ .

5. I'm the beautiful result of sun and rain. I am a _____ .

6. Although we do not weigh very much, we do a terrific job at keeping certain animals warm. We are _____ .

7. I'm what's left after your piece of cornbread has been eaten. I am _____ .

8. Although I am clothing, you wouldn't wear me out of the house. I am _____ .

Word Bank				
bluejays	dumpster	matchbox	angel	feathers
caterpillar	dragon	oceans	snowflake	crayons
pajamas	crumbs	rainbow	lessons	noodles

Name _____

The Gourmet Grubber

The Grubber Sweet Shop was being rebuilt thanks to the Duke of Hampshire. In the candy box below are some of the sweets now sold there. Help organize the candies by numbering them in alphabetical order.

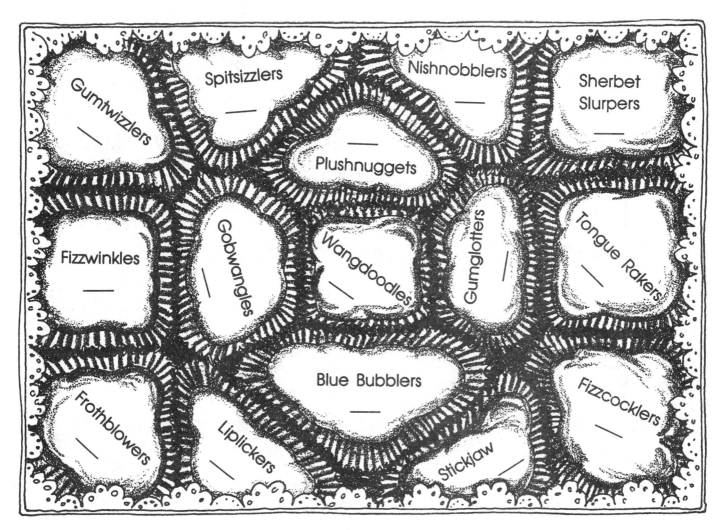

1. Underline all 3-syllable candies in red.
2. Circle all 4-syllable candies in green.
3. Draw a yellow box around the candies that start with the letter "g."
4. Put an orange X above the candy that does not end with the letter "s."
5. Draw a purple line above the words that have more than one "s."
6. Circle in blue the candy that has this color in its name.
7. Draw a pink X after the candy name that you like best.

Name _____

What's Missing?

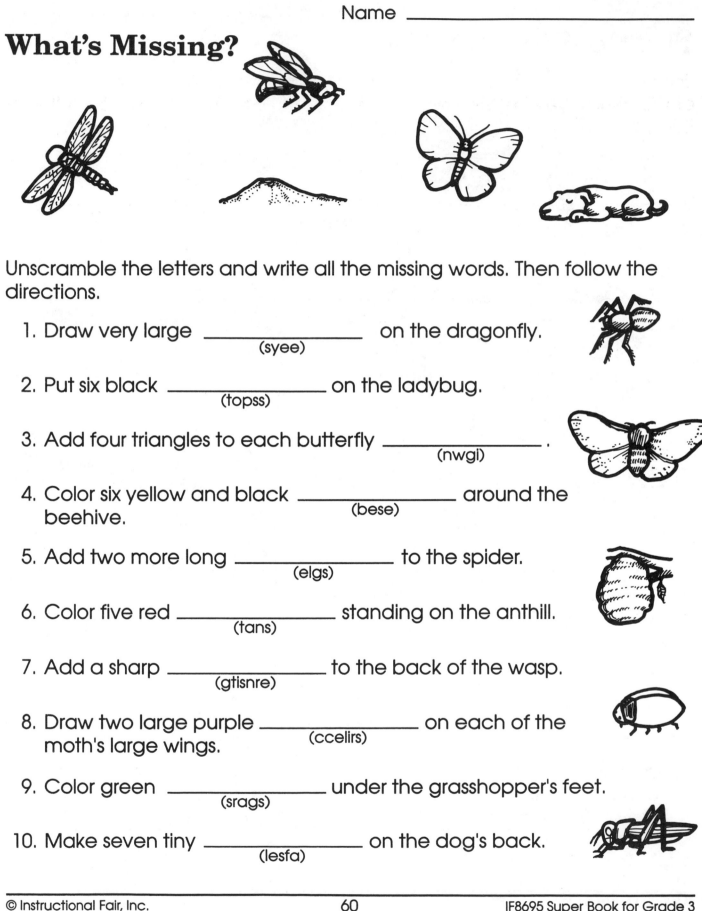

Unscramble the letters and write all the missing words. Then follow the directions.

1. Draw very large _____ on the dragonfly.
   (syee)

2. Put six black _____ on the ladybug.
   (topss)

3. Add four triangles to each butterfly _____ .
   (nwgi)

4. Color six yellow and black _____ around the beehive.
   (bese)

5. Add two more long _____ to the spider.
   (elgs)

6. Color five red _____ standing on the anthill.
   (tans)

7. Add a sharp _____ to the back of the wasp.
   (gtisnre)

8. Draw two large purple _____ on each of the moth's large wings.
   (ccelirs)

9. Color green _____ under the grasshopper's feet.
   (srags)

10. Make seven tiny _____ on the dog's back.
    (lesfa)

Name _____

Step-by-Step

Because Ut had just moved to America, she didn't know how to do some of the things we do. Write complete sentences telling Ut how to do these things.

How to Roller Skate

_____
_____
_____
_____
_____
_____

How to Make a Banana Split

_____
_____
_____
_____
_____
_____

How to Play Tic-Tac-Toe

_____
_____
_____
_____
_____
_____

Name _____

What a Day!

Read the story that goes with each picture. Write the word which best describes each day on the line.

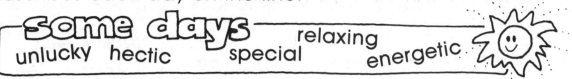

some days
unlucky   hectic   special   relaxing   energetic

At 9:00 Bob played tennis with his brother. At 11:00 he went swimming with friends. At 1:00 he mowed the yard and trimmed the shrubs.

Bob had an _____ day.

At 8:00 Sally dropped her books in the mud on the way to school. At 11:00 she spilled her milk on her clothes. At 4:00 she knocked a lamp off a table.

Sally had an _____ day.

At 10:00 Kirk got out of bed. At 12:00 he ate lunch while watching TV. At 2:00 he read a book while lying in a hammock. At 5:00 he rode his bike to a friend's house.

Kirk had a _____ day.

At 9:00 Kim went shopping with her mom. At 12:00 they ate lunch at her favorite restaurant. At 2:00 they saw a movie. At 5:00 Kim had a birthday party.

Kim had a _____ day.

At 8:00 Tom went to the store for his mom. At 10:00 he took his little brother to the dentist. At 1:00 he cleaned his room. At 2:00 he took his books to the library.

Tom had a _____ day.

Name _____

Brand News

Read the information on each label. Underline the correct sentence to tell the main idea of each package.

This cake will taste good because it is iced at the factory.

This is a quick and easy cake to eat because it has already been prepared and frozen.

This gum tastes great and makes bubbles even though it doesn't have sugar.

The more sugar a gum contains, the larger the bubbles it will make.

This baby food will look white because the color of the food has been removed.

This baby food is nutritional and is the natural color of the food.

This spaghetti is speedy because it just must be heated to serve.

This spaghetti is speedy because it came in an easy-open can.

This aspirin is not to be taken by children.

Adults take this aspirin once every six hours, but children take only one a day.

Name _____

Next ...

Read each sentence. Write two sentences which tell two different things that could happen.

1. The smoke from the oven rose in the air toward the smoke detector.

next: 1. _____
       2. _____

2. The crowd cheered wildly as the football player ran toward the goal line.

next: 1. _____
       2. _____

3. Bob and Kelly were on their way to the movie when Kelly realized she had left her money at home.

next: 1. _____
       2. _____

4. The diver was looking for the old sunken ship when he spotted a huge grey mass ahead.

next: 1. _____
       2. _____

5. When Rob arrived for the museum tour, he found that the tour had started ten minutes earlier.

next: 1. _____
       2. _____

6. Just as Sam was to go on stage for the class play, he realized he had forgotten his lines.

next: 1. _____
       2. _____

Name _____

Think About It!

Arthur, the director of a play, had to handle many problems. Think about each problem and then write what you would have done to help each character solve it.

Sue Ellen didn't talk loudly enough.

_____
_____
_____
_____

Buster could not remember what to say.

_____
_____
_____
_____

Muffy kept dropping the basket filled with cranberries.

_____
_____
_____

Is That a Fact!

Name _____

Read each sentence. If it states a fact, write the word **fact** on the line. If it states an opinion, write the word **opinion** on the line.

1. Eighth graders are too old to be rolling snowballs.   _____

2. A town square is part of a town.   _____

3. Enough snow can fall in one night to become a foot deep.   _____

4. Mr. Wetzel sells the best candy in the world.   _____

5. A fence is usually strong enough to stop a snowball.   _____

6. Winter is the season after fall and before spring.   _____

7. Everyone likes to play in the snow.   _____

8. Warm weather will make snow melt.   _____

9. Emmett always makes the biggest and best snowballs.   _____

10. It is hard for wild animals to find food in the snow.   _____

Now Really!

Name _____

Read each sentence. Draw and color an Easter egg on the line only if it tells something that could really happen.

1. Rabbits are good soccer players. _____

2. Chickens lay lots of eggs. _____

3. Farmers can lock rabbits in cages. _____

4. Children can decorate eggs. _____

5. Only one colony of rabbits decorates eggs for the Easter Bunny. _____

6. All rabbits learn how to decorate eggs in school. _____

7. A soccer player listens to the coach. _____

8. Chickens are good coaches. _____

9. Rabbits eat carrots. _____

10. Rabbits stuff baskets with eggs and jelly beans. _____

Name _____

A Penny for Your Thoughts

A **phrase** is an *incomplete* thought—it doesn't make sense all by itself. A **sentence**, on the other hand, is a *complete* thought.

Circle **phrase** or **sentence** to show whether each group of words below is an incomplete or a complete thought.

1.	day of feasting in the village	phrase	sentence
2.	it was a string of blue beads	phrase	sentence
3.	the chief was pleased	phrase	sentence
4.	played drums and danced	phrase	sentence
5.	he looked at the ship	phrase	sentence
6.	pointed to the north	phrase	sentence
7.	rowed toward the ship	phrase	sentence
8.	we will tell the chief	phrase	sentence
9.	she is sad	phrase	sentence
10.	going back to England	phrase	sentence

Copy each of the five sentences above using capital letters and periods.

_____
_____
_____
_____
_____

Add words to the phrases above to make complete thoughts. Don't forget to begin each sentence with a capital letter and end it with a period!

_____
_____
_____
_____
_____

Name _____

First Things First . . . But Not Always!

Below each sentence fill in the circle to show which event happened first. Remember that **sometimes** what happened first might be at the end of the sentence!

1. Henry walked straight to the diorama, then leaned over the counter.
   - ○ Henry walked straight to the diorama.
   - ○ Henry leaned over the counter.

2. Henry opened one of the cabinets and took out a jar of peanut butter.
   - ○ Henry opened one of the cabinets.
   - ○ Henry took out a jar of peanut butter.

3. Before eating his sandwich, Henry poured himself a glass of milk.
   - ○ Henry ate his sandwich.
   - ○ Henry poured himself a glass of milk.

4. Tom and Lucy climbed into the jack-o'-lantern as soon as Henry closed the bathroom door.
   - ○ Tom and Lucy climbed into the jack-o'-lantern.
   - ○ Henry closed the bathroom door.

5. After they had climbed to the top of the roof, Tom watched the yard, and Lucy watched the sky.
   - ○ They climbed to the top of the roof.
   - ○ Tom watched the yard, and Lucy watched the sky.

6. Finally, the Littles gave up and went back to their apartment.
   - ○ The Littles gave up.
   - ○ The Littles went back to their apartment.

7. Everyone noticed that things looked different because Uncle Nick had tidied up the living room.
   - ○ Everyone noticed that things looked different.
   - ○ Uncle Nick tidied up the living room.

Name _____

Super Cookies!

Super Cookies

First mix
  1 cup sugar
  1 cup brown sugar
  1 cup butter
  2 teaspoons vanilla
Next add
  4 eggs
Mix in
  4 cups of flour
  3 teaspoons baking powder
  1 teaspoon salt
Stir in
  1½ cups milk
Then stir in
  1 cup chocolate pieces
  1 cup shredded coconut
  1 cup chopped cherries
  1 cup chopped nuts
Bake at 350° for 10 minutes.
Sprinkle on powdered sugar.

Number the directions in the correct order. Use the recipe to help you.

_____ Bake the cookies for 10 minutes. Remove the pan from the oven.

_____ Roll the dough into small balls.

_____ When the cookies are cool, enjoy eating them.

_____ Read the recipe first.

_____ Put the pan in 350° oven and set the timer.

_____ Mix the sugar, brown sugar, butter and vanilla until smooth.

_____ Pour in the milk and stir carefully.

_____ Take out all the ingredients and put them next to the utensils.

_____ Place the balls of dough on a greased pan. Be sure there is a space between each ball.

_____ Stir in the chocolate pieces, coconut, cherries and nuts. Mix well.

_____ Then stir in the flour, baking powder and salt.

_____ Get the measuring cups, spoons, bowls, mixer and pans ready.

_____ Remove the cookies from the pan and sprinkle powdered sugar on top of them.

_____ Add the eggs and mix well.

• Try the recipe!

Name _____

Waterworks

Use the diagram to help you number the sentences in the correct order to tell how water is purified.

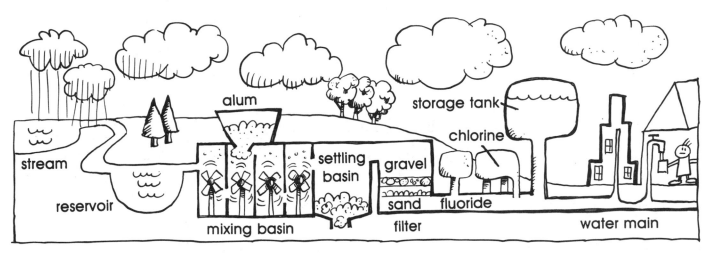

_____ Smaller pipes carry the water to the faucets in our homes.

_____ As the water flows through the filter, the alum and dirt sink to the bottom of the settling basin.

_____ The water in the reservoir goes through a large pipe into a mixing basin.

_____ Now that the water is as clean as possible it is stored in a huge storage tank.

_____ First raindrops fall into streams, lakes and rivers.

_____ Water leaves the storage tank through water mains.

_____ A chemical called alum is added to take the dirt out of the water.

_____ Turn the faucet handle and you have water.

_____ The clear, filtered water passes through a pipe where fluoride and chlorine are added.

_____ Then the streams and rivers flow into a reservoir.

_____ Smaller pipes carry the water from the water main to our homes.

This Is Where It's At!

Name _____

Read each sentence. Write the word **who, what, when, where** or **why** to show what the underlined words tell you.

1. <u>King Shabazz</u> didn't believe in Spring.   _____

2. King and Tony would sit <u>on the steps of the apartment</u> and talk about Spring.   _____

3. <u>One day</u> they decided to try to find Spring.   _____

4. They stopped <u>at the streetlight.</u>   _____

5. King <u>cleaned his shades.</u>   _____

6. The streetlight changed <u>so they</u> ran across the street.   _____

7. <u>The bar-b-q</u> smelled good.   _____

8. <u>After they passed the apartments,</u> they saw a red car in a vacant lot.   _____

9. The boys ran to look inside the car <u>because they wanted to see where the birds had been.</u>   _____

10. King and Tony were happy <u>because they had found Spring.</u>   _____

Name _____

In a Class by Himself!

Read each phrase.
If it tells **who**, color the space **brown**.
If it tells **what**, color the space **yellow**.
If it tells **when**, color the space **green**.
If it tells **where**, color the space **blue**.
If it tells **why**, color the space **purple**.

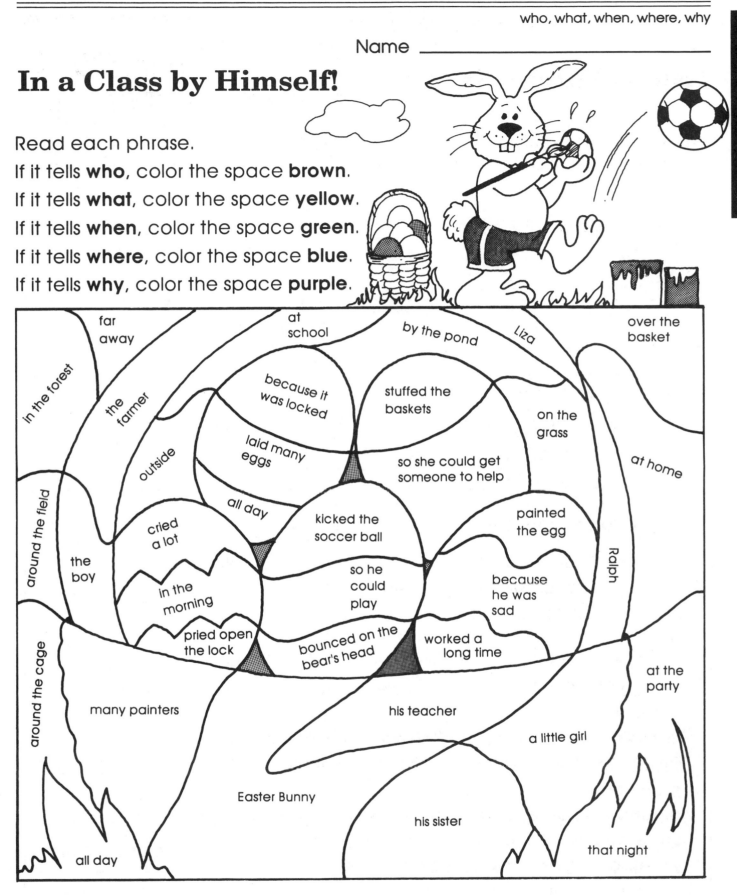

Read All About It!

Name _____

On the lines to the right of the story write the correct category— **who, what, when, where, why** — for each underlined word or phrase.

Huckleberry Heights Daily Herald

SPECIAL WEATHER REPORT

Volume MMI • No. 2   **Editor: I.N. Thenews**

Snowstorm Turns Streets into Skating Rink

(1) <u>Late last night</u> a (2) <u>major blizzard</u> closed most of (3) <u>the roads</u> here (4) <u>in Huckleberry Heights</u>. (5) <u>Early this morning</u>, (6) <u>the superintendent</u> announced that all schools (7) <u>in the area</u> would be closed (8) <u>due to the bad weather</u>. (9) <u>By noon</u>, the snowplows had cleared most of (10) <u>the snow</u>, but (11) <u>people</u> were warned not to drive (12) <u>because of the dangerously icy streets</u>. This, however, didn't keep (13) <u>the children</u> of Huckleberry Heights from getting around. Almost all of them put on their (14) <u>ice skates</u> and were seen sailing (15) <u>down the streets</u> during (16) <u>most of the afternoon</u>.

1. _____
2. _____
3. _____
4. _____
5. _____
6. _____
7. _____
8. _____
9. _____
10. _____
11. _____
12. _____
13. _____
14. _____
15. _____
16. _____

Name _____

What's It All About?

Underline the **topic sentence** – the sentence that most completely tells what the paragraph is all about – in each paragraph. Then write two phrases that are **supporting details** – they explain or tell about the topic sentence.

1. It happened exactly as Silla said it would. She gave birth to seven beautiful, healthy rabbits at the next full moon. The kits had small, mouse-like ears and were completely deaf. Their eyes were closed tight, and they couldn't see a thing. Their bodies were bare and they needed the warmth provided by the nest their mother had prepared.

   Supporting detail – _____

   Supporting detail – _____

2. Rabbits like to live together in a group. They dig their burrows like underground apartments where they will always have lots of neighbors. They help each other take care of the young. When the weather turns cold, they snuggle up together to keep each other warm.

   Supporting detail – _____

   Supporting detail – _____

3. Rahm and Silla scratched a hole in the sandy wall of the burrow with their front feet. Then they used their back feet to push the loose ground back into the tunnel. Silla smoothed down the walls and then pulled wool out of her fur to line the floor. They both worked hard to prepare a nursery for the babies who were soon to be born.

   Supporting detail – _____

   Supporting detail – _____

AND NOW . . . On the back write a paragraph about yourself when you were young. Be sure to include a topic sentence and several complete sentences that offer supporting details. You might also draw a picture to go with your paragraph.

Name _____

Soaring A-"Cross" Words

Read the clue. Find the word in the Word Bank. Write it in the puzzle.

Across

1. An exciting time
3. The child of your aunt and uncle
5. Your mother's mother
9. Place where boats sail near land
10. A very large town
11. Feel
12. Your mother or father's brother

Down

1. Your mother or father's sister
2. To help you remember
4. Another language
6. To answer
7. Places where things are made
8. A machine for lifting

Word Bank

city	aunt	crane
factories	touch	harbor
Spanish	uncle	remind
cousin	reply	grandma
adventure		

Name _____

Say What You Mean!

Write the vocabulary word from the Word Bank that means the same as each group of words.

1. changes, alters, varies _____

2. frail, tender, fragile _____

3. eliminate, scrap, reject _____

4. anger, fury, temper _____

5. withdraw, depart, retire _____

6. protect, guard, defend _____

7. worn, ripped, torn _____

8. unbelieving, doubtful, skeptical _____

9. common, usual, general _____

10. pause, delay, stall _____

11. bravery, boldness, fearlessness _____

12. transfer, move, disturb _____

13. great, immense, enormous _____

14. rude, ill-behaved, disrespectful _____

15. swallow, gobble, eat _____

16. deserted, vacant, unoccupied _____

17. explode, pop, blast _____

18. fighters, soldiers, combatants _____

19. tear, rip, shred _____

20. trash, junk, rubbish _____

Word Bank

suspicious	courage	discard	hesitate
retreat	transforms	shield	impolite
devour	delicate	rage	abandoned
ordinary	tattered	fray	dislodge
vast	debris	warriors	burst

Name _____

An A-"Mazing" Rabbit!

Help Ralph find his soccer ball. Read the clues. Find the definition in the maze and write the word on the line. Then draw a line through the maze in the same order as your answers.

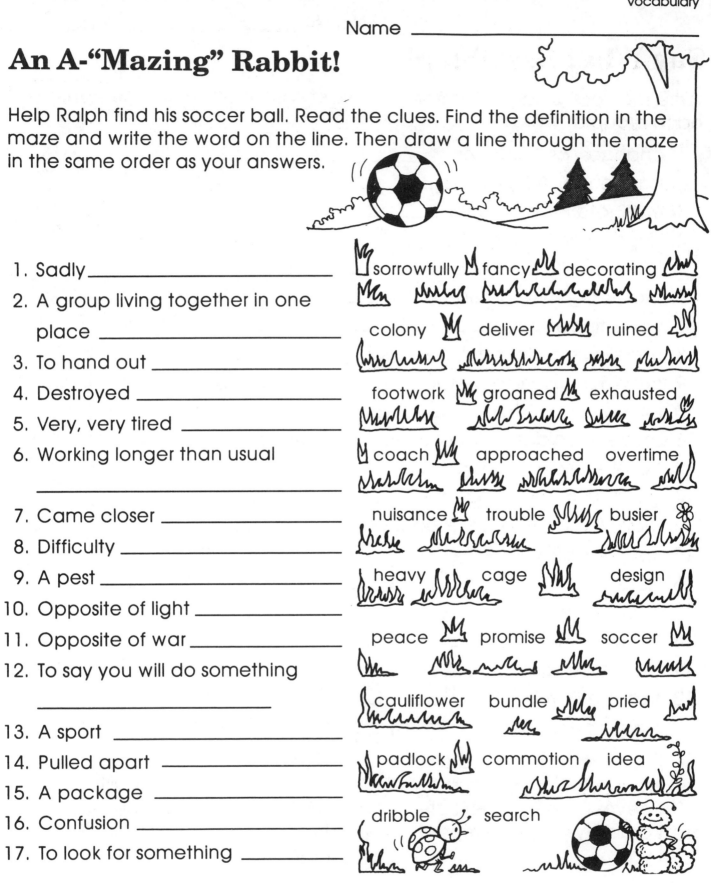

1. Sadly _____
2. A group living together in one
   place _____
3. To hand out _____
4. Destroyed _____
5. Very, very tired _____
6. Working longer than usual
   _____
7. Came closer _____
8. Difficulty _____
9. A pest _____
10. Opposite of light _____
11. Opposite of war _____
12. To say you will do something
    _____
13. A sport _____
14. Pulled apart _____
15. A package _____
16. Confusion _____
17. To look for something _____

sorrowfully   fancy   decorating

colony   deliver   ruined

footwork   groaned   exhausted

coach   approached   overtime

nuisance   trouble   busier

heavy   cage   design

peace   promise   soccer

cauliflower   bundle   pried

padlock   commotion   idea

dribble   search

Good-by, Jennie!

Name _____

Many foreign words have worked their way into our American language. Match each word or phrase below with its meaning. You may use a dictionary for help.

1. au revoir (French) _____
2. Gesundheit (German) _____
3. crepe (French) _____
4. tortilla (Spanish) _____
5. pita (Greek) _____
6. chopsticks (Asian) _____
7. oui (French) _____
8. sarong (Malaysian) _____
9. amigo (Spanish) _____
10. rendezvous (French) _____
11. babushka (Russian) _____
12. lasagna (Italian) _____
13. madam (French) _____
14. guacamole (Spanish) _____
15. torte (German) _____
16. foyer (French) _____
17. beret (French) _____

a. a lobby or entryway
b. a flat bread made from corn or flour
c. thin sticks used for eating
d. a married woman
e. a dip made with avocado
f. a scarf worn on the head
g. fabric wrapped to wear as a skirt
h. friend
i. yes
j. a rich layer cake
k. a meeting place
l. a flat hat
m. good-by
n. a dish made with long, flat noodles
o. thin cloth or pancake
p. round bread with pocket
q. "Good health!" to someone who sneezed

A NOW ... D You may have noticed that a few of these words have to do with food. Which ethnic foods do you enjoy most?

Name _____

Fable-ology

Create your own fable about how an animal acquired a particular physical feature. Remember to have the animal learn a lesson. Illustrate your fable.

How the _____ **Got Its** _____

Long, long ago there lived a _____

_____

_____

_____

_____

_____

_____

_____

_____

_____

_____

Moral: _____

_____

Name _____

Mouse on the Moon

Stories are always more exciting when you can picture them happening in your mind. Descriptive words such as adverbs and adjectives help make the story more exciting. Imagine that the moon is really made of cheese, and that you are a mouse exploring it for the first time. With a partner, write two descriptive words for each category below. Then, use all of them in a story.

What I smell:
1. _____
2. _____

What I see:
1. _____
2. _____

What I hear:
1. _____
2. _____

What I feel:
1. _____
2. _____

What I taste:
1. _____
2. _____

_____
title

_____
_____
_____
_____
_____
_____
_____
_____
_____
_____
_____
_____
_____

Name _____

Star Gazing

The Indians loved to watch the moon and the stars. Following the example, write a poem about the sun, moon, or stars.

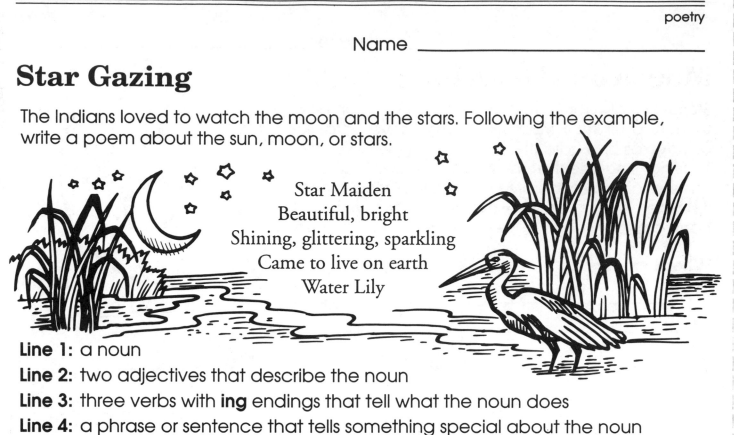

Star Maiden
Beautiful, bright
Shining, glittering, sparkling
Came to live on earth
Water Lily

Line 1: a noun
Line 2: two adjectives that describe the noun
Line 3: three verbs with **ing** endings that tell what the noun does
Line 4: a phrase or sentence that tells something special about the noun
Line 5: a synonym for the noun. Repeat the noun if there is no synonym.

_____

_____

_____

_____

_____

Name _____

Your Turn in the Poets Gallery

Fill in the blanks to make your own silly poems. The number at the end of each line tells the total number of syllables the line should have. Then draw a picture in each frame for the Poets Gallery.

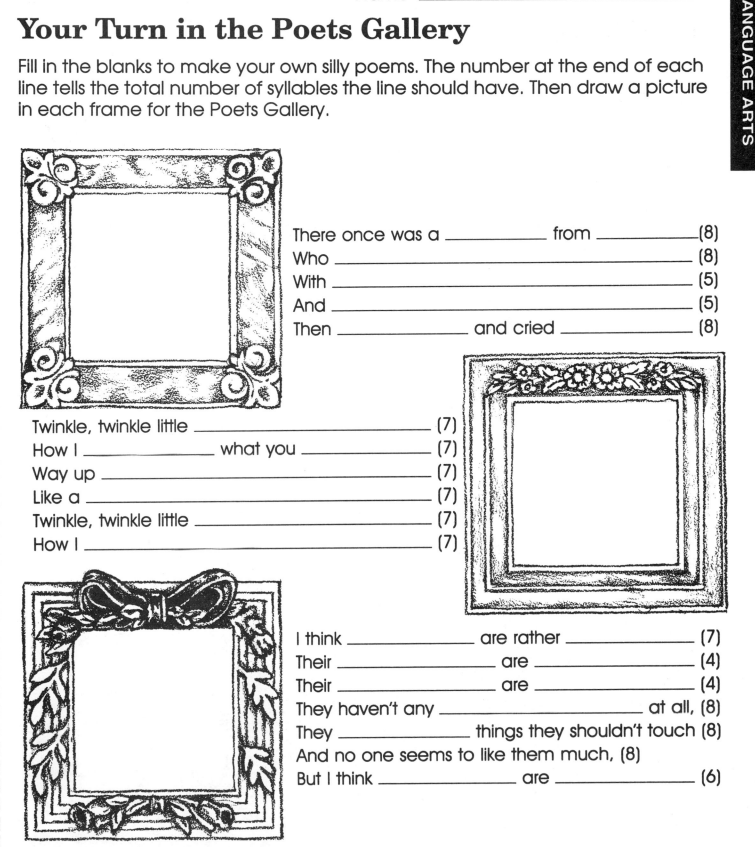

There once was a _____ from _____ (8)
Who _____ (8)
With _____ (5)
And _____ (5)
Then _____ and cried _____ (8)

Twinkle, twinkle little _____ (7)
How I _____ what you _____ (7)
Way up _____ (7)
Like a _____ (7)
Twinkle, twinkle little _____ (7)
How I _____ (7)

I think _____ are rather _____ (7)
Their _____ are _____ (4)
Their _____ are _____ (4)
They haven't any _____ at all, (8)
They _____ things they shouldn't touch (8)
And no one seems to like them much, (8)
But I think _____ are _____ (6)

Name _____

Now Hiring

This is a job application to become a maid.
Please print neatly!

Name _____ _____ _____
         Last   First   Middle

Address _____

City, State, Zip Code _____

Previous experience that would make you a good maid:

_____

_____

_____

Services you perform: _____

Hours you could work: _____

Vacation dates you prefer: _____

Salary required: _____

References (People who could tell us about you):

_____

_____

_____

_____

Signature

_____

Name _____

Dewey Decimal System

The Dewey Decimal System is used in most libraries to put books in order. This makes it easier for you to find the book you need.

Someone copied the system on a piece of scratch paper with the numbers in the wrong order. Number the system in order starting with 000-099.

Dewey Decimal	Types of Books
_____ 600-699	farming, medicine, building and cooking
_____ 300-399	jobs, education and customs
_____ 000-099	encyclopedias, almanacs and books of facts
_____ 900-999	people, places and events in history
_____ 400-499	dictionaries and languages
_____ 700-799	painting, music, dancing, sports and games
_____ 500-599	animals, math, stars and chemistry
_____ 200-299	religions
_____ 800-899	stories, poems and plays
_____ 100-199	great ideas and logical thinking

Read the titles. Write the Dewey Decimal numbers for each book.

_____ *Tap Dancing*

_____ *Star Gazer*

_____ *Poems about Animals*

_____ *Cookie Cookbook Just for Kids*

_____ *The Spanish Language Made Easy*

Name _____

Skipping Through the Tens

Skip count by tens. Begin with the number on the first line. Write each number that follows.

0, ___ , ___ , ___ , ___ , ___ , ___ , ___ , ___ , ___ , 100

3, ___ , ___ , ___ , ___ , 53 , ___ , ___ , ___ , ___ , 103

1, ___ , ___ , ___ , ___ , ___ , ___ , 81 , ___ , ___

8, ___ , ___ , ___ , ___ , 68 , ___ , ___ , ___ , ___

6, ___ , ___ , ___ , ___ , ___ , ___ , ___ , ___ , ___

4, ___ , ___ , ___ , ___ , ___ , ___ , ___ , ___ , 104

2, ___ , ___ , ___ , ___ , ___ , ___ , ___ , 92 , ___

5, ___ , ___ , ___ , 45 , ___ , ___ , ___ , ___ , ___

7, ___ , ___ , ___ , ___ , ___ , 77 , ___ , ___ , ___

9, ___ , ___ , ___ , ___ , ___ , ___ , ___ , ___ , ___

What is ten more than ...

26 ____   29 ____

44 ____   77 ____

53 ____   91 ____

24 ____   49 ____

66 ____   35 ____

54 ____   82 ____

Name _____

Counting to 100

By twos:

		6	8				16			22			
30							44						56
				66						78			
							100						

By threes:

3	6					21						39	
				57						75			
	90				102								

By fours:

4	8								40				
60							88			100			

On the back, count by fives to 100. Can you count by sixes? Try it.

MATH

Name _____

Outstanding Elephant Math

Connect the dots in order.

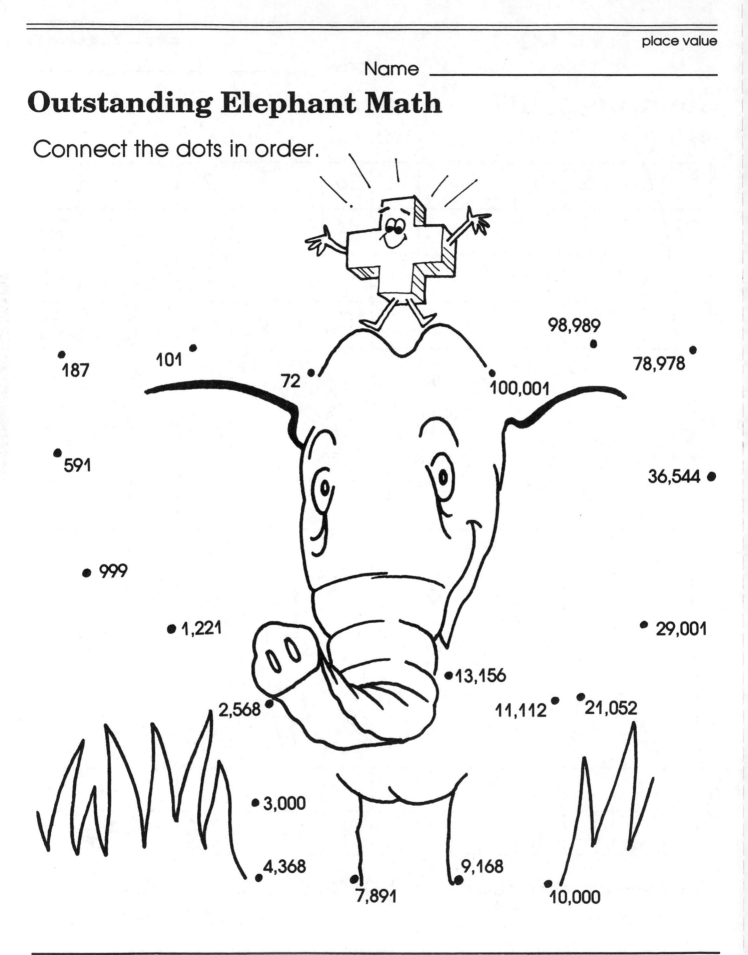

187

101

72

98,989

78,978

100,001

591

36,544

999

29,001

1,221

13,156

2,568

11,112

21,052

3,000

4,368

7,891

9,168

10,000

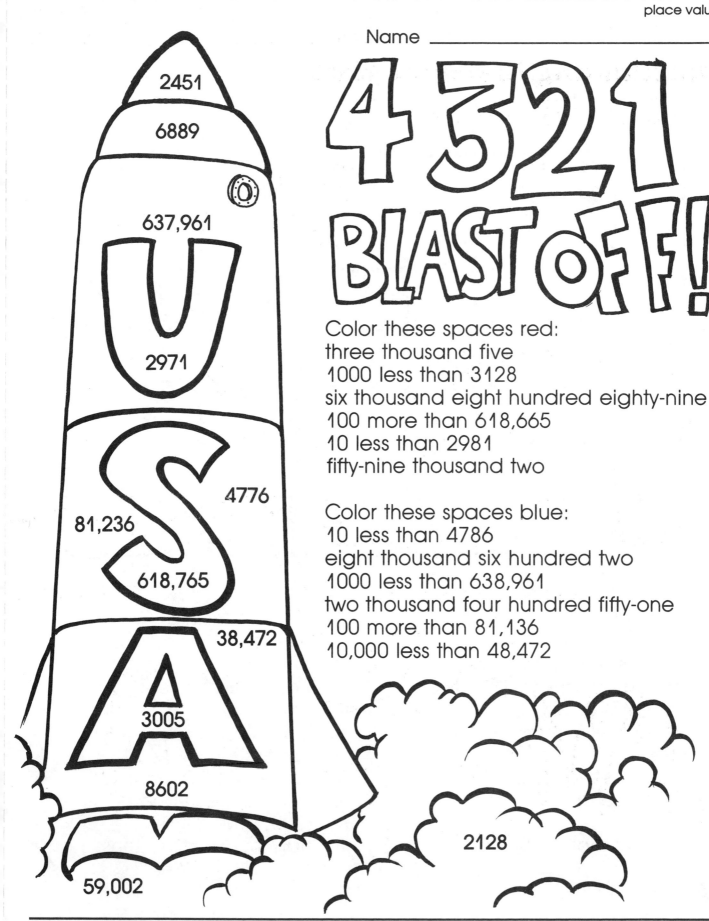

4 3 2 1 BLAST OFF!

Color these spaces red:
three thousand five
1000 less than 3128
six thousand eight hundred eighty-nine
100 more than 618,665
10 less than 2981
fifty-nine thousand two

Color these spaces blue:
10 less than 4786
eight thousand six hundred two
1000 less than 638,961
two thousand four hundred fifty-one
100 more than 81,136
10,000 less than 48,472

MATH

Numbers on rocket:
2451
6889
637,961
2971
4776
81,236
618,765
38,472
3005
8602
59,002
2128

Name _____

Place Value Puzzle

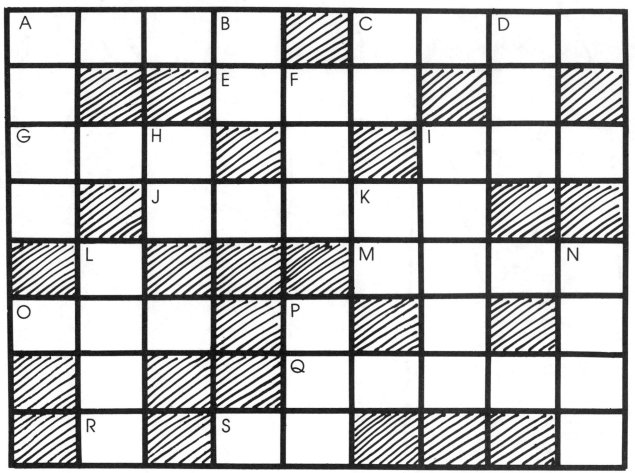

ACROSS

A. 3 thousand 5 hundred 9
C. 100 less than 8754
E. one hundred sixty-two
G. seven hundred eighty-two
I. 100, 150, 200, ___
J. 1, 2, 3, 4, 5 mixed up
L. two
M. 100 less than 9704
O. three zeros
P. eight
Q. 10,000 more than 56,480
R. one
S. 1 ten, 1 one

DOWN

A. 10 more than 3769
B. ninety-one
C. 28 backwards
D. 5 hundreds, 8 tens, 5 ones
F. 100 less than 773
H. 5, 10, 15, 20, ___
I. ten less than 24,684
K. 2 tens, 9 ones
L. two thousand one
N. 1000, 2000, 3000, ___
P. eight hundreds, 6 tens, 1 one

Name _____

Write That Number

Write the following numbers using digits.

1. six hundred fifty thousand, two hundred twenty-five _____

2. nine hundred ninety-nine thousand, nine hundred ninety-nine _____

3. one hundred six thousand, four hundred thirty-seven _____

4. three hundred fifty-six thousand, two hundred two _____

5. Write the smallest number you can using the digits 6, 9, 3, 5, 1, 9. The smallest number is _____ .

6. Write the largest number you can using the digits 6, 9, 3, 5, 1, 9. The largest number is _____ .

7. Write the number that is two more than 356,909. _____

8. Write the number that is five less than 448,394. _____

9. Write the number that is ten more than 285,634. _____

10. Write the number that is ten less than 395,025. _____

Write the following numbers in word form.

11. 3,208 _____

12. 13,656 _____

13. 451,867 _____

Name _____

Mushrooming Addition

Add   52 + 28 = 80
      28 + 91 = 119
      119 + 80 = ?

Follow arrows.

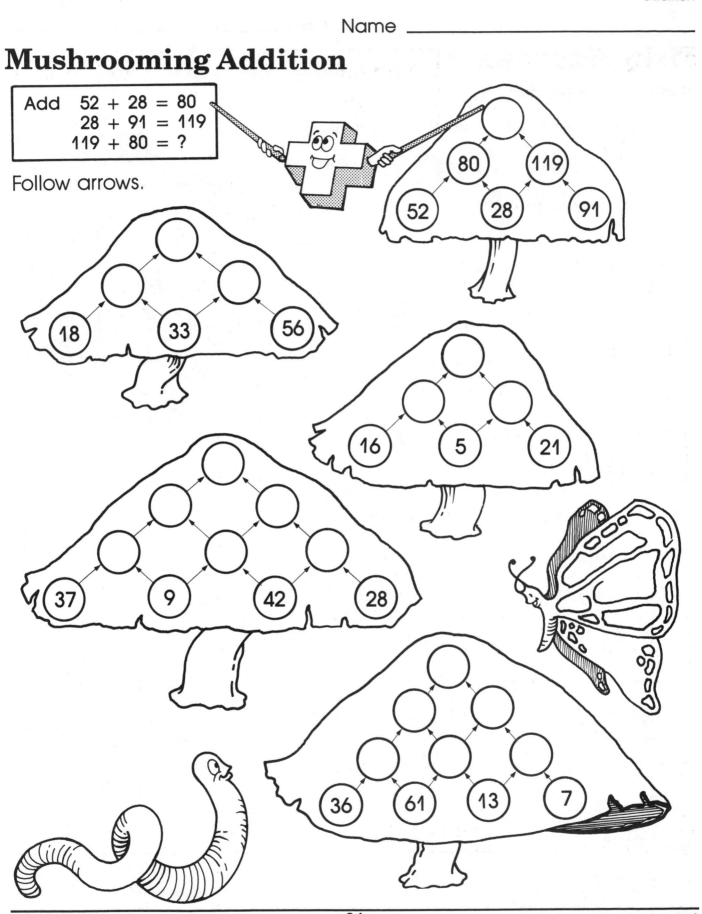

Name _____

Fishy Addition

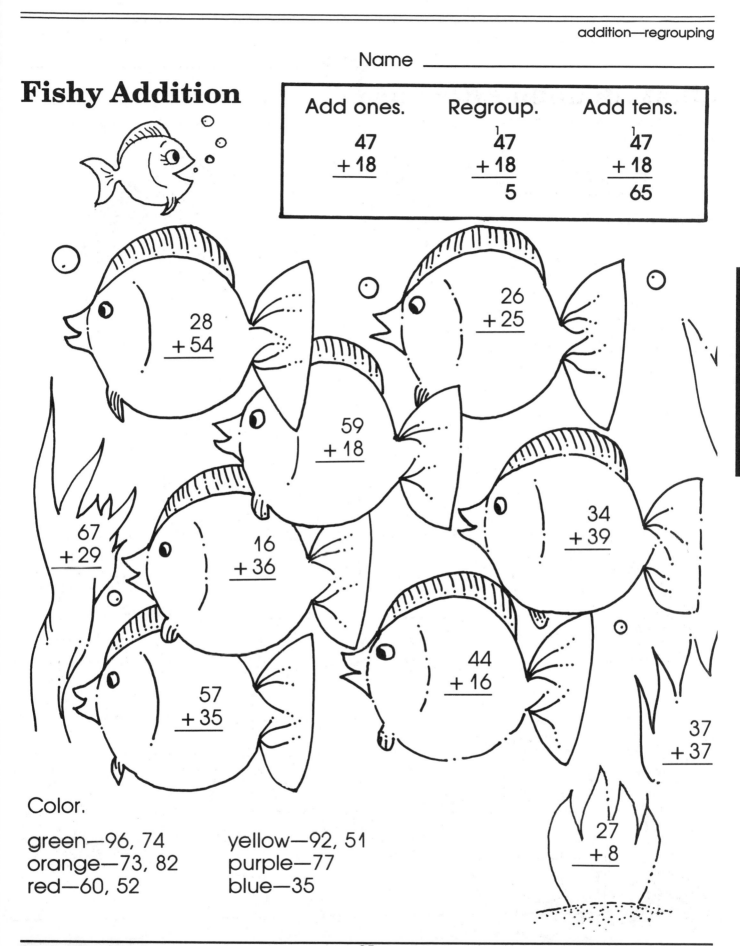

Add ones.	Regroup.	Add tens.
47 + 18	47 + 18 5	47 + 18 65

28
+ 54

26
+ 25

59
+ 18

67
+ 29

34
+ 39

16
+ 36

57
+ 35

44
+ 16

37
+ 37

27
+ 8

Color.

green—96, 74   yellow—92, 51
orange—73, 82   purple—77
red—60, 52   blue—35

IF8695 Super Book for Grade 3

Name _____

Make the Windows Shine!

Add. Each problem you complete makes the window "squeaky" clean.

$$476 + 319$$ $$248 + 629$$ $$327 + 544$$

$$572 + 318$$ $$815 + 177$$ $$527 + 144$$

$$429 + 343$$ $$462 + 319$$ $$462 + 529$$ $$648 + 238$$

$$756 + 127$$ $$563 + 208$$ $$646 + 248$$ $$924 + 66$$

$$628 + 259$$ $$526 + 347$$ $$927 + 46$$ $$765 + 218$$

Name _____

Addition Ace

Add. The pilot will remain in the air for as long as it takes to complete these problems.

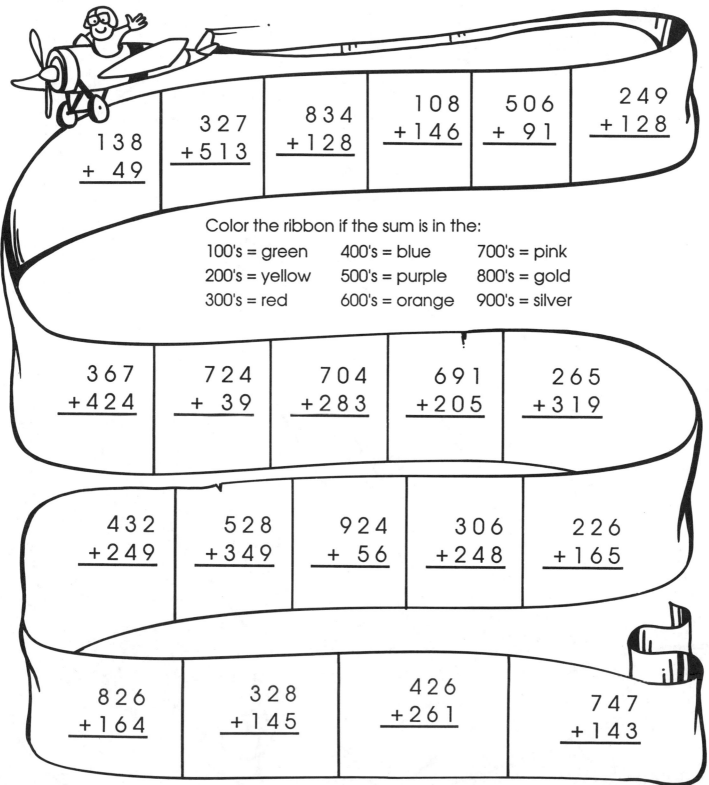

```
138      327      834      108      506      249
+ 49     +513     +128     +146     + 91     +128
```

Color the ribbon if the sum is in the:

100's = green	400's = blue	700's = pink
200's = yellow	500's = purple	800's = gold
300's = red	600's = orange	900's = silver

```
367      724      704      691      265
+424     + 39     +283     +205     +319
```

```
432      528      924      306      226
+249     +349     + 56     +248     +165
```

```
826      328      426           747
+164     +145     +261          +143
```

Name _____

Space Shuttle Addition

Experience addition in space as the payload specialist under zero gravity conditions.

$$\begin{array}{r} 371 \\ +439 \\ \hline \end{array}$$

$$\begin{array}{r} 629 \\ +184 \\ \hline \end{array}$$

$$\begin{array}{r} 264 \\ +483 \\ \hline \end{array}$$

$$\begin{array}{r} 146 \\ +587 \\ \hline \end{array}$$

$$\begin{array}{r} 438 \\ +290 \\ \hline \end{array}$$

$$\begin{array}{r} 362 \\ +459 \\ \hline \end{array}$$

$$\begin{array}{r} 347 \\ +328 \\ \hline \end{array}$$

$$\begin{array}{r} 528 \\ +391 \\ \hline \end{array}$$

$$\begin{array}{r} 327 \\ +649 \\ \hline \end{array}$$

$$\begin{array}{r} 382 \\ +249 \\ \hline \end{array}$$

$$\begin{array}{r} 283 \\ +346 \\ \hline \end{array}$$

$$\begin{array}{r} 465 \\ +193 \\ \hline \end{array}$$

$$\begin{array}{r} 409 \\ +292 \\ \hline \end{array}$$

$$\begin{array}{r} 566 \\ +283 \\ \hline \end{array}$$

$$\begin{array}{r} 423 \\ +392 \\ \hline \end{array}$$

$$\begin{array}{r} 283 \\ +519 \\ \hline \end{array}$$

$$\begin{array}{r} 625 \\ +246 \\ \hline \end{array}$$

$$\begin{array}{r} 498 \\ +123 \\ \hline \end{array}$$

Name _____

Let's Climb to the Top!

$$328 \atop +449$$

$$409 \atop +736$$

$$921 \atop +87$$

$$562 \atop +614$$

$$207 \atop +913$$

$$982 \atop +220$$

$$246 \atop +492$$

$$824 \atop +597$$

$$621 \atop +489$$

$$826 \atop +95$$

$$462 \atop +781$$

$$547 \atop +782$$

$$284 \atop +493$$

$$200 \atop +489$$

$$506 \atop +214$$

$$429 \atop +636$$

$$684 \atop +519$$

$$425 \atop +594$$

$$536 \atop +184$$

$$623 \atop +192$$

IF8695 Super Book for Grade 3

Picnic Problems

Help the ant find a path to the picnic. Work the problems. Shade the box if an answer has a 9 in it.

836 + 90	536 +248	952 + 8	362 + 47	486 +293	368 +529
789 526 +214	2846 +6478	932 +365	374 +299	835 +552	956 874 + 65
4768 +2894	38 456 +3894	4507 +2743	404 +289	1843 +6752	4367 +3571
639 + 77	587 342 +679	5379 1865 +2348	450 +145	594 +278	459 +367
29 875 +2341	387 29 +5614	462 379 +248			

Name _____

Bubble Math

Add the problems inside these bubbles.

5642 +1819

4629 +1258

2647 +3281

3426 +2841

3690 +2434

4625 +1817

6843 +2391

6241 +2363

5942 +1829

5642 +2919

2648 +1923

4826 +2098

2641 +6259

8465 +1386

7205 +1839

2643 +7427

5246 +3187

4265 +3827

9124 +1348

3142 +2639

These bubbles all popped in order from least to greatest. Number from 1 to 20 the order in which they popped starting with the smallest sum.

MATH

Name _____

Yummy Additions

Add ones. Regroup.	Add tens. Regroup.	Add hundreds. Regroup.	Add thousands. Regroup.
7465 + 4978 3	7465 + 4978 43	7465 + 4978 443	7465 + 4978 12443

Do the problems. Color an answer containing a **3**–brown, **4**–red, **5**–yellow.

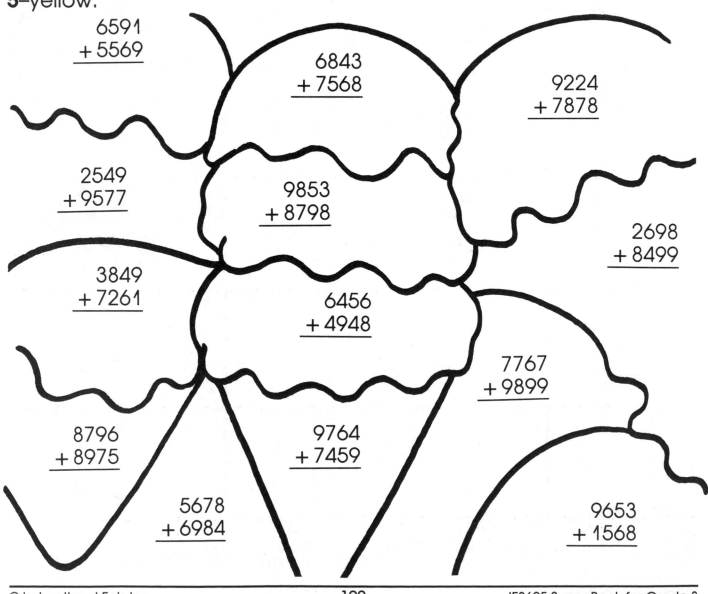

6591
+ 5569

6843
+ 7568

9224
+ 7878

2549
+ 9577

9853
+ 8798

2698
+ 8499

3849
+ 7261

6456
+ 4948

7767
+ 9899

8796
+ 8975

9764
+ 7459

9653
+ 1568

5678
+ 6984

Name _____

Mountaintop Getaway

Work all problems. Find a path to the cabin by
shading in all answers that have a 3 in them.

	98 − 52	46 − 12	68 − 17
79 − 53	65 − 23	63 − 31	86 − 32
59 − 45	75 − 64	67 − 24	97 − 54	55 − 43
87 − 65	44 − 32	57 − 24	88 − 25	75 − 61	48 − 26
69 − 25	95 − 24	48 − 13	58 − 16	35 − 13	39 − 17

SECRET
PATHS

103

MATH

Name _____

Hats, Hats, Hats

Calculate the difference in each hat below.

736
−629

466
−327

837
−529

742
−428

784
−565

673
−458

648
−426

982
−665

947
−729

543
−426

928
−619

847
−628

427
−318

524
−318

245
−126

852
−328

545
−221

Name _____

Soaring to the Stars

Connect the dots to form two stars. Begin one star with the subtraction problem whose difference is 100 and end with the problem whose difference is 109. Begin the other with 110 and end with 120. Color the pictures.

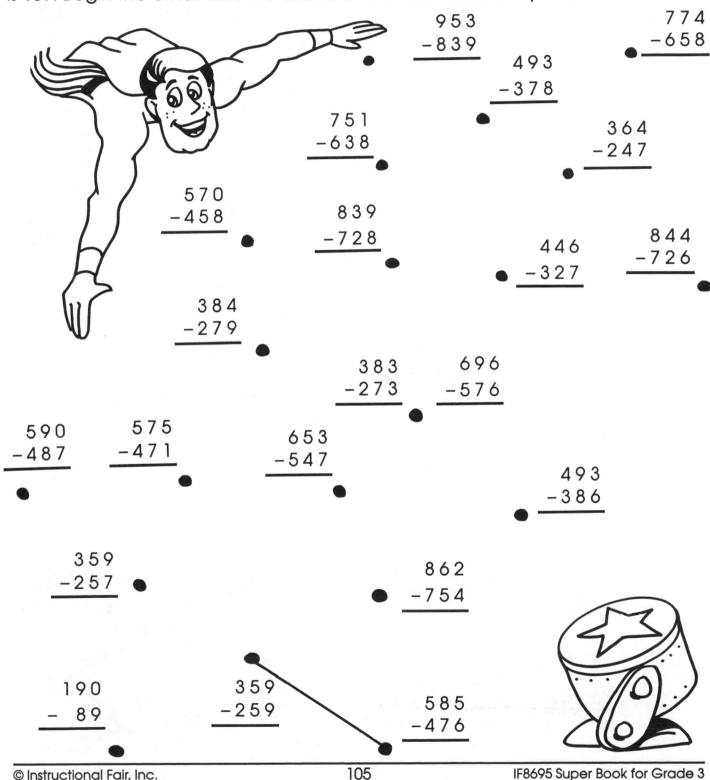

$$953 - 839$$

$$774 - 658$$

$$493 - 378$$

$$364 - 247$$

$$751 - 638$$

$$570 - 458$$

$$839 - 728$$

$$446 - 327$$

$$844 - 726$$

$$384 - 279$$

$$383 - 273$$

$$696 - 576$$

$$590 - 487$$

$$575 - 471$$

$$653 - 547$$

$$493 - 386$$

$$359 - 257$$

$$862 - 754$$

$$190 - 89$$

$$359 - 259$$

$$585 - 476$$

MATH

Name _____

Dino-Might

Whenever you're using "kid transportation," what is the best thing to do? To find out, work the problems. Then write the letters on the matching blanks.

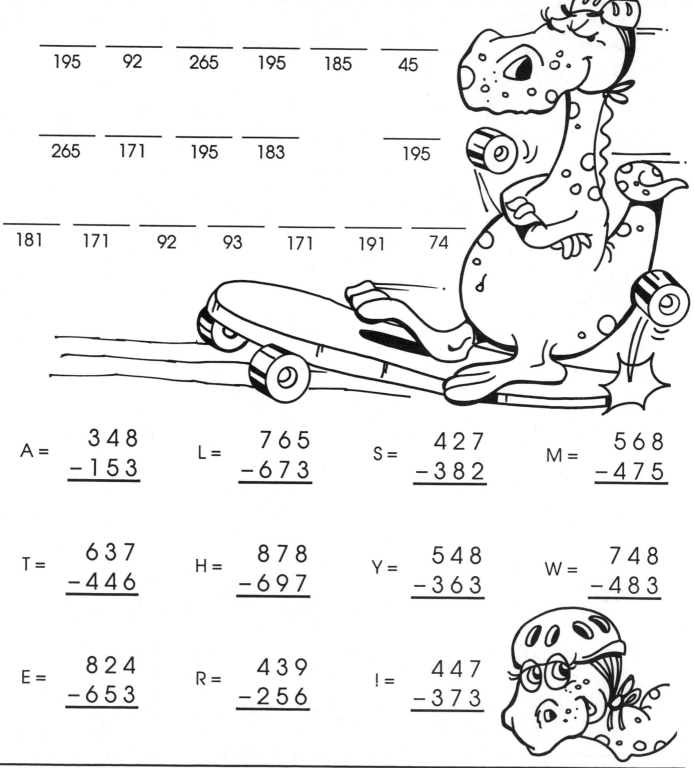

____ ____ ____ ____ ____ ____
195   92   265   195   185   45

____ ____ ____ ____   ____
265   171   195   183   195

____ ____ ____ ____ ____ ____ ____
181   171   92   93   171   191   74

A = 348
    −153

L = 765
    −673

S = 427
    −382

M = 568
    −475

T = 637
    −446

H = 878
    −697

Y = 548
    −363

W = 748
    −483

E = 824
    −653

R = 439
    −256

! = 447
    −373

IF8695 Super Book for Grade 3

Name _____

Find the Hidden Instrument

Solve each problem. Color each shape according to the key below. 482

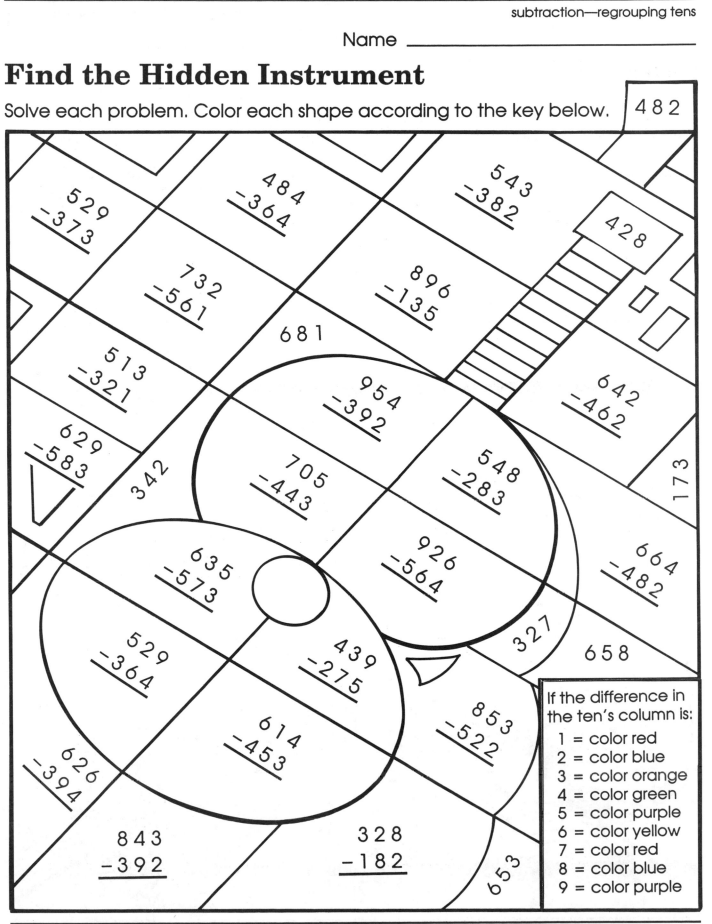

$$\begin{array}{r} 529 \\ -373 \\ \hline \end{array}$$

$$\begin{array}{r} 484 \\ -364 \\ \hline \end{array}$$

$$\begin{array}{r} 543 \\ -382 \\ \hline \end{array}$$

428

$$\begin{array}{r} 732 \\ -561 \\ \hline \end{array}$$

$$\begin{array}{r} 896 \\ -135 \\ \hline \end{array}$$

$$\begin{array}{r} 513 \\ -321 \\ \hline \end{array}$$

681

$$\begin{array}{r} 642 \\ -462 \\ \hline \end{array}$$

$$\begin{array}{r} 629 \\ -583 \\ \hline \end{array}$$

342

$$\begin{array}{r} 954 \\ -392 \\ \hline \end{array}$$

$$\begin{array}{r} 705 \\ -443 \\ \hline \end{array}$$

$$\begin{array}{r} 548 \\ -283 \\ \hline \end{array}$$

173

$$\begin{array}{r} 926 \\ -564 \\ \hline \end{array}$$

$$\begin{array}{r} 664 \\ -482 \\ \hline \end{array}$$

$$\begin{array}{r} 635 \\ -573 \\ \hline \end{array}$$

$$\begin{array}{r} 529 \\ -364 \\ \hline \end{array}$$

$$\begin{array}{r} 439 \\ -275 \\ \hline \end{array}$$

327

658

$$\begin{array}{r} 614 \\ -453 \\ \hline \end{array}$$

$$\begin{array}{r} 853 \\ -522 \\ \hline \end{array}$$

$$\begin{array}{r} 626 \\ -394 \\ \hline \end{array}$$

$$\begin{array}{r} 843 \\ -392 \\ \hline \end{array}$$

$$\begin{array}{r} 328 \\ -182 \\ \hline \end{array}$$

653

If the difference in
the ten's column is:

1 = color red
2 = color blue
3 = color orange
4 = color green
5 = color purple
6 = color yellow
7 = color red
8 = color blue
9 = color purple

Name _____

Sailing Through Subtraction

Start at the bottom and work your way up the sails.

```
  542        638              836        737
- 383      - 453            - 478      - 448
_____      _____            _____      _____


  243        567              984        468
- 154      - 384            - 643      - 399
_____      _____            _____      _____

  524        674              374        246
- 342      - 495            - 185      - 158
_____      _____            _____      _____


  852        736              642        435
- 464      - 557            - 557      - 286
_____      _____            _____      _____
```

IF8695 Super Book for Grade 3

Name _____

Gobble, Gobble

If answer has a **3** in it, color it orange, **4**-red, **5**-purple, **6**-brown, **7**-yellow, **8**-blue and **9**-green.

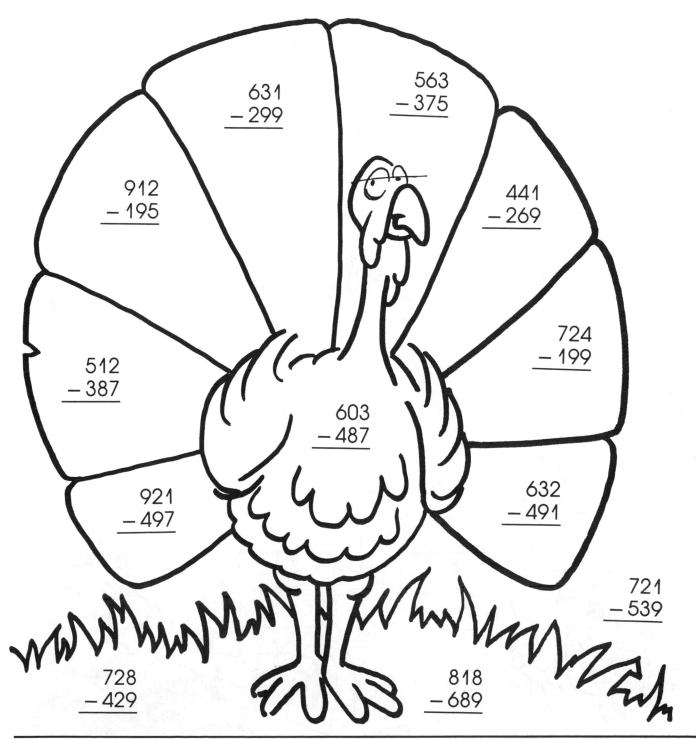

Name _____

Round and Round She Goes . . .

Take a ride around this Ferris wheel.

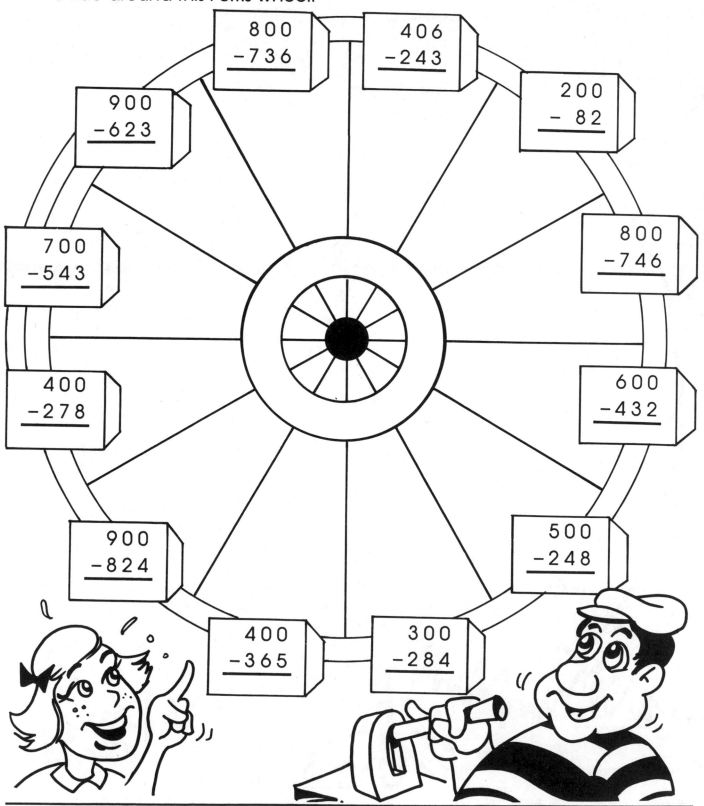

Name _____

Kite Craze!

These subtraction problems are flying high.

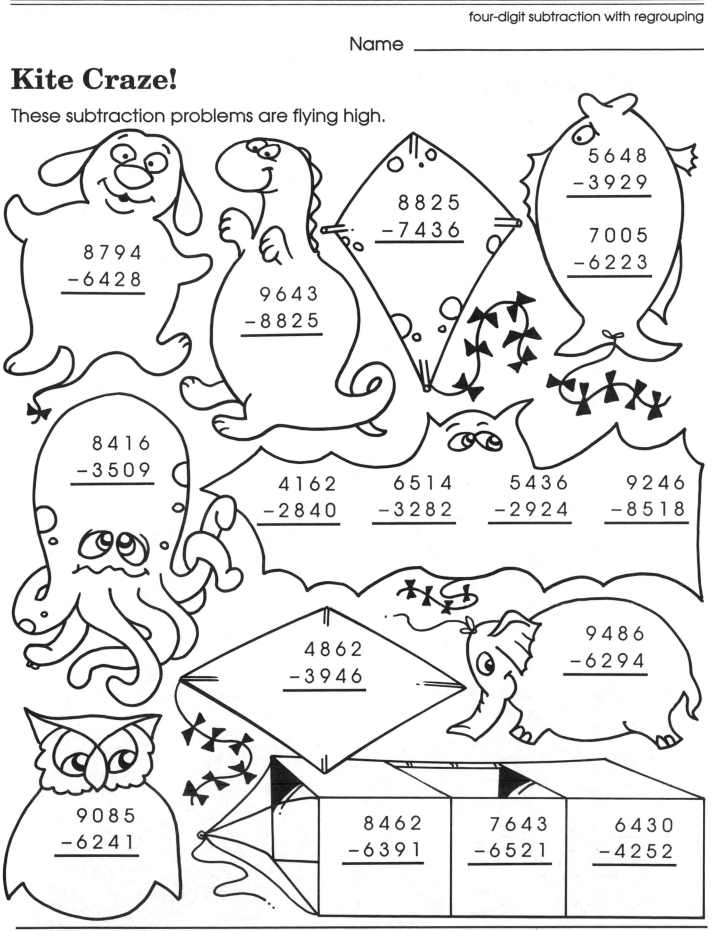

$$\begin{array}{r} 8794 \\ -6428 \\ \hline \end{array}$$

$$\begin{array}{r} 9643 \\ -8825 \\ \hline \end{array}$$

$$\begin{array}{r} 8825 \\ -7436 \\ \hline \end{array}$$

$$\begin{array}{r} 5648 \\ -3929 \\ \hline \end{array}$$

$$\begin{array}{r} 7005 \\ -6223 \\ \hline \end{array}$$

$$\begin{array}{r} 8416 \\ -3509 \\ \hline \end{array}$$

$$\begin{array}{r} 4162 \\ -2840 \\ \hline \end{array}$$

$$\begin{array}{r} 6514 \\ -3282 \\ \hline \end{array}$$

$$\begin{array}{r} 5436 \\ -2924 \\ \hline \end{array}$$

$$\begin{array}{r} 9246 \\ -8518 \\ \hline \end{array}$$

$$\begin{array}{r} 4862 \\ -3946 \\ \hline \end{array}$$

$$\begin{array}{r} 9486 \\ -6294 \\ \hline \end{array}$$

$$\begin{array}{r} 9085 \\ -6241 \\ \hline \end{array}$$

$$\begin{array}{r} 8462 \\ -6391 \\ \hline \end{array}$$

$$\begin{array}{r} 7643 \\ -6521 \\ \hline \end{array}$$

$$\begin{array}{r} 6430 \\ -4252 \\ \hline \end{array}$$

MATH

Name _____

Subtraction on Stage!

These subtraction problems are heading west. Solve 'em. It'll be a bouncy ride.
Just hold on!

```
  5648        2148        7641        7648
 -2425       - 825       -5246       -3289
```

```
  5408        8209        8419        6249
 -1291       -4182       -2182       -1526
```

```
  6428        4287        7645        2016
 -4159       -2492       -2826       -1021
```

```
                                     7689
                                    -2845
```

```
  8247        9047        5231
 -6459       -6152       -1642
```

Name _____

Subtraction Search

Work each problem. Find the answer in the chart and circle it. Answers are in a straight line, but may go in any direction.

2	1	6	3	2	7	5
6	3	3	2	1	0	8
2	2	1	6	3	3	4
0	2	2	6	5	0	6
8	5	4	2	0	8	7
8	9	0	6	1	5	6
3	2	8	4	4	2	1
8	3	4	8	8	5	0
8	1	9	8	7	2	9
3	4	5	8	5	6	7
8	1	3	7	0	4	2
9	3	2	1	7	0	2

$$\begin{array}{r} 6003 \\ -2737 \\ \hline \end{array} \qquad \begin{array}{r} 5040 \\ -3338 \\ \hline \end{array} \qquad \begin{array}{r} 9000 \\ -5725 \\ \hline \end{array}$$

$$\begin{array}{r} 7200 \\ -4356 \\ \hline \end{array} \qquad \begin{array}{r} 3406 \\ -1298 \\ \hline \end{array} \qquad \begin{array}{r} 5602 \\ -3138 \\ \hline \end{array}$$

$$\begin{array}{r} 7006 \\ -5429 \\ \hline \end{array} \qquad \begin{array}{r} 3006 \\ -2798 \\ \hline \end{array} \qquad \begin{array}{r} 3605 \\ -2718 \\ \hline \end{array}$$

$$\begin{array}{r} 5904 \\ -3917 \\ \hline \end{array} \quad \begin{array}{r} 5039 \\ -1954 \\ \hline \end{array} \quad \begin{array}{r} 8704 \\ -2496 \\ \hline \end{array} \quad \begin{array}{r} 4081 \\ -3594 \\ \hline \end{array} \quad \begin{array}{r} 6508 \\ -399 \\ \hline \end{array} \quad \begin{array}{r} 5039 \\ -2467 \\ \hline \end{array}$$

$$\begin{array}{r} 9006 \\ -575 \\ \hline \end{array} \quad \begin{array}{r} 5001 \\ -2351 \\ \hline \end{array} \quad \begin{array}{r} 8002 \\ -5686 \\ \hline \end{array} \quad \begin{array}{r} 6058 \\ -2175 \\ \hline \end{array} \quad \begin{array}{r} 9504 \\ -7368 \\ \hline \end{array} \quad \begin{array}{r} 7290 \\ -1801 \\ \hline \end{array}$$

MATH

Name _____

Dial Carefully

Add or subtract. Write each answer in the puzzle.

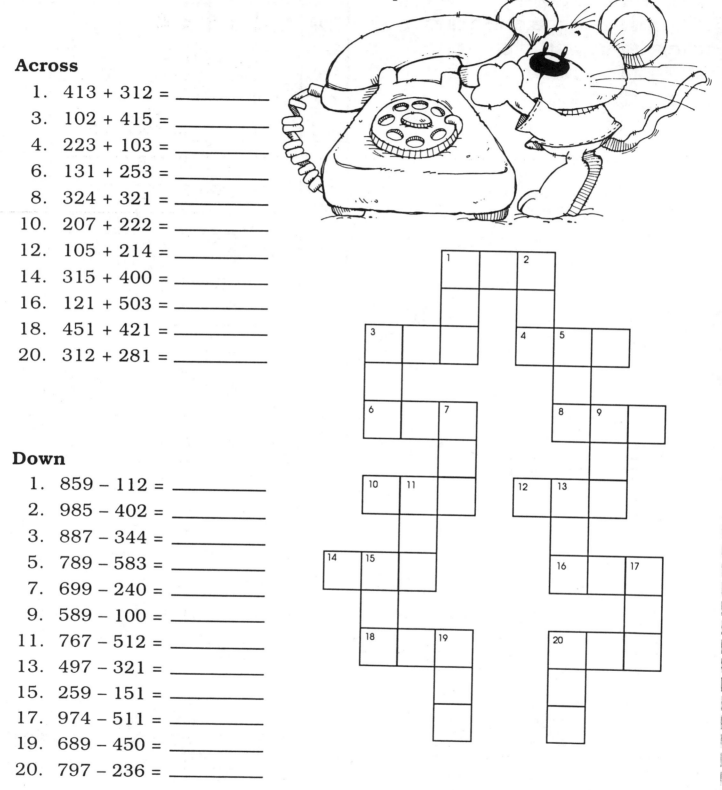

Across

1. 413 + 312 = _____
3. 102 + 415 = _____
4. 223 + 103 = _____
6. 131 + 253 = _____
8. 324 + 321 = _____
10. 207 + 222 = _____
12. 105 + 214 = _____
14. 315 + 400 = _____
16. 121 + 503 = _____
18. 451 + 421 = _____
20. 312 + 281 = _____

Down

1. 859 − 112 = _____
2. 985 − 402 = _____
3. 887 − 344 = _____
5. 789 − 583 = _____
7. 699 − 240 = _____
9. 589 − 100 = _____
11. 767 − 512 = _____
13. 497 − 321 = _____
15. 259 − 151 = _____
17. 974 − 511 = _____
19. 689 − 450 = _____
20. 797 − 236 = _____

Name _____

Wormy Apples

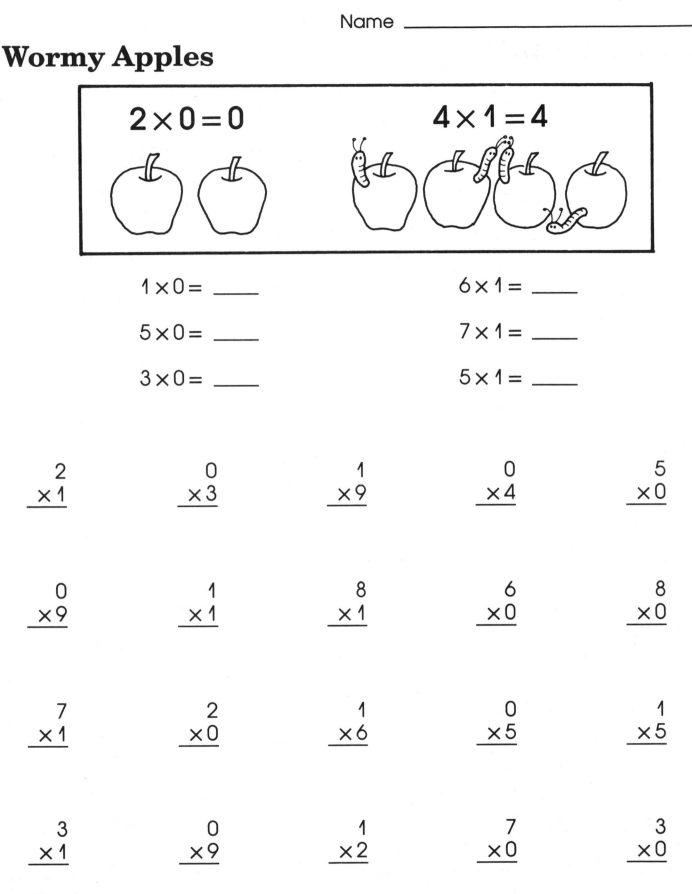

$2 \times 0 = 0$ $4 \times 1 = 4$

$1 \times 0 = $ _____ $6 \times 1 = $ _____

$5 \times 0 = $ _____ $7 \times 1 = $ _____

$3 \times 0 = $ _____ $5 \times 1 = $ _____

$$\begin{array}{r} 2 \\ \times 1 \\ \hline \end{array} \qquad \begin{array}{r} 0 \\ \times 3 \\ \hline \end{array} \qquad \begin{array}{r} 1 \\ \times 9 \\ \hline \end{array} \qquad \begin{array}{r} 0 \\ \times 4 \\ \hline \end{array} \qquad \begin{array}{r} 5 \\ \times 0 \\ \hline \end{array}$$

$$\begin{array}{r} 0 \\ \times 9 \\ \hline \end{array} \qquad \begin{array}{r} 1 \\ \times 1 \\ \hline \end{array} \qquad \begin{array}{r} 8 \\ \times 1 \\ \hline \end{array} \qquad \begin{array}{r} 6 \\ \times 0 \\ \hline \end{array} \qquad \begin{array}{r} 8 \\ \times 0 \\ \hline \end{array}$$

$$\begin{array}{r} 7 \\ \times 1 \\ \hline \end{array} \qquad \begin{array}{r} 2 \\ \times 0 \\ \hline \end{array} \qquad \begin{array}{r} 1 \\ \times 6 \\ \hline \end{array} \qquad \begin{array}{r} 0 \\ \times 5 \\ \hline \end{array} \qquad \begin{array}{r} 1 \\ \times 5 \\ \hline \end{array}$$

$$\begin{array}{r} 3 \\ \times 1 \\ \hline \end{array} \qquad \begin{array}{r} 0 \\ \times 9 \\ \hline \end{array} \qquad \begin{array}{r} 1 \\ \times 2 \\ \hline \end{array} \qquad \begin{array}{r} 7 \\ \times 0 \\ \hline \end{array} \qquad \begin{array}{r} 3 \\ \times 0 \\ \hline \end{array}$$

Name _____

Factor Fun

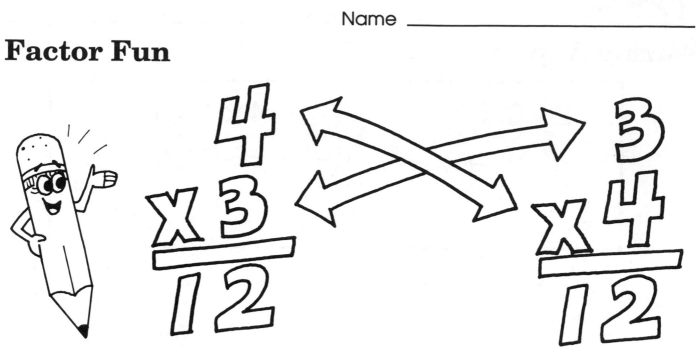

If you change the order of the factors, you have the same product.

7 ×3	3 ×7	6 ×5	5 ×6	2 ×3	3 ×2

$4 \times 6 =$ _____ $2 \times 9 =$ _____ $8 \times 4 =$ _____

$6 \times 4 =$ _____ $9 \times 2 =$ _____ $4 \times 8 =$ _____

7 ×2	2 ×7	3 ×6	6 ×3	9 ×4	4 ×9

$8 \times 3 =$ _____ $5 \times 2 =$ _____ $9 \times 3 =$ _____

$3 \times 8 =$ _____ $2 \times 5 =$ _____ $3 \times 9 =$ _____

Name _____

The Aliens Are Coming!

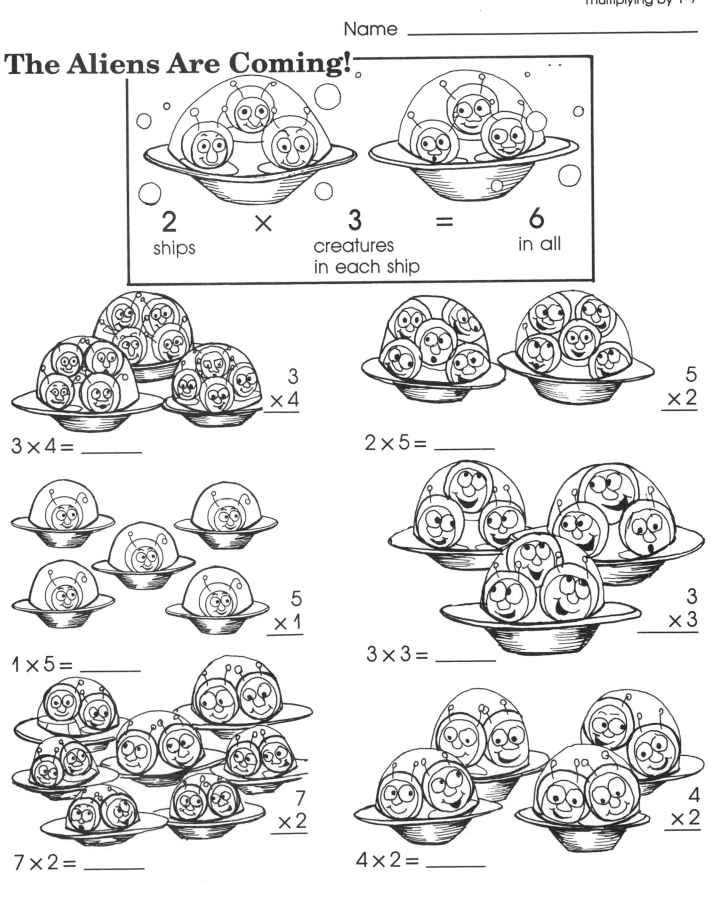

2 × 3 = 6
ships   creatures   in all
          in each ship

3 × 4 = _____
$$\begin{array}{r} 3 \\ \times 4 \\ \hline \end{array}$$

2 × 5 = _____
$$\begin{array}{r} 5 \\ \times 2 \\ \hline \end{array}$$

1 × 5 = _____
$$\begin{array}{r} 5 \\ \times 1 \\ \hline \end{array}$$

3 × 3 = _____
$$\begin{array}{r} 3 \\ \times 3 \\ \hline \end{array}$$

7 × 2 = _____
$$\begin{array}{r} 7 \\ \times 2 \\ \hline \end{array}$$

4 × 2 = _____
$$\begin{array}{r} 4 \\ \times 2 \\ \hline \end{array}$$

MATH

Name _____

Racing to the Finish

WINNER

3 × 5

$$\begin{array}{r} 5 \\ \times 3 \\ \hline \end{array}$$
$$\begin{array}{r} 2 \\ \times 8 \\ \hline \end{array}$$
$$\begin{array}{r} 4 \\ \times 6 \\ \hline \end{array}$$
$$\begin{array}{r} 9 \\ \times 3 \\ \hline \end{array}$$

$$\begin{array}{r} 7 \\ \times 5 \\ \hline \end{array}$$
$$\begin{array}{r} 3 \\ \times 9 \\ \hline \end{array}$$
$$\begin{array}{r} 4 \\ \times 2 \\ \hline \end{array}$$
$$\begin{array}{r} 6 \\ \times 2 \\ \hline \end{array}$$
$$\begin{array}{r} 4 \\ \times 4 \\ \hline \end{array}$$
$$\begin{array}{r} 0 \\ \times 6 \\ \hline \end{array}$$

$$\begin{array}{r} 3 \\ \times 2 \\ \hline \end{array}$$
$$\begin{array}{r} 7 \\ \times 2 \\ \hline \end{array}$$
$$\begin{array}{r} 6 \\ \times 5 \\ \hline \end{array}$$
$$\begin{array}{r} 3 \\ \times 4 \\ \hline \end{array}$$
$$\begin{array}{r} 8 \\ \times 3 \\ \hline \end{array}$$
$$\begin{array}{r} 4 \\ \times 5 \\ \hline \end{array}$$

$$\begin{array}{r} 5 \\ \times 2 \\ \hline \end{array}$$
$$\begin{array}{r} 7 \\ \times 4 \\ \hline \end{array}$$
$$\begin{array}{r} 6 \\ \times 3 \\ \hline \end{array}$$
$$\begin{array}{r} 4 \\ \times 8 \\ \hline \end{array}$$
$$\begin{array}{r} 2 \\ \times 2 \\ \hline \end{array}$$
$$\begin{array}{r} 8 \\ \times 5 \\ \hline \end{array}$$

$$\begin{array}{r} 3 \\ \times 7 \\ \hline \end{array}$$
$$\begin{array}{r} 5 \\ \times 5 \\ \hline \end{array}$$
$$\begin{array}{r} 5 \\ \times 9 \\ \hline \end{array}$$
$$\begin{array}{r} 9 \\ \times 2 \\ \hline \end{array}$$
$$\begin{array}{r} 4 \\ \times 6 \\ \hline \end{array}$$
$$\begin{array}{r} 9 \\ \times 4 \\ \hline \end{array}$$

Name _____

Double Trouble

Solve each multiplication problem. Below each answer, write the letter from the code that matches. Read the coded question and write the answer in the space provided.

1	4	9	16	25	36	49	64	81	100	121	144
e	g	h	i	n	o	s	t	u	w	x	y

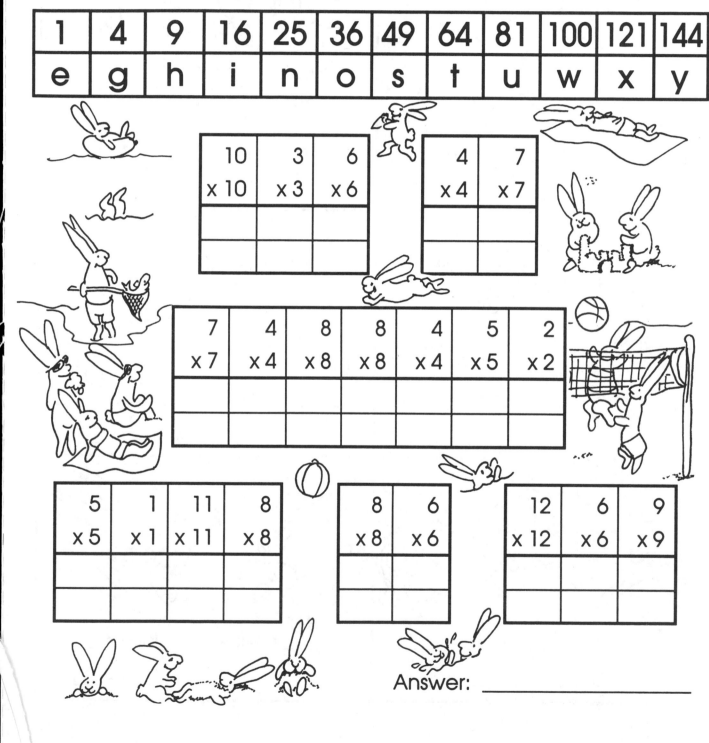

10 x 10	3 x 3	6 x 6

4 x 4	7 x 7

7 x 7	4 x 4	8 x 8	8 x 8	4 x 4	5 x 5	2 x 2

5 x 5	1 x 1	11 x 11	8 x 8

8 x 8	6 x 6

12 x 12	6 x 6	9 x 9

Answer: _____

MATH

Name _____

Count the Legs!

Multiply to find the number of legs. Write the problem twice.

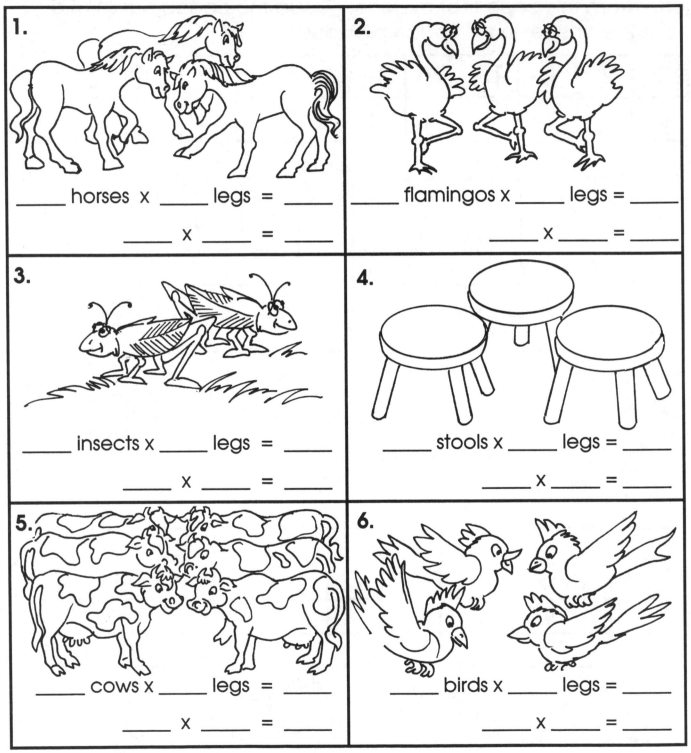

1.

____ horses x ____ legs = ____

____ x ____ = ____

2.

____ flamingos x ____ legs = ____

____ x ____ = ____

3.

____ insects x ____ legs = ____

____ x ____ = ____

4.

____ stools x ____ legs = ____

____ x ____ = ____

5.

____ cows x ____ legs = ____

____ x ____ = ____

6.

____ birds x ____ legs = ____

____ x ____ = ____

Name _____

Bows, Bows, Bows

$$15 \div 3 = 5 \text{ sets}$$
in   in
all each
     set

$$\overset{5 \text{ sets}}{3\overline{)15 \text{ in all}}}$$
in
each
set

$8 \div 2 =$ _____ $2\overline{)8}$ $12 \div 4 =$ _____ $4\overline{)12}$

$21 \div 3 =$ _____ $3\overline{)21}$ $18 \div 3 =$ _____ $3\overline{)18}$

$20 \div 5 =$ _____ $5\overline{)20}$ $16 \div 4 =$ _____ $4\overline{)16}$

$14 \div 7 =$ _____ $7\overline{)14}$ $12 \div 2 =$ _____ $2\overline{)12}$

$18 \div 2 =$ _____ $2\overline{)18}$ $24 \div 6 =$ _____ $6\overline{)24}$

MATH

Name _____

Blastoff!

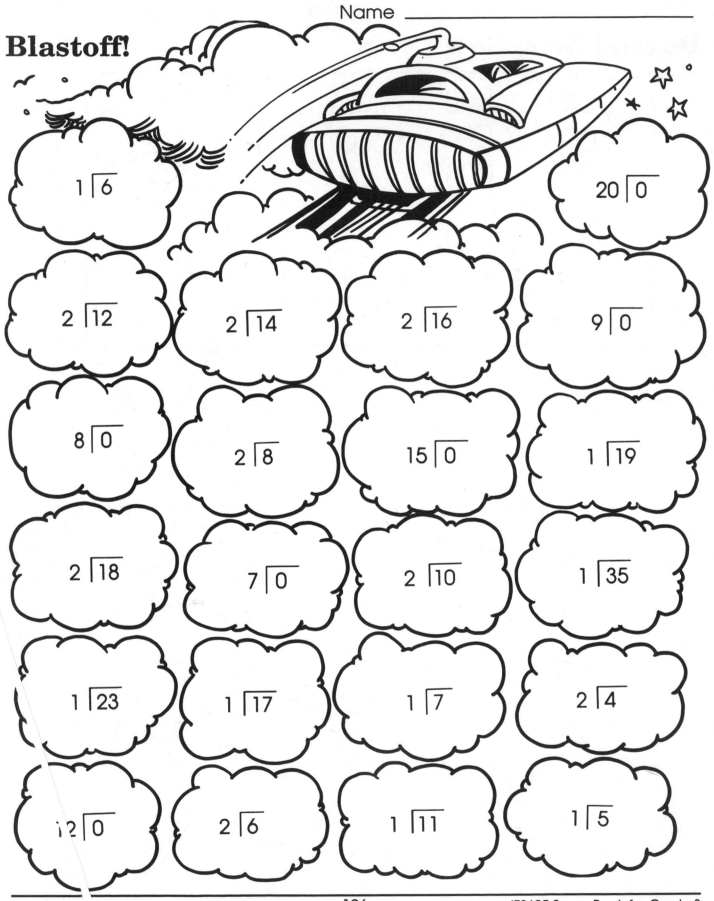

$1 \overline{)6}$

$20 \overline{)0}$

$2 \overline{)12}$

$2 \overline{)14}$

$2 \overline{)16}$

$9 \overline{)0}$

$8 \overline{)0}$

$2 \overline{)8}$

$15 \overline{)0}$

$1 \overline{)19}$

$2 \overline{)18}$

$7 \overline{)0}$

$2 \overline{)10}$

$1 \overline{)35}$

$1 \overline{)23}$

$1 \overline{)17}$

$1 \overline{)7}$

$2 \overline{)4}$

$12 \overline{)0}$

$2 \overline{)6}$

$1 \overline{)11}$

$1 \overline{)5}$

Name _____

Jersey Division

Arrange jersey digits in the balls to get correct answer.

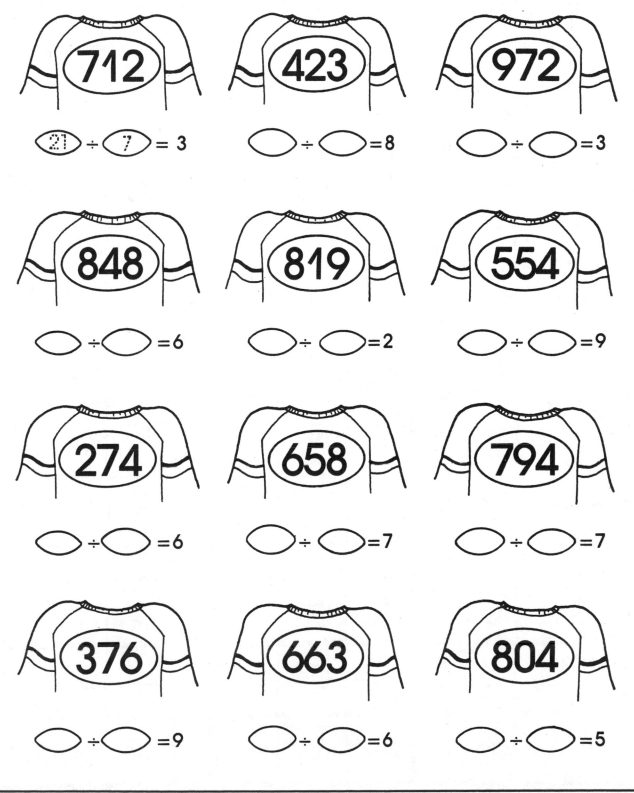

712 $21 \div 7 = 3$

423 $\bigcirc \div \bigcirc = 8$

972 $\bigcirc \div \bigcirc = 3$

848 $\bigcirc \div \bigcirc = 6$

819 $\bigcirc \div \bigcirc = 2$

554 $\bigcirc \div \bigcirc = 9$

274 $\bigcirc \div \bigcirc = 6$

658 $\bigcirc \div \bigcirc = 7$

794 $\bigcirc \div \bigcirc = 7$

376 $\bigcirc \div \bigcirc = 9$

663 $\bigcirc \div \bigcirc = 6$

804 $\bigcirc \div \bigcirc = 5$

MATH

Name _____

Division Tic-Tac-Toe

9, 7, 5, 3 = X

8, 6, 4, 2 = O

X on odd answers   O on even answers

$4\overline{)36}$	$4\overline{)24}$	$10 \div 5$	$4\overline{)32}$	$12 \div 4$	$5\overline{)30}$	$24 \div 4$	$5\overline{)45}$	$28 \div 4$
$5\overline{)40}$	$32 \div 4$	$25 \div 5$	$4\overline{)28}$	$4\overline{)20}$	$20 \div 4$	$5\overline{)45}$	$5\overline{)20}$	$8 \div 4$
$35 \div 5$	$20 \div 4$	$12 \div 4$	$20 \div 5$	$10 \div 5$	$15 \div 5$	$4\overline{)16}$	$5\overline{)15}$	$30 \div 5$
$25 \div 5$	$4\overline{)8}$	$16 \div 4$	$5\overline{)10}$	$4\overline{)8}$	$24 \div 4$	$8 \div 4$	$45 \div 5$	$4\overline{)16}$
$32 \div 4$	$5\overline{)20}$	$5\overline{)35}$	$4\overline{)36}$	$5\overline{)35}$	$4\overline{)32}$	$5\overline{)25}$	$36 \div 4$	$4\overline{)24}$
$40 \div 5$	$4\overline{)12}$	$15 \div 5$	$45 \div 5$	$5\overline{)30}$	$4\overline{)12}$	$5\overline{)10}$	$25 \div 5$	$4\overline{)36}$
$4\overline{)12}$	$5\overline{)10}$	$5\overline{)45}$	$36 \div 4$	$4\overline{)28}$	$16 \div 4$	$28 \div 4$	$5\overline{)30}$	$45 \div 5$
$30 \div 5$	$5\overline{)25}$	$35 \div 5$	$24 \div 4$	$5\overline{)35}$	$5\overline{)40}$	$16 \div 4$	$32 \div 4$	$15 \div 5$
$4\overline{)32}$	$8 \div 4$	$5\overline{)20}$	$5\overline{)25}$	$8 \div 4$	$36 \div 4$	$4\overline{)20}$	$4\overline{)12}$	$4\overline{)8}$

Name ______________________

Mr. R Means Business

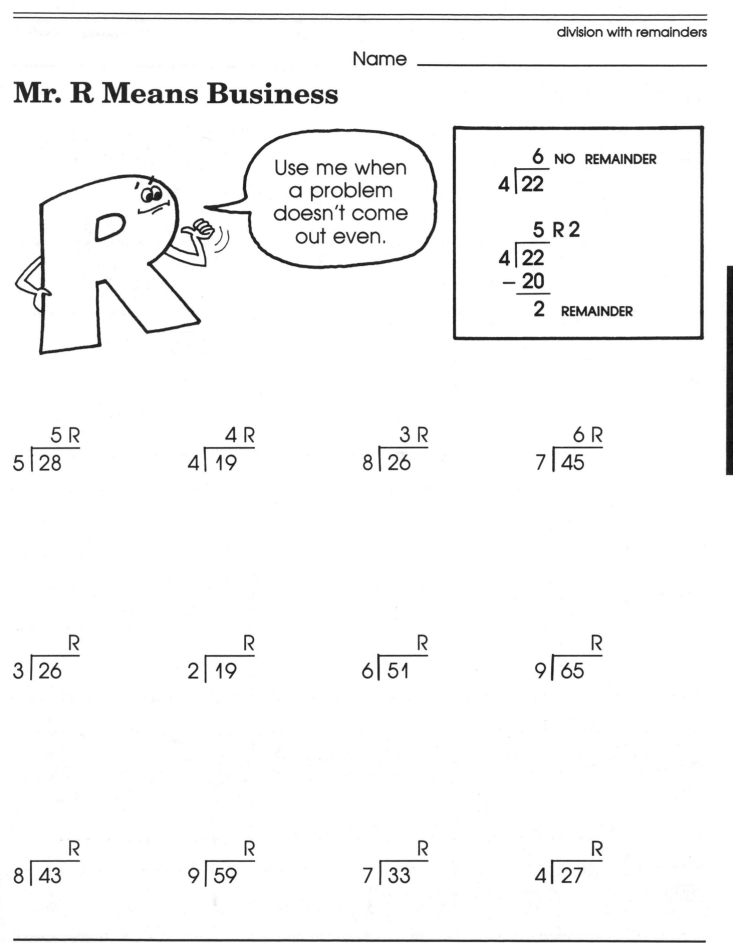

Use me when a problem doesn't come out even.

```
    6  NO REMAINDER
4 | 22

    5 R 2
4 | 22
  - 20
     2  REMAINDER
```


$5\overline{)28}$ = 5 R	$4\overline{)19}$ = 4 R	$8\overline{)26}$ = 3 R	$7\overline{)45}$ = 6 R
$3\overline{)26}$ = R	$2\overline{)19}$ = R	$6\overline{)51}$ = R	$9\overline{)65}$ = R
$8\overline{)43}$ = R	$9\overline{)59}$ = R	$7\overline{)33}$ = R	$4\overline{)27}$ = R

Name _____

Make It Fair

Circle the items and then write two division problems to go with each picture.

There are six children. Circle the number of cookies each child will get if the cookies are divided equally.

_____   _____

There are eight dogs. Circle the dog biscuits each dog will get if the dog biscuits are divided equally.

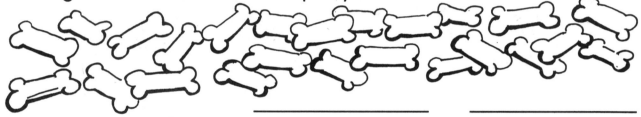

_____   _____

Divide the pepperoni so that five pizzas will have the same amount.

_____   _____

Separate the books so that there will be the same number of books on three shelves.

_____   _____

On the back of this page, draw pictures of your own and write division sentences to go with them.

Hmm, What Should I Do?

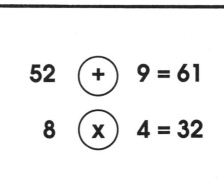

$$52 \; \bigoplus \; 9 = 61$$

$$8 \; \bigotimes \; 4 = 32$$

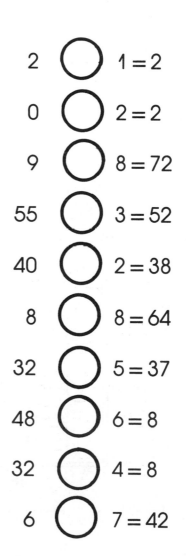
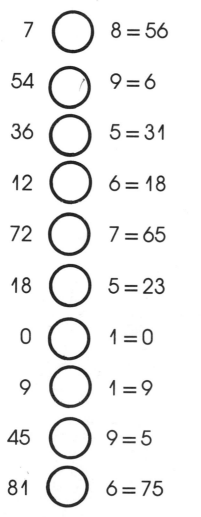

MATH

Write the correct symbols in the circles.

7 ◯ 8 = 56   2 ◯ 1 = 2

54 ◯ 9 = 6   0 ◯ 2 = 2

36 ◯ 5 = 31   9 ◯ 8 = 72

12 ◯ 6 = 18   55 ◯ 3 = 52

72 ◯ 7 = 65   40 ◯ 2 = 38

18 ◯ 5 = 23   8 ◯ 8 = 64

0 ◯ 1 = 0   32 ◯ 5 = 37

9 ◯ 1 = 9   48 ◯ 6 = 8

45 ◯ 9 = 5   32 ◯ 4 = 8

81 ◯ 6 = 75   6 ◯ 7 = 42

Name _____

Easy Street

Easy does it! What is each house worth?
Count the money in each house on Easy
Street. Write the amount on the line.

Example

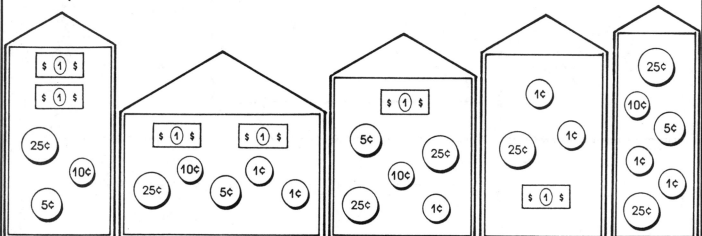

$2.40   _____   _____   _____   _____

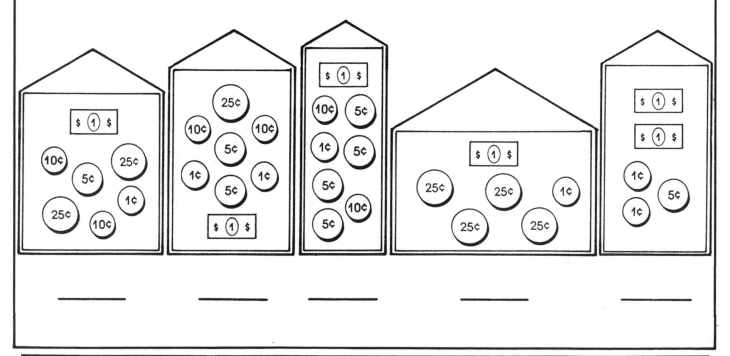

_____   _____   _____   _____   _____

Name _____

Your Answer's Safe with Me

Find the right "combination" to open each safe. Draw the bills and coins needed to make each amount.

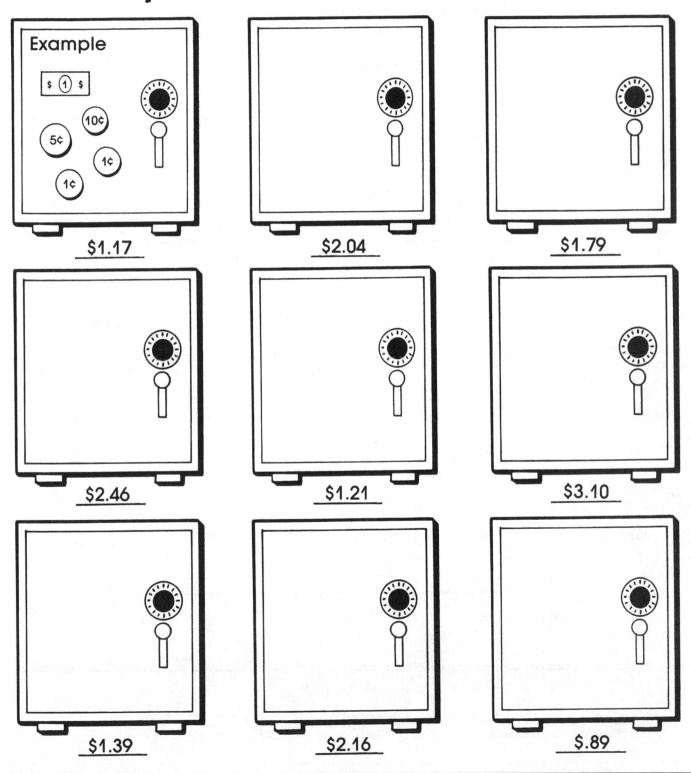

Example

$ 1 $

10¢

5¢

1¢

1¢

$1.17

$2.04

$1.79

$2.46

$1.21

$3.10

$1.39

$2.16

$.89

MATH

Name _____

A Collection of Coins

Figure out which coins are needed to make the given amount.

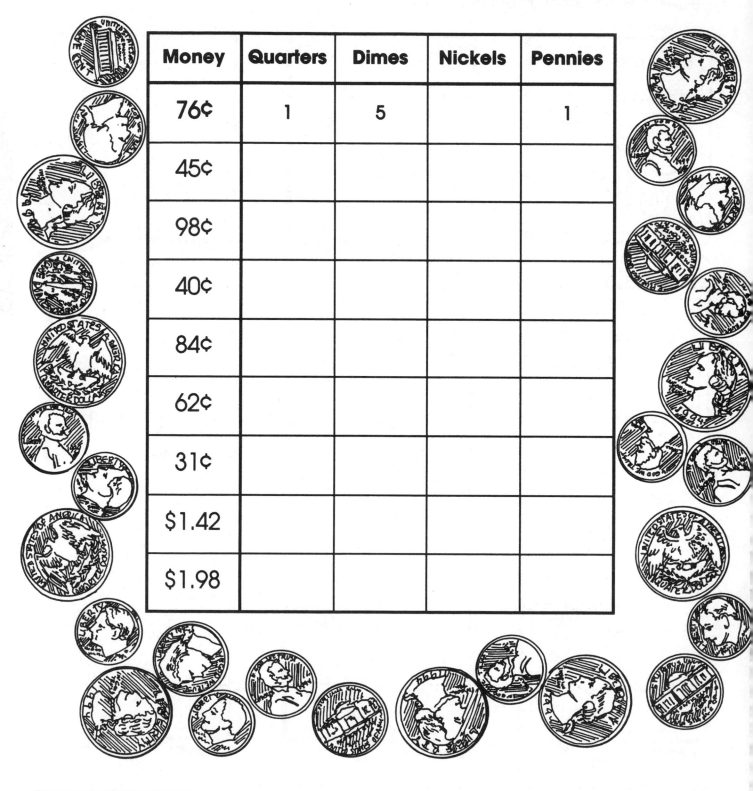

Money	Quarters	Dimes	Nickels	Pennies
76¢	1	5		1
45¢				
98¢				
40¢				
84¢				
62¢				
31¢				
$1.42				
$1.98				

Name _____

Pizza "Dough" Business

The number of pieces tells you how many coins to use. Write in the amounts to equal the total price of these pizzas.

Name _____

How Many Coins?

Take the fewest coins possible to equal the amount shown in each box. Put the coins in the box. Record the coins.

17¢

coins:

98¢

coins:

24¢

coins:

63¢

coins:

58¢

coins:

35¢

coins:

IF8695 Super Book for Grade 3

Making Change

When you do not have the exact change to buy something at a store, the clerk must give you change. The first amount of money is what you give the clerk. The second amount is what the item costs. In the box, list the least amount of coins and bills you will receive in change. Write your own problems in boxes 9 and 10.

	Amount I Have	Cost of Item	Change
1	$3.75	$3.54	
2	$10.00	$5.63	
3	$7.00	$6.05	
4	$6.50	$7.25	
5	$7.50	$6.13	
6	$0.75	$0.37	
7	$7.00	$6.99	
8	$15.00	$12.75	
9			
10			

© Instructional Fair, Inc.   139   IF8695 Super Book for Grade 3

Name _____

Monetary Message

What's the smartest thing to do with your money? To find out, use the key at the bottom of the page to match the letters with the sums in the blanks provided.

| _____ | _____ | _____ | _____ | | _____ | _____ | _____ |
| $42.71 | $33.94 | $50.42 | $100.73 | | $45.70 | $2.39 | $1.55 |

| _____ | _____ | _____ | | _____ | _____ | | _____ | _____ | _____ | _____ |
| $33.94 | $26.13 | $88.02 | | $45.70 | $2.39 | | $51.12 | $45.70 | $11.01 | $11.01 |

| _____ | _____ | _____ | | _____ | _____ | _____ |
| $33.94 | $88.02 | $88.02 | | $55.76 | $42.79 | $6.84 |

V = $\begin{array}{r} \$42.13 \\ +\ \ 8.29 \\ \hline \end{array}$
A = $\begin{array}{r} \$\ 4.56 \\ +\ 29.38 \\ \hline \end{array}$
N = $\begin{array}{r} \$\ \ 4.65 \\ +\ 21.48 \\ \hline \end{array}$
, = $\begin{array}{r} \$\ \ \ .09 \\ 1.25 \\ +\ \ \ .21 \\ \hline \end{array}$

P = $\begin{array}{r} \$\ 9.31 \\ +\ 33.48 \\ \hline \end{array}$
L = $\begin{array}{r} \$\ 6.73 \\ +\ \ 4.28 \\ \hline \end{array}$
E = $\begin{array}{r} \$\ 81.49 \\ +\ 19.24 \\ \hline \end{array}$

T = $\begin{array}{r} \$\ \ \ .42 \\ 1.94 \\ +\ \ \ .03 \\ \hline \end{array}$

U = $\begin{array}{r} \$\ 50.84 \\ +\ \ \ 4.92 \\ \hline \end{array}$
I = $\begin{array}{r} \$\ 7.49 \\ +\ 38.21 \\ \hline \end{array}$
S = $\begin{array}{r} \$\ 23.46 \\ +\ 19.25 \\ \hline \end{array}$

D = $\begin{array}{r} \$\ 3.04 \\ +\ 84.98 \\ \hline \end{array}$
W = $\begin{array}{r} \$\ 1.89 \\ +\ 49.23 \\ \hline \end{array}$
! = $\begin{array}{r} \$\ 4.35 \\ +\ 2.49 \\ \hline \end{array}$

Name _____

Add 'Em Up!

Write in the prices and then add. Regroup when needed. Choose the items to be added together in problems 13-18.

Picture items with prices:
- skateboard $29.32
- watch $4.37
- hot dog $.69
- dictionary $8.43
- kite $4.84
- rocket $3.84
- guitar $34.99
- hat $2.41
- radio $43.09
- goldfish $.84
- purse $3.09
- rollerblades $84.36

1. skateboard
   + hat
   ____

2. dictionary
   + radio
   ____

3. purse
   + goldfish
   ____

4. hot dog
   + watch
   ____

5. dictionary
   + kite
   ____

6. rollerblades
   + guitar
   ____

7. hot dog
   + rocket
   ____

8. skateboard
   + goldfish
   ____

9. hat
   + kite
   ____

10. radio
   + guitar
   ____

11. rocket
   + goldfish
   ____

12. skateboard
   + rollerblades
   ____

13. _____
   + _____

14. _____
   + _____

15. _____
   + _____

16. _____
   + _____

17. _____
   + _____

18. _____
   + _____

MATH

Name _____

Spending Spree

Use the clues to figure out what each child bought. Then, subtract to find out how much change each had left.

Clue:

1. Katelyn started with: $23.45 — She likes to keep warm!

2. David began with: $40.25 — He loves to see things zoom into the sky!

3. Mark started with: $50.37 — He likes to travel places with his hands free and a breeze in his face!

4. Eva started with: $14.84 — She loves to practice her jumping and exercise at the same time!

5. Earl arrived with: $26.42 — He loves to learn about interesting things!

6. Bill brought: $61.49 — He wants to see the heavens for himself!

7. Michelle brought: $40.29 — Fuzzy companions make such great friends!

8. Cheryl started with: $16.80 — She loves to hear music that is soft and beautiful!

9. Heather arrived with: $20.48 — She loves to put it down on paper for everyone to see!

$9.31

$12.49

$52.28

$15.29

$2.43

$13.45

$21.52

$32.51

$3.95

$47.29

Name _____

Dessert Included

Brenda and Doug really like chocolate — chocolate-covered raisins, chocolate candy, chocolate cake, hot chocolate! Most of all, they are very fond of chocolate sundaes with chocolate chip ice cream. When they find out that the Eats and Sweets Restaurant is offering a free chocolate dessert with any meal costing exactly $5.00, they decide to go there for dinner.

Menu

Meat

Chicken	$1.95
Roast Beef	$3.05
Shrimp	$3.50
Roast Pork	$2.75

Potatoes/Vegetables

Mashed Potatoes	$1.00
French Fries	$.85
Sweet Corn	$.65
Green Beans	$.50

Salads

Cole Slaw	$.60
Potato Salad	$.95
Dinner Salad	$.75
Macaroni Salad	$1.10

Drinks

White Milk	$.40
Chocolate Milk	$.45
Orange Juice	$.95
Soda Pop	$.55

Choosing one item from each of the four categories, list four different meals they could eat for exactly $5.00, and then receive the free dessert.

Meal # 1 _____ , _____ , _____ , _____

Meal # 2 _____ , _____ , _____ , _____

Meal # 3 _____ , _____ , _____ , _____

Meal # 4 _____ , _____ , _____ , _____

Big Discount

Name _____

The Terrific Toy Company is celebrating its 50th anniversary. All of the toys are discounted.

Original Cost of Toy	Discount
$3.00 – $5.00	$1.00
$6.00 – $10.00	$2.00
$11.00 – $15.00	$3.00
$16.00 – $20.00	$4.00
$21.00 – $25.00	$5.00

As a special bonus, if your bill **after** the discount is exactly $50.00, you also get a free movie video called "Toyland."

Look carefully at the toys and their original prices listed below.

Puzzle – $3.00

Action Figure – $6.00

Board Game – $8.00

Basketball – $10.00

Football – $12.00

Talking Doll – $15.00

Deluxe Blocks – $20.00

Teddy Bear – $22.00

Video Game – $24.00

Remote-Controlled Car – $25.00

Using the discount prices, decide which four toys you might buy in order to get the free movie video. Figure out two solutions. Do not choose any toy more than once.

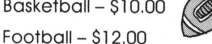

Solution number 1: _____ , _____ , _____ , _____

Solution number 2: _____ , _____ , _____ , _____

Mind-Bogglers

These problems will boggle your mind. Don't give up. Try different problem-solving strategies to help you find the answers.

1. Marta receives an allowance of $2.25 a week. This week her mom pays her in nickels, dimes and quarters. She received more dimes than quarters.

   What coins did her mom use to pay her? _____

   Strategy I used: _____

2. You are asked to draw a picture of a dinosaur. You make the head 1/3 as long as the body. You draw the tail as long as the head and the body combined. The total length of the dinosaur is 56 inches. How long did you make each part of the dinosaur?

   head _____ tail _____ body _____

   Strategy I used: _____

3. Mr. Whitman takes his family on a trip to the amusement park. He brings $75 with him to buy the entrance tickets, food and souvenirs for the family. The tickets to get into the amusement park are $12.75 for adults and $8.45 for children. How much money will Mr. Whitman have for food and souvenirs after he buys entrance tickets for himself, Mrs. Whitman and their two children? _____

   Strategy I used: _____

4. There are eight tables in the classroom. Normally, the teacher has two students sitting on each side. Today, she is going to do a special project so she pushes all eight tables together in a long row. How many students can sit at the long table? _____

   Strategy I used: _____

5. Mr. Jonyou gives his three children a weekly allowance. He pays them in dollar bills. Tony is the first to get paid. He receives half the number of dollar bills his dad has. Joe gets his allowance second. He receives half of the remaining dollar bills plus one. Mr. Jonyou now has $2 left, which is Carmen's allowance. How much allowance do Tony and Joe receive?

   Tony _____ Joe _____

   Strategy I used: _____

Vote for Me!

Name _____

Middletown School had an election to choose the new members of the Student Council. Grace, Bernie, Laurie, Sherry, and Sam all ran for the office of president.

On the chart below are the five students' names with three numbers after each name. The numbers represent the votes each might have received.

Grace	21	36	39
Bernie	47	32	26
Laurie	25	44	38
Sherry	34	37	40
Sam	48	33	29

Use the information and the clues below to see who became president, and how many votes he or she received.

- The winning number of votes was an even number.
- The winning number of votes was between 30 and 40.
- The two digits added together are greater than 10.

_____ became the president of the Student Council with _____ votes.

Who would have become president
if the winning number was **odd** and
the other clues remained the same? _____

Name _____

How Many Outfits?

Suppose you had two pairs of jeans (one blue and the other gray) and three shirts (blue, red and green). How many different outfits could you wear? Use the pictures to help you with the answer.

Your friend has six sweaters and five shirts. How many different combinations of shirts and sweaters does she have? Draw your own pictures to help you figure out the answer.

Your dad has five shirts and six ties. How many different ways can he wear his shirts and ties? Draw pictures if you need to do so.

On the back of this paper, make up your own story problems.

Name _____

Emery Prepares for His Party

Read each story problem carefully. What is the question? What information is given that will help with the answer? Will drawing a picture help? Remember that solving story problems takes time.

1. If Emery needed 329 knives, 329 forks and 329 spoons, how many pieces of silverware did Emery need altogether? _____

2. Emery cooked 329 eggs for his guests. How many dozen eggs did he need to buy? _____

3. Emery baked tarts for dessert. The recipe he followed yielded eight tarts. How many batches of tarts would he have to make to get 329 tarts?

   _____

4. If each recipe called for two eggs, how many eggs would Emery need to make the tarts? To solve this problem, you will need the information from problem 3. _____

5. Before Emery peeled his potatoes, he weighed them. He discovered that there were five potatoes in each pound. He planned on preparing enough potatoes to feed 330 people one each. How many pounds of potatoes would he need? _____

6. The guests sat at 54 tables. Each table had two vases. Emery put five flowers in each vase. How many flowers did he have to pick? _____

7. Write you own story problem about Emery Raccoon and his party.

Name _____

Solving Math Problems

Solving a mystery is like solving a math problem. Jenny Archer had a mystery that she wasn't certain how to solve. Just as she tried several methods in order to solve her mystery, solving math problems may take many tries. Solve the problems below.

1. Your dad wants to deposit money in his bank account. The bank is a very busy place. He has to stand in line. There are 6 people in front of him and 8 people behind him. How many people are standing in line? _____

2. A jogger can jog 1.5 miles in 12 minutes. He jogged for 30 minutes. How far did he jog? _____

3. Your parents are trying to save money to buy something very special. If they save $2 in January, $4 in February, $8 in March, and so on, how much money will they save in a year? _____

4. When you go to a fancy restaurant, it is customary to leave a 15% tip for the server. This means that you pay the bill for your food plus you leave 15% of that bill. If your meal cost $6.00, how much should you leave for a tip?

_____

Name _____

Racing Chimps

One chimpanzee in the forest always liked to brag that it could get more fruit than any other animal in the forest. So an older and wiser chimpanzee decided to challenge him to a race.

"Let us see who can bring back more bananas in one hour," said the older chimp. The race began.

Quickly, the younger chimp picked a bunch of five bananas and carried it back. He continued doing this every five minutes.

The older chimp was not quite as fast. Every ten minutes he carried back eight bananas.

After 45 minutes the young chimp decided to stop and eat one of his bananas before continuing. By the time he finished, the hour was over and the older chimp called out, "The race is over. My pile of bananas is bigger. I have won the race!"

Using the information above, figure out how many bananas were in each pile, and which chimp won the race.

The younger chimp had _____ bananas in his pile.

The older chimp had _____ bananas in his pile.

The winner was the _____ chimp!

Name _____

The Lion Dance

The Lion Dance, which started in China, became a Japanese folk dance. In this dance many people line up under a long piece of colorful cloth. The person in front wears a mask of a lion's head. As a group, the line of people dance in the streets around the town.

In this Lion Dance the children lined up in this order: 2 boys, 2 girls, 2 boys, 2 girls. The order remained the same through the entire line.

- Masato, a Japanese boy, stood behind the fifth boy. Find and circle his left foot.

- Koko, a Japanese girl, stood in front of the seventh boy. Put a box around her left foot.

- If every two children needed a 4-foot section of the cloth, and the lion's head was 4 feet long, how many feet long is the entire costume?

_____ feet

Challenge!

- How many yards long is the entire lion costume?

_____ yards

Name _____

How Far Is It?

Drawing pictures can be a good problem-solving strategy. If you wish, use another sheet of paper to draw pictures to help you solve the problems below. Each problem requires three answers.

1. Jimmy has to walk 12 blocks to get to the park where he likes to play ball. It takes him 3 minutes to walk one block. How many minutes will it take him to walk to the park?

Distance_____ Speed_____ Time_____

2. An airplane leaves the airport at 9:00 a.m. It flies at 200 miles per hour. When it lands at 11:00 a.m., how far will it have gone?

Distance_____ Speed_____ Time_____

3. Tad rides his bike to his grandmother's house. It takes him 45 minutes to ride there. She lives 5 miles from his house. How many minutes does it take him to ride one mile?

Distance_____ Speed_____ Time_____

4. Rachael loves to visit her grandparents who live 150 miles from her house. When they make the trip, her dad drives. He averages 50 miles an hour. How many hours will the trip take?

Distance_____

Speed_____

Time_____

5. It is 50 miles between Dakota City and Blue Falls. It takes Mr. Oliver one hour to make the drive. How fast does he drive?

Distance_____ Speed_____ Time_____

Name _____

Fraction Fun

4 gloves are shaded.
9 gloves in all.

$\frac{4}{9}$ of the gloves are shaded.

TOYS

What fraction of the balls are shaded? _____

cars?_____

teddy bears?_____

trains?_____

rabbits?_____

dolls?_____

hats?_____

airplanes?_____

boats?_____

Name _____

More Fractions

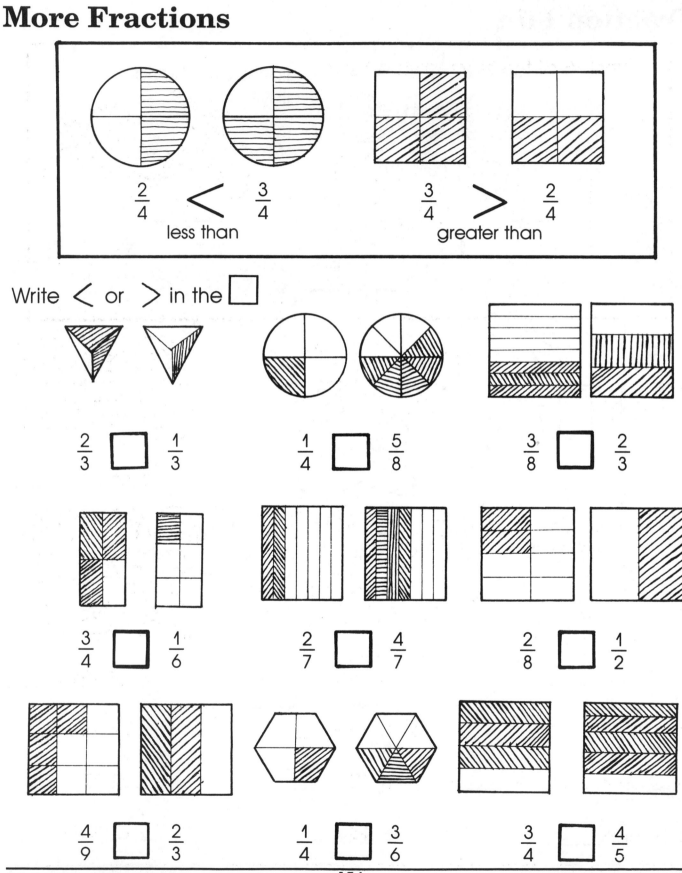

$\frac{2}{4}$ **<** $\frac{3}{4}$
less than

$\frac{3}{4}$ **>** $\frac{2}{4}$
greater than

Write **<** or **>** in the ☐

$\frac{2}{3}$ ☐ $\frac{1}{3}$

$\frac{1}{4}$ ☐ $\frac{5}{8}$

$\frac{3}{8}$ ☐ $\frac{2}{3}$

$\frac{3}{4}$ ☐ $\frac{1}{6}$

$\frac{2}{7}$ ☐ $\frac{4}{7}$

$\frac{2}{8}$ ☐ $\frac{1}{2}$

$\frac{4}{9}$ ☐ $\frac{2}{3}$

$\frac{1}{4}$ ☐ $\frac{3}{6}$

$\frac{3}{4}$ ☐ $\frac{4}{5}$

Name _____

Star Gazing

To find ½ of the stars, divide by 2.

$\frac{1}{2}$ of $10 = 5$

$\frac{1}{2}$ of $6 =$ _____

$\frac{1}{2}$ of $8 =$ _____

$\frac{1}{3}$ of $9 =$ _____

$\frac{1}{5}$ of $10 =$ _____

$\frac{1}{3}$ of $15 =$ _____

$\frac{1}{6}$ of $18 =$ _____

$\frac{1}{5}$ of $20 =$ _____

$\frac{1}{4}$ of $8 =$ _____

$\frac{1}{2}$ of $16 =$ _____

$\frac{1}{4}$ of $12 =$ _____

$\frac{1}{6}$ of $18 =$ _____

$\frac{1}{6}$ of $12 =$ _____

$\frac{1}{3}$ of $24 =$ _____

$\frac{1}{3}$ of $27 =$ _____

$\frac{1}{4}$ of $24 =$ _____

MATH

Name _____

Oh, Those Worms!

Color the worms to show the fractions.

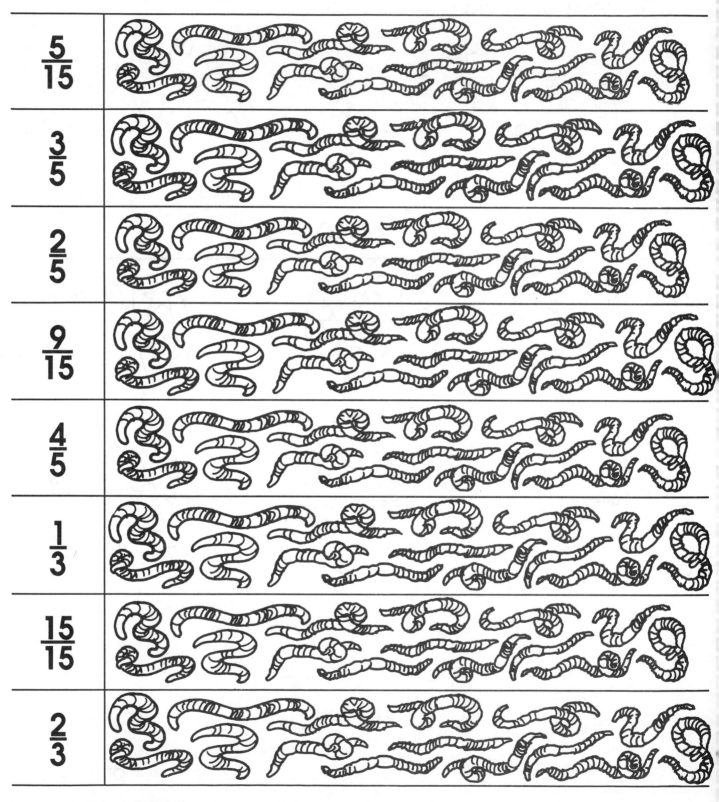

IF8695 Super Book for Grade 3

Name _____

The Mystery of the Missing Sweets

Some mysterious person is sneaking away with pieces of desserts from Sam Sillicook's Diner. Help him figure out how much is missing.

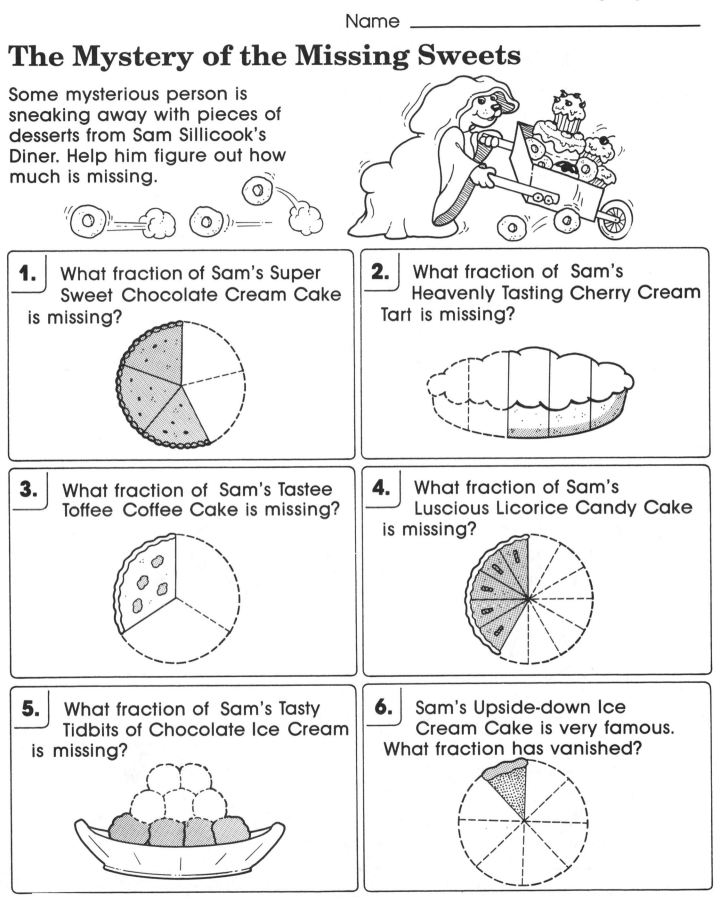

1. What fraction of Sam's Super Sweet Chocolate Cream Cake is missing?

2. What fraction of Sam's Heavenly Tasting Cherry Cream Tart is missing?

3. What fraction of Sam's Tastee Toffee Coffee Cake is missing?

4. What fraction of Sam's Luscious Licorice Candy Cake is missing?

5. What fraction of Sam's Tasty Tidbits of Chocolate Ice Cream is missing?

6. Sam's Upside-down Ice Cream Cake is very famous. What fraction has vanished?

MATH

Name _____

Solar Scholars

Keep your sunny side up! Write the time.

8:20

Name _____

Time on My Hands

Draw the hour and minute hands.

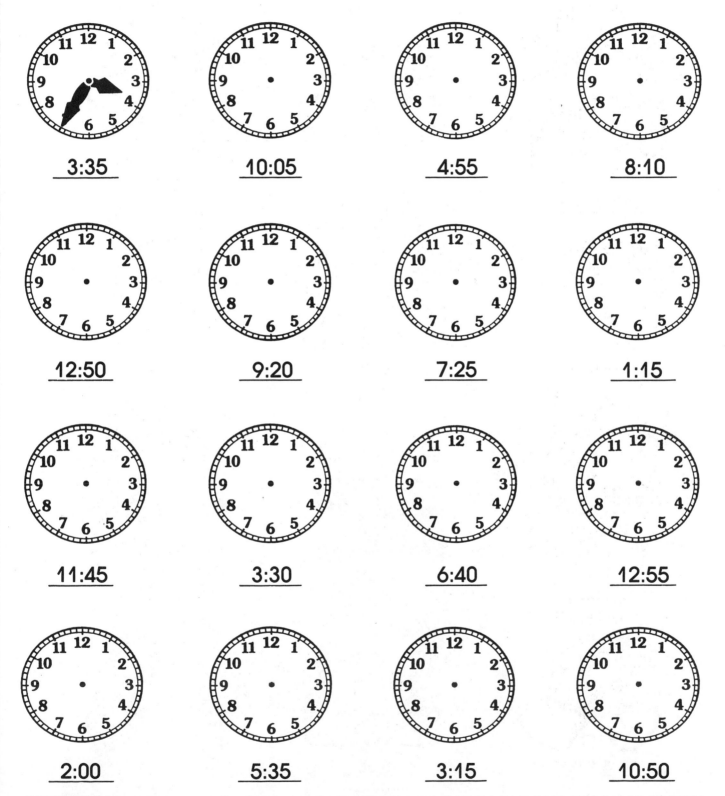

3:35

10:05

4:55

8:10

12:50

9:20

7:25

1:15

11:45

3:30

6:40

12:55

2:00

5:35

3:15

10:50

MATH

Minute Men

Name _____

Add the clock hands to these "Minute Men" clocks.

Example

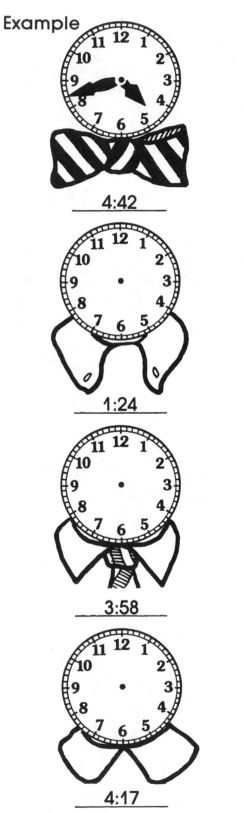

4:42

9:03

6:51

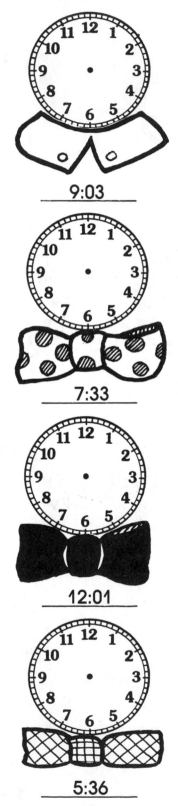

1:24

7:33

10:11

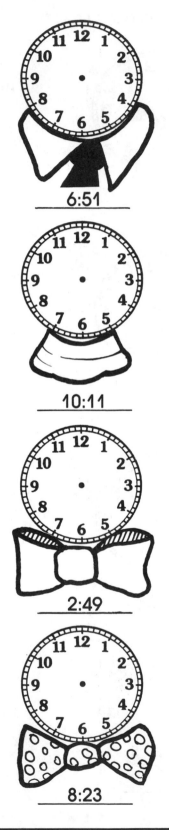

3:58

12:01

2:49

4:17

5:36

8:23

Name _____

Take Time for These

Be right on time! Write the exact time shown on these clocks.

6:47

Name _____

Monkeying Around

Nat can't tell time. He thinks that a minute is some kind of insect and that a clock is a new kind of soccer ball. He needs your help to solve these problems.

1. Nat is supposed to be at school in 10 minutes. What time should he get there?

_____

2. Nat started breakfast at 7:10 a.m. It took him 15 minutes to eat. Mark the time he finished.

3. Nat will leave school in 5 minutes. What time will it be then?

_____

4. Nat and his brother Not Nit Wit will eat dinner in 15 minutes. When will that be?

_____

5. It is now 6:45 p.m. Nat must start his homework in 5 minutes. Mark the starting time on the clock.

6. Nat will go to the park in 15 minutes. It is now 1:25 p.m. Mark the time he will go to the park.

Name _____

Daily Schedule

Fill in your own grade, teacher and room number. Next write the times and subjects that are listed in the order they would take place during a school day.

Subjects/Activity	Times
Art	2:30 p.m.
Reading	8:30 a.m.
Spelling	8:15 a.m.
Science	11:15 a.m.
Health	11:45 a.m.
Social Studies	1:40 p.m.
English	10:00 a.m.
Handwriting	9:30 a.m.
Physical Education	1:15 p.m.
Music	2:00 p.m.
Library	12:45 p.m.
Lunch	12:00 p.m.
Recess	9:45 a.m.
Attendance/Flag Salute	8:00 a.m.
Math	10:30 a.m.
Dismissal	3:00 p.m.

Daily Schedule

Grade ____   Teacher _____

Room _____

Time	Subject/Activity

MATH

How long is the listed lunch period? _____

How long is the listed recess? _____

What subject do you like the best? _____

What subject do you like the least? _____

Name _____

Timely Fun

Make an estimate of how many times you can do each activity in one minute. Then, time yourself and see how close you came.

Say the alphabet.

ABCDEFGHIJKLMNOPQRSTUVWXYZ

Estimate: _____
Actual: _____

Clap your hands.

Estimate: _____
Actual: _____

Do jumping jacks.

Estimate: _____
Actual: _____

Count to 20.

6 5 4 3 2 1
7
8
9 10 11 12 13 14 15 16 17 18 19 20

Estimate: _____
Actual: _____

Hop on one foot.

Estimate: _____
Actual: _____

Count backward from 20 to 1.

16 15 14 13
17 12 11
18
20 19

Estimate: _____
Actual: _____

IF8695 Super Book for Grade 3

Feeding Time

Name _____

Ken and Angie enjoyed watching the animals being fed at the zoo. However, when they arrived, they were a little confused by the signs.

Help them figure out the feeding time for each kind of animal. Be sure to include if it's A.M. or P.M.

Seals: Feeding time is two hours after the monkeys.

_____ : _____

Tigers: Feeding time is two hours after 9:00 A.M.

_____ : _____

Lions: Feeding time is 1:00 P.M.

Giraffes: Feeding time is one hour before the elephants.

_____ : _____

Monkeys: Feeding time is three hours before the giraffes.

_____ : _____

Elephants: Feeding time is three hours after the lions.

_____ : _____

MATH

Now trace the path in the zoo that Ken and Angie would take so that they could see all the animals being fed.

FEEDING TIMES

ZOO ENTRANCE

ZOO EXIT

Perfect Symmetry

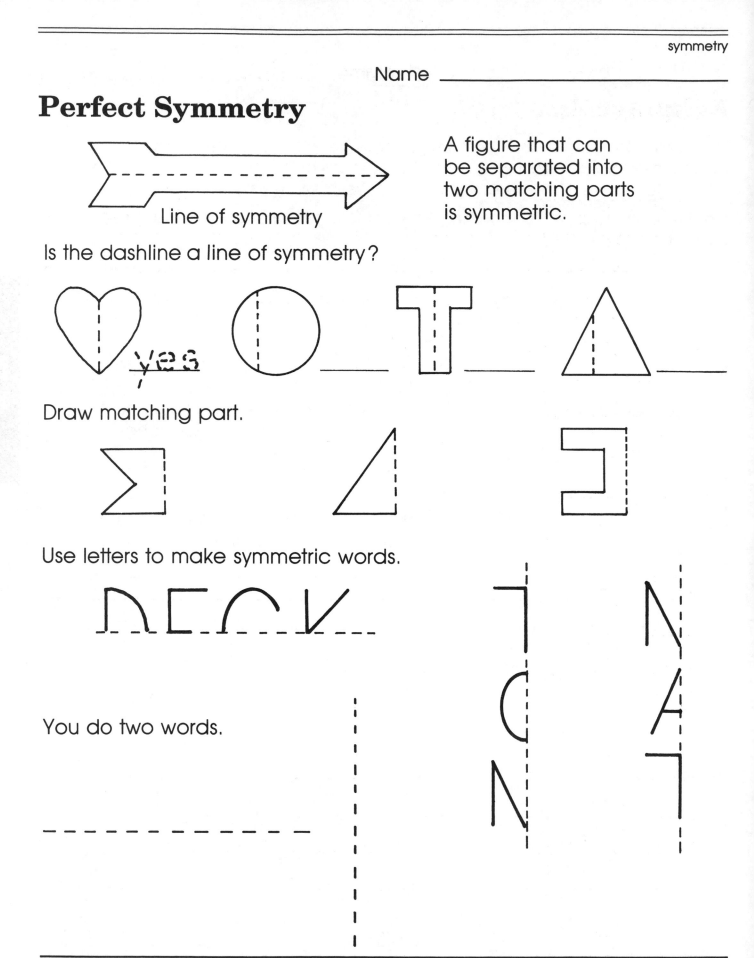

Line of symmetry

A figure that can be separated into two matching parts is symmetric.

Is the dashline a line of symmetry?

yes

_____ T _____ _____

Draw matching part.

Use letters to make symmetric words.

DECK

You do two words.

Name _____

A Square Activity

The **area** is the number of square units contained in a surface. Find the area by counting the square units.

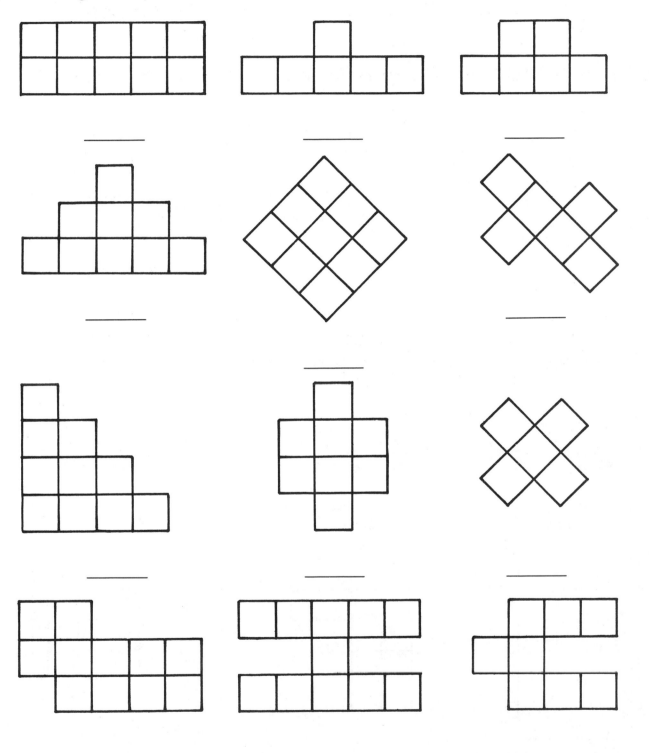

Name _____

Perimeter Problems

The **perimeter** is the distance around a figure. Find the perimeters for the figures below.

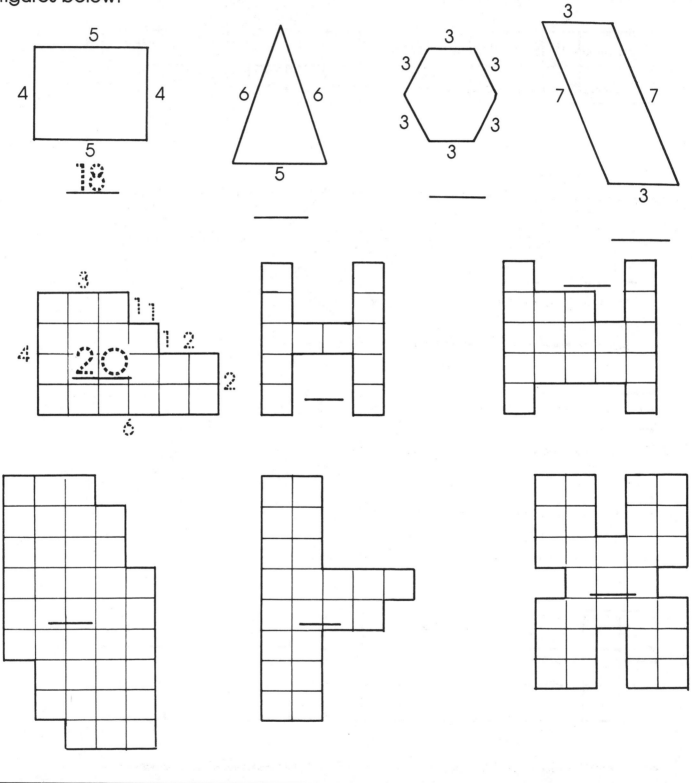

Name _____

Sawing Logs

Measure the logs to the nearest centimeter.

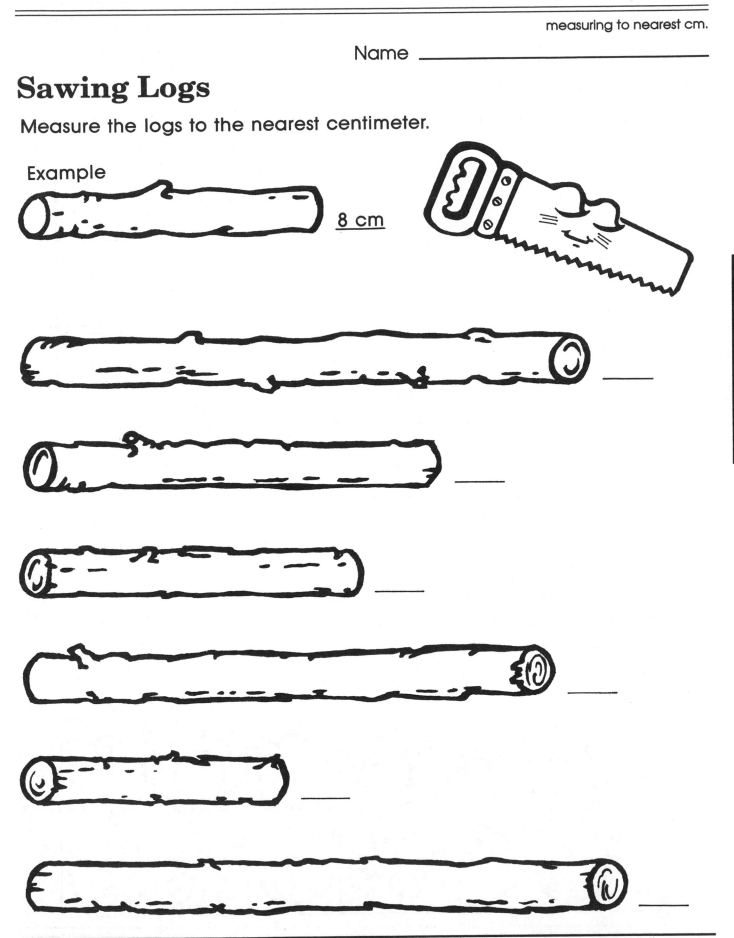

Example

8 cm

MATH

Name _____

Flower Graph

Cut out and match the flowers to the graph.

Daisies					
Sunflowers					
Tulips					
Roses					

How many tulips? ____ Sunflowers? ____ Roses? ____ Daisies? ____
How many more tulips than roses? ____
How many more daisies than sunflowers? ____
How many sunflowers and tulips? ____
How many roses and daisies? ____

Name _____

Potato Face

Read the line graphs to draw the potato faces.

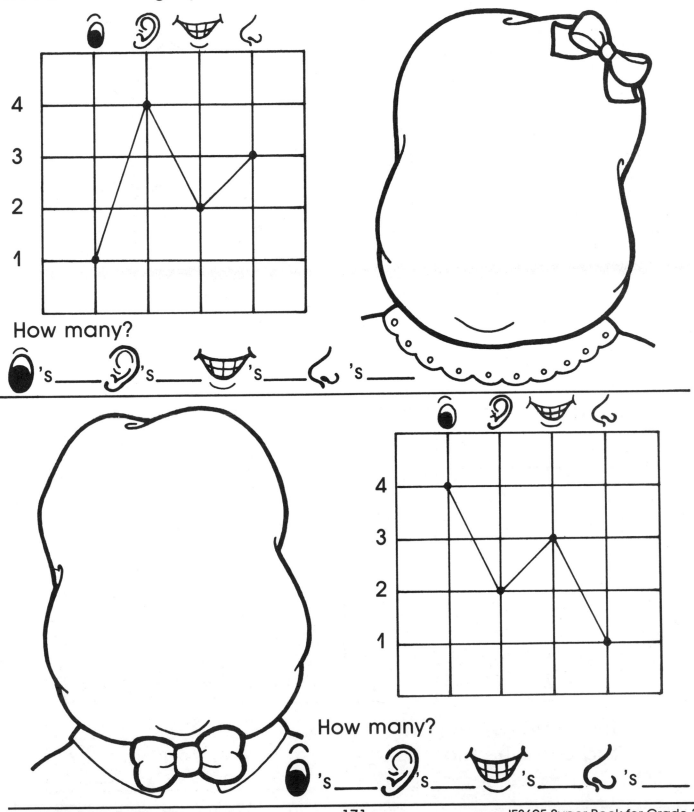

How many?

👁's____ 👂's____ 😁's____ 👃's____

How many?

👁's____ 👂's____ 😁's____ 👃's____

MATH

Name _____

Frog Bubbles

Color the picture.

Finish the line graph to show how many bubbles.

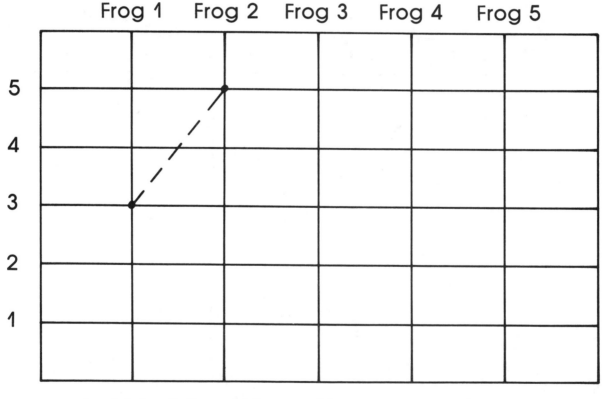

How many bubbles? Frog 1? ____ 2? ____ 3? ____ 4? ____ 5? ____
Which frog blew the most bubbles? ____ Which frog blew the least? ____

Name _____

Candy Sales

Every year the students sell candy as a fund-raising project. These are the results of the sales for this year.

Grade Level	Number of Sales
Kindergarten	40
First	70
Second	50
Third	80
Fourth	85
Fifth	75

Make a bar graph to show the number of sales made at each grade level.

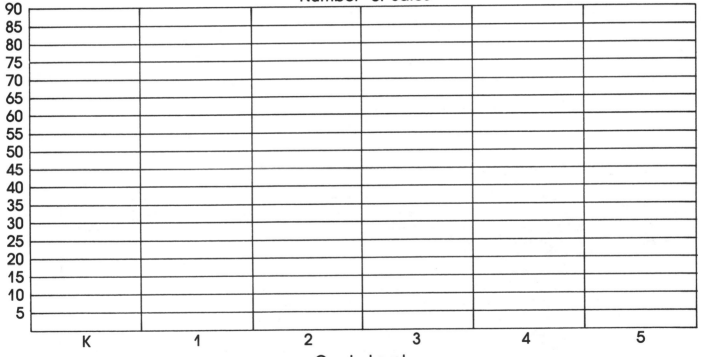

Number of Sales

Grade Level

Write the grade levels in order starting with the one that sold the most.

1. _____
2. _____
3. _____
4. _____
5. _____
6. _____

Name _____

Hot Lunch Favorites

The cooks in the cafeteria asked each third and fourth grade class to rate the hot lunches. They wanted to know which food the children liked the best.

The table shows how the students rated the lunches.
Hint: Each 👤 equals 2 students

Food	Number of Students Who Liked It Best
hamburgers	👤 👤 👤 👤 👤
hot dogs	👤 👤 👤 👤 👤 👤 👤
tacos	👤 👤 👤 👤 👤
chili	
soup and sandwiches	👤
spaghetti	👤 👤
fried chicken	👤 👤 👤 👤
fish sticks	👤 👤 👤

Make a bar graph to show the information on the table. Remember - each 👤 equals 2 people. The first one is done for you.

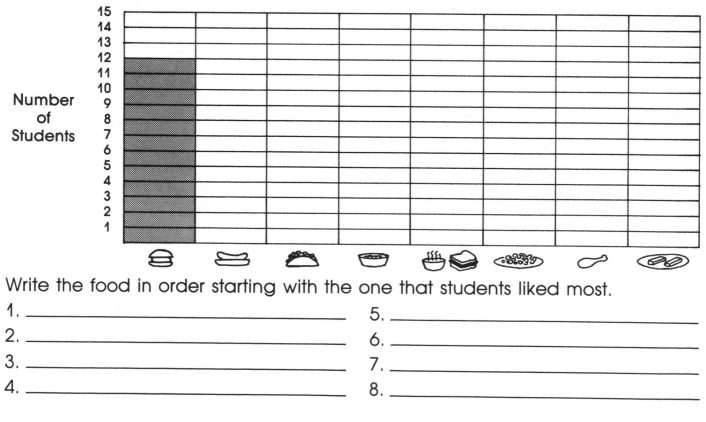

Write the food in order starting with the one that students liked most.

1. _____   5. _____

2. _____   6. _____

3. _____   7. _____

4. _____   8. _____

Name _____

Tooth Talk

Study the drawing of the tooth to help you fill in the blanks.

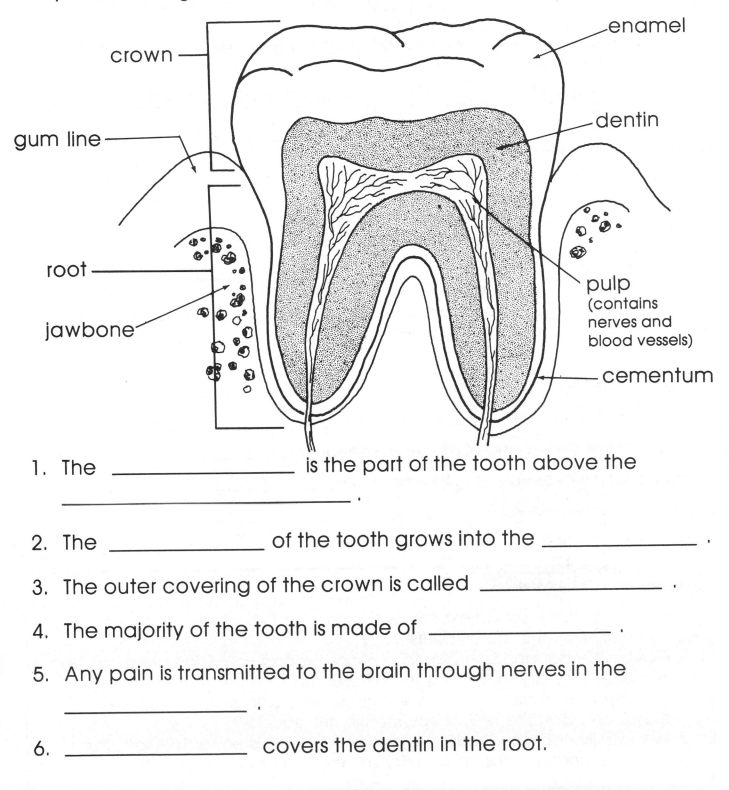

1. The _____ is the part of the tooth above the

   _____ .

2. The _____ of the tooth grows into the _____ .

3. The outer covering of the crown is called _____ .

4. The majority of the tooth is made of _____ .

5. Any pain is transmitted to the brain through nerves in the

   _____ .

6. _____ covers the dentin in the root.

Name _____

Quiet, Please!

A large jet plane rumbles as it takes off down the runway. You can feel the ground vibrate. The plane is also filling the air with vibrations. When the vibrations reach your ear, you hear them as sound.

Your **outer ear** collects the vibrations just like a funnel. The vibrations strike your **eardrum,** making it vibrate too. These vibrations are passed through a series of three small bones. The last bone vibrates against a snail-shaped tube. This tube is called the **cochlea.** It is filled with liquid. Small hair-like sensors in the cochlea pick up the vibrations and send it to the **auditory nerve.** The auditory nerve sends the sound message to your brain.

Label the parts of the ear using the words in bold.

Sounds Around Us

1. What is the loudest sound you have ever heard? _____

2. What is the softest sound you have ever heard? _____

3. What sound wakes you up in the morning? _____

4. What sound relaxes you? _____

5. What sound frightens you? _____

Something Special

Try some of these sound experiments with your classmates. Keep your eyes closed for all of the experiments!

1. Cover one ear and listen for the sounds around you. Then uncover your ear and listen again. What is the difference?

2. Choose one student to make several sounds with objects found in the classroom. Can the rest of you identify the sounds?

3. We usually hear the loudest sounds around us. Listen for the soft, "far away" sounds. List the sounds. Try this experiment outside.

Name _____

Strong Bones

The skeleton is a framework of 206 bones that has three main jobs: to hold your body up, to protect your inner organs, and to produce new blood cells inside the bones. That means our bones must be healthy. The outer part of our bones contains calcium, which keeps our bones strong. What would happen if our bones lacked calcium? Try the experiment below with a partner to find out.

Materials Needed

a chicken bone
a glass jar with a lid
1 cup vinegar

Procedure

1. Clean the chicken bone.
2. Place the bone in the jar and cover it with vinegar.
3. Cover tightly.
4. Let it sit for two weeks.

After two weeks:
How has the chicken bone changed? _____

_____

What would happen to your body without calcium? _____

_____

Rickets is a disease caused by too little calcium in your body. Calcium is found in many of the foods we eat. Check the labels of several foods. List at least ten that contain calcium.

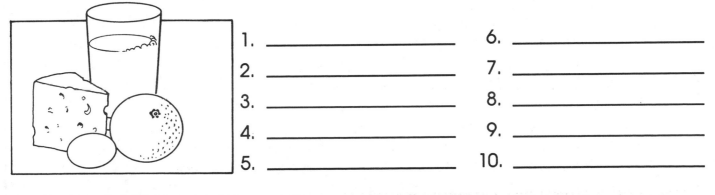

1. _____   6. _____
2. _____   7. _____
3. _____   8. _____
4. _____   9. _____
5. _____   10. _____

SCIENCE

Name _____

Build a Blood Cell!

We cannot live without blood. Our blood is made of millions of cells. There are red blood cells, white blood cells, and cells called platelets. They are so tiny that you cannot see them without a microscope.

Red blood cells carry oxygen from the lungs to the body's tissues and remove carbon dioxide. White blood cells protect the body from disease. Platelets help damaged blood vessels to stop bleeding. Each blood cell has its own parts. Look at the picture below and study the parts of the red blood cells. Remember, this is much bigger than a real cell.

Follow these directions to make a red blood cell.

Materials Needed
1 plastic bag that seals
1 dark button
½ cup prepared red Jell-O™

hemoglobin

membrane

nucleus

membrane

Platelets

Directions
1. Put the Jell-O™ in the bag.
2. Place the button in the bag.
3. Squeeze the button to the center of the bag.

Red blood cell
(erythrocytes)

White blood cell
(lymphocyte)

Draw your red blood cell and label its parts.

Name _____

Ingenious Genes

Your body is made up of cells. Each cell holds threadlike structures called chromosomes that contain genes. Genes are inherited from your parents and determine how you will look. This is why we often look like our parents. Some genes are stronger, or dominant, and some are carried down through generations. Below is a table listing the characteristics of a mother and a father. See if you can find all of the possible combinations for their children. There are 16 possibilities!

	hair	eyes	skin color	height
Mom	blonde	green	dark	short
Dad	red	blue	fair	tall

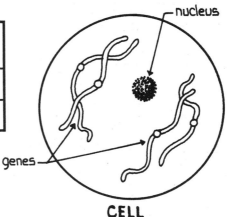

CELL

Examples:

blonde hair	blonde hair
green eyes	blue eyes
dark skin	dark skin
short	tall

_____

_____

_____

Complete the chart below for your mother and father. Then, find all of the combinations that determine how you could have looked! (You may have fewer than 16 if any traits are the same.)

	hair	eyes	skin color	height
Mom				
Dad				

_____

_____

Name _____

Just Swallow It!

Use this diagram to help you number the sentences in the correct order to show what happens when you swallow a bite of food.

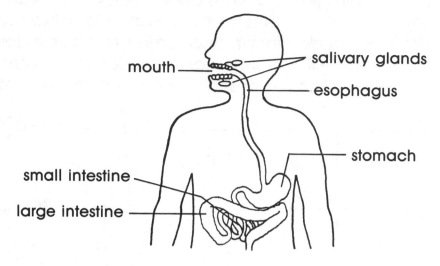

_____ While your teeth are breaking the food into tiny pieces, saliva is making the food softer.

_____ Whatever the body cannot use goes into the large intestine.

_____ While the food is in your stomach, more juices help to dissolve it.

_____ First you must pick up your sandwich in your hand.

_____ When the food in your mouth is soft enough, you swallow it.

_____ Move your hand to your mouth.

_____ When the food has dissolved in your stomach, it goes to your small intestine.

_____ Put a corner of the sandwich in your mouth.

_____ As you swallow your food, it moves down the esophagus to your stomach.

_____ Use your teeth to take a bite of the sandwich.

_____ While the food is in your small intestine, the body absorbs whatever it needs.

What happens when you try to swallow too big of a bite?

_____

Write a sentence about a kind of food that is good for your body.

_____

_____

Name _____

Going Around in Circles!

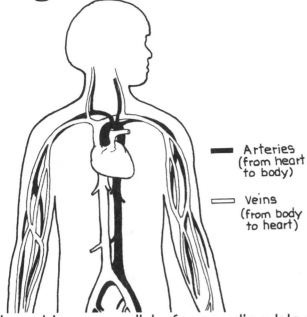

Arteries
(from heart
to body)

Veins
(from body
to heart)

The circulatory system is responsible for moving blood throughout your body. It is blood that carries food and oxygen to your body's cells and carries away carbon dioxide and other wastes. This system also carries disease-fighting substances that help prevent you from getting sick.

The main components of your body's circulatory system are: the heart, blood vessels, blood, and the lymphatic system. Your heart controls this system.

The heart is responsible for sending blood mixed with oxygen to the rest of your body through blood vessels called arteries. Blood vessels called veins return blood to your heart. Your veins look blue because the blood in them has no oxygen. Back toward the heart, the blood gathers more oxygen as it passes through your lungs and becomes red. This cycle occurs about one time every minute. It is your heart's constant pumping that keeps your blood circulating.

Use the information above to solve the puzzle.

Across
2. The _____ controls the circulatory system.
4. Blood without oxygen is _____ .
6. Arteries carry blood mixed with _____ from the heart to the rest of your body.
7. _____ carry blood to the heart.

Down
1. _____ carry blood away from the heart.
3. Blood is _____ when it contains oxygen.
5. Blood gets oxygen from your _____.

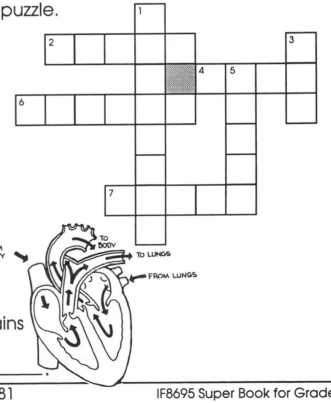

Name _____

Backbone or No Backbone?

Which part of your body helps you stand tall or sit up straight? It is your backbone. You are a member of a large group of animals that all have backbones. Animals with backbones are called **vertebrates.** Birds, fish, reptiles, amphibians, and mammals are all vertebrates.

Some animals do not have backbones. These animals are called **invertebrates.** Worms, centipedes, and insects are all invertebrates.

Classifying

Find the five vertebrates and five invertebrates hidden in the wordsearch. Then write them in the correct group.

Invertebrates

1. _____

2. _____

3. _____

4. _____

5. _____

```
B R A B B I T B U D
E A G I R A F F E L
E W O F H E P R U W
T O G K L C M O T H
L R N F R Y S G I A
E M L I O N O J E L
R S P I D E R M R E
```

Vertebrates

1. _____

2. _____

3. _____

4. _____

5. _____

Your neighborhood has many animals in or near it. Add their names to the lists.

Invertebrates

6. _____

7. _____

8. _____

9. _____

10. _____

Vertebrates

6. _____

7. _____

8. _____

9. _____

10. _____

Find Out

There are many more invertebrates than vertebrates. Nine out of ten animals is an invertebrate. Which group has the largest animals? Which group has the smallest animals?

Name _____

Insects in Winter

In the summertime, insects can be seen buzzing and fluttering around us. But as winter's cold weather begins, suddenly the insects seem to disappear. Do you know where they go?

Many insects, such as flies and mosquitoes, find a warm place to spend the winter. They live in cellars, barns, attics, caves and tree holes.

Beetles and ants try to dig deep into the ground. Some beetles stack up in piles under rocks or dead leaves.

In the fall, female grasshoppers and crickets lay their eggs and die. The eggs hatch in the spring.

Bees also try to protect themselves from the winter cold. Honeybees gather in a ball in the middle of their hive. The bees stay in this tight ball trying to stay warm.

Winter is very hard for insects, but each spring the survivors come out and the buzzing and fluttering begins again.

Write.

When cold weather begins, _____ seem to disappear.

Unscramble and check.

_____ and_____ find a warm place in:

q u t M s o e o s i   s f i l e

☐ beds   ☐ barns   ☐ caves   ☐ cellars   ☐ attics   ☐ sweaters

Circle Yes or No.

I n the winter, insects look for a warm place to live.   Yes   No

n oise, such as buzzing, can be heard all winter long.   Yes   No

S ome beetles and ants dig deep into the ground.   Yes   No

e very insect finds a warm home for the winter.   Yes   No

G rickets and grasshoppers lay their eggs and die.   Yes   No

T he honeybees gather in a ball in their hive.   Yes   No

S urvivors of the cold weather come out each spring.   Yes   No

SCIENCE

Name _____

Six-Legged Friends

The largest group of animals belongs to the group called invertebrates–or animals without backbones. This large group is the **insect** group.

Insects are easy to tell apart from other animals. Adult insects have three body parts and six legs. The first body part is the **head.** On the head are the mouth, eyes, and antennae. The second body part is the **thorax.** On it are the legs and wings. The third part is the **abdomen.** On it are small openings for breathing.

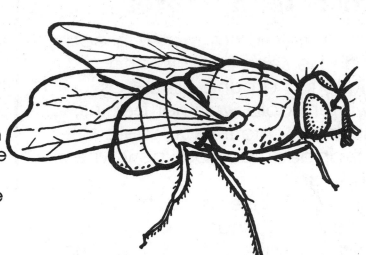

Color the body parts of the insect above. head–red, thorax–yellow, abdomen–blue

Draw an insect below. Make your insect a one-of-a-kind. Be sure it has the correct number of body parts, legs, wings, and antennae. Fill in the information.

Insect's name_____

Length_____

Where found _____

Food_____

Warning: _____

_____

_____

_____

Find Out

Many people think that spiders are insects. Spiders and insects are alike in many ways, but spiders are not insects. Find out how the two are different.

Name _____

Go Bats for Bats

Bats live all over the world. The bats found in the rainforest play an important role because they control insects and pollinate and disperse seeds for avocados, bananas, cashews, figs, peaches and other fruits. However, the bats that live in the rainforest are in danger due to the increasing destruction of their habitat. This could mean that our supply of fruits, nuts and spices could decrease and possibly vanish if the destruction continues. Read the description of each bat below. Notice how each one is different and has special features to help it survive. Put the letter of each description next to the bat it describes and the bat's food.

A. Notice the long nose and tongue this bat uses to dip into the durian blossom.

B. This bat's large ears and nose flap enable it to locate insects at night.

C. With its long feet and claws, this bat captures certain small prey.

D. The long snout on this bat helps it eat fruit like figs.

Food

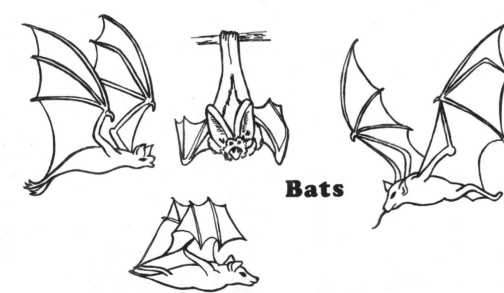

Bats

Once you have matched up the bats and their food, cut all the pictures apart. Glue each bat to a piece of construction paper. Glue the food it eats to the back. Punch a hole in each piece of construction paper. Put a piece of string through each piece of paper and tie the bats to a hanger. Now, you have a bat mobile to hang from the ceiling.

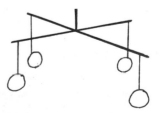

Name _____

A Sampling of Snakes

The Snake House is a very popular place to visit at the zoo. There are many different types and sizes of snakes. Some snakes are poisonous while others are not. Some snakes are harmless to most creatures, and some are very dangerous.

The five snakes described here are held in the cages below.

Decide which snake belongs in each cage by using the clues given here and beneath the boxes. Then write each name in the correct cage.

The King Cobra is the longest poisonous snake in the world. One of these snakes measured almost 19 feet long. It comes from southeast Asia and the Philippines.

The Gaboon Viper, a very poisonous snake, has the longest fangs of all snakes (nearly 2 inches). It comes from tropical Africa.

The Reticulated Python is the longest snake of all. One specimen measured 32 feet 9½ inches. It comes from southeast Asia, Indonesia, and the Philippines. It crushes its prey to death.

The Black Mamba, the fastest-moving land snake, can move at speeds of 10–12 m.p.h. It lives in the eastern part of tropical Africa.

The Anaconda is almost twice as heavy as a reticulated python of the same length. One anaconda that was almost 28 feet long weighed nearly 500 pounds.

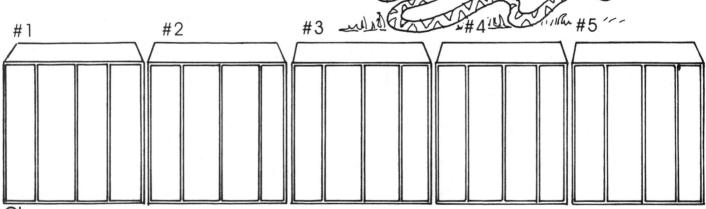

Clues:

- The snake in cage #5 moves the fastest on land.
- The longest snake of all is between the snake that comes from tropical Africa and the longest poisonous snake.
- The very heavy snake is to the left of the longest poisonous snake.

Name _____

From Egg to Tadpole to Frog

The poem below tells about the changes that occur in frogs during their life cycles. In every line, there is one word that doesn't make sense. Find the correct word in the Word Bank and write it in the puzzle. **Hint:** The correct word rhymes with it.

The Life Cycle of a Frog

There is jelly on the legs (13)
   To protect the entire match. (11)
It takes tree to twenty-five days (7↓)
   Until they're ready to catch. (5)

Out comes a pollihog (18)
   When the time is just bright. (8)
It breathes using hills (14)
   And its size is very light. (4)

It loses its long scale (9)
   After pegs begin to grow. (1)
Digestion and breathing strange (12)
   In a process fast and glow. (2)

What helps a frog to seethe (3)
   Is its thin and moist chin. (6↓)
It also uses rungs (15)
   To let the hair in. (10)

Some frogs can skim like a duck. (6→)
   And some can mop like a rabbit. (16)
Others climb bees like a squirrel (7→)
   Which may seem a bunny habit. (17)

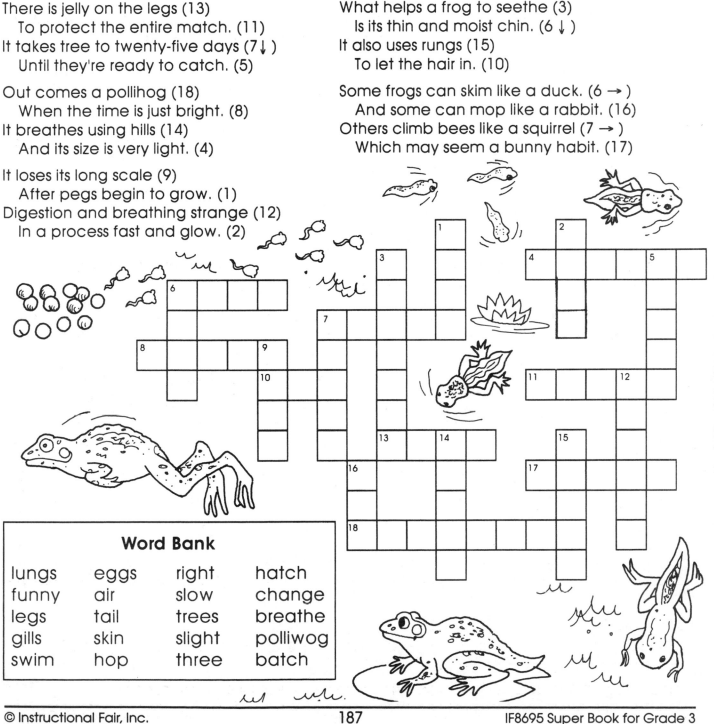

Word Bank

lungs	eggs	right	hatch
funny	air	slow	change
legs	tail	trees	breathe
gills	skin	slight	polliwog
swim	hop	three	batch

IF8695 Super Book for Grade 3

SCIENCE

Name _____

The Mighty Bear

Bears are large and powerful animals. Depending on the type of bear, they can weigh from 60 to 2,000 pounds.

Listed below are four different kinds of bears. The lengths of these bears are 3 feet, 5 feet, 8 feet, and 9 feet. Use the clues to match each bear to its length. Write the answers in the blanks.

Clues:

Alaskan brown bear + American black bear = 14 feet

Polar bear + Alaskan brown bear = 17 feet

American black bear + Sun bear = 8 feet

The Alaskan brown bear is _____ feet in length.

The American black bear is _____ feet in length.

The polar bear is _____ feet in length.

The sun bear is _____ feet in length.

Name _____

Toadly Froggin' Around

Harry and Song Lee loved frogs and similar creatures. Read the information about frogs and toads. Then write **true** or **false** in front of each statement.

Frogs and Toads

Both frogs and toads are amphibians. Amphibians spend part of their lives as water animals and part as land animals. In the early stages of their lives, amphibians breathe through gills, while as adults they develop lungs. Most amphibians lay eggs near water. Newly hatched frogs and toads both have tails that they later lose. Both often have poison glands in their skin to protect them from their enemies.

Frogs and toads are different in several ways. Most toads are broader, darker, and flatter. Their skin is drier. Toads are usually covered with warts while frogs have smooth skin. Most toads live on land while most frogs prefer being in or near the water.

_____ 1. Both frogs and toads usually lay eggs near water.

_____ 2. Most frogs have drier skin than toads.

_____ 3. Very young amphibians breathe with lungs.

_____ 4. Frogs tend to be lighter in color.

_____ 5. An adult frog's tail helps support him while sitting.

_____ 6. Poison glands often protect frogs from an enemy.

_____ 7. A toad's skin is often bumpy.

_____ 8. Frogs and toads are both amphibians.

SCIENCE

Name _____

A Re-Appearing Act

The starfish is a very interesting sea animal. Most starfish have five "arms" on their bodies. When a starfish is in danger, it can drop off its arms to escape. It then grows new arms to replace the missing ones. Also, if a starfish is cut in two, each of the pieces may grow into a new starfish.

Use the information above to solve these puzzles.

Puzzle #1 – This starfish originally had five arms. If two of these arms were broken off and grew back twice and the other three were dropped off and grew back five times each, how many arms did this starfish have during its lifetime? _____

Puzzle #2 – At first, this starfish had ten arms. It was then cut in half. Each of the halves grew new arms again so that they had the same number as the original starfish. Eventually, the same thing happened again to both new starfish. How many arms were involved in all? _____

Puzzle #3 – This starfish had 24 arms when it was born. If ½ of these arms broke off and grew back 4 times and ¼ of the original arms dropped off and grew back 3 times, how many arms did this starfish have during its lifetime? _____

Name _____

Butterflies and Moths

People sometimes confuse butterflies with moths, but there are some important differences.

Butterflies . . .
- fly by day.
- antennae have knobs.
- have thin, hairless bodies.
- rest with their wings held upright.

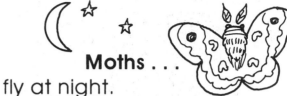

Moths . . .
- fly at night.
- antennae have no knobs.
- have plump, furry bodies.
- rest with their wings spread out flat.

Suppose you decided to start a butterfly and/or moth collection. Each mounting page would be divided into 16 sections. Large butterflies or moths would require two sections to mount. Small butterflies or moths would require only one.

If you had three large butterflies for this page and the rest were small, how many small butterflies could you mount? _____

Draw and color these butterflies on the page.

If you had four large moths, and you didn't want any of them to be next to each other, how would you mount them with smaller moths so that all of the sections would be used? Draw and color them on this page.

SCIENCE

Name _____

Secret Code for Worm Lovers

To decode the secret words, use the code below.

A	B	C	D	E	F	G	H	I	J	K	L	M
1	2	3	4	5	6	7	8	9	10	11	12	13

N	O	P	Q	R	S	T	U	V	W	X	Y	Z
14	15	16	17	18	19	20	21	22	23	24	25	26

1. Earthworms can also be called __ __ __ __ __
   14 9 7 8 20

   __ __ __ __ __ __ __ __.
   3 18 1 23 12 5 18 19

2. Earthworms have no __ __ __ __ or __ __ __ __.
   5 1 18 19   5 25 5 19

3. Sections of an earthworm are called __ __ __ __ __ __ __ __.
   19 5 7 13 5 14 20 19

4. Earthworms __ __ __ __ __ __ __ through their __ __ __ __.
   2 18 5 1 20 8 5   19 11 9 14

5. Earthworms eat __ __ __ __.
   19 15 9 12

6. As they __ __ __ __ __ __ through the soil, they give plants the __ __ __
   2 21 18 18 15 23   1 9 18
   that they need.

Name _____

Man's Best Friend

Dogs have been called "Man's Best Friend," and there are many good reasons for this. Dogs have been friendly with humans for over 10,000 years. Dogs have helped with hunting and herding. They have helped guide blind people and have also helped the police do detective work. Most often, they are kept as pets to provide both friendship and protection.

There are over 130 breeds of dogs in the United States. Certain breeds are more popular than others. According to the 1990 registrations, the following were the most popular breeds:

Golden Retriever
Cocker Spaniel
Rottweiler
Poodle
Labrador Retriever

Use the clues below to discover the order of the dogs' popularity. Then write each dog's name in the correct ribbon.

- "I'm the third most popular dog. My name is similar to something that forms during a rainstorm."

- "My name includes one of man's most precious metals, and I rank fourth."

- "I have the most vowels in my name, and I rank second."

- "I don't consider it a rotten deal to follow gold."

- "I rank first, which makes me proud as a peacock."

First Place   Second Place   Third Place   Fourth Place   Fifth Place

Name _____

A Shark's Fringe Benefit

The largest carnivorous (flesh-eating) fish that can be dangerous to man is the great white shark. Although it doesn't have a very large brain, it has excellent senses.

Great white sharks have several rows of jagged-edged teeth. New teeth replace worn or broken teeth. The replacement teeth move from inside the mouth to the outer edge.

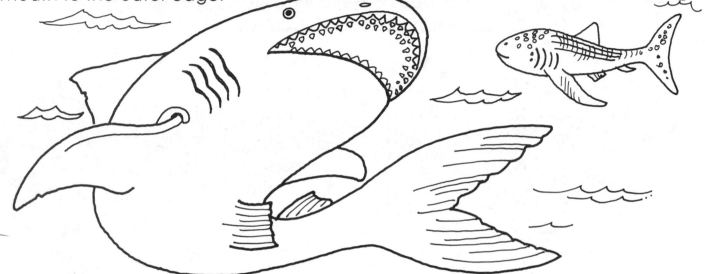

Imagine this. A shark had three rows containing two dozen teeth each on the bottom jaw and three rows containing two dozen teeth each on the top jaw.

First, the shark broke off 8 top teeth and wore down 10 bottom teeth, and these were replaced by new teeth.

Next, it wore down 6 top teeth and 4 bottom teeth and these were replaced by new teeth.

Finally, the shark broke off 9 top teeth and 9 bottom teeth and these were replaced.

How many total teeth had the shark had in its mouth at one time or another?

_____

Pretend the "Good Fairy" put 25¢ under the shark's pillow for each tooth that

was broken off. How much money would she leave? $ _____

       IF8695 Super Book for Grade 3

Name _____

Endangered Animal Acrostic

Using the animal names below, write the answers to the following definitions in the spaces provided. The circled letters are used as clues for your answers.

blue whale	jaguar	pronghorn
cheetah	okapi	polar bear
vicuna	yak	giant panda

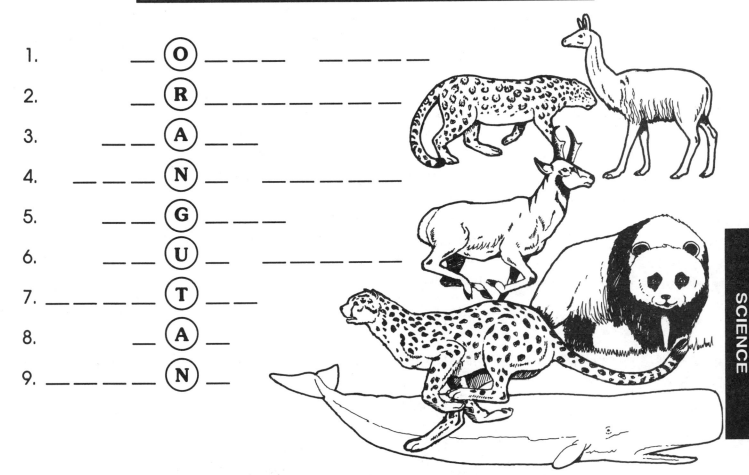

1. __ (O) __ __ __   __ __ __ __
2. __ (R) __ __ __ __ __ __
3. __ __ (A) __ __
4. __ __ __ (N) __   __ __ __ __
5. __ __ (G) __ __
6. __ __ (U) __ __   __ __ __ __ __
7. __ __ __ __ (T) __ __
8. __ __ (A) __ __
9. __ __ __ __ __ (N) __

1. large animal with white coat
2. upright horns and sheeplike feet
3. only living relative of the giraffe
4. lives in bamboo forests in southwestern China
5. largest wild cat in the Western Hemisphere

6. largest animal on Earth
7. cat that can run over 60 miles per hour
8. species of wild cattle in Tibet
9. member of the camel family in South America

SCIENCE

Name _____

Puzzling Problems

Which dinosaur's name means "iguana tooth?" To find out the answer, read each statement about dinosaurs below. If the statement is false, darken the letter in the circle to the left of that statement. The remaining letters will spell out the answer.

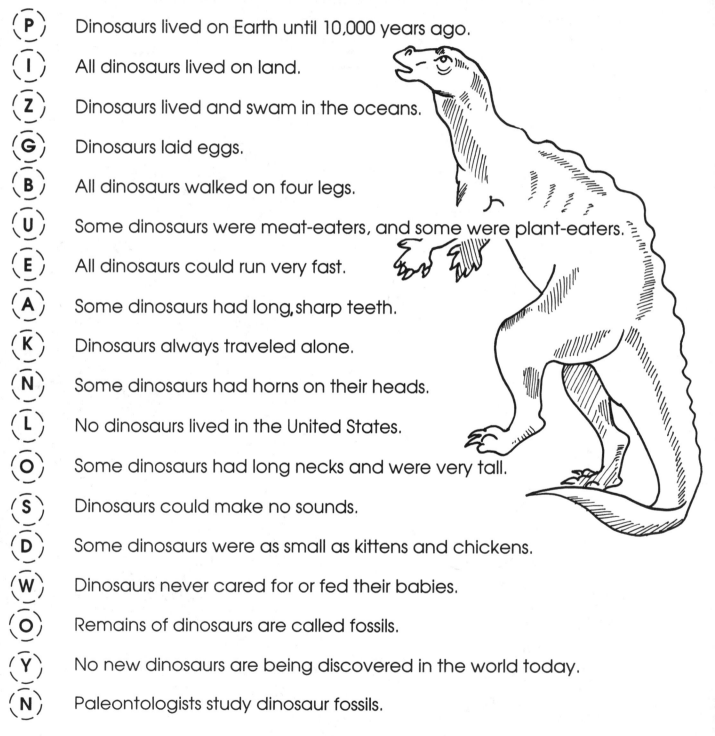

(P) Dinosaurs lived on Earth until 10,000 years ago.

(I) All dinosaurs lived on land.

(Z) Dinosaurs lived and swam in the oceans.

(G) Dinosaurs laid eggs.

(B) All dinosaurs walked on four legs.

(U) Some dinosaurs were meat-eaters, and some were plant-eaters.

(E) All dinosaurs could run very fast.

(A) Some dinosaurs had long, sharp teeth.

(K) Dinosaurs always traveled alone.

(N) Some dinosaurs had horns on their heads.

(L) No dinosaurs lived in the United States.

(O) Some dinosaurs had long necks and were very tall.

(S) Dinosaurs could make no sounds.

(D) Some dinosaurs were as small as kittens and chickens.

(W) Dinosaurs never cared for or fed their babies.

(O) Remains of dinosaurs are called fossils.

(Y) No new dinosaurs are being discovered in the world today.

(N) Paleontologists study dinosaur fossils.

Name _____

A Hidden Dinosaur

I have a big skull with a beak like a parrot's. What am I? To answer this question, circle the correct answer under each question below. Then, follow the directions.

1. A dinosaur that has three horns on its head would be the:
   a. Triceratops - Mark out all letter B's below.
   b. Diplodocus - Mark out all letter P's below.
   c. Brachiosaurus - Mark out all letter R's below.

2. A large plant-eating dinosaur is the:
   a. Tyrannosaurus - Mark out all letter T's below.
   b. Deinonychus - Mark out all letter O's below.
   c. Apatosaurus - Mark out all letter N's below.

3. A dinosaur with large bony plates on its back is the:
   a. Iguanodon - Mark out all letter C's below.
   b. Stegosaurus - Mark out all letter D's below.
   c. Galapagos tortoise - Mark out all letter A's below.

4. A dinosaur with tiny front arms and a huge skull is the:
   a. Tyrannosaurus - Mark out all letter L's below.
   b. Ankylosaurus - Mark out all letter S's below.
   c. Triceratops - Mark out all letter E's below.

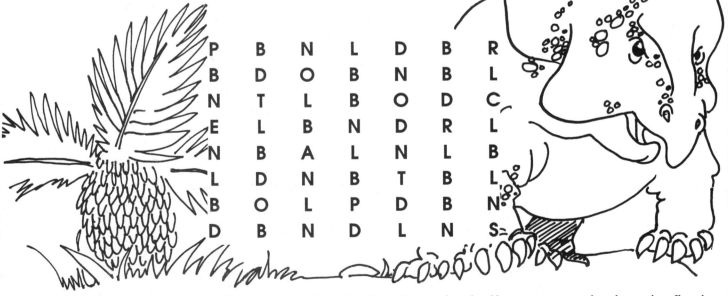

P	B	N	L	D	B	R
B	D	O	B	N	B	L
N	T	L	B	O	D	C
E	L	B	N	D	R	L
N	B	A	L	N	L	B
L	D	N	B	T	B	L
B	O	L	P	D	B	N
D	B	N	D	L	N	S

Start at the top. Write the remaining letters in order in the spaces below to find out the name of the hidden dinosaur.

__ __ __ __ __ __ __ __ __ __ __ __ __ __

Name _____

How Long Were the Dinosaurs?

Dinosaurs varied greatly in size. Some were up to 90 feet long! Use a dinosaur encyclopedia or other reference materials to find the lengths of some dinosaurs. Write the names of the dinosaurs along the bottom of the line graph. Color in the lengths (in feet) with different colored pens or crayons.

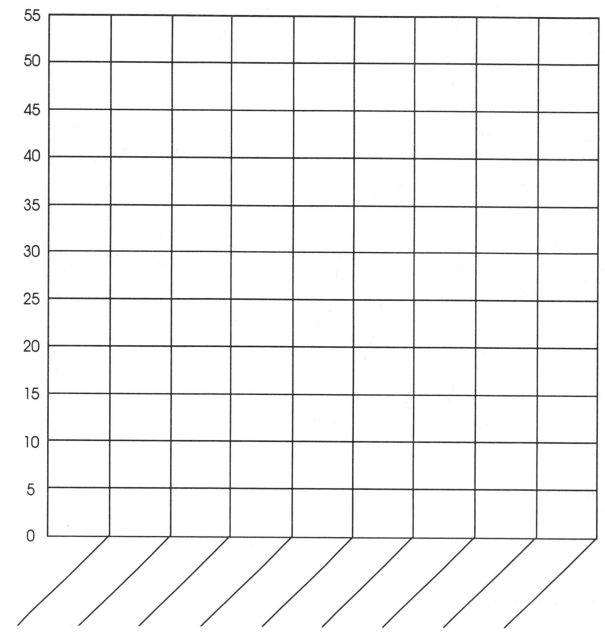

Dinosaur Length in Feet

Dinosaur Names

Name _____

Dinosaur Diagram

A Venn diagram is a great tool to use to compare things. Use the one below to compare two dinosaurs. Fill in the Iguanodon with characteristics common only to it. Fill in the Triceratops with characteristics common only to the Triceratops. Above **Same**, write characteristics that both dinosaurs share. Write a story about your findings on the lines below.

Different   **Same**   **Different**

SCIENCE

_____
_____
_____
_____
_____
_____
_____
_____
_____

Name _____

A Dinosaur Tale

Study the dinosaurs illustrated below. Then complete each category with words that you associate with these animals. A few examples are already written under each heading. Use the words to compose a poem or short story about these dinosaurs. You can write your own composition or poem or you can share your ideas with other students and write a group composition or poem. Read your work aloud.

Nouns	Verbs	Adjectives
tail	walk	huge
teeth	run	spiked
head	eat	sharp

Title: _____

_____

_____

_____

_____

_____

_____

_____

Name _____

Get a Clue!

Get a Clue! is a fun way to gain information about dinosaurs. To play, read the 16 clues below about a certain dinosaur. Use your science book or other resource materials and your own logical thinking to guess the name of the dinosaur. When you are finished, write your own clues about another dinosaur. Give it to another student to see if he/she can guess the answer.

I am a dinosaur.

1. My name means "three-horned face."
2. My skull is 7 or 8 feet long.
3. I have a beaked mouth like a parrot.
4. I eat plants.
5. I walk on all four legs.
6. I am 30 feet long.
7. I weigh up to 10 tons.
8. I am one of the last dinosaurs to live.
9. I have 3 claws on my front feet.
10. I live in Canada and the U.S.
11. I have a thick neck frill.
12. I have 3 horns on my skull.
13. I am the best-known horned dinosaur.
14. I use my horns for protection.
15. I have a small hoof on each toe.
16. I was named by O. C. Marsh in 1889.

I am a _____ .

I am a dinosaur.

1. _____
2. _____
3. _____
4. _____
5. _____

6. _____
7. _____
8. _____
9. _____
10. _____

I am a _____ .

SCIENCE

Name _____

The End of the Dinosaurs

What could have killed all the dinosaurs? Scientists are not really sure. They have many different **theories,** or explanations, for why the dinosaurs died out.

Several theories are listed below. Each theory has a **cause** and an **effect.** A cause is "a change that happened on earth" and an effect is "what resulted from the change on earth." Draw a line from each cause to its effect.

Cause

A huge meteor hit the earth, starting fires and making a thick cloud of dust and smoke that covered the earth.

Small, fast mammals that liked to eat eggs quickly spread around the world.

New kinds of flowering plants started to grow on the earth. These plants had poison in them that the dinosaurs could not taste.

When dinosaurs were living, the earth was warm all year long. Suddenly the earth became cooler with cold winter months.

Effect

Dinosaurs were cold-blooded and they couldn't find places to hibernate. They had no fur or feathers to keep them warm. They froze to death.

The sunlight was blocked and plants couldn't grow. The dinosaurs starved to death.

Fewer and fewer baby dinosaurs were born.

The dinosaurs ate poison without even knowing it and they died.

Name _____

Animal Mysteries

As long as people have studied animals, there have been mysteries about why animals act in certain ways.

One mystery has to do with some animals' strange behavior **before** earthquakes. Horse and cattle stampedes, screeching seabirds, howling dogs, even animals coming out of hibernation early, are examples of this mysterious behavior.

Another mystery involves birds and ants. No one can explain why a bird will pick up an ant in its beak and rub the ant over its feathers again and again. This is called "anting," and birds have been known to do this for an hour without stopping.

One animal mystery is very sad. For hundreds of years, some whales have mysteriously swam from the ocean onto a beach where they would die. Reports of "beached whales" occur about five times a year some- where in the world.

There are hundreds of other animal mysteries—such as how and why animals hibernate— that scientists have not solved. Can you think of another animal mystery?

3 Animal Mysteries

Write.

1. Some animals act strangely before an_____.

Check.

This strange behavior includes: ☐ laughing birds ☐ howling dogs

☐ horse and cattle stampedes ☐ barking whales

☐ leaving hibernation early ☐ screeching seabirds

Write.

2. This mystery is about _____ rubbing _____ over their feathers.

Write.

3. A sad mystery is about _____ swimming onto

a _____ and dying.

• Write a solution to one of the animal mysteries.

203   IF8695 Super Book for Grade 3

SCIENCE

Name _____

Hibernation

Have you ever wondered why some animals hibernate? Hibernation is a long sleep that some animals go into for the winter.

Animals get their warmth and energy from food. Some animals cannot find enough food in the winter. They must eat large amounts of food in the fall. Their bodies store this food as fat. Then in winter, they sleep in hibernation. Their bodies live on the stored fat. Since their bodies need much less food during hibernation, they can stay alive without eating new food during the winter.

Some animals that hibernate are: bats, chipmunks, bears, snakes and turtles.

Underline.

Hibernation   is a sleep that some animals go into for the winter.
                is the time of year to gather food for the winter.

Yes or No.

Animals get their warmth and energy from food.   Yes   No
Some animals cannot find enough food in the winter.   Yes   No
Animals hibernate because they are lazy.   Yes   No
Animals need less food while they are hibernating.   Yes   No

Match.

Animals that hibernate . . .
    eat and store food   in the winter.
    go to sleep   in the fall.

Color the animals that hibernate.

Name _____

Rain in the Rainforest

At least 80 inches of rain falls and thundershowers may occur for 200 or more days each year in a rainforest. Rainforests need a lot of rain so that the plants native to them do not dry out. Fill in the precipitation graph below with the average rainfall of a typical tropical rainforest. The amounts are listed beneath the graph.

```
         0  2  4  6  8  10  12  14  16  18  20  22  24  26  28  30

JANUARY

FEBRUARY

MARCH

APRIL

MAY

JUNE

JULY

AUGUST

SEPTEMBER

OCTOBER

NOVEMBER

DECEMBER
```

J	F	M	A	M	J	J	A	S	O	N	D
24"	20"	13"	11"	10"	7"	8"	9"	9"	11"	14"	18"

What was the total rainfall for the year in this rainforest? _____

What is the total rainfall for a year in your area? _____

SCIENCE

Name _____

Lightning

Lightning is a flash of light caused by electricity in the sky. Clouds are made of many water droplets. All of these droplets together contain a large electrical charge. Sometimes these clouds set off a huge spark of electricity called lightning. Lightning travels very fast. As it cuts through the air, it can cause thunder.

Lightning takes various forms. Some lightning looks like a zigzag in the sky. Sheet lightning spreads and lights the sky. Ball lightning looks like a ball of fire.

Underline.

Lightning is a flash of light   caused by sunshine.
caused by electricity in the sky.

Yes or No

Sometimes clouds set off a huge spark of electricity.	Yes	No
Lightning is caused by dry weather.	Yes	No
Lightning travels very fast.	Yes	No
Lightning can cause thunder.	Yes	No

Unscramble and write in the puzzle above.

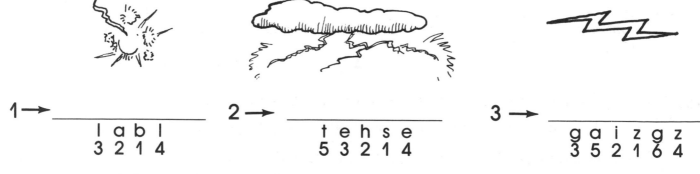

1 → _____
l a b l
3 2 1 4

2 → _____
t e h s e
5 3 2 1 4

3 → _____
g a i z g z
3 5 2 1 6 4

• Draw a picture of a sky with the three kinds of lightning.

Name _____

A Funnel Cloud—Danger!

Did you know that a tornado is the most violent windstorm on Earth? A tornado is a whirling, twisting storm that is shaped like a funnel 🌀 .

A tornado usually occurs in the spring on a hot day. It begins with thunderclouds and thunder. A cloud becomes very dark. The bottom of the cloud begins to twist and form a funnel. Rain and lightning begin. The funnel cloud drops from the dark storm clouds. It moves down toward the ground.

A tornado is very dangerous. It can destroy almost everything in its path.

SCIENCE

Circle.

A   thunder
    tornado   is the most violent windstorm on Earth.

Check.

Which words describe a tornado?

☐ whirling   ☐ twisting   ☐ icy   ☐ funnel-shaped   ☐ dangerous

Underline.

A funnel shape is: ◯   ▢   ⬭   ▽   〰

Write and Circle.

A tornado usually occurs in the _____ on a   cool   day.
                                  autumn   spring   hot

Write 1-2-3 below and in the picture above.

◯ The funnel cloud drops down to the ground.
◯ A tornado begins with dark thunderclouds.
◯ The dark clouds begin to twist and form a funnel.

Name _____

The Eye of the Storm

A hurricane is a powerful storm that forms over some parts of an ocean. A hurricane can be several hundred miles wide.

A hurricane has two main parts: the eye and the wall cloud. The eye is the center of the storm. In the eye, the weather is calm. The storm around the eye is called the wall cloud. It has strong winds and heavy rain. In some hurricanes, the wind can blow 150 miles an hour!

As the storm moves across the water, it causes giant waves in the ocean. As the storm moves over land it can cause floods, destroy buildings and kill people who have not taken shelter.

eye

wall clouds

Circle.

A hurricane has two main parts: tornado
                                    wall cloud
                                    eye

Write.

| wall cloud |
| eye |

_____ The calm center of the hurricane

_____ The wind and rainstorm around the eye

Check:

A hurricane ☐ can be several hundred miles wide.
            ☐ can have winds that move 150 miles an hour.
            ☐ is a small storm.
            ☐ can cause giant waves in the ocean.
            ☐ can cause floods and hurt people.

Name _____

Soil Study

Soil basically falls into three groups: sand, clay, and loam. Yet soils look much the same on the surface.

Soil is made of small pieces of broken rock. Wind, water, heat, cold, plants, and animals help to break up the rocks in the soil. Sometimes soil contains pieces of decayed plants and animals.

Take two tall, thin jars outside and look at soil in two different places. In each place, use the jar to dig up a soil plug. To do this, twist the jar as you push it in the soil. Then carefully pull the jar up. Tap out one plug of soil on a large piece of paper. Someone may have

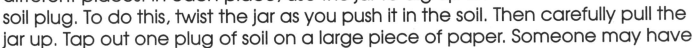

to help you by running a knife around the mouth of the jar. Look at your soil with a magnifying glass. Feel it with your fingers. Record what you see and feel in the chart below. Repeat these steps with the other plug of soil.

Use another jar to collect one more plug of soil. Take it to school to share with the class. It will be interesting to look at each other's soil. Repeat the same steps as you did with the first two plugs of soil. Then record these findings on the chart.

Rank the three soil samples below according to their color, texture, and the amounts of moisture and decayed plants present in them. Write about any other interesting characteristics the soil samples contain.

Where I Found the Soil	Color	Texture	Dry or Wet?	Decayed Plants Present?	Other Interesting Characteristics

SCIENCE

Name _____

Tidal Waves

Tidal waves are large, destructive waves that can crash onto land like a bomb. They are so strong that they can travel into a town and tear large buildings down. These waves happen only 2 or 3 times a year and are caused by underwater landslides, earthquakes, or hurricanes. Use this information to complete the line graph.

Location	Height	Location	Height
Portugal	50 feet	Japan (1896)	100 feet
Hawaii	20 feet	Chile	35 feet
Alaska	60 feet	Northern Chile	70 feet
Japan (1933)	96 feet		

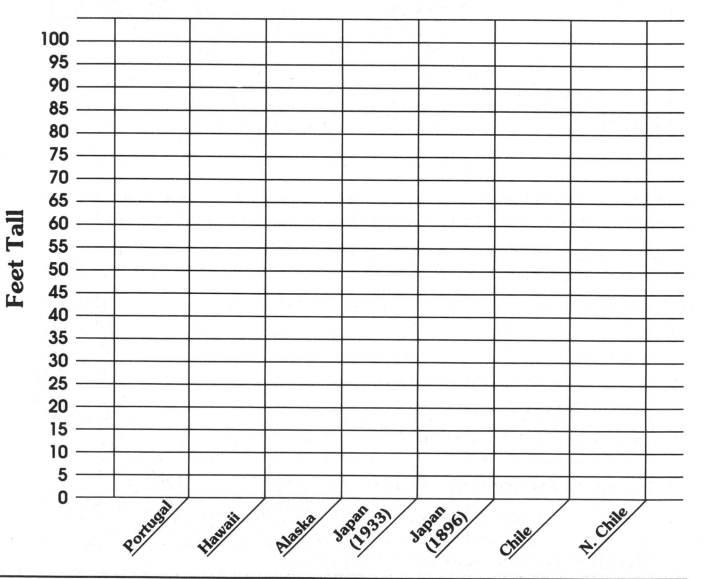

Name _____

Volcanic Activity

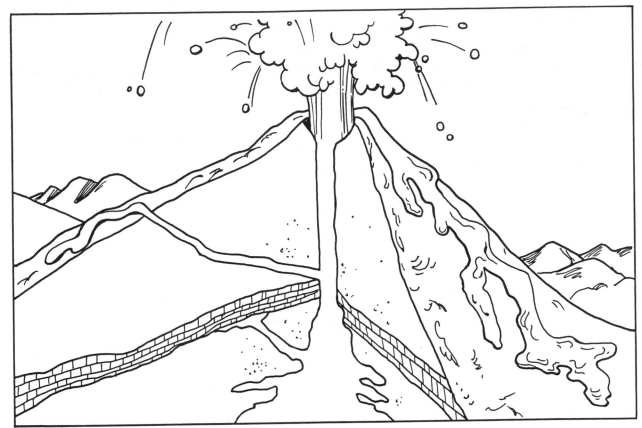

Indonesia is comprised of the world's largest group of islands. These islands are located on the equator in the Indian Ocean between Asia and Australia.

Children living in Indonesia study about the land around them. This includes volcanoes because there are about 60 active volcanoes on the islands.

Use the clues below to label the parts of the volcano.

1. The magma is the hot liquid in the center of the earth. Color it red.

2. The conduit is the passage that leads up the mountain. Color it red also.

3. Rock makes up the outer part of the mountain. Color the rock brown.

4. The vent is the opening. Circle it.

5. The lava is the liquid that runs down the side of the mountain. Color the lava orange and draw more lava at the vent.

Name _____

The Solar System

Our solar system is made up of the sun and all the objects that go around, or orbit, the sun.

The sun is the only star in our solar system. It gives heat and light to the nine planets in the solar system. The planets and their moons all orbit the sun.

The time it takes for each planet to orbit the sun is called a year. A year on Earth is 365 days. Planets closer to the sun have shorter years. Their orbit is shorter. Planets farther from the sun take longer to orbit, so their years are longer. A year on Pluto is 248 of our years!

Asteroids, comets and meteors are also part of our solar system.

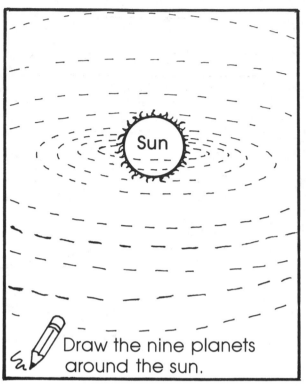

Draw the nine planets around the sun.

Underline.

The solar system is: the sun without the nine planets.
                        the sun and all the objects that orbit the sun.

Check.

☐ is the center of our solar system.
☐ is the only star in our solar system.
☐ is a planet in our solar system.
☐ gives heat and light to our solar system.

Write.

A _____ is the time it takes for a planet to orbit the sun.
  month   year

Match.

Planets closer to the sun . . .   have a longer year.
Planets farther from the sun . . .   have a shorter year.

Name _____

Sun – sational Puzzle

Use words from the Word Box to complete the crossword puzzle about the sun.

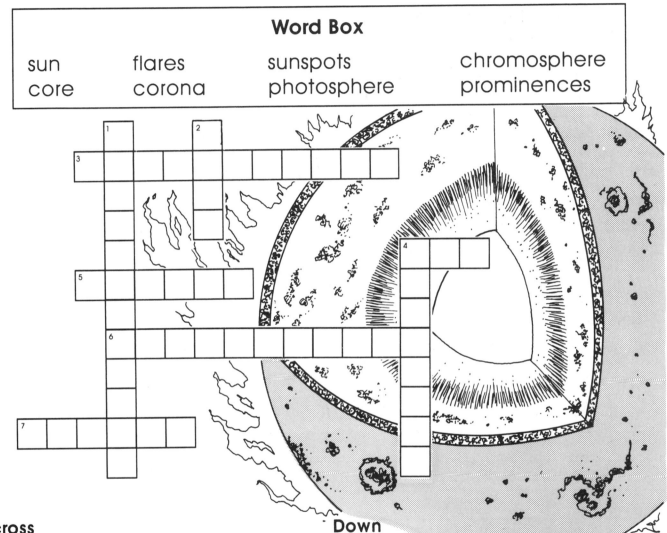

Word Box

sun	flares	sunspots	chromosphere
core	corona	photosphere	prominences

Across

3. the part of the sun you can see

4. huge glowing ball of gases at the center of our solar system

5. the region of the sun's atmosphere above the chromosphere

6. big, bright arches of gas

7. flashes of light on the sun's surface

Down

1. the middle part of the sun's atmosphere

2. the center of the sun

4. dark patches that sometimes appear on the sun

Name _____

A Time Capsule on the Moon

Scientists have studied the rocky surface of the moon from samples that astronauts brought back to Earth. They found out that the moon is probably 4 1/2 billion years old! Because the moon has no rain or wind, everything stays the same on the surface. The U.S. flags placed on the moon should stay for millions of years. That means future visitors will see them long after we're gone. What do you think would be important to show people millions of years from now? Design a space time capsule to be sealed and left on the moon. What will you put in it? Why?

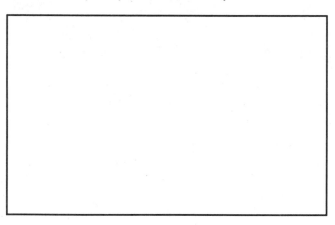

_____

_____

_____

_____

_____

_____

_____

_____

Bring some of these items to share with the class and make a class time capsule. Seal it until the end of the year.

Name _____

Man on the Moon

Earth's closest neighbor in space is the moon. The moon is very different from the earth. It has no wind, no air, and no water. The sky around the moon always looks black, and stars can always be seen. Because there is a lot less gravity on the moon, astronauts can jump much farther there than on Earth. There are large holes, called **craters**, on the moon.

Pretend you are an astronaut and you have just landed on the moon. You see many craters all around you.

Suppose you begin to travel in the order of the numbered craters on the moon. With your first step you jump from crater #1, over crater #2 and land on crater #3. You continue skipping over one crater with every step, until you come back to where you started. With a red crayon color the craters you landed on.

Now imagine that you started on crater #1, jumped over two craters at a time, and landed on #4. Continue following this pattern until you reach #16 and mark each of the craters you landed on with an X.

Which two craters would you have landed on both times?

Craters # _____ and # _____

Name _____

Where Will It Lead?

Read the list of famous events in American space exploration. Number them in the correct order.

	Year	Event	Spacecraft
_____	1981	first space shuttle	Columbia
_____	1961	first American in space	Freedom 7
_____	1971	first drive on the moon	Apollo 15
_____	1962	orbit earth three times	Friendship 7
_____	1973	astronauts live in space station	Skylab
_____	1965	first walk in space	Gemini 4
_____	1975	Americans and Russians meet in space	Apollo-Soyuz
_____	1969	first walk on the moon	Apollo 11
_____	1983	first American woman in space	Discovery

Make a time line to show the order of these events in American space exploration. Write each year in the top box, each event in the square and each spacecraft name in the bottom box. The first one is done for you.

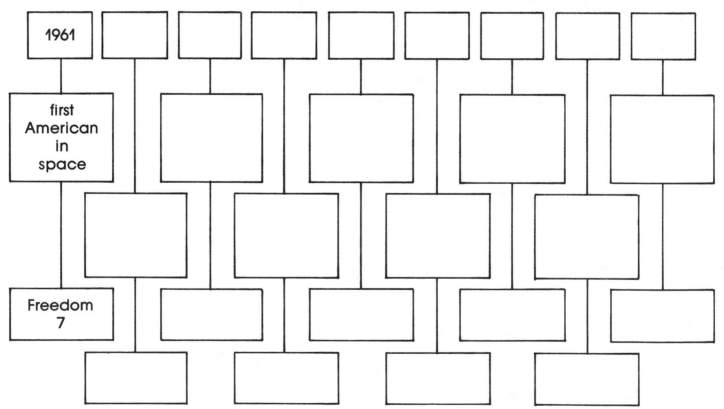

Name _____

A Black Hole

Have you ever heard of a mysterious black hole? Some scientists believe that a black hole is an invisible object somewhere in space. The scientists believe that it has such a strong pull toward it, called gravity, that nothing can escape from it!

These scientists believe that a black hole is a star that collapsed. The collapse made its pull even stronger. It seems invisible because even its own starlight cannot escape! It is believed that anything in space that comes near the black hole will be pulled into it forever. Some scientists believe there are many black holes in our galaxy.

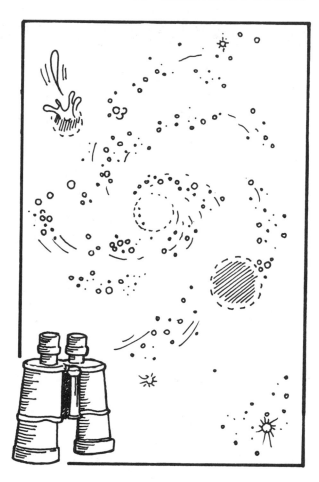

SCIENCE

Check.

Some scientists believe that:

- [ ] a black hole is an invisible object in space.
- [ ] a black hole is a collapsed star.
- [ ] a black hole is a path to the other side of the Earth.
- [ ] a black hole has a very strong pull toward it.
- [ ] a black hole will not let its own light escape.

Write.

| A - gravity |
| B - collapse |

____ To fall or cave in

____ A strong pull from an object in space

Draw a spaceship being pulled into the black hole.

- Draw what you think the inside of a black hole would be like.

Name _____

The Milky Way Galaxy

The Milky Way galaxy is made up of the Earth, its solar system and all the stars you can see at night. There are over 100 billion stars in the Milky Way!

The Milky Way is shaped much like a record. It has a center which the outer part goes around.

The Milky Way is always spinning slowly through space. It is so large that it would take 200 million years for the galaxy to turn one complete time.

Many stars in the Milky Way are in clusters. Some star clusters contain up to one million stars!

Our solar system

Put a red circle around our solar system.

Check.
The Milky Way galaxy is made up of

☐ Earth.
☐ no sun.
☐ our solar system.
☐ 100 billion stars.

Yes or No
The Milky Way is shaped like a pencil.   Yes   No
The Milky Way is always slowly moving in space.   Yes   No
Many stars in the Milky Way are in clusters.   Yes   No
Some star clusters have one million stars.   Yes   No

Circle.
It would take   200   90   600   million years for the galaxy to spin once.

Underline.
Which object is the Milky Way shaped much like?

 record   ruler

Name _____

How Big?

Planets vary greatly in size. Look at the list of planets and their diameters.

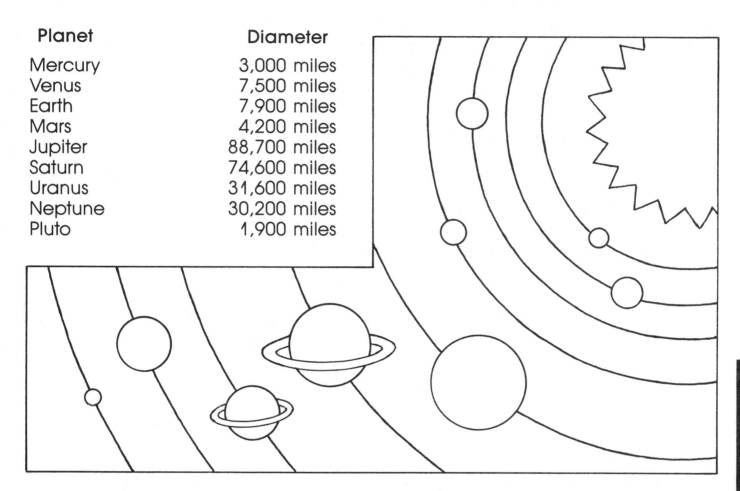

Planet	Diameter
Mercury	3,000 miles
Venus	7,500 miles
Earth	7,900 miles
Mars	4,200 miles
Jupiter	88,700 miles
Saturn	74,600 miles
Uranus	31,600 miles
Neptune	30,200 miles
Pluto	1,900 miles

Write the names of the planets in order by size starting with the planet that has the largest diameter.

1. _____
2. _____
3. _____
4. _____
5. _____
6. _____
7. _____
8. _____
9. _____

SCIENCE

Name _____

Mercury

Mercury is one of the smallest of the nine planets in our solar system. It is also the nearest planet to the sun.

Mercury spins very slowly. The side next to the sun gets very hot before it turns away from the sun. The other side freezes while away from the sun. As the planet slowly spins, the frozen side then becomes burning hot and the hot side becomes freezing cold.

Even though Mercury spins slowly, it moves around the sun very quickly. That is why it was named Mercury— after the Roman messenger for the gods.

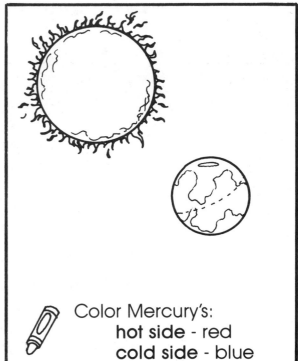

Color Mercury's:
hot side - red
cold side - blue

Underline.

Mercury is the largest planet in our solar system.
is one of the smallest planets in our solar system.

Write.

Mercury is the _____ planet to the sun.
darkest   nearest

Match.

How does spinning slowly affect the temperature on Mercury?

The side next to the sun   is freezing cold.

The side away from the sun   is burning hot.

Circle.

Mercury moves quickly   around the sun. Mercury spins very lightly.
quietly   slowly.

Check.

Mercury was named for the ☐ famous Roman speaker.
☐ Roman messenger for the gods.

Name _____

Venus

Venus is the nearest planet to Earth. Because it is the easiest planet to see in the sky, it has been called the Morning Star and Evening Star. The Romans named Venus after their goddess of love and beauty.

Venus is covered with thick clouds. The sun's heat is trapped by the clouds. The temperature on Venus is nearly 900 degrees!

Space probes have been sent to study Venus. They have reported information to scientists. But they can only last a few hours on Venus because of the high temperature.

Venus turns in the opposite direction from Earth. So, on Venus, the sun rises in the west and sets in the east!

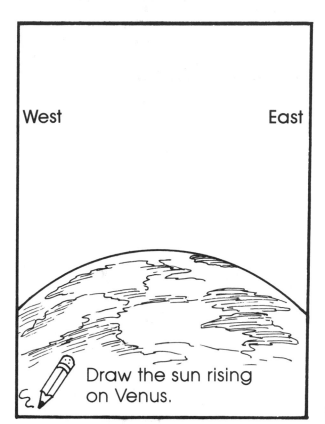

West   East

Draw the sun rising on Venus.

Unscramble and Circle.

_____ is the   friendliest   planet to Earth.
e s V u n   nearest
2 5 1 4 3

Check.

It is called the   ☐ Evening Sun
                    ☐ Morning Star   because it is so easy to see.
                    ☐ Evening Star

Circle.

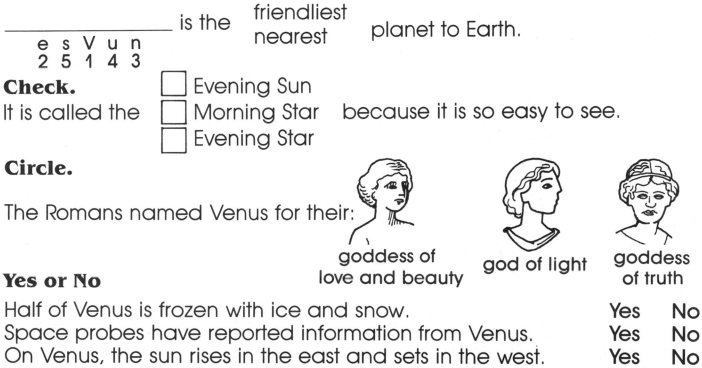

The Romans named Venus for their:

goddess of   god of light   goddess
love and beauty   of truth

Yes or No

Half of Venus is frozen with ice and snow.   Yes   No
Space probes have reported information from Venus.   Yes   No
On Venus, the sun rises in the east and sets in the west.   Yes   No

SCIENCE

Name _____

The Red Planet

Mars is the fourth planet from the sun at 141,600,000 miles away. The diameter of Mars is 4,200 miles. Mars is often called the Red Planet because rocks on the surface contain limonite, which is similar to rust. The planet has large deserts with huge dust storms. You can create your own landscape of Mars. Here's how:

Materials Needed
1 shoe box
sand
pebbles
foil
spray bottle of water
2 steel wool cleaning pads
   (without soap)

Directions
1. Line the box with foil.
2. Fill it with sand.
3. Cut the steel wool into small pieces and mix with sand.
4. Place rocks and pebbles on top.
5. Make dried-out river beds using your fingers.
6. Spray water to cover sand and keep wet for a few days.
7. Record with descriptions below.

Day 1	Day 2	Day 3
Day 4	Day 4	Day 6

Name _____

Jupiter

Jupiter is the largest planet in our solar system. It has sixteen moons. Jupiter is the second brightest planet— only Venus is brighter.

Jupiter is bigger and heavier than all of the other planets together. It is covered with thick clouds. Many loose rocks and dust particles form a ring around Jupiter.

One of the most fascinating things about Jupiter is its Great Red Spot. The Great Red Spot of Jupiter is a huge storm in the atmosphere. It looks like a red ball. This giant storm is larger than Earth! Every six days it goes completely around Jupiter.

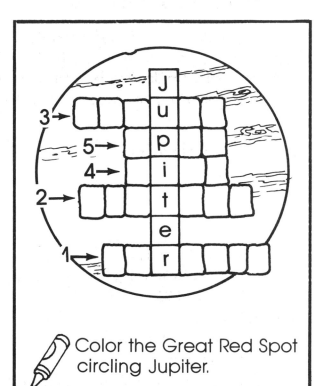

Color the Great Red Spot circling Jupiter.

Unscramble and write in puzzle.

1→ Jupiter is the _____ planet in our solar system. 2→ Jupiter

e t s l r g a
5 7 6 1 3 4 2

has _____ moons. 3→Jupiter is covered with thick

t n x s e i e
4 7 3 1 5 2 6

_____. 4→ Loose rocks and dust form a _____ around

d s o c l u
5 6 3 1 2 4

g i r n
4 2 1 3

Jupiter. 5→ The Great Red _____ of Jupiter is a huge storm.

t S o p
4 1 3 2

Circle and Write.

Jupiter is the second largest / brightest planet.

Jupiter is _____ and lighter / heavier than all planets together.

bigger   redder

SCIENCE

Name _____

Saturn

Saturn is probably most famous for its rings. The rings which circle Saturn are made of billions of tiny pieces of ice and dust. Although these rings are very wide, they are very thin. If you look at the rings from the side, they are almost too thin to be seen.

Saturn is the second largest planet in our solar system. It is so big that 758 Earths could fit inside it!

Saturn is covered by clouds. Strong, fast winds move the clouds quickly across the planet.

Saturn has 22 moons! Its largest moon is called Titan.

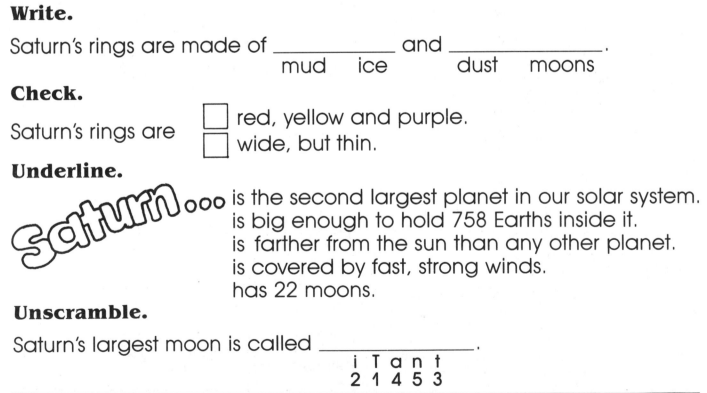

Draw 22 moons around Saturn!

Circle.

Saturn is most famous for its   spots.   rings.

Write.

Saturn's rings are made of _____ and _____.

mud   ice   dust   moons

Check.

Saturn's rings are   ☐ red, yellow and purple.
                     ☐ wide, but thin.

Underline.

Saturn °°° is the second largest planet in our solar system.
is big enough to hold 758 Earths inside it.
is farther from the sun than any other planet.
is covered by fast, strong winds.
has 22 moons.

Unscramble.

Saturn's largest moon is called _____.

i T a n t
2 1 4 5 3

Name _____

Uranus

Did you know that Uranus was first thought to be a comet? Many scientists studied the mystery "comet." It was soon decided that Uranus was a planet. It was the first planet to be discovered through a telescope.

Scientists believe that Uranus is made of rock and metal with gas and ice surrounding it.

Even through a telescope, Uranus is not easy to see. That is because it is almost two billion miles from the sun that lights it. It takes Uranus 84 Earth years to orbit the sun!

Scientists know that Uranus has five moons and is circled by nine thin rings. But there are still many mysteries about this faraway planet.

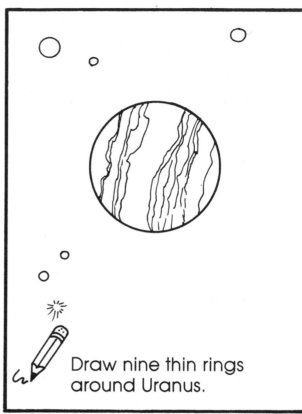

Draw nine thin rings around Uranus.

Circle.

Uranus was first thought to be a   moon.
                                         comet.

Write.

Uranus was the first planet to be discovered through a _____.
                                                          telescope TV

Check.

Scientists believe that Uranus is made of:

☐ rock   ☐ oil   ☐ metal   ☐ oceans   ☐ gas   ☐ ice

Match.

two billion miles   . . . the number of Uranus' moons

84 Earth years   . . . the distance of Uranus from the sun

five   . . . the number of Uranus' rings

nine   . . . the time it takes Uranus to orbit the sun

Name _____

Neptune

Neptune is the eighth planet from the sun. It is difficult to see Neptune—even through a telescope. It is almost three billion miles from Earth.

Scientists believe that Neptune is much like Uranus—made of rock, iron, ice and gases.

Neptune has two moons. Scientists believe that it may also have rings.

Neptune is so far away from the sun that it takes 164 Earth years for it to orbit the sun just once!

Neptune is a cold and distant planet that scientists still know very little about.

Draw 2 moons around Neptune.

Write, Circle or Unscramble.

N eptune is the   sixth / eighth   planet from the sun.

E arth is almost three _____ miles from Neptune.
million   billion

P eople know   very little / very much   about Neptune.

T elescopes are used to see Neptune.   **Yes   No**

U ranus and Neptune are made of: rock   soap   gases   ice

N eptune is a _____ and _____ planet.
warm   cold   distant   near

E very orbit around the _____ takes Neptune 164 Earth years.
u s n
2 1 3

Name _____

Pluto

Pluto is the ninth planet from the sun. It is farther from the sun than any other planet.

If you stood on Pluto, the sun would look just like a bright star in the sky. Pluto is so far away that it gets little of the sun's heat. That is why it is freezing cold on Pluto.

Some scientists think that Pluto was once one of Neptune's moons that escaped from orbit and drifted into space. Other scientists believe it has always been a planet in our solar system.

Pluto is so far away from the sun that it takes 247 Earth years just to orbit the sun once!

Draw how the sun would look from Pluto.

Unscramble and Circle.

_____ is the
seventh
ninth
planet from the sun.

l t P o u
2 4 1 5 3

Pluto is
closest
farther
from the _____ than any other planet.

n u s
3 2 1

Check.

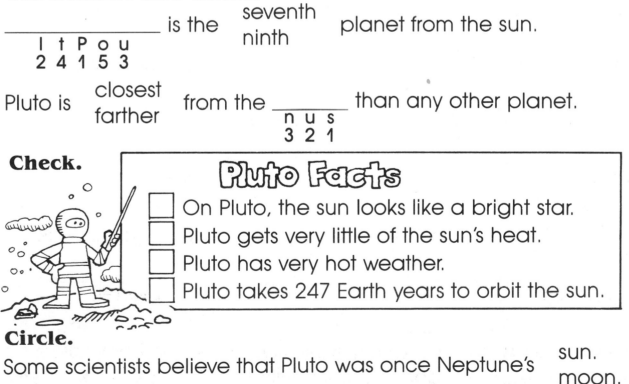

Pluto Facts

☐ On Pluto, the sun looks like a bright star.
☐ Pluto gets very little of the sun's heat.
☐ Pluto has very hot weather.
☐ Pluto takes 247 Earth years to orbit the sun.

Circle.

Some scientists believe that Pluto was once Neptune's
sun.
moon.

SCIENCE

Constellations

On a clear night, you can see about two thousand stars in the sky. Scientists can use giant telescopes to see billions of stars.

Stars in groups form pictures called constellations. These constellations have been recognized for years. Ancient people named many constellations for animals, heroes and mythical creatures. Many of these names are still used.

Some constellations can be seen every night of the year. Others change with the seasons.

Since all stars are constantly moving, these same constellations that we now see will be changed thousands of years from now.

Connect the stars to form the constellation called the Little Dipper.

Write.

Stars in groups form pictures called _____.

telescopes   constellations

Check.

Ancient people named many constellations for:

☐ animals   ☐ heroes   ☐ oceans   ☐ mythical creatures

Match.

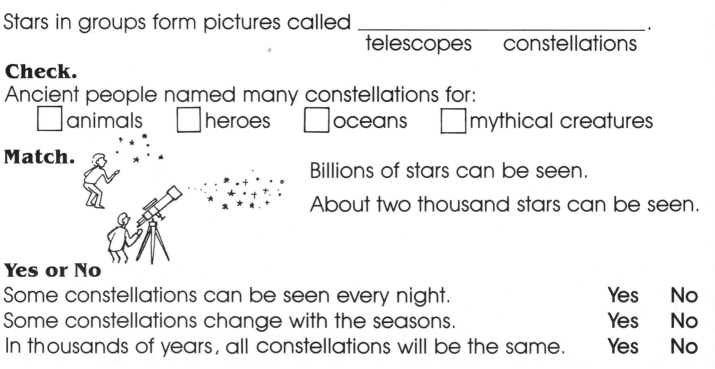

Billions of stars can be seen.

About two thousand stars can be seen.

Yes or No

Some constellations can be seen every night.	Yes	No
Some constellations change with the seasons.	Yes	No
In thousands of years, all constellations will be the same.	Yes	No

Name _____

Leaning into Summer

Why isn't it summer all year long? The seasons change because the Earth is tilted like the leaning Tower of Pisa. As the Earth orbits the sun, it stays tilting in the same direction in space.

Let's look at the seasons in the Northern Hemisphere. When the North Pole is tilting toward the sun, the days become warmer and longer. It is summer. Six months later, the North Pole tilts away from the sun. The days become cooler and shorter. It is winter.

Label the Northern Hemisphere's seasons on the chart below. Write a make-believe weather forecast for each season. Each forecast should show what the weather is like in your region for that season.

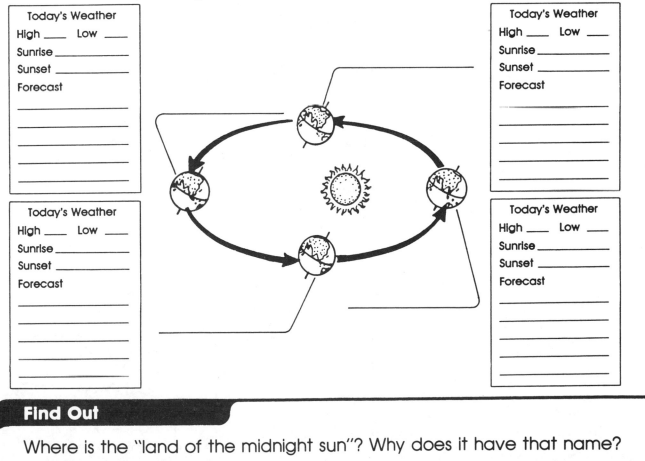

Today's Weather
High _____ Low _____
Sunrise _____
Sunset _____
Forecast
_____
_____
_____
_____
_____
_____

Today's Weather
High _____ Low _____
Sunrise _____
Sunset _____
Forecast
_____
_____
_____
_____
_____
_____

Today's Weather
High _____ Low _____
Sunrise _____
Sunset _____
Forecast
_____
_____
_____
_____
_____
_____

Today's Weather
High _____ Low _____
Sunrise _____
Sunset _____
Forecast
_____
_____
_____
_____
_____
_____

Find Out

Where is the "land of the midnight sun"? Why does it have that name?

SCIENCE

Name _____

The Moon's "Faces"

As the moon orbits the Earth, we often see different amounts of the moon's lighted part. Sometimes it looks like a circle, half-circle, or thin, curved sliver. These different shapes are the moon's **phases**.

Cut out the moon's phases as seen from Earth at the bottom of the page. Paste them in the correct box. Label the pictures using the words in the Word Bank. Use your science book to help you.

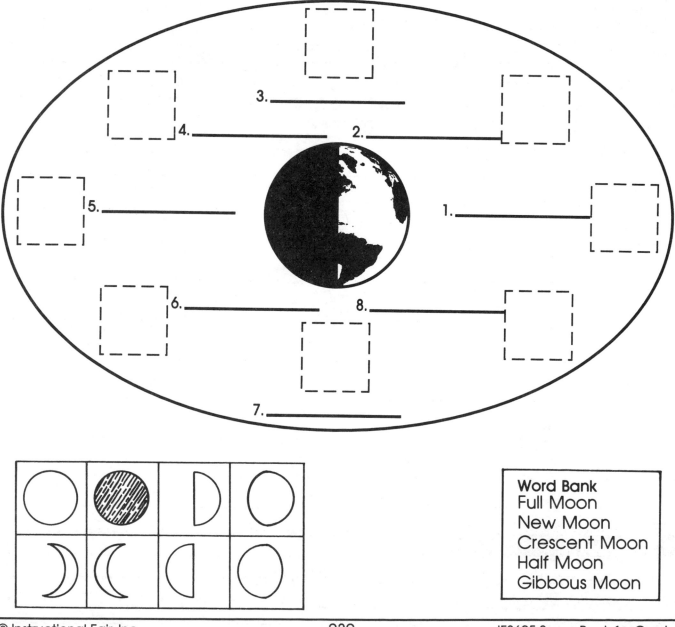

Word Bank
Full Moon
New Moon
Crescent Moon
Half Moon
Gibbous Moon

Name _____

Fatty Foods

Many of the foods we eat contain fat.
Try this fat test on several foods.

Materials Needed

6" x 6" pieces of brown paper bags (one per student)
6 containers each containing 1/4 cup of the following:
    water, oil, peanut butter, soft cheese,
    orange juice, soft margarine
6 toothpicks (one in each container)

Directions

- Predict which foods contain fat on the chart below.
- Use the toothpick from each container to make a spot on your bag. Be careful to use small amounts so they won't run together.
- Wait several minutes and check the spots. Those with fat will leave a greasy spot.
- Record your observations.

Name of Food	I Predict . . .		I Observed . . .	
	Fat	No Fat	Fat	No Fat

Which food seemed to have the most fat? Why?_____

Which food surprised you? _____

Which of the foods do you eat often? _____

What could you eat instead of the fatty foods? _____

On the back of this page, draw the path of these foods through the digestive system.

SCIENCE

Name _____

My Body Homework

To keep your body working and looking its best, you should start good habits now and keep them as you grow older. Use this checklist to keep yourself on track for the next week. Keep it on your bathroom mirror or next to your bed where it will remind you to do your "homework!"

	Sun.	Mon.	Tues.	Wed.	Thurs.	Fri.	Sat.
I slept at least 8 hours.							
I ate a healthy breakfast.							
I brushed my teeth this morning.							
I ate a healthy lunch.							
I washed my hands after using the bathroom.							
I exercised at least 30 minutes today.							
I drank at least 6 glasses of water.							
I stood and sat up straight.							
I ate a healthy dinner.							
I bathed.							
I brushed my teeth this evening.							

Name _____

What I Look for in a Friend

What I Look for in a Friend	What I Do Not Look for in a Friend
1.	1.
2.	2.
3.	3.
4.	4.

SOCIAL STUDIES

Name _____

Story Plan About Friends

Setting

Where the story takes place _____
_____

When the story takes place _____
_____

Characters in the story _____
_____

The problem in the story is _____
_____
_____
_____

Steps to solve the problem:

First, the friends _____
_____

Next, the friends _____
_____

Finally, the friends _____
_____

The story ends _____
_____
_____
_____

Name _____

Your Family

1. What is a family? _____
   _____
   _____
   _____

2. What is the purpose of a family? _____
   _____
   _____
   _____

3. Who in your family do you go to . . .
   when you are sick? _____
   for help with homework? _____
   for advice? _____
   when you are afraid? _____
   when you want something? _____
   when you are unhappy? _____
   when you have had a bad day? _____
   Have you always gone to the same person in each situation or do you go
   to different people in the family at different times? _____
   Explain your answer. _____
   _____
   _____

4. What does your family do for recreation? _____
   _____
   _____

5. Compare your family with others. How is it the same? How is it different?
   _____
   _____

6. Do you think families around the world are like families you know?
   Explain your answer. _____
   _____
   _____
   _____

SOCIAL STUDIES

Name _____

What Do You See?

Look at the pictures below. Write three sentences about each one concerning (1) the appearance of the person(s), (2) the means of transportation and (3) the landscape.

_____
_____
_____
_____
_____
_____
_____

_____
_____
_____
_____
_____
_____

_____
_____
_____
_____
_____
_____

Draw a picture in the box of you going somewhere. Write three sentences describing yourself.

_____
_____
_____

Name ____________________

The Secret Message

One morning in late June, Sally, Jim, and Lee Cruise found a very strange note on the breakfast table. It looked like a secret code. Suddenly, Lee realized that it was a rebus. Each line contained one word in the message. Help the Cruise children read the rebus.

L + ( – j) + 's = ____________

s + ( – b) = ____________

( – rap) + ( – n) = ____________

( – ) + t + ( – b) = ____________

(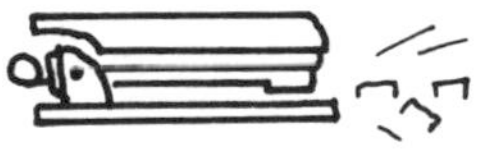 – pler) + ( – ir) + s = ____________

Then Mom and Dad yelled, "Surprise! Do you want to go?"

The excited children answered their parents' question with a rebus of their own. Fill in the missing blanks.

Y + ( – CH – S) = ____________ !

Name _____

The Best Way to Tell It

There are many vehicles that can be used to convey a message, such as a telephone, a fax machine, a radio, etc. Tell by which vehicle you think the information below would best be delivered. In some instances, there may be more than one choice.

You will be late coming home from school.

_____

How you looked when you were a baby

_____

An urgent need for help _____

How the world looked 5,000,000 years ago _____

The first Thanksgiving _____

National news _____

A make-believe story _____

Asking someone to visit your home on their vacation _____

A garage sale _____

Something that happened "once upon a time" _____

A funny experience _____

What you saw _____

A baseball game _____

An adventure in space _____

A series of strange events and their solutions _____

Tell someone you missed them. _____

_____

Your dog ran away. _____

_____

A true story _____

_____

Name _____

It Says the Same Thing Differently

Translate and write the rebus message. Then do what it tells you to do on this line:

_____

W + [image] - P + [image] - NT   [image] - YO + [image] - N

_____   _____

[image] + [image] - ILN   [image] + [image] - TE + [image] - OOR

_____   _____

Use the Code Key below to translate the message under it.

A	B	C	D	E	F	G	H	I	J	K	L	M	N	O	P	Q	R	S	T	U	V	W	X	Y	Z
/	Ʒ	ᗡ	ᴄ	⊐	⌐	⌐	−	=	‖	⌈	>	⌈	m	n	·	C	⟩	Ƨ	S	⊓	∧	⼱	:	▽	ᕐ

⌈⊐⊓⊓⊐Ʒᕐ   ‖⊓   ᕐ·m⊐   /⌈C=/Ʒ⊐⊓ᕐ

_____

⌈···⟩   ⌈‖‖⟩⊐   ⌈⊐⊓⊓⊐Ʒᕐ   ⼱⊐   ⟩⊓·⼱

_____   _____

‖⊓   ·⊓=⊐ᕐᕐ   /⌈C=/Ʒ⊐⊓ᕐ

_____   _____ .

Make a code of your own. Fill in the Code Key below with a symbol to represent each letter. Write a direction using your code.

A	B	C	D	E	F	G	H	I	J	K	L	M	N	O	P	Q	R	S	T	U	V	W	X	Y	Z

_____

_____

SOCIAL STUDIES

Name _____

Symbol-Sign Communication

Here are some familiar symbol-signs:

Handicapped

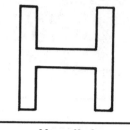

Hospital

No Parking

Railroad Crossing

Design, draw and color symbol-signs for the following:

Children's Playground	**Watch Your Step**	**Monkey House**	**Bicycle Path**
Blind Corner	**Narrow Bridge**	**Library**	**Picnic Area**
Protect Earth - Recycle	**Fishing Only From 5:00-7:00 p.m.**	**Wildflower Sanctuary**	**Dogs Must Be On Leash**

Name _____

Land Ho!

Read each clue. Find the matching word in the Word Bank. Write it in the puzzle.

Across

1. Opposite of south
4. Raised land smaller than mountain
5. Opposite of east
6. A very high hill
10. Water with land all around it
11. Water is on three sides of this landform
12. Opposite of west
14. A very large piece of land

Down

2. Large body of salt water
3. Flat land that is higher than the land around it
7. Water is all around this land
8. Very dry, sandy land
9. A large stream of water
11. Flat land
13. Opposite of north

Word Bank

continent   lake   plain
desert   mountain   plateau
east   north   river
hill   ocean   south
island   peninsula   west

Name _____

The Long Climb

Mom, Dad, Sally, Lee, and Jim started their vacation by visiting some places in the state of New York.

They decided to visit the Statue of Liberty. Two sets of parallel stairways rise from the statue's base to its crown. First Dad gave the children clues so they could find out how many steps are in each stairway.

Clue 1: The number is between 160 and 170.
Clue 2: It is an even number.
Clue 3: If you add the 3 digits in the number, the answer is 15. How many steps are in each stairway? _____

Next, Dad asked them to figure out the statue's height in inches from its base to its torch.

Clue 1: The number is less than 1,820 and more than 1,800.
Clue 2: It is an odd number.
Clue 3: The sum of the digits is 13.

The Statue of Liberty is _____ inches tall.

Finally, Dad had them compute the statue's weight in tons.

Clue 1: The number is between 200 and 250.
Clue 2: It is divisible by 5.
Clue 3: The sum of the digits is 9.

The Statue of Liberty weighs _____ tons.

Extra: The Statue of Liberty weighs _____ pounds.

Name _____

Music in the Air

While in New York City, the Cruise family saw a famous play on Broadway. Both Sally and Lee thought it was funny, and Jim really enjoyed the music.

To find out the name of the musical, read the sentence hidden in the chart below. Look up, down and sideways, connecting all the letters into words as you go.

Write the sentence here: _____

_____

Name _____

A Family Tree

The Cruise family stopped at Ellis Island, an old immigration station located in the New York Harbor. Mom and Dad reminded the children that America is a land of immigrants. Immigrants are individuals and families from other countries who have decided to live in America.

Mom told the children that people can show who belongs in their family by drawing a family tree. Each branch represents a member of the family.

Sally, Lee, and Jim decided that they would like to make a family tree. It would include their names; the names of their parents; both sets of grandparents, the Cruises and the Flyers; their dad's sister, Alice; her husband, John Jones; and their two children, Molly and Mark.

How many branches would the tree need? _____

Complete the family tree by drawing a branch for each family member. Write each person's name on a branch.

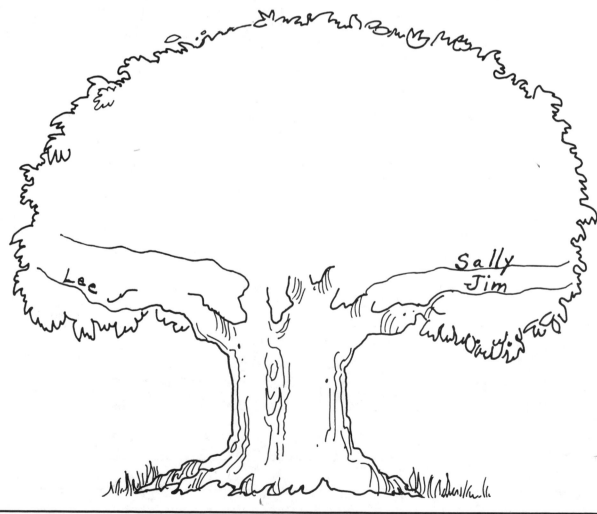

Name _____

Plymouth Rock

In Plymouth, Massachusetts, the Cruise family was able to see the famous rock which marks the Pilgrims' landing in America in 1620. The graphite boulder with the date carved on it is named "Plymouth Rock." It lies near the water's edge.

Lee decided to play with some of the other rocks in the bay. The rocks he chose were all about the same size.

First, Lee placed the rocks flat on the ground and started forming a triangle. It looked like this:

If Lee continued to follow the pattern and added rocks at the bottom of the triangle until he formed ten rows, how many rocks would he need? _____

Next, Lee created a four-sided hollow box. Each side was three rocks high and three rocks across like this:

How many rocks did Lee use? _____

Finally, Lee stacked rocks in a three-sided pyramid like the one shown here:

How many rocks did it take to form the pyramid? _____

245

IF8695 Super Book for Grade 3

SOCIAL STUDIES

Name _____

A Relaxing Ride

In Pennsylvania, the Cruise family visited Pennsylvania Dutch country. They rode through beautiful farmlands in a horse and buggy.

The horse and buggy followed a path from the farmhouse to the barn. Look carefully at the paths and count how many different ways they could travel.

They could travel _____ ways to get from the farmhouse to the barn.

 IF8695 Super Book for Grade 3

Name _____

Our Capital

Washington, D.C., our nation's capital, has many popular tourist attractions.

Sally Cruise really wanted to visit the Lincoln Memorial because she had studied about our 16th President in school this year.

As she looked up at the large statue of Lincoln, Sally looked closely at the base. She noticed that it looked like it was made up of many rectangular shapes.

Count all the rectangles shown in the base of the statue. Do not count any shaded areas. _____

SOCIAL STUDIES

The White House

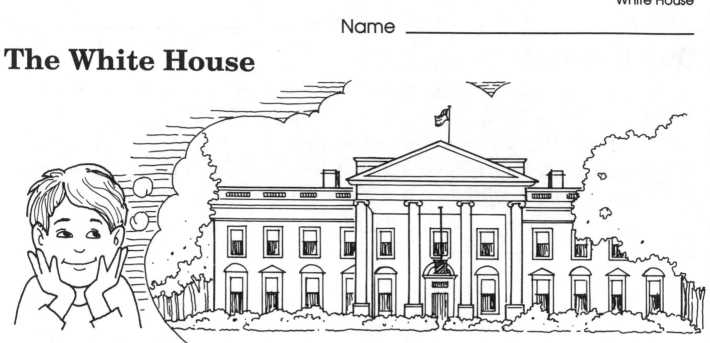

Jim Cruise really enjoyed his family's visit to the White House. Everything seemed so large and majestic. He remembered studying about some of the important events that have taken place there. Jim recalled that the White House has been the home of every President in American history except George Washington.

Jim has even thought about becoming the President of the U.S. himself. He knows that the President of the United States may not serve more than two terms in office. A term is four years.

Help Jim answer questions about his possible future election.

Our 42nd President was elected in 1992. If each future President is only elected to **one** term of four years, which President would Jim become if he were elected in the year 2040? _____

Our 42nd President was elected in 1992. If each future President is elected to **two** terms in office, which President would Jim become if he were elected in the year 2040? _____

Our 42nd President was elected in 1992. If in the future, all but two Presidents serve two terms, what President would Jim become if he were elected in the year 2040? _____

Name _____

Where's Our Mummy?

Chicago, Illinois, is a city with many interesting things to do. The Cruise family visited a zoo, an aquarium, a museum, and a planetarium.

The last place they went was the Field Museum of Natural History. Everyone agreed that their favorite exhibit was the Egyptian mummies. They learned that scientists today have discovered how the Egyptians of long ago made the mummies.

As they looked around at the mummy cases, each family member chose a favorite mummy. Use the clues to match each family member with his or her favorite mummy.

Clue 1: Mom liked a mummy on one end.

Clue 2: Dad liked the mummy that stood between Sally's and Lee's.

Clue 3: Jim's favorite mummy stood to the left of Sally's.

Clue 4: Mom's favorite mummy was separated from Dad's by two mummies.

_____'s   _____'s   _____'s   _____'s   _____'s
favorite   favorite   favorite   favorite   favorite

SOCIAL STUDIES

Name _____

Frontier Town

Dodge City, Kansas is an old western frontier town which attracts many tourists. On Front Street, each family member imagined himself or herself riding into town over 120 years ago. Dad thought about how tired he would have been just finishing a long cattle drive. Jim and Lee pictured themselves atop horses and not their ten-speed bikes. Mom and Sally thought about riding horses wearing long, full dresses on a hot, summer day.

As they looked at the buildings in town, they noticed signs posted in each window. The businesses were open only on certain days of the week.

Read the signs to help the family figure out which day of the week Dodge City really is a "Ghost Town," because all the stores are closed.

The day of the week on which

all of the shops are closed is _____ .

Name _____

Your State

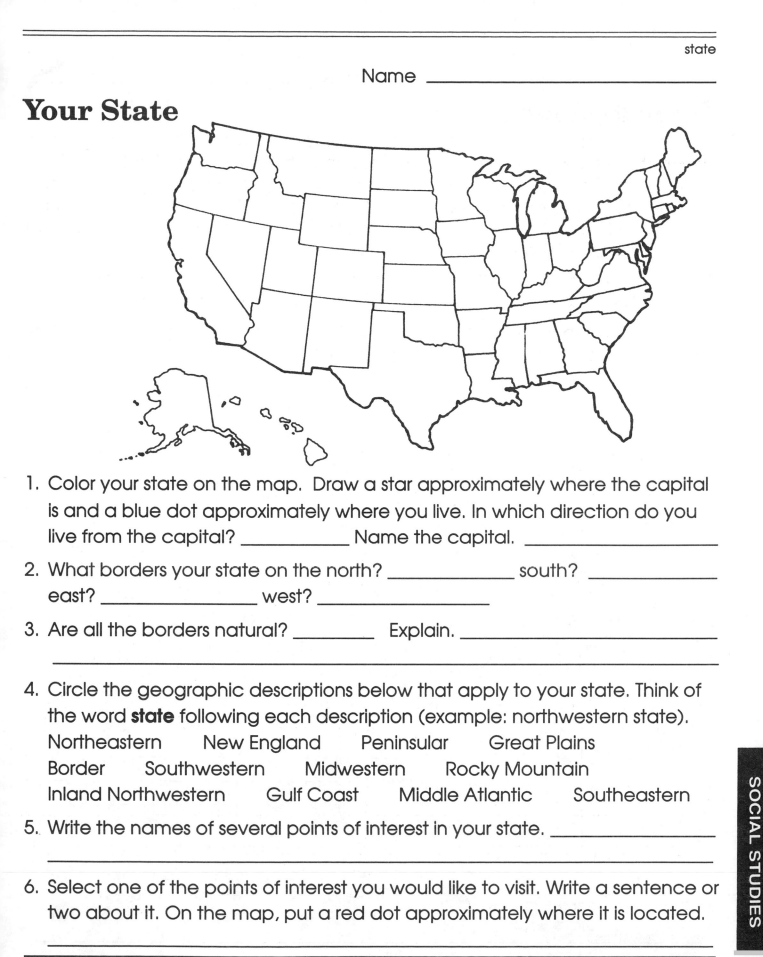

1. Color your state on the map. Draw a star approximately where the capital is and a blue dot approximately where you live. In which direction do you live from the capital? _____ Name the capital. _____

2. What borders your state on the north? _____ south? _____ east? _____ west? _____

3. Are all the borders natural? _____ Explain. _____
   _____

4. Circle the geographic descriptions below that apply to your state. Think of the word **state** following each description (example: northwestern state).
   Northeastern   New England   Peninsular   Great Plains
   Border   Southwestern   Midwestern   Rocky Mountain
   Inland Northwestern   Gulf Coast   Middle Atlantic   Southeastern

5. Write the names of several points of interest in your state. _____
   _____

6. Select one of the points of interest you would like to visit. Write a sentence or two about it. On the map, put a red dot approximately where it is located.
   _____

       IF8695 Super Book for Grade 3

SOCIAL STUDIES

Name _____

State Symbols

My state is _____ .

Draw pictures of three of the state's symbols: bird, flower and tree.
Write the name of each symbol on the line under it.

Bird _____	**Flower** _____	**Tree** _____

Other state symbols: _____

Draw a picture of the
state flag. If the flag is
different on each side,
draw one side here and
the other side on the
back of this paper.

State Flag

Write a description of the state seal.

_____

_____

_____

_____

_____

Draw the seal in the circle to the left. If the
two sides are different, draw the other side
on the back of this paper.

State Seal

Name _____

Briefly Addressed

Write the postal abbreviation for each state.

1. Washington	_____	26. Oregon	_____
2. California	_____	27. Idaho	_____
3. Nevada	_____	28. Arizona	_____
4. Montana	_____	29. Wyoming	_____
5. Utah	_____	30. Colorado	_____
6. New Mexico	_____	31. North Dakota	_____
7. South Dakota	_____	32. Nebraska	_____
8. Kansas	_____	33. Oklahoma	_____
9. Texas	_____	34. Minnesota	_____
10. Iowa	_____	35. Missouri	_____
11. Arkansas	_____	36. Louisiana	_____
12. Wisconsin	_____	37. Illinois	_____
13. Mississippi	_____	38. Indiana	_____
14. Ohio	_____	39. Kentucky	_____
15. Tennessee	_____	40. Alabama	_____
16. Pennsylvania	_____	41. New York	_____
17. Vermont	_____	42. New Hampshire	_____
18. Maine	_____	43. Massachusetts	_____
19. Rhode Island	_____	44. Connecticut	_____
20. New Jersey	_____	45. Delaware	_____
21. Maryland	_____	46. Virginia	_____
22. West Virginia	_____	47. North Carolina	_____
23. South Carolina	_____	48. Georgia	_____
24. Florida	_____	49. Michigan	_____
25. Alaska	_____	50. Hawaii	_____

SOCIAL STUDIES

Name _____

Baseball, U.S.A.

Locate the cities that have Major League Baseball teams on the map. Draw the symbol for each where it belongs.

National League
EAST

★ Philadelphia, PA (Phillies)
🧢 St. Louis, MO (Cardinals)
M Montreal (Expos)
🐱 Chicago, IL (Cubs)
☠ Pittsburgh, PA (Pirates)
🐟 Miami , FL (Marlins)
🍎 New York, NY (Mets)

WEST

G San Francisco, CA (Giants)
⚾ Atlanta, GA (Braves)
LA Los Angeles, CA (Dodgers)
✗ Houston, TX (Astros)
⊕ Cincinnati, OH (Reds)
P San Diego, CA (Padres)
⛰ Denver, CO (Rockies)

American League
EAST

T Toronto (Blue Jays)
NY New York, NY (Yankees)
⊛ Detroit, MI (Tigers)
🐤 Baltimore, MD (Orioles)
🧦 Boston, MA (Red Sox)
ℓ Cleveland, OH (Indians)
B Milwaukee, WI (Brewers)

WEST

🧦 Chicago, IL (White Sox)
👑 Kansas City, KS (Royals)
R Arlington, TX (Rangers)
O Anaheim, CA (Angels)
🚢 Seattle, WA (Mariners)
A Oakland, CA (A's)
⚭ Minneapolis, MN (Twins)

Name _____

North, South, East, and West

Pretend you are flying in an airplane with the wind blowing sharply in your face. You are flying from Chicago to Nashville. In what direction are you traveling?

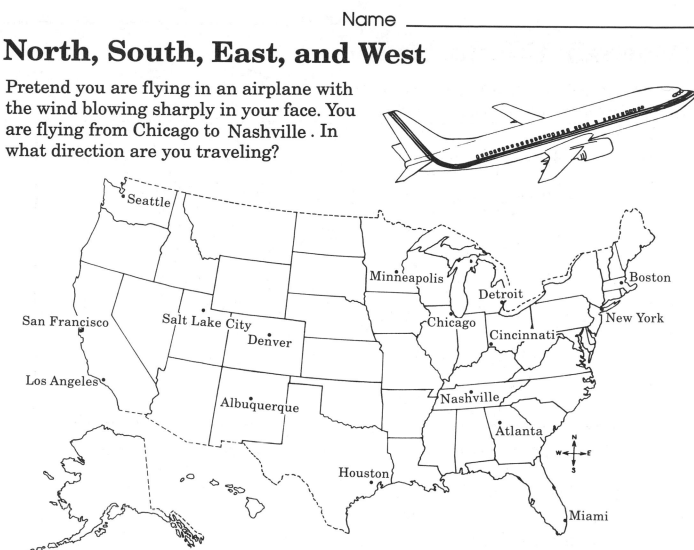

If you said, "south," to the above question, you are correct!

Write the direction you would be traveling for each set of cities. Use the four cardinal directions—north, south, east, and west.

Atlanta to Los Angeles _____   Houston to Minneapolis _____

Seattle to Los Angeles _____   Miami to New York _____

San Francisco to Nashville _____   Detroit to New York _____

Denver to Salt Lake City _____   Boston to Minneapolis _____

Cincinnati to Detroit _____   Atlanta to Albuquerque _____

Chicago to Nashville _____   Nashville to Miami _____

SOCIAL STUDIES

Name _____

Drawing a Compass Rose

The maps of the early explorers were beautiful pieces of art. Their maps would often have pictures of fire-breathing dragons and sea monsters warning of dangers where they were traveling.

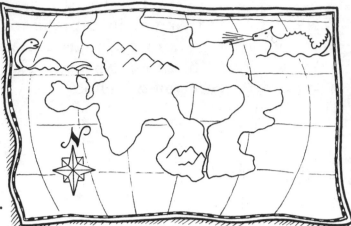

In a corner of their map would be a beautiful **compass rose**. The compass rose indicated the four **cardinal directions**—north, south, east, and west.

Follow the steps below to draw a compass rose in the upper right-hand corner of the map. Indicate the cardinal directions on your rose.

After completing the compass rose, draw a map of your own make-believe land.

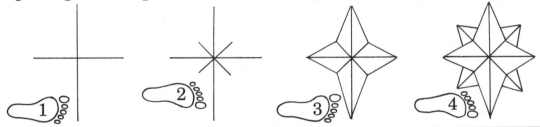

Name _____

Making a Compass

A compass is a magnet that can identify geographic direction. It is very easy to make your own compass and a lot of fun too!

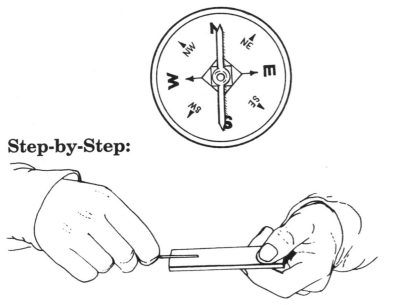

Step-by-Step:

You will need:
 magnet
 steel sewing needle
 piece of thin plastic foam
  (from fast-food packaging)
 shallow glass or plastic bowl
 masking tape
 water

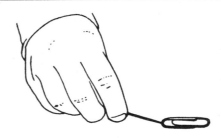

1. Pull the sewing needle toward you across the magnet. Repeat this 20 times. Be sure to always pull in the same direction.

2. Test your needle on a steel object. If it is not yet magnetized, repeat step #1, until it is.

3. Tape the needle to a small piece of plastic foam.

4. Float your magnet in a dish of water.

What did you find out?

Wait for your floating needle to stop spinning. In what direction is it pointing?

_____

Try giving the floating needle a little spin. Wait for it to stop spinning. Now what direction is it pointing? _____

SOCIAL STUDIES

Name _____

Dream Town

You are the city planner and have been chosen to map out a new "dream town." What will make your community a great place to live?

Your new town will have shopping malls, parks, factories, streets, railroads, an airport, and whatever else you would like to add.

You will need:
large piece of white drawing paper or poster board
crayons or markers
ruler

Step-by-Step:
1. Cut out the Map Key and glue it on a corner of the large sheet of paper.
2. Draw the natural features like rivers, oceans, lakes, and hills or mountains.
3. Draw the streets and highways.
4. Draw the homes, factories, shopping centers, police station, etc., using the symbols from the Map Key.

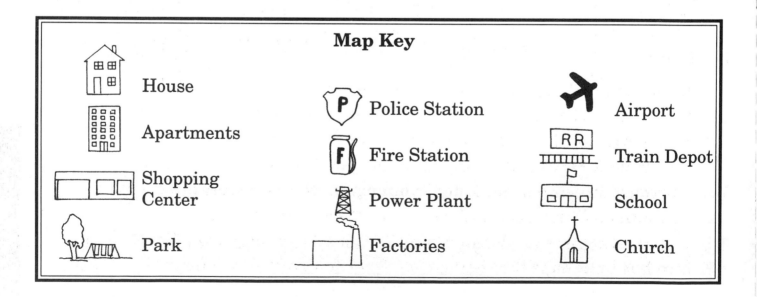

Map Key

House
Apartments
Shopping Center
Park

Police Station
Fire Station
Power Plant
Factories

Airport
Train Depot
School
Church

Name _____

A Walk Around Town

Let's take a walk around the town of Forest Grove. Use a marker or crayon to trace your route.

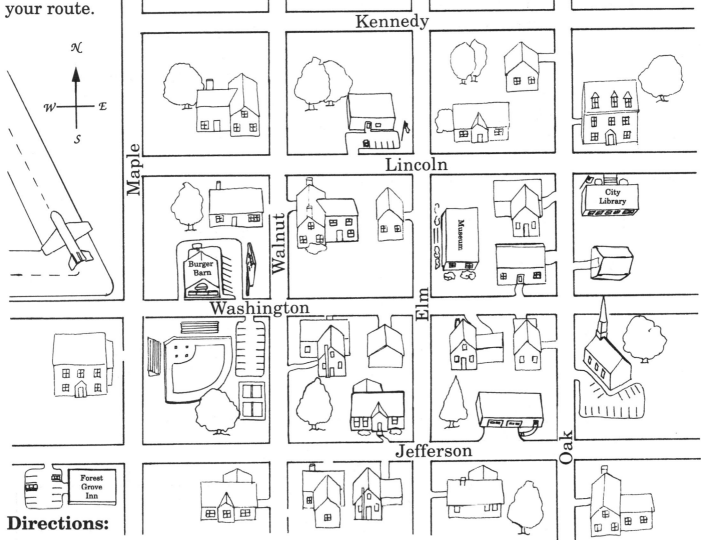

Directions:

1. Begin your walking tour at Forest Grove Inn.
2. Walk two blocks east to Elm Street.
3. Turn north on Elm Street. Walk to the Museum.
4. Go 1/2 block north to the corner of Elm and Lincoln.
5. Turn east on Lincoln. Walk until you come to the City Library.
6. Go south on Oak Street until you reach Washington Street.
7. Turn west on Washington and walk 2 1/2 blocks to the Burger Barn.
8. Lunch is over. Take the shortest way back to Forest Grove Inn.

     IF8695 Super Book for Grade 3

SOCIAL STUDIES

Near School

Geographers can tell us how places are the same and how they are different. Where you live is different from where your friend lives. Maybe you live southwest of school while your friend lives north of the school.

Write the names and draw pictures of landmarks that are found near your school. Place each one on the chart in its correct location relative to your school.

Northwest	North	Northeast
West	School	East
Southwest	South	Southeast

Name _____

Do You Have the Time?

The earth spins on its axis in a west to east direction. This causes our day to begin with the sun rising in the east and setting in the west. Different areas of the United States can have different amounts of daylight at the same moment in time. For instance, when the sun is rising in New York, it is still dark in California.

A **time zone** is an area in which everyone has the same time. Every zone is one hour different from its neighbor. There are 24 time zones around the world. There are six time zones in the United States. The map above shows the four zones that cover the 48 contiguous states.

When it is 6 o'clock in New York, what time is it in . . .

Chicago? _____   Los Angeles? _____   Denver? _____

What is the name of the time zone in which you live? _____

Name three other states in your time zone. _____

_____   _____

261   IF8695 Super Book for Grade 3

SOCIAL STUDIES

Name _____

They Showed the Way

Meriwether Lewis and William Clark were chosen by President Jefferson to find a route to the Pacific Ocean. They had to draw maps of the land, record weather conditions and write about the plants and animals that they found along the way. People wanted to know what it was like west of the Mississippi River. On May 14, 1804 they started their expedition. They arrived at the Pacific Ocean on November 7, 1805. They set up a camp which they named Fort Clatsop.

Write the names of the states in the order Lewis and Clark traveled through them on their expedition from St. Louis, Missouri to Fort Clatsop, Oregon.

1. _____   5. _____   8. _____
2. _____   6. _____   9. _____
3. _____   7. _____   10. _____
4. _____

• How long did the trip take? _____

Name _____

Totem Poles

Many Native American tribes painted symbols to tell stories. Others weaved designs into blankets to remind them of legends. The tribes in Washington State and parts of Alaska carved their family crests into trees. We call these totem poles. You can make a personal totem pole too. Draw your totem pole on another sheet of paper.

1. For the bottom of your totem pole, draw a human figure. It could be you.

2. On the top of the human figure, draw a symbol of your father's occupation.

3. Above that, draw a symbol to depict your mother. The symbol could show her occupation or it could show something she does that has special meaning to you.

4. Next draw a favorite animal, which will be your family's crest. It could be your family pet or an animal your family especially likes, such as a special bird.

5. The next section should include a symbol of the type of job you want to do when you become an adult.

6. Next think of a hobby that you really enjoy, such as a sport, music, or computers. Draw this.

7. On top of your totem pole, draw a symbol that stands for something very important to you.

8. Now go back and color your totem pole.

9. Then think of a way to make your totem pole out of scraps of construction paper, tissue paper, and other odds and ends.

10. Use your design to create a 3-D totem pole. Give it to your teacher for display.

SOCIAL STUDIES

Name _____

The Makah and Nootka Whalers

Although many tribes of the Northwest Coastal area used whales as a source of food and supplies, only the Makah and Nootka tribes actually hunted them at sea. These Indians trained and purified themselves for three months before the hunt. Then they set out in canoes. When a whale was spotted, the chief had the honor of striking with the first harpoon. All others then joined in until the whale was exhausted and eventually died. Finally, the Indians tied the mouth shut so the whale's lungs couldn't fill with water and sink, and the whale was towed back to shore.

Imagine the difficulty of hunting an animal the size of a whale! To help you visualize this incredible feat, use encyclopedias to find the length in meters of the whales listed below. Then write these lengths in feet and list a comparison to help you imagine the size.

Type of Whale	Length in Meters	Length in Feet	That's about as long as ...
blue			
humpback			
killer			
sperm			

Fun Fact: An entire tribe could live a whole year on only 2-4 whales!

Name _____

Native American Drum

The Eastern Woodland tribes lived in the woods and depended greatly on hunting. They practiced dances and songs from the time they were children. The drum was an important part of their ceremonies. Children learned to make their own drums using the five steps below. Number the steps for making a drum in the correct order. Then draw a picture to illustrate each step. Draw your completed drum in the last box.

____ Cut two pieces of hide for the top and bottom.

____ Carve out the center of a tree trunk.

____ Paint the drum.

____ Punch holes around the cut hide.

____ Use yarn to tie the hides to the drum.

1.	2.
3.	4.
5.	

SOCIAL STUDIES

Name _____

The Hunters

Although they farmed and ate other foods besides meat, hunting was very important to most Woodland Indians, especially during the winter.

The information below shows the game that was caught by two Eastern Woodland tribes. Use the imformation to complete a double bar graph comparing the successes of the two tribes. Be sure to use a different color for each tribe.

Iroquois Tribe

Mohawk Tribe

* Each print represents 4 animals caught.

Bear	
Beaver	
Deer	
Moose	
Rabbit	

0   2   4   6   8   10   12   14   16   18   20   22   24   26   28   30

[ ] **Iroquois**   [ ] **Mohawk**

Name _____

Southwest Symbols

The tribes who lived in this area made pictures called pictographs to tell stories of hunting, farming, trading, traveling and battling with other tribes.

You can write an Indian story on another sheet of paper using symbols for the most important parts. Be sure to use words between the symbols to create complete sentences! The key has been started for you, but add your own symbols as you use them in the story.

Ex: As the ⌖ rose into the sky, the great 👤 rode off toward the ⛰.

Symbol Key

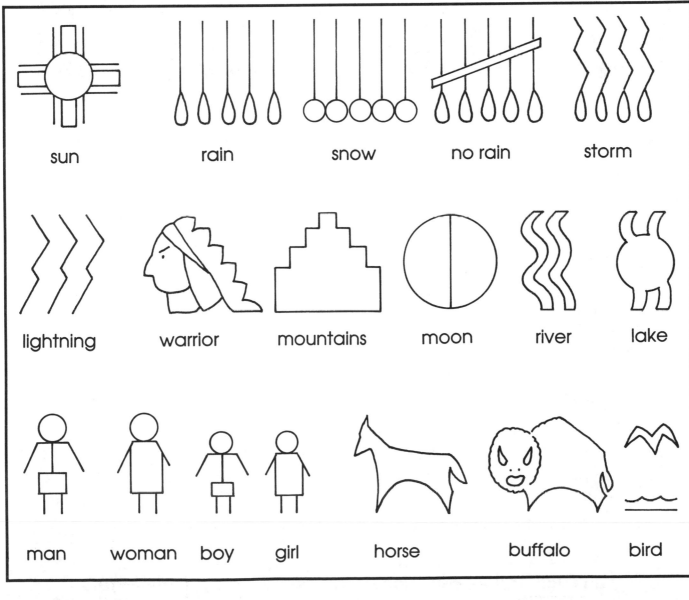

sun	rain	snow	no rain	storm
lightning	warrior	mountains	moon	river	lake
man	woman	boy	girl	horse	buffalo	bird

Name _____

The Buffalo Hunters

The Plains Indians' survival depended on the buffalo. They killed only as many as they needed and wasted none of the animal.

Below is a list of some buffalo body parts. Make a logical guess as to the function of each. Then use an encyclopedia to find the actual uses. You may be very surprised!

Your Logical Guess

clothing, tepees, drums •   • teeth

decorations •   • brain

bowls for cooking •   • tongue

cups, spoons •   • hide

jewelry •   • large intestine

strings on bows •   • horns

bags for storage •   • muscles

ropes, belts •   • stomach

food •   • hair

tanning mixture for leather •   • tail

Name another buffalo part and its function. _____

Fun Fact: The Plains Indians had over 500 uses for the buffalo.

Name _____

Canada, Geographically Speaking

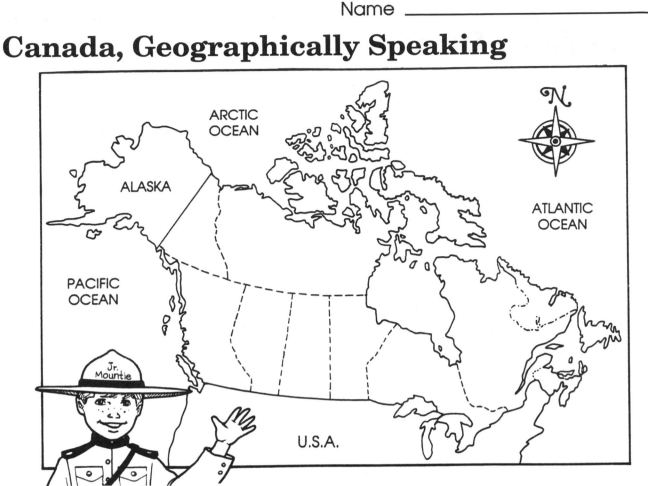

Unlike the United States, Canada is not divided into states. Follow the directions to label the ten provinces and two territories that make up Canada.

1. The Yukon Territory is connected to Alaska. The Northwest Territory is the large area to its east. Label them.
2. British Columbia is south of Yukon. Label the province and color it yellow.
3. East of British Columbia is Alberta. Label it and color it red.
4. The province between Alberta and Manitoba is called Saskatchewan. This is where Big Foot supposedly lives. Draw him there and label the provinces.
5. Winnepeg is a city in Manitoba. Label the city and color the province brown.
6. The province north of the Great Lakes is Ontario. Color it orange.
7. The largest province is Quebec. Label the province and color it green.
8. New Brunswick borders Quebec on the southeast, and Nova Scotia is attached to it. Label them and color them purple.
9. Nestled above the two provinces is Prince Edward Island. Color this province black.
10. The last province is Newfoundland. This province borders Quebec and includes the large island near it. Label both parts.

SOCIAL STUDIES

Name _____

Montreal, the Heart of French Canada

Canada's largest province, Quebec, is unique because most of its inhabitants speak French. The people there have long been referred to as French-Canadians. They are quite proud of their French heritage, often referring to themselves as "pure wool."

Montreal is Quebec's most famous city and is often called the "Heart of French Canada." By day or night, it is an exciting city with fine universities, the National Hockey League (Montreal Canadiens), incredible museums, and the one-of-a-kind *Cirque du Soleil*.

Cirque du Soleil means Circus of the Sun. This circus is unique because it only has human performers; no animals. Quebec funds a school called the École Nationale de Cirque. With an enrollment of 20 youngsters, the school provides an academic education while the students learn the arts of the big top on the trapeze, stilts, trampoline, and tightrope.

Pretend that you are a student at the school. Write about what a typical day is like for you. Draw yourself performing below.

Name _____

Bolivia

Bolivia is located in South America and is about twice the size of Texas. Children here go to school from 9 a.m. to 4 p.m. They have a long vacation in June and July, but for them this is winter break. They have another long break from October to December. This is summer in Bolivia!

Think about yourself during summer and winter vacations. Then, follow these directions:

1. Write your name in the chart below.
2. Draw yourself during summer break in the first box.
3. Draw something Porfirio might do in July.
4. Draw yourself during winter break in the third box.
5. Draw something Porfirio might do in December.
6. Color each picture.

What do you notice about the pictures? Why are the seasons opposite? Write your answers on the back.

	_____(your name)	Porfirio (Bolivian boy)
July	1.	2.
December	3.	4.

SOCIAL STUDIES

Name _____

Animals in the Rainforest

Brazil is located in South America. Many of its people are very poor. This country is partially covered by rainforests in which thousands of different plants and animals live. However, many of these animals could become extinct because of the destruction of the rainforests for their lumber. Follow the directions below to discover some of the animals that live in the rainforest.

1. Draw a jungle pig (called a tapir) hiding in the leaves.
2. Draw a jaguar lying on the ground.
3. Draw a parrot in the trees.
4. Draw an anaconda snake on the riverbank.
5. Draw spiders on the trees and on the ground.
6. Draw fish in the river.
7. Draw an alligator in the river.
8. Draw butterflies in the air.
9. Draw an Indian in the trees.
10. Color your rainforest and its animals.

Name _____

Chewing Pleasures

Chewing gum is probably something you enjoy. Did you ever wonder about its history? Chewing gummy substances dates back hundreds of years. Early Greeks and American Indians chewed resin from the bark of trees. In the mid-1800s, sweetened par-affin wax came to be favored over resin.

Today gum has an "international flavor." Gum base, the chewy ingredient, comes mainly from the Ama-zon Valley in Brazil. Natural resins, which make the gum feel better when you chew it, come from southern United States.

Exact recipes are top-secret information. Manufac-turers are continually improving their products. They also have to design appealing packages so you will want to buy them! That is why companies put baseball cards in some of the packages.

Some people have been against chewing gum. They thought it kept students from concentrating in school. Others thought that if you swallowed gum it would clog up your stomach. Research says that chewing gum actually reduces tension and improves concentration. Gum is a low-calorie snack and it helps prevent tooth decay and promotes sweeter breath.

Interview people to find out why they chew gum. Each space equals one person's answer.

Why We Chew Gum										
Enjoyment										
Tastes Good										
Helps Concentration										
Freshens Breath										
Cleans Teeth										
	1	2	3	4	5	6	7	8	9	10

Compile your information and make a group graph.

SOCIAL STUDIES

Name _____

Central America

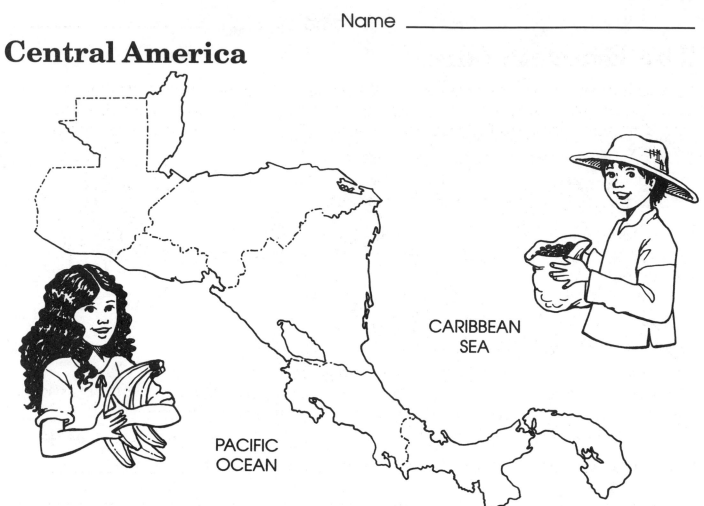

CARIBBEAN
SEA

PACIFIC
OCEAN

The land connecting North and South America is called Central America. This is where Costa Rica and six other countries are located. Follow the directions below to label the countries and some of their products.

1. Draw a cotton plant in Belize. It's the northernmost country.

2. Draw a cotton plant in Guatemala. It borders Belize.

3. El Salvador grows many coffee beans. Draw a cup of coffee in this country that is southeast of Guatemala.

4. Silver is mined in Honduras, north of El Salvador. Color this country silver.

5. Nicaragua contains gold mines. Color this country bordering Honduras gold.

6. Children from Costa Rica love the bananas grown there. Draw a banana.

7. Panama's fishermen catch many shrimp. Draw some shrimp in this southern-most country. If you look closely, you will see a break in the land through which ships can pass. This is the Panama Canal. Label it also.

The U.S. helped clear the land that was once where the canal is now. Why do you think they wanted to help? Write your answer on the back of this paper.

Name _____

The Emerald Isle

Ireland is often called the Emerald Isle because of its rolling green farmland and countryside. This is why we wear green on St. Patrick's Day, an Irish holiday. Sean and Kathleen want you to follow the directions below to make today a special Irish day.

1. Write the name of three crayons that have a green tint. _____

   _____

2. Name two people wearing green today. _____

   _____

3. Write three words you can spell with the letters in IRELAND. _____

   _____

4. Write the title of a book that has the word *green* in it. _____

   _____

5. Name four green animals. _____

   _____

6. What do scientists call trees that stay green all winter? _____

7. List two things in your classroom that are entirely green. _____

8. Name your favorite green food. _____

9. Draw a leprechaun on the back of your paper.

10. Use only green crayons for the rest of the school day.

SOCIAL STUDIES

Name _____

Number, Please!

The population of Israel is a mixture of people from over 70 countries. Use the telephone puzzle below to dial and meet a few!

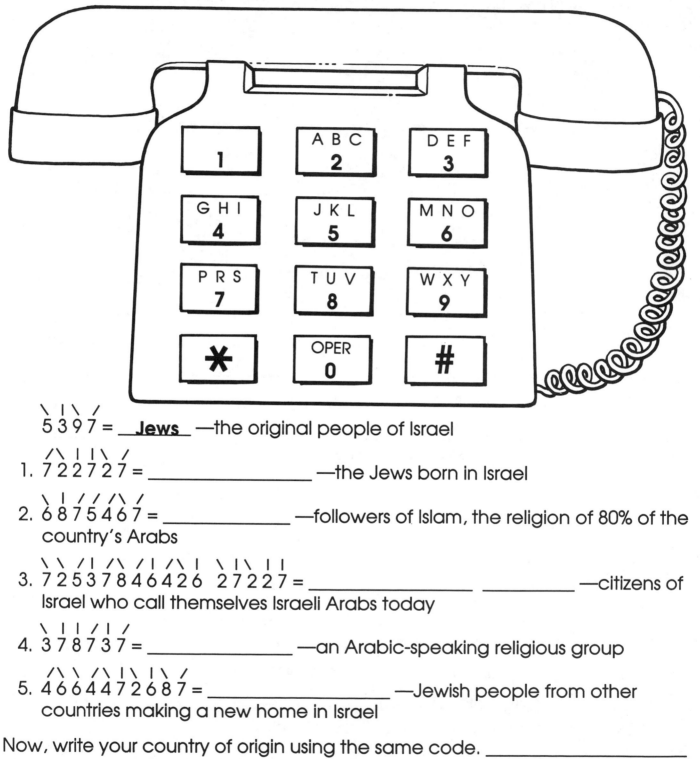

5 3 9 7 = __Jews__ —the original people of Israel

1. 7 2 2 7 2 7 = _____ —the Jews born in Israel

2. 6 8 7 5 4 6 7 = _____ —followers of Islam, the religion of 80% of the country's Arabs

3. 7 2 5 3 7 8 4 6 4 2 6 2 7 2 2 7 = _____ _____ —citizens of Israel who call themselves Israeli Arabs today

4. 3 7 8 7 3 7 = _____ —an Arabic-speaking religious group

5. 4 6 6 4 4 7 2 6 8 7 = _____ —Jewish people from other countries making a new home in Israel

Now, write your country of origin using the same code. _____

Name _____

A Journey to Japan

Follow the directions to complete the map of Japan, Mieko's homeland.

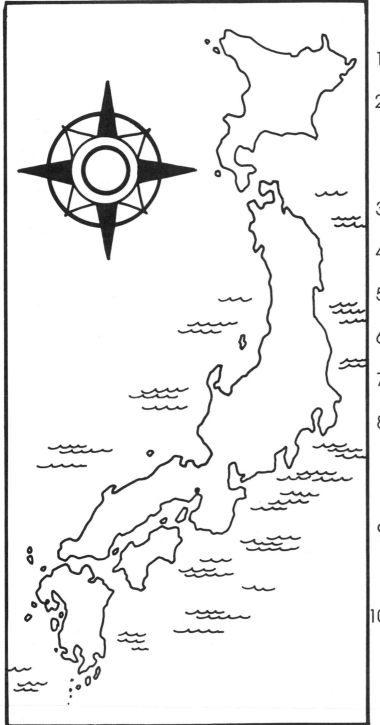

1. Add the eight directional letters to the compass rose.
2. Label the islands in capital letters:
   KYUSHU – southernmost
   HOKKAIDO – northernmost
   HONSHU – south of Hokkaido
   SHIKOKU – north of Kyushu
3. Add a red ★ and label the capital city, Tokyo.
4. Draw a mountain at Mount Fuji's location.
5. Label **Nagasaki** by the dot on Kyushu Island.
6. Label the **Sea of Japan** and the **Pacific Ocean**. Add blue waves.
7. Label **Osaka** by the dot on Honshu Island.
8. Outline the islands in these colors:
   Hokkaido – orange
   Honshu – green
   Shikoku – red
   Kyushu – yellow
9. Along the northern edge of the box, label the map **JAPAN**, using a different color for each letter.
10. Draw the flag of Japan.

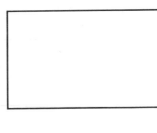

SOCIAL STUDIES

Name _____

Written Japanese

When Laura visited a Japanese classroom, she could not read anything that was written. She learned that written Japanese is considered to be one of the most difficult writing systems in the world. It is a combination of Japanese phonetic symbols as well as Chinese characters. Each character is a symbol that stands for a complete word or syllable. However difficult, almost all Japanese people 15 years of age or older can read and write.

Use the following Japanese characters to write a story about a big man. Use the characters in your story whenever possible.

大	人	木	森	山	門
big	man	tree	forest	mountain	gate

The 大 人 _____

_____

_____

_____

_____

_____

_____

_____

Name _____

Raising a Family in Kenya

As members of the more progressive Njoroge Tribe, Omar's parents have a dream. They want to see their four children through secondary school. That will require great sacrifice for them as their coffee crop only earned them $120 after expenses last year.

Omar and his family live a very simple life. Omar's father raises coffee plants on their one-acre farm. Omar's mother and father work very hard to earn the money to send Omar and his brother and two sisters to school. It costs $75 a year for primary school for each child. To earn more money, Omar's father works as a stonemason for $5 a day. Omar's mother works at a larger farm for $2 a day.

1. How many days will Omar's father have to work as a stonemason to pay for one year of Omar's primary school? (Hint: Count by 5's.) _____

2. How many days will Omar's father have to work to pay for the other 3 children's primary school each year? (Hint: Add your answer from #1 three times.) _____

3. One pair of children's shoes cost $10. How many days will Omar's mother have to work to buy him a pair of shoes? (Hint: Count by 2's.) _____

4. How many days will Omar's mother have to work to buy the other 3 children new pairs of shoes? (Hint: Add your answer to #3 three times.) _____

5. How much will it cost to buy shoes for all four children. (Hint: Count by 10's.) _____

SOCIAL STUDIES

Name _____

Tortillas, Anyone?

Juan lives in Mexico. The main food crop grown there is corn. Even though it is grown on half of Mexico's cultivated land, corn is still imported because the demand for it is so high. Since ancient times, corn has been used to make flat pancakes called tortillas. Sometimes they are folded and stuffed with different foods to make tacos. Throughout Mexico, you will see stands on the street serving tortillas and tacos. Juan's mother folds the tortillas and fills them with meat, goat cheese, beans, hot sauce, and lettuce.

Scientists have been unable to trace the ancestry of modern corn directly to a wild plant. But they do know that Indians in what is now Central or Southern Mexico gathered corn from wild plants about 10,000 years ago. About 5000 B.C., the Indians learned how to grow their own corn. That is how it came to be called Indian corn.

The words in dark type below make each of the sentences untrue. Rewrite the sentences so they are true. On another sheet of paper, draw all the things you would want to include in a super delicious taco. Be creative!

1. Tacos are made from **wheat bread**.

   _____

2. The Indians that gathered corn from wild plants lived in **northern Mexico**.

   _____

3. Tortillas are made from **wheat**.

   _____

4. The stands on the streets of Mexico serve **hot dogs.**

   _____

5. Corn is often called **Italian** corn.

   _____

6. About **10,000** B.C., Indians learned to grow corn themselves.

   _____

7. Much corn is **exported** to Mexico.

   _____

8. Corn is used to make flat **sandwiches** called tortillas.

   _____

Name _____

Life in the Village

Juan's house is made of clay. The clay was mixed together with straw and water and shaped into bricks. His roof is made of red tiles that are sloped to let the rain run off easily.

In the back of Juan's house is a shady patio. It has a wall around it to form a courtyard. At night, the cow and burro join the chickens and turkeys there.

The house has a hard-packed dirt floor. Juan's mother or father builds a cooking fire on the floor. It is built near the door so the smoke can go out the door and windows on either side of the door. That is where Juan's mother makes the tortillas that he loves. It is 10-year-old Maria's job to sweep the floor and bring cool water to drink from the village fountain. She helps her mother wash the family's clothes in the river.

Juan helps his father with his clay animals that he makes to sell at the village market during fiestas. Some day Juan wants to be a potter like his father. Juan has already sold some vases at the market. On a sheet of white paper, draw and decorate a colorful vase that Juan might have made.

Draw a picture of Juan's house and yard below. Reread the paragraphs above to include as much detail as possible. When you draw the front door, draw what you can see inside of it.

SOCIAL STUDIES

Name _____

New Zealand

canton ⌐

New Zealand is an island southeast of Australia. The people there speak English because most of their ancestors were from England. Children there, as in the U.S., face their flag when they say their pledge. You can make a New Zealand flag by following the directions below.

1. In the middle of the small box (the canton), draw a red stripe from the top to the bottom.

2. Draw a red stripe across the middle of the canton area.

3. Still in the canton area, draw a red stripe diagonally from corner to corner.

4. Draw a red stripe diagonally the other way.

5. Color white stripes on both sides of the red stripes.

6. Draw four stars to the right of the canton.

7. Color the stars red.

8. Outline the stars in white.

9. Color the entire background blue.

10. Look at a British flag. What do you notice?

Name _____

Operation Bootstrap

Puerto Rico is a small island located about 1,000 miles southeast of Florida. The people there are U.S. citizens though they cannot vote in presidential elections and do not pay federal income taxes. The country is poor, but their program "Operation Bootstrap" is helping manufacturing to grow. José has been given the task of making a bar graph about his country's employment. Follow the directions to help him complete the graph.

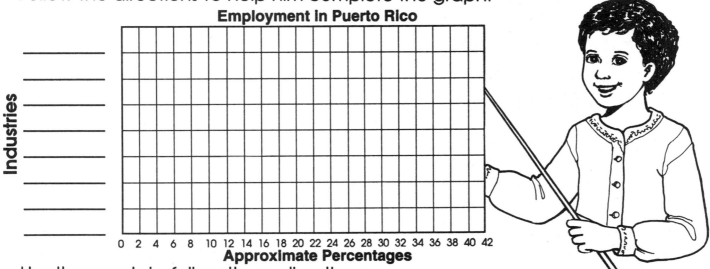

Use the graph to follow these directions.

1. Agriculture accounts for 5 percent of all employment. Label it and fill in the bar graph.
2. Construction employs about the same percentage of people as agriculture.
3. Finance, insurance and real estate is one category. It employs 2 percent less people than does agriculture. Label it and fill in the bar graph.
4. Government employs the highest number of workers. It employs 42 percent of all workers. Label this category and fill in the bar graph.
5. Manufacturing accounts for a high amount of employment, but it employs 21 percent less than the government does. Label and fill in the bar graph.
6. Wholesale and retail trade employs about 13 percent more people than does construction. Label and fill in the bar graph.
7. Transportation and communication employs 1 percent less than agriculture does. Label and fill in the bar graph.
8. The last category is utilities and mining. It employs 2 percent less people than transportation and communication. Label and fill in the bar graph.

SOCIAL STUDIES

Name _____

Chinese Lion Dance

Children in Taiwan go to school from Monday through Saturday! They study all of the subjects that you do, including physical education. They sometimes learn the Chinese Lion Dance, which is done with two or more children carrying a costume like the one below. Complete the picture above by following the directions.

1. Color its face green.
2. Color its mouth red.
3. Color its nose purple.
4. Color its hair yellow.
5. Draw and color the rest of the lion's body.
6. Draw the legs of two children underneath the lion costume.

On the back of this paper, design another lion costume. Use at least five crayons to color your design.

Name _____

Desert Attire

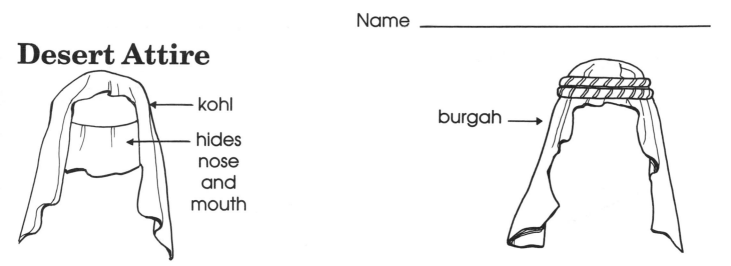

Tunisia is located in northeastern Africa. Much of the land is desert, so the people must protect themselves from sun and blowing sand. For this reason, many children wear special head coverings like the ones pictured. Finish the picture above by following the directions.

1. Use pencil to draw a boy wearing the burgah.
2. Draw a girl wearing the kohl.
3. Draw a white robe on the boy.
4. Draw a black robe on the girl.
5. Draw desert sand under their feet.
6. Draw the blazing sun.
7. Draw a camel nearby.
8. Color the boy and the girl.

It is an Arabian custom for the girls to keep their noses and mouths covered. Why do you think they do this?

SOCIAL STUDIES

Name _____

Everybody Grows Rice

Although Asian countries grow ninety percent of the world's rice, it is grown in many other countries, including the United States. Write the names of the rice-producing countries in the puzzle.

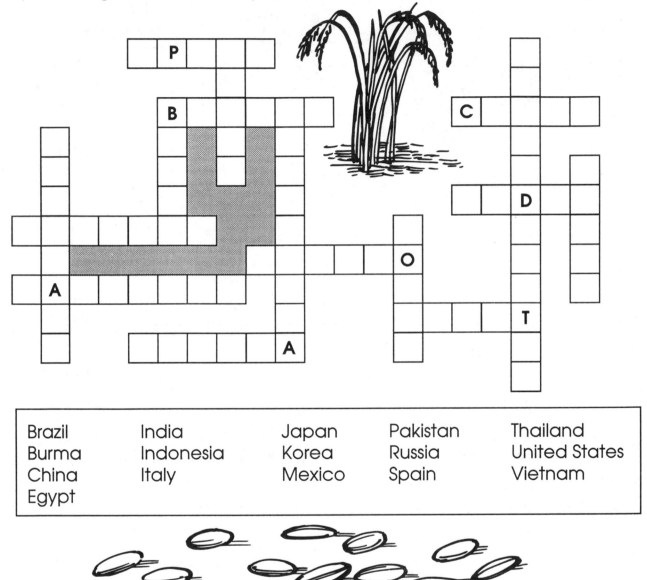

Brazil	India	Japan	Pakistan	Thailand
Burma	Indonesia	Korea	Russia	United States
China	Italy	Mexico	Spain	Vietnam
Egypt				

AND NOW Find out more about one of these rice-producing countries. Draw and label a map showing the regions in that country where rice is grown. Label the capital city. Show the type of dress worn by the people of the country.

Name _____

Hip, Hip, Hooray for Holidays

Choose a word from the Word Box to complete each sentence. Then write the word in the puzzle.

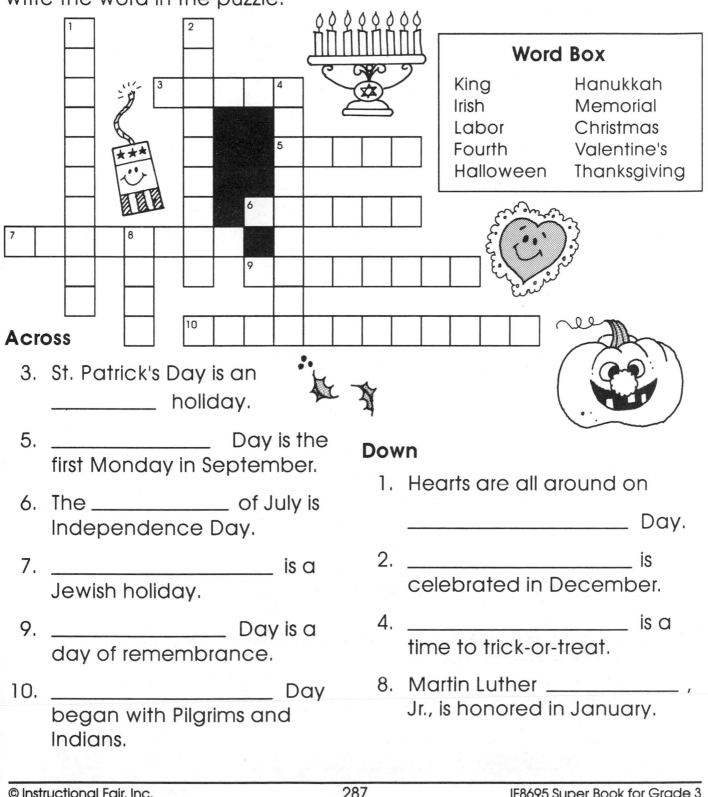

Word Box

King	Hanukkah
Irish	Memorial
Labor	Christmas
Fourth	Valentine's
Halloween	Thanksgiving

Across

3. St. Patrick's Day is an _____ holiday.

5. _____ Day is the first Monday in September.

6. The _____ of July is Independence Day.

7. _____ is a Jewish holiday.

9. _____ Day is a day of remembrance.

10. _____ Day began with Pilgrims and Indians.

Down

1. Hearts are all around on _____ Day.

2. _____ is celebrated in December.

4. _____ is a time to trick-or-treat.

8. Martin Luther _____, Jr., is honored in January.

SOCIAL STUDIES

Name _____

Let's Celebrate!

In each calendar month below, write all the holidays you and your family celebrate and their dates. Include family celebrations like birthdays and anniversaries and national, religious, state and community holidays.

January	February	March

April	May	June

July	August	September

October	November	December

Answer Key

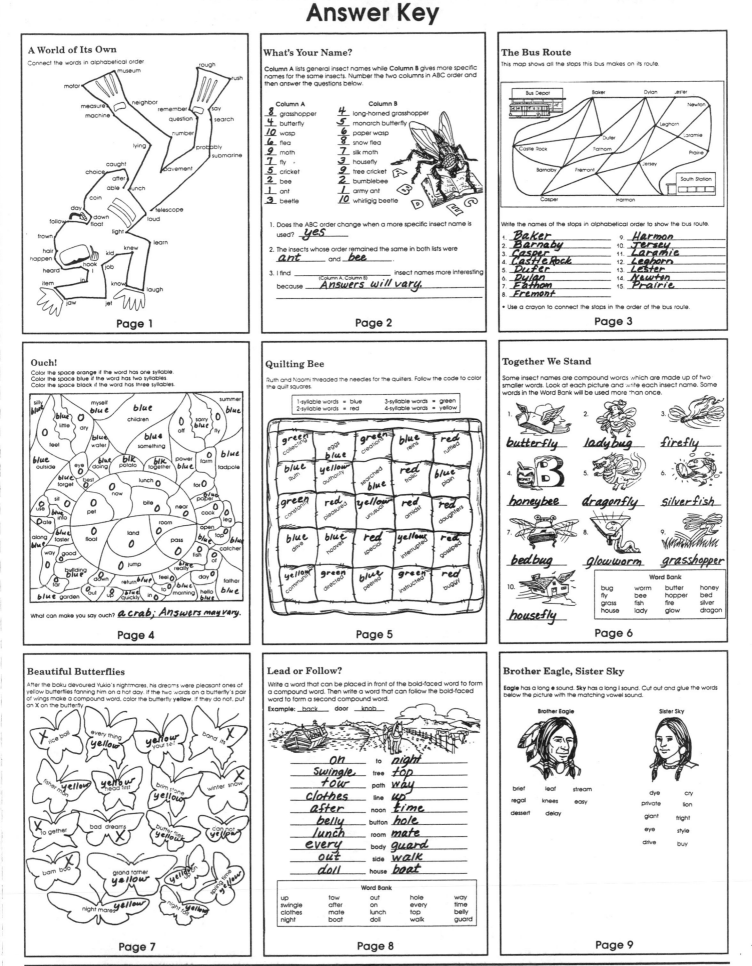

A World of Its Own

Connect the words in alphabetical order

museum, rough, rush, motor, neighbor, measure, remember, say, search, machine, question, number, lying, probably, submarine, caught, pavement, choice, after, able, lunch, coin, telescope, day, down, loud, follow, float, light, learn, frown, knew, hair, kid, happen, hook, job, heard, in, item, know, laugh, jaw, jet

Page 1

What's Your Name?

Column A lists general insect names while Column B gives more specific names for the same insects. Number the two columns in ABC order and then answer the questions below.

Column A		Column B	
8	grasshopper	4	long-horned grasshopper
4	butterfly	5	monarch butterfly
10	wasp	6	paper wasp
6	flea	8	snow flea
9	moth	7	silk moth
7	fly	3	housefly
5	cricket	9	tree cricket
2	bee	2	bumblebee
1	ant	1	army ant
3	beetle	10	whirligig beetle

1. Does the ABC order change when a more specific insect name is used? **yes**

2. The insects whose order remained the same in both lists were **ant** and **bee**.

3. I find _____ (Column A, Column B) insect names more interesting because **Answers will vary.**

Page 2

The Bus Route

This map shows all the stops this bus makes on its route.

Bus Depot, Baker, Dylan, Lester, Newton, Leghorn, Laramie, Dufer, Fatnom, Prairie, Castle Rock, Jersey, Barnaby, Fremont, South Station, Casper, Harmon

Write the names of the stops in alphabetical order to show the bus route.

1. Baker
2. Barnaby
3. Casper
4. Castle Rock
5. Dufer
6. Dylan
7. Fatham
8. Fremont
9. Harmon
10. Jersey
11. Laramie
12. Leghorn
13. Lester
14. Newton
15. Prairie

• Use a crayon to connect the stops in the order of the bus route.

Page 3

Ouch!

Color the space orange if the word has one syllable.
Color the space blue if the word has two syllables.
Color the space black if the word has three syllables.

What can make you say ouch? **a crab; Answers may vary.**

Page 4

Quilting Bee

Ruth and Naomi threaded the needles for the quilters. Follow the code to color the quilt squares.

1-syllable words = blue   3-syllable words = green
2-syllable words = red   4-syllable words = yellow

Page 5

Together We Stand

Some insect names are compound words which are made up of two smaller words. Look at each picture and write each insect name. Some words in the Word Bank will be used more than once.

1. butterfly
2. ladybug
3. firefly
4. honeybee
5. dragonfly
6. silverfish
7. bedbug
8. glowworm
9. grasshopper
10. housefly

Word Bank

bug	worm	butter	honey
fly	bee	hopper	bed
grass	fish	fire	silver
house	lady	glow	dragon

Page 6

Beautiful Butterflies

After the baku devoured Yukio's nightmares, his dreams were pleasant ones of yellow butterflies fanning him on a hot day. If the two words on a butterfly's pair of wings make a compound word, color the butterfly yellow. If they do not, put an X on the butterfly.

X rice ball, every thing / yellow, your self / yellow, band its X, fisher man / yellow, head first / yellow, brim stone / yellow, winter snow X, to gether / yellow, bad dreams, butter flies / yellow, can not / yellow X, bam boo X, grand father / yellow, up on / yellow, spring time / yellow, night mares / yellow, night fall / yellow

Page 7

Lead or Follow?

Write a word that can be placed in front of the bold-faced word to form a compound word. Then write a word that can follow the bold-faced word to form a second compound word.

Example: back **door** knob

on	**to**	night
swingle	**tree**	top
tow	**path**	way
clothes	**line**	up
after	**noon**	time
belly	**button**	hole
lunch	**room**	mate
every	**body**	guard
out	**side**	walk
doll	**house**	boat

Word Bank

up	tow	out	hole	way
swingle	after	on	every	time
clothes	mate	lunch	top	belly
night	boat	doll	walk	guard

Page 8

Brother Eagle, Sister Sky

Eagle has a long e sound. Sky has a long i sound. Cut out and glue the words below the picture with the matching vowel sound.

Brother Eagle: brief, leaf, stream, regal, knees, easy, dessert, delay

Sister Sky: dye, cry, private, lion, giant, fright, eye, style, drive, buy

Page 9

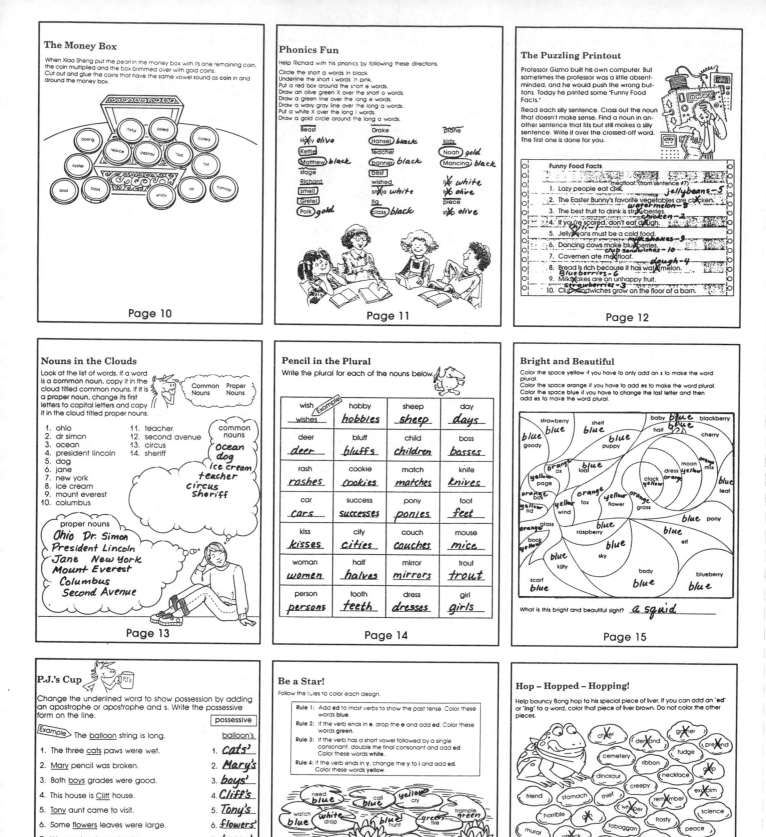

Page 10 — The Money Box

When Xiao Sheng put the pearl in the money box with its one remaining coin, the coin multiplied and the box brimmed over with gold coins.
Cut out and glue the coins that have the same vowel sound as **coin** in and around the money box.

Coins: royal, soiled, coiled, boiling, rejoice, destroy, toys, oyster, foil, spoil, boys, enjoy, oil, convoy

Page 11 — Phonics Fun

Help Richard with his phonics by following these directions.

Circle the short a words in black.
Underline the short i words in pink.
Put a red box around the short e words.
Draw an olive green X over the short o words.
Draw a green line over the long e words.
Draw a wavy gray line over the long a words.
Put a white X over the long i words.
Draw a gold circle around the long o words.

Beast Drake plane
Holly *olive* Hansel *black* kids
Kettle teacher Noah *gold*
Matthew *black* banner *black* Mancino *black*
stage best
Richard wished life *white*
smell smile *white* log *olive*
Gretel flag piece
Polk *gold* class *black* stick *olive*

Page 12 — The Puzzling Printout

Professor Gizmo built his own computer. But sometimes the professor was a little absent-minded, and he would push the wrong buttons. Today he printed some "Funny Food Facts."

Read each silly sentence. Cross out the noun that doesn't make sense. Find a noun in another sentence that fits but still makes a silly sentence. Write it over the crossed-off word. The first one is done for you.

Funny Food Facts

1. Lazy people eat chili. *meatloaf (from sentence #7)* *jellybeans–5*
2. The Easter Bunny's favorite vegetables are chicken. *watermelon–8*
3. The best fruit to drink is strawberries. *chicken–2*
4. If you're scared, don't eat dough.
5. Jellybeans must be a cold food. *milkshakes–9*
6. Dancing cows make blueberries. *club sandwiches–10*
7. Cavemen ate meatloaf. *dough–4*
8. Bread is rich because it has watermelon. *Blueberries–6*
9. Milkshakes are an unhappy fruit. *strawberries–3*
10. Club sandwiches grow on the floor of a barn.

Page 13 — Nouns in the Clouds

Look at the list of words. If a word is a common noun, copy it in the cloud titled common nouns. If it is a proper noun, change its first letters to capital letters and copy it in the cloud titled proper nouns.

1. ohio
2. dr simon
3. ocean
4. president lincoln
5. dog
6. jane
7. new york
8. ice cream
9. mount everest
10. columbus
11. teacher
12. second avenue
13. circus
14. sheriff

common nouns: Ocean, dog, Ice cream, teacher, circus, Sheriff

proper nouns: Ohio, Dr. Simon, President Lincoln, Jane, New York, Mount Everest, Columbus, Second Avenue

Page 14 — Pencil in the Plural

Write the plural for each of the nouns below.

wish (Example)	hobby	sheep	day
wishes	hobbies	sheep	days
deer	bluff	child	boss
deer	bluffs	children	bosses
rash	cookie	match	knife
rashes	cookies	matches	knives
car	success	pony	foot
cars	successes	ponies	feet
kiss	city	couch	mouse
kisses	cities	couches	mice
woman	half	mirror	trout
women	halves	mirrors	trout
person	tooth	dress	girl
persons	teeth	dresses	girls

Page 15 — Bright and Beautiful

Color the space yellow if you have to only add an s to make the word plural.
Color the space orange if you have to add es to make the word plural.
Color the space blue if you have to change the last letter and then add es to make the word plural.

What is this bright and beautiful sight? *a squid*

Page 16 — P.J.'s Cup

Change the underlined word to show possession by adding an apostrophe or apostrophe and s. Write the possessive form on the line.

Example: The balloon string is long. → balloon's

1. The three cats paws were wet. — cats'
2. Mary pencil was broken. — Mary's
3. Both boys grades were good. — boys'
4. This house is Cliff house. — Cliff's
5. Tony aunt came to visit. — Tony's
6. Some flowers leaves were large. — flowers'
7. We saw two bears tracks. — bears'
8. The children room was messy. — children's
9. My sister birthday is today. — sister's
10. The clowns acts made us laugh. — clowns'
11. Charlie Brown filled Snoopy dish. — Snoopy's
12. Mark joined the game with the boys. — boys
13. The baseball players uniforms are clean. — players'
14. The dog dish was empty. — dog's

Page 17 — Be a Star!

Follow the rules to color each design.

Rule 1: Add ed to most verbs to show the past tense. Color these words **blue**.
Rule 2: If the verb ends in e, drop the e and add ed. Color these words **green**.
Rule 3: If the verb has a short vowel followed by a single consonant, double the final consonant and add ed. Color these words **white**.
Rule 4: If the verb ends in y, change the y to i and add ed. Color these words **yellow**.

Page 18 — Hop – Hopped – Hopping!

Help bouncy Bong hop to his special piece of liver. If you can add an "ed" or "ing" to a word, color that piece of liver brown. Do not color the other pieces.

Bong is certainly a frog of action. All of the words he hopped on are ...
verbs or action words

IF8695 Super Book for Grade 3

Little Words Mean a Lot

A pronoun is a word that takes the place of a noun. Above each underlined word below, write a pronoun from the Word Box that could replace it.

Word Box

she   it   her   we   he   his   I   him   they   your

1. Uncle Nick shouted at Mus Mus as **he** ~~Uncle Nick~~ walked to the kitchen.
2. **She** Lucy ran to **her** Lucy's mother in tears.
3. **They** The Littles crowded up to the kitchen door.
4. Granny Little said, "**I** ~~Granny Little~~ wouldn't believe it if **I** ~~Granny Little~~ didn't see it with these old eyes."
5. Lucy said, "Mus Mus is a cute name." **It**
6. **They** Will and Tom have gone to get some leftovers.
7. **He** Uncle Nick kept on writing **his** Uncle Nick's life story.
8. **She** Mrs. Little whispered, "Don't bother **him** Uncle Nick."
9. Granny Little turned **her** Granny Little's back on Uncle Nick.
10. **We** Tom told Uncle Nick, "Lucy and Tom want to read **your** Uncle Nick's book."

Page 19

Words of Worth

The words below are adjectives. They describe nouns (persons, places or things). Write a noun to go with each adjective. Then draw its picture in each Indian shield. *Words and pictures will vary*

howling   shallow
pounding   smart
straight   frail

Page 20

Marvelous Modifiers

WET PAINT

Words that describe are called adjectives. Circle the adjectives in the sentences below.
1. Lucas stared at the **cool white** paint in the can.
2. The **green** grass was marked with bits of **white** paint.
3. The **naughty** twins needed a **warm soapy** bath.
4. The painters worked with **large** rollers.
5. Lucas thought it was a **great** joke.

For each noun below, write two descriptive adjectives. Then write a sentence using all three words. *Answers will vary.*

1. marshmallows
2. airplane
3. beach
4. summer
5. teacher

AND NOW... Some adjectives like good and bad, big and little, happy and sad are overused. Make a list of more descriptive adjectives that could be used in place of these words. Compare your list with the lists of other classmates.

Page 21

Where's That Monkey?

In the sentences below, write an adverb on the line to complete each sentence. The word in parentheses tells the kind of adverb to write. Do not use an adverb more than once. *Answers will vary.*

Example → The car is ___here___ . (where)
1. Our team played ___ . (when)
2. Brian writes ___ . (how)
3. The cows move ___ . (how)
4. Melissa will dance ___ . (when)
5. My dog went ___ . (where)
6. We ran ___ . (how)
7. The choir sang ___ . (how)
8. The cat purred ___ . (where)
9. Hilary spoke ___ . (how)
10. We'll go on our vacation ___ . (when)
11. The sign goes ___ . (where)
12. Mother brought the groceries ___ . (where)
13. David read the directions ___ . (how)
14. We'll be leaving ___ . (when)
15. We have three bedrooms ___ . (where)
16. Our family goes on a vacation ___ . (when)
17. Jim ran ___ down the street. (how)
18. They ___ laid the baby in the crib. (how)
19. The man went ___ with his paper. (where)

Page 22

Speech Puzzle

Unscramble each word to name the parts of speech. Write each word in the correct puzzle spaces.

adjective
verb
interjection
pronoun
adverb
article
noun
conjunction

1 ↓ A ___ is a word that names a person, place or thing.
   o n u n   Ex: man, city, chair
2 ↑ A ___ is a word used in place of a noun. Ex: he, she, it
   o o p u r n n
3 → An ___ is a word that describes a noun or pronoun.
   d e c v t e i i a   Ex: happy
4 ↓ A ___ is a word that shows action or that something is.
   r v b e   Ex: leap, be
5 → An ___ is a word that tells how, when or where about a
   v r a b e d   verb.   Ex: quickly
6 ↓ An ___ is a kind of adjective that says a noun will follow.
   a i e r c l t   Ex: the, a, an
7 ↓ ___ is an exclamation followed by an
   t r e t o j e i n c i n   exclamation point or comma. Ex: Ouch!
8 → A ___ is a word that connects other words.
   o u c n o n i c t n i   Ex: and, or

Page 23

Abracadabra

Write a complete sentence using each of the following subjects. *Sentences will vary.*

Example → The magician performs difficult tricks
1. The truck
2. Mr. and Mrs. Turner
3. The clowns
4. Fresh strawberries
5. Our team
6. A large crowd
7. Pancakes
8. All of the joggers
9. The skeleton

Write a complete sentence using each of the following predicates.

Example → The busy street ___ was noisy.
1. ___ was funny.
2. ___ will be ready.
3. ___ went too quickly.
4. ___ is on the corner.
5. ___ were ruined.
6. ___ still exists.
7. ___ was fun.
8. ___ were on my desk.
9. ___ turned to gold.

Page 24

Capital Review

A B C D E F

In the sentences below, circle the words that should begin with a capital letter.

Example → (Is) (I) (Love) (Lucy) still on television?
1. "(After) lunch," said (Sue), "(let's) go shopping."
2. (I) learned a lot from the book, (Inside) the (Personal) (Computer).
3. (My) class from (Hudson) (School) went to (Forest) (Park).
4. (Carlos) speaks (Spanish), (French) and (English).
5. (The) (Carter) family lives on (Terrace) (Drive).
6. "(The) new kid on the (Block)" is a great story.
7. (We) saw the movie "(Ghostbusters)" last (Saturday).
8. (Christopher) (Columbus) discovered (America) in 1492.
9. (I) was born (June) 12, 1965, in (Denver), (Colorado).
10. (Next) (Thursday), (Mr.) and (Mrs.) (Evans) have an anniversary.
11. (My) brother will attend (Harvard) (College) in (Boston).
12. (The) letter to (Montie) ended, "(Love) from (Aunt) (Rose)."
13. (In) (Hawaii), (Kamehameha) (Day) is celebrated each (June).
14. (Mrs.) (Hardy) said, "(Don't) be late for the party."
15. (Stone) (Brother) (Hardware) is on (Elm) (Street).

Page 25

Patriotic Punctuation

Decide which punctuation mark should follow each sentence. Add it. Then draw its design in the matching numbered area on the flag.

statement (.)
command (.)
question (?)
exclamation (!)

1. Phoebe was thirteen years old.
2. Finally, everyone would be free!
3. Trust no one.
4. Where was Mr. Hickey?
5. Should she go back to Queen's Head?
6. You must find out who it is.
7. Run, get my father.
8. Phoebe packed and headed for Mortier House.
9. Mr. Green never spoke to Phoebe at all.
10. Thomas was "T".
11. Should Phoebe tell Mr. Hickey the secret?
12. Go feed the seed to the chickens.
13. Did you air and turn Mrs. Washington's quilt?
14. Mr. Hickey has put poison in your dinner.
15. She placed the peas on the general's plate.
16. What jest is this?
17. My very favorite, June peas!

Punctuation may vary.

Page 26

Sealed with a Kiss

Read the letter Ut sent to Vietnam.

january 20 1993

dearest mother

i find america to be a beautiful country i even saw many flakes of snow fall on the ground

father my brother my sisters and i miss you greatly i look at your picture often but sometimes i am so lonely i will try to be your angel child

love
ut

Rewrite the letter correctly with capital letters and punctuation.

January 20, 1993

Dearest Mother,
I find America to be a beautiful country. I even saw many flakes of snow fall on the ground.
Father, my brother, my sisters, and I miss you greatly. I look at your picture often, but sometimes I am so lonely. I will try to be your angel child.
Love,
Ut

Page 27

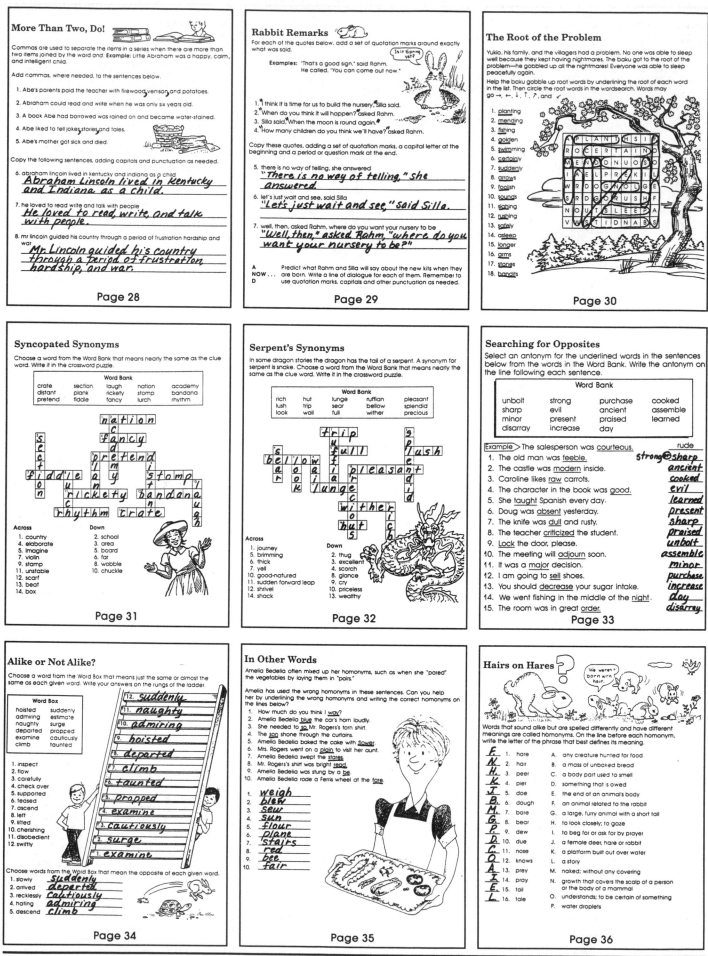

More Than Two, Do!

Commas are used to separate the items in a series when there are more than two items joined by the word *and*. **Example:** Little Abraham was a happy, calm, and intelligent child.

Add commas, where needed, to the sentences below.

1. Abe's parents paid the teacher with firewood, venison, and potatoes.
2. Abraham could read and write when he was only six years old.
3. A book Abe had borrowed was rained on and became water-stained.
4. Abe liked to tell jokes, stories, and tales.
5. Abe's mother got sick and died.

Copy the following sentences, adding capitals and punctuation as needed.

6. abraham lincoln lived in kentucky and indiana as a child.

Abraham Lincoln lived in Kentucky and Indiana as a child.

7. he loved to read write and talk with people.

He loved to read, write, and talk with people.

8. mr lincoln guided his country through a period of frustration hardship and war.

Mr. Lincoln guided his country through a period of frustration, hardship, and war.

Page 28

Rabbit Remarks

For each of the quotes below, add a set of quotation marks around exactly what was said.

Examples: "That's a good sign," said Rahm.
He called, "You can come out now."

1. I think it is time for us to build the nursery, Silla said.
2. When do you think it will happen? asked Rahm.
3. Silla said, When the moon is round again.
4. How many children do you think we'll have? asked Rahm.

Copy these quotes, adding a set of quotation marks, a capital letter at the beginning and a period or question mark at the end.

5. there is no way of telling, she answered

"There is no way of telling," she answered.

6. let's just wait and see, said Silla

"Let's just wait and see," said Silla.

7. well, then, asked Rahm, where do you want your nursery to be

"Well, then," asked Rahm, "where do you want your nursery to be?"

A NOW... D Predict what Rahm and Silla will say about the new kits when they are born. Write a line of dialogue for each of them. Remember to use quotation marks, capitals and other punctuation as needed.

Page 29

The Root of the Problem

Yukio, his family, and the villagers had a problem. No one was able to sleep well because they kept having nightmares. The baku got to the root of the problem—he gobbled up all the nightmares! Everyone was able to sleep peacefully again.

Help the baku gobble up root words by underlining the root of each word in the list. Then circle the root words in the wordsearch. Words may go →, ←, ↓, ↑, ↗, and ↘.

1. planting
2. mending
3. fishing
4. golden
5. swimming
6. certainly
7. suddenly
8. arrows
9. foolish
10. sounds
11. sighing
12. rushing
13. safely
14. asleep
15. longer
16. arms
17. stones
18. bandits

Page 30

Syncopated Synonyms

Choose a word from the Word Bank that means nearly the same as the clue word. Write it in the crossword puzzle.

Word Bank

crate	section	laugh	nation	academy
distant	plank	rickety	stomp	bandana
pretend	fiddle	fancy	lurch	rhythm

Across
1. country
4. elaborate
5. imagine
7. violin
9. stamp
11. unstable
12. scarf
13. beat
14. box

Down
2. school
3. area
5. board
6. far
8. wobble
10. chuckle

Page 31

Serpent's Synonyms

In some dragon stories the dragon has the tail of a serpent. A synonym for serpent is snake. Choose a word from the Word Bank that means nearly the same as the clue word. Write it in the crossword puzzle.

Word Bank

rich	hut	lunge	ruffian	pleasant
lush	trip	sear	bellow	splendid
look	wail	full	wither	precious

Across
1. journey
5. brimming
6. thick
7. yell
10. good-natured
11. sudden forward leap
12. shrivel
14. shack

Down
2. thug
3. excellent
4. scorch
8. glance
9. cry
10. priceless
13. wealthy

Page 32

Searching for Opposites

Select an antonym for the underlined words in the sentences below from the words in the Word Bank. Write the antonym on the line following each sentence.

Word Bank

unbolt	strong	purchase	cooked
sharp	evil	ancient	assemble
minor	present	praised	learned
disarray	increase	day	

Example The salesperson was courteous. — rude

1. The old man was feeble. — strong
2. The castle was modern inside. — ancient
3. Caroline likes raw carrots. — cooked
4. The character in the book was good. — evil
5. She taught Spanish every day. — learned
6. Doug was absent yesterday. — present
7. The knife was dull and rusty. — sharp
8. The teacher criticized the student. — praised
9. Lock the door, please. — unbolt
10. The meeting will adjourn soon. — assemble
11. It was a major decision. — minor
12. I am going to sell shoes. — purchase
13. You should decrease your sugar intake. — increase
14. We went fishing in the middle of the night. — day
15. The room was in great order. — disarray

Page 33

Alike or Not Alike?

Choose a word from the Word Box that means just the same or almost the same as each given word. Write your answers on the rungs of the ladder.

Word Box

hoisted	suddenly
admiring	estimate
naughty	surge
departed	propped
examine	cautiously
climb	taunted

1. inspect
2. flow
3. carefully
4. check over
5. supported
6. teased
7. ascend
8. left
9. lifted
10. cherishing
11. disobedient
12. swiftly

12. suddenly
11. naughty
10. admiring
9. hoisted
8. departed
7. climb
6. taunted
5. propped
4. examine
3. cautiously
2. surge
1. examine

Choose words from the Word Box that mean the opposite of each given word.

1. slowly — suddenly
2. arrived — departed
3. recklessly — cautiously
4. hating — admiring
5. descend — climb

Page 34

In Other Words

Amelia Bedelia often mixed up her homonyms, such as when she "pared" the vegetables by laying them in "pairs."

Amelia has used the wrong homonyms in these sentences. Can you help her by underlining the wrong homonyms and writing the correct homonyms on the lines below?

1. How much do you think I way?
2. Amelia Bedelia blue the car's horn loudly.
3. She needed to so Mr. Rogers's torn shirt.
4. The son shone through the curtains.
5. Amelia Bedelia baked the cake with flower.
6. Mrs. Rogers went on a plain to visit her aunt.
7. Amelia Bedelia swept the stares.
8. Mr. Rogers's shirt was bright read.
9. Amelia Bedelia was stung by a be.
10. Amelia Bedelia rode a Ferris wheel at the fare.

1. weigh
2. blew
3. sew
4. sun
5. flour
6. plane
7. stairs
8. red
9. bee
10. fair

Page 35

Hairs on Hares

We weren't born with hair.

Words that sound alike but are spelled differently and have different meanings are called homonyms. On the line before each homonym, write the letter of the phrase that best defines its meaning.

F 1. hare — A. any creature hunted for food
N 2. hair — B. a mass of unbaked bread
H 3. peer — C. a body part used to smell
K 4. pier — D. something that is owed
J 5. doe — E. the end of an animal's body
B 6. dough — F. an animal related to the rabbit
M 7. bare — G. a large, furry animal with a short tail
G 8. bear — H. to look closely; to gaze
P 9. dew — I. to beg for or ask for by prayer
D 10. due — J. a female deer, hare or rabbit
C 11. nose — K. a platform built out over water
O 12. knows — L. a story
A 13. prey — M. naked; without any covering
I 14. pray — N. growth that covers the scalp of a person or the body of a mammal
E 15. tail — O. understands; to be certain of something
L 16. tale — P. water droplets

Page 36

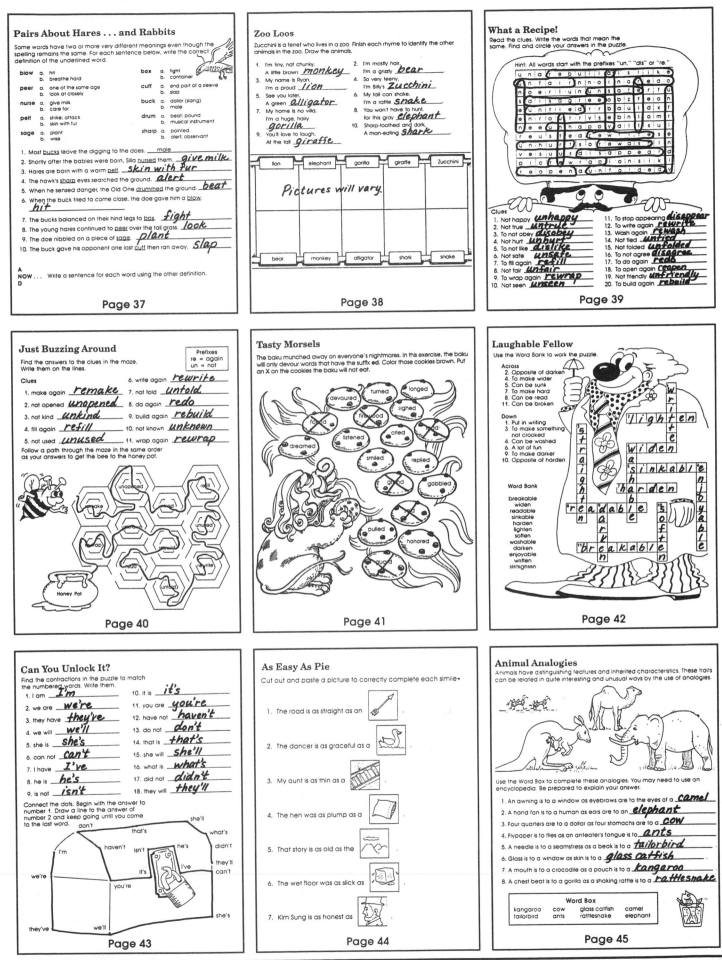

Pairs About Hares . . . and Rabbits

Some words have two or more very different meanings even though the spelling remains the same. For each sentence below, write the correct definition of the underlined word.

blow a. hit
b. breathe hard

peer a. one of the same age
b. look at closely

nurse a. give milk
b. care for

pelt a. strike; attack
b. skin with fur

sage a. plant
b. wise

box a. fight
b. container

cuff a. end part of a sleeve
b. slap

buck a. dollar (slang)
b. male

drum a. beat; pound
b. musical instrument

sharp a. pointed
b. alert; observant

1. Most bucks leave the digging to the does. _male_
2. Shortly after the babies were born, Silla nursed them. _give milk_
3. Hares are born with a warm pelt. _skin with fur_
4. The hawk's sharp eyes searched the ground. _alert_
5. When he sensed danger, the Old One drummed the ground. _beat_
6. When the buck tried to come close, the doe gave him a blow. _hit_
7. The bucks balanced on their hind legs to box. _fight_
8. The young hares continued to peer over the tall grass. _look_
9. The doe nibbled on a piece of sage. _plant_
10. The buck gave his opponent one last cuff then ran away. _slap_

A NOW... Write a sentence for each word using the other definition.

Page 37

Zoo Loos

Zucchini is a ferret who lives in a zoo. Finish each rhyme to identify the other animals in the zoo. Draw the animals.

1. I'm tiny, not chunky, A little brown _monkey_
2. I'm mostly hair, I'm a grizzly _bear_
3. My name is Ryan, I'm a proud _lion_
4. So very teeny, I'm Billy's _Zucchini_
5. See you later, A green _alligator_
6. My tail can shake, I'm a rattle _snake_
7. My home is no villa, I'm a huge, hairy _gorilla_
8. You won't have to hunt, for this gray _elephant_
9. You'll love to laugh, At the tall _giraffe_
10. Sharp-toothed and dark, A man-eating _shark_

lion	elephant	gorilla	giraffe	Zucchini

Pictures will vary.

bear	monkey	alligator	shark	snake

Page 38

What a Recipe!

Read the clues. Write the words that mean the same. Find and circle your answers in the puzzle.

Hint: All words start with the prefixes "un," "dis" or "re."

Clues

1. Not happy _unhappy_
2. Not true _untrue_
3. To not obey _disobey_
4. Not hurt _unhurt_
5. To not like _dislike_
6. Not safe _unsafe_
7. To fill again _refill_
8. Not fair _unfair_
9. To wrap again _rewrap_
10. Not seen _unseen_
11. To stop appearing _disappear_
12. To write again _rewrite_
13. Wash again _rewash_
14. Not tied _untied_
15. Not folded _unfolded_
16. To not agree _disagree_
17. To do again _redo_
18. To open again _reopen_
19. Not friendly _unfriendly_
20. To build again _rebuild_

Page 39

Just Buzzing Around

Find the answers to the clues in the maze. Write them on the lines.

Prefixes
re = again
un = not

Clues

1. make again _remake_
2. not opened _unopened_
3. not kind _unkind_
4. fill again _refill_
5. not used _unused_
6. write again _rewrite_
7. not told _untold_
8. do again _redo_
9. build again _rebuild_
10. not known _unknown_
11. wrap again _rewrap_

Follow a path through the maze in the same order as your answers to get the bee to the honey pot.

Honey Pot

Page 40

Tasty Morsels

The baku munched away on everyone's nightmares. In this exercise, the baku will only devour words that have the suffix ed. Color those cookies brown. Put an X on the cookies the baku will not eat.

turned, longed, devoured, sighed, folded, firewood, listened, cried, dreamed, smiled, replied, ground, gobbled, pulled, honored

Page 41

Laughable Fellow

Use the Word Bank to work the puzzle.

Across
2. Opposite of darken
4. To make wider
5. Can be sunk
7. To make hard
8. Can be read
11. Can be broken

Down
1. Put in writing
3. To make something not crooked
4. Can be washed
6. A lot of fun
9. To make darker
10. Opposite of harden

Word Bank
breakable
widen
readable
sinkable
harden
lighten
soften
washable
darken
enjoyable
written
straighten

lighten, written, straight, widen, washable, sinkable, enjoyable, harden, readable, soften, breakable

Page 42

Can You Unlock It?

Find the contractions in the puzzle to match the numbered words. Write them.

1. I am _I'm_
2. we are _we're_
3. they have _they've_
4. we will _we'll_
5. she is _she's_
6. can not _can't_
7. I have _I've_
8. he is _he's_
9. is not _isn't_
10. it is _it's_
11. you are _you're_
12. have not _haven't_
13. do not _don't_
14. that is _that's_
15. she will _she'll_
16. what is _what's_
17. did not _didn't_
18. they will _they'll_

Connect the dots. Begin with the word number 1. Draw a line to the answer of number 2 and keep going until you come to the last word.

she'll, that's, what's, haven't, isn't, he's, didn't, I'm, it's, they'll, can't, I've, we're, you're, they've, we'll, she's

Page 43

As Easy As Pie

Cut out and paste a picture to correctly complete each simile.

1. The road is as straight as an
2. The dancer is as graceful as a
3. My aunt is as thin as a
4. The hen was as plump as a
5. That story is as old as the
6. The wet floor was as slick as
7. Kim Sung is as honest as

Page 44

Animal Analogies

Animals have distinguishing features and inherited characteristics. These traits can be related in quite interesting and unusual ways by the use of analogies.

Use the Word Box to complete these analogies. You may need to use an encyclopedia. Be prepared to explain your answer.

1. An awning is to a window as eyebrows are to the eyes of a _camel_
2. A hand fan is to a human as ears are to an _elephant_
3. Four quarters are to a dollar as four stomachs are to a _cow_
4. Flypaper is to flies as an anteater's tongue is to _ants_
5. A needle is to a seamstress as a beak is to a _tailorbird_
6. Glass is to a window as skin is to a _glass catfish_
7. A mouth is to a crocodile as a pouch is to a _kangaroo_
8. A chest beat is to a gorilla as a shaking rattle is to a _rattlesnake_

Word Box
kangaroo, cow, glass catfish, camel, tailorbird, ants, rattlesnake, elephant

Page 45

What's the Connection?

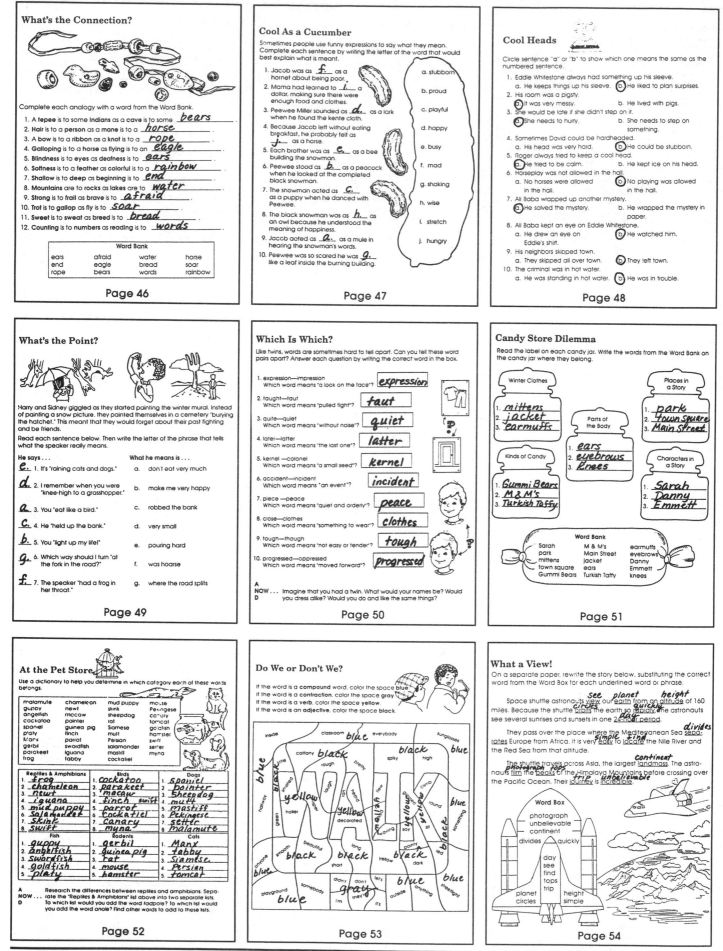

Complete each analogy with a word from the Word Bank.

1. A **tepee** is to some **Indians** as a **cave** is to some ___bears___
2. **Hair** is to a **person** as a **mane** is to a ___horse___
3. A **bow** is to a **ribbon** as a **knot** is to a ___rope___
4. **Galloping** is to a **horse** as **flying** is to an ___eagle___
5. **Blindness** is to **eyes** as **deafness** is to ___ears___
6. **Softness** is to a **feather** as **colorful** is to a ___rainbow___
7. **Shallow** is to **deep** as **beginning** is to ___end___
8. **Mountains** are to **rocks** as **lakes** are to ___water___
9. **Strong** is to **frail** as **brave** is to ___afraid___
10. **Trot** is to **gallop** as **fly** is to ___soar___
11. **Sweet** is to **sweat** as **breed** is to ___bread___
12. **Counting** is to **numbers** as **reading** is to ___words___

Word Bank			
ears	afraid	water	horse
end	eagle	bread	soar
rope	bears	words	rainbow

Page 46

Cool As a Cucumber

Sometimes people use funny expressions to say what they mean. Complete each sentence by writing the letter of the word that would best explain what is meant.

1. Jacob was as __f.__ as a hornet about being poor.
2. Mama had learned to __i.__ a dollar, making sure there were enough food and clothes.
3. Peewee Miller sounded as __d.__ as a lark when he found the kente cloth.
4. Because Jacob left without eating breakfast, he probably felt as __j.__ as a horse.
5. Each brother was as __e.__ as a bee building the snowman.
6. Peewee stood as __b.__ as a peacock when he looked at the completed black snowman.
7. The snowman acted as __c.__ as a puppy when he danced with Peewee.
8. The black snowman was as __h.__ as an owl because he understood the meaning of happiness.
9. Jacob acted as __a.__ as a mule in hearing the snowman's words.
10. Peewee was so scared he was __g.__ like a leaf inside the burning building.

a. stubborn
b. proud
c. playful
d. happy
e. busy
f. mad
g. shaking
h. wise
i. stretch
j. hungry

Page 47

Cool Heads

Circle sentence "a" or "b" to show which one means the same as the numbered sentence.

1. Eddie Whitestone always had something up his sleeve.
   a. He keeps things up his sleeve.   **(b.)** He liked to plan surprises.
2. His room was a pigsty.
   (a.) It was very messy.   b. He lived with pigs.
3. She would be late if she didn't step on it.
   (a.) She needs to hurry.   b. She needs to step on something.
4. Sometimes David could be hardheaded.
   a. His head was very hard.   **(b.)** He could be stubborn.
5. Roger always tried to keep a cool head.
   (a.) He tried to be calm.   b. He kept ice on his head.
6. Horseplay was not allowed in the hall.
   a. No horses were allowed in the hall.   **(b.)** No playing was allowed in the hall.
7. Ali Baba wrapped up another mystery.
   (a.) He solved the mystery.   b. He wrapped the mystery in paper.
8. Ali Baba kept an eye on Eddie Whitestone.
   a. He drew an eye on Eddie's shirt.   **(b.)** He watched him.
9. His neighbors skipped town.
   a. They skipped all over town.   **(b.)** They left town.
10. The criminal was in hot water.
   a. He was standing in hot water.   **(b.)** He was in trouble.

Page 48

What's the Point?

Harry and Sidney giggled as they started painting the winter mural. Instead of painting a snow picture, they painted themselves in a cemetery "burying the hatchet." This meant that they would forget about their past fighting and be friends.

Read each sentence below. Then write the letter of the phrase that tells what the speaker really means.

He says... **What he means is...**

__e.__ 1. It's "raining cats and dogs."   a. don't eat very much
__d.__ 2. I remember when you were "knee-high to a grasshopper."   b. make me very happy
__a.__ 3. You "eat like a bird."   c. robbed the bank
__c.__ 4. He "held up the bank."   d. very small
__b.__ 5. You "light up my life!"   e. pouring hard
__g.__ 6. Which way should I turn "at the fork in the road?"   f. was hoarse
__f.__ 7. The speaker "had a frog in her throat."   g. where the road splits

Page 49

Which Is Which?

Like twins, words are sometimes hard to tell apart. Can you tell these word pairs apart? Answer each question by writing the correct word in the box.

1. expression—impression
   Which word means "a look on the face"?   **expression**
2. taught—taut
   Which word means "pulled tight"?   **taut**
3. quite—quiet
   Which word means "without noise"?   **quiet**
4. later—latter
   Which word means "the last one"?   **latter**
5. kernel—colonel
   Which word means "a small seed"?   **kernel**
6. accident—incident
   Which word means "an event"?   **incident**
7. piece—peace
   Which word means "quiet and orderly"?   **peace**
8. close—clothes
   Which word means "something to wear"?   **clothes**
9. tough—though
   Which word means "not easy or tender"?   **tough**
10. progressed—oppressed
   Which word means "moved forward"?   **progressed**

A
NOW... Imagine that you had a twin. What would your names be? Would
D   you dress alike? Would you do and like the same things?

Page 50

Candy Store Dilemma

Read the label on each candy jar. Write the words from the Word Bank on the candy jar where they belong.

Winter Clothes
1. mittens
2. jacket
3. earmuffs

Places in a Story
1. park
2. town square
3. Main Street

Parts of the Body
ears
eyebrows
knees

Kinds of Candy
1. Gummi Bears
2. M&M's
3. Turkish Taffy

Characters in a Story
1. Sarah
2. Danny
3. Emmett

Word Bank		
Sarah	M & M's	earmuffs
park	Main Street	eyebrows
mittens	jacket	Danny
town square	ears	Emmett
Gummi Bears	Turkish Taffy	knees

Page 51

At the Pet Store

Use a dictionary to help you determine in which category each of these words belongs.

malamute	chameleon	mud puppy	mouse
guppy	newt	skink	Pekingese
angelfish	macaw	sheepdog	canary
cockatoo	pointer	rat	tomcat
spaniel	guinea pig	Siamese	goldfish
platy	finch	mutt	hamster
Manx	parrot	Persian	swift
gerbil	swordfish	salamander	setter
parakeet	iguana	mastiff	myna
frog	tabby	cockatiel	

Reptiles & Amphibians	Birds	Dogs
1. frog	1. cockatoo	1. spaniel
2. chameleon	2. parakeet	2. pointer
3. newt	3. macaw	3. sheepdog
4. iguana	4. finch swift	4. mutt
5. mud puppy	5. parrot	5. mastiff
6. salamander	6. cockatiel	6. Pekingese
7. skink	7. canary	7. setter
8. swift	8. myna	8. malamute

Fish	Rodents	Cats
1. guppy	1. gerbil	1. Manx
2. angelfish	2. guinea pig	2. tabby
3. swordfish	3. rat	3. Siamese
4. goldfish	4. mouse	4. Persian
5. platy	5. hamster	5. tomcat

A
NOW... Research the differences between reptiles and amphibians. Separate the "Reptiles & Amphibians" list above into two separate lists.
D   To which list would you add the word tadpole? To which list would you add the word anole? Find other words to add to these lists.

Page 52

Do We or Don't We?

If the word is a **compound word**, color the space blue.
If the word is a **contraction**, color the space gray.
If the word is a **verb**, color the space yellow.
If the word is an **adjective**, color the space black.

Page 53

What a View!

On a separate paper, rewrite the story below, substituting the correct word from the Word Box for each underlined word or phrase.

Space shuttle astronauts _view_ our _earth_ from an _altitude_ of 160 miles. Because the shuttle _orbits_ the earth so _rapidly_ the astronauts see several sunrises and sunsets in one _24-hour period_.

They pass over the place where the Mediterranean Sea _separates_ Europe from Africa. It is very _easy_ to _locate_ the Nile River and the Red Sea from that altitude.

The shuttle travels across Asia, the largest _landmass_. The astronauts _film_ the _peaks_ of the Himalaya Mountains before crossing over the Pacific Ocean. Their _journey_ is _incredible_.

(handwritten substitutions: see, planet, height, circles, quickly, day, divides, simple, find, continent, photograph, trip, unbelievable)

Word Box	
photograph	
unbelievable	
continent	
divides	quickly
day	
see	
find	
tops	
planet	
circles	
trip	
height	simple

Page 54

IF8695 Super Book for Grade 3

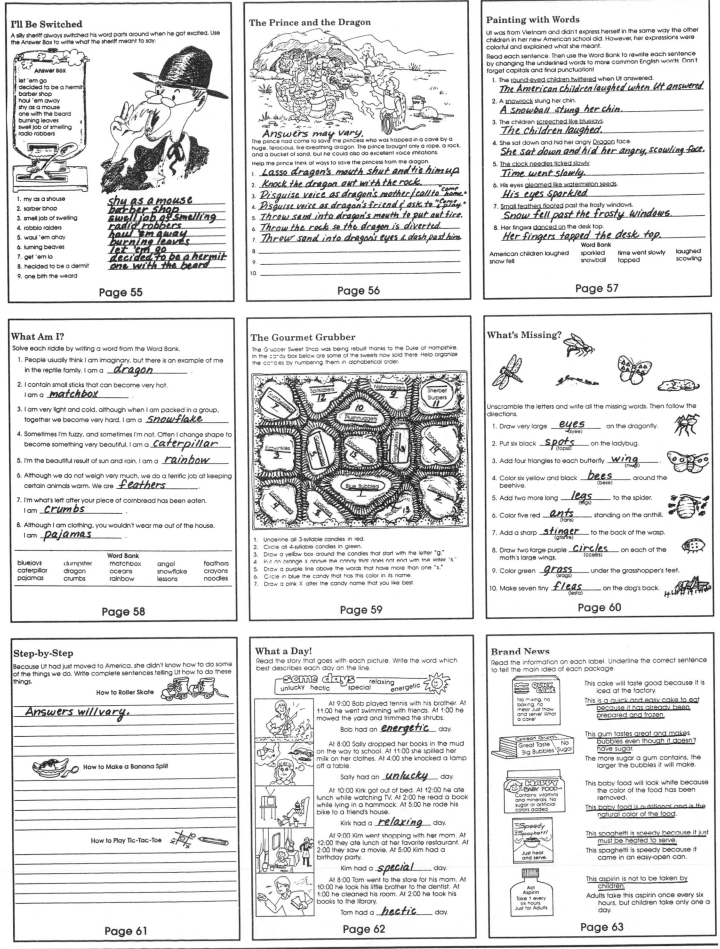

I'll Be Switched

A silly sheriff always switched his word parts around when he got excited. Use the Answer Box to write what the sheriff meant to say.

Answer Box
let 'em go
decided to be a hermit
barber shop
haul 'em away
shy as a mouse
one with the beard
burning leaves
swell job of smelling
radio robbers

1. my as a shouse — *shy as a mouse*
2. sarber bhop — *barber shop*
3. smell job of swelling — *swell job of smelling*
4. robblo raiders — *radio robbers*
5. waul 'em ahay — *haul 'em away*
6. lurning beaves — *burning leaves*
7. get 'em lo — *let 'em go*
8. hecided to be a dermit — *decided to be a hermit*
9. one bith the weard — *one with the beard*

Page 55

The Prince and the Dragon

Answers may vary

The prince had come to save the princess who was trapped in a cave by a huge, ferocious, fire-breathing dragon. The prince brought only a rope, a rock, and a bucket of sand, but he could also do excellent voice imitations.

Help the prince think of ways to save the princess from the dragon.

1. *Lasso dragon's mouth shut and tie him up*
2. *Knock the dragon out with the rock.*
3. *Disguise voice as dragon's mother & call to "come home."*
4. *Disguise voice as dragon's friend & ask to "come & play."*
5. *Throw sand into dragon's mouth to put out fire.*
6. *Throw the rock so the dragon is diverted.*
7. *Throw sand into dragon's eyes & dash past him.*
8. _____
9. _____
10. _____

Page 56

Painting with Words

Ut was from Vietnam and didn't express herself in the same way the other children in her new American school did. However, her expressions were colorful and explained what she meant.

Read each sentence. Then use the Word Bank to rewrite each sentence by changing the underlined words to more common English words. Don't forget capitals and final punctuation!

1. The round-eyed children twittered when Ut answered.
The American children laughed when Ut answered.

2. A snowrock stung her chin.
A snowball stung her chin.

3. The children screeched like bluejays.
The children laughed.

4. She sat down and hid her angry Dragon face.
She sat down and hid her angry, scowling face.

5. The clock needles ticked slowly.
Time went slowly.

6. His eyes gleamed like watermelon seeds.
His eyes sparkled.

7. Small feathers floated past the frosty windows.
Snow fell past the frosty windows.

8. Her fingers danced on the desk top.
Her fingers tapped the desk top.

Word Bank

American children laughed — sparkled — time went slowly — laughed
snow fell — snowball — tapped — scowling

Page 57

What Am I?

Solve each riddle by writing a word from the Word Bank.

1. People usually think I am imaginary, but there is an example of me in the reptile family. I am a *dragon*
2. I contain small sticks that can become very hot. I am a *matchbox*
3. I am very light and cold, although when I am packed in a group, together we become very hard. I am a *snowflake*
4. Sometimes I'm fuzzy, and sometimes I'm not. Often I change shape to become something very beautiful. I am a *caterpillar*
5. I'm the beautiful result of sun and rain. I am a *rainbow*
6. Although we do not weigh very much, we do a terrific job at keeping certain animals warm. We are *feathers*
7. I'm what's left after your piece of cornbread has been eaten. I am *crumbs*
8. Although I am clothing, you wouldn't wear me out of the house. I am *pajamas*

Word Bank

bluejays — dumpster — matchbox — angel — feathers
caterpillar — dragon — oceans — snowflake — crayons
pajamas — crumbs — rainbow — lessons — noodles

Page 58

The Gourmet Grubber

The Grubber Sweet Shop was being rebuilt thanks to the Duke of Hampshire. In the candy box below are some of the sweets now sold there. Help organize the candies by numbering them in alphabetical order.

1. Underline all 3-syllable candies in red.
2. Circle all 4-syllable candies in green.
3. Draw a yellow box around the candies that start with the letter "g."
4. Put an orange X above the candy that does not end with the letter "s."
5. Draw a purple line above the words that have more than one "s."
6. Circle in blue the candy that has this color in its name.
7. Draw a pink X after the candy name that you like best.

Page 59

What's Missing?

Unscramble the letters and write all the missing words. Then follow the directions.

1. Draw very large *eyes* (syee) on the dragonfly.
2. Put six black *spots* (topss) on the ladybug.
3. Add four triangles to each butterfly *wing* (nwgi).
4. Color six yellow and black *bees* (bese) around the beehive.
5. Add two more long *legs* (elgs) to the spider.
6. Color five red *ants* (tans) standing on the anthill.
7. Add a sharp *stinger* (gtsrine) to the back of the wasp.
8. Draw two large purple *circles* (ccelirs) on each of the moth's large wings.
9. Color green *grass* (srags) under the grasshopper's feet.
10. Make seven tiny *fleas* (lesfa) on the dog's back.

Page 60

Step-by-Step

Because Ut had just moved to America, she didn't know how to do some of the things we do. Write complete sentences telling Ut how to do these things.

How to Roller Skate

Answers will vary.

How to Make a Banana Split

How to Play Tic-Tac-Toe

Page 61

What a Day!

Read the story that goes with each picture. Write the word which best describes each day on the line.

Some days unlucky hectic special relaxing energetic

At 9:00 Bob played tennis with his brother. At 11:00 he went swimming with friends. At 1:00 he mowed the yard and trimmed the shrubs.
Bob had an *energetic* day.

At 8:00 Sally dropped her books in the mud on the way to school. At 11:00 she spilled her milk on her clothes. At 4:00 she knocked a lamp off a table.
Sally had an *unlucky* day.

At 10:00 Kirk got out of bed. At 12:00 he ate lunch while watching TV. At 2:00 he read a book while lying in a hammock. At 5:00 he rode his bike to a friend's house.
Kirk had a *relaxing* day.

At 9:00 Kim went shopping with her mom. At 12:00 they ate lunch at her favorite restaurant. At 2:00 they saw a movie. At 5:00 Kim had a birthday party.
Kim had a *special* day.

At 8:00 Tom went to the store for his mom. At 10:00 he took his little brother to the dentist. At 1:00 he cleaned his room. At 2:00 he took his books to the library.
Tom had a *hectic* day.

Page 62

Brand News

Read the information on each label. Underline the correct sentence to tell the main idea of each package.

This cake will taste good because it is iced at the factory.
This is a quick and easy cake to eat because it has already been prepared and frozen.

This gum tastes great and makes bubbles even though it doesn't have sugar.
The more sugar a gum contains, the larger the bubbles it will make.

This baby food will look white because the color of the food has been removed.
This baby food is nutritional and is the natural color of the food.

This spaghetti is speedy because it just must be heated to serve.
This spaghetti is speedy because it came in an easy-open can.

This aspirin is not to be taken by children.
Adults take this aspirin once every six hours, but children take only one a day.

Page 63

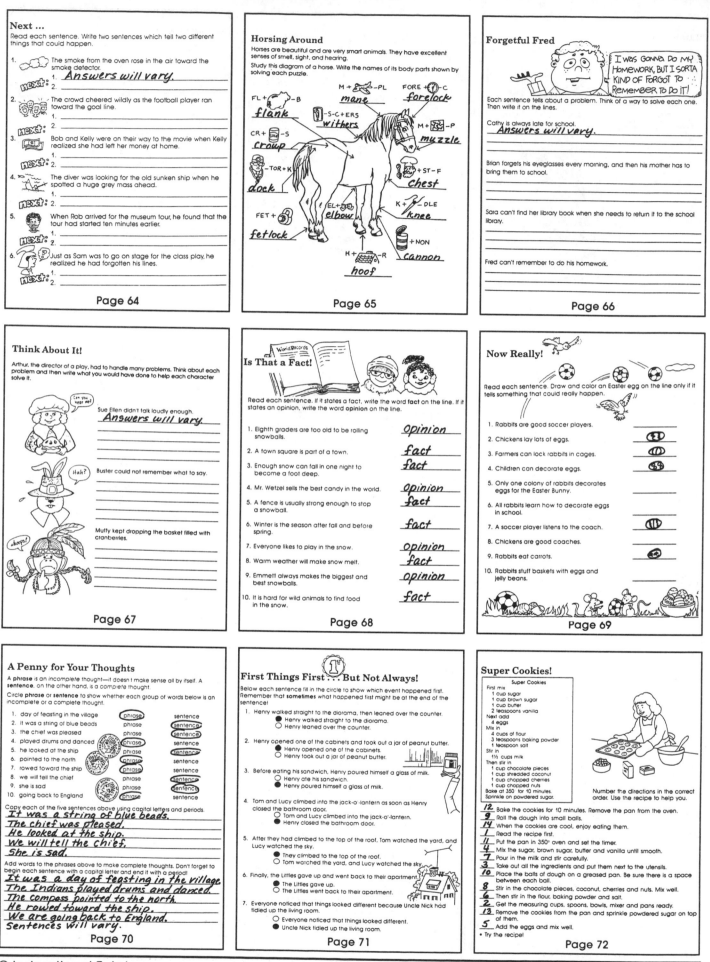

Next ...

Read each sentence. Write two sentences which tell two different things that could happen.

1. The smoke from the oven rose in the air toward the smoke detector.
   1. *Answers will vary.*

2. The crowd cheered wildly as the football player ran toward the goal line.
   1.

3. Bob and Kelly were on their way to the movie when Kelly realized she had left her money at home.
   2.

4. The diver was looking for the old sunken ship when he spotted a huge grey mass ahead.
   2.

5. When Rob arrived for the museum tour, he found that the tour had started ten minutes earlier.
   2.

6. Just as Sam was to go on stage for the class play, he realized he had forgotten his lines.
   1.
   2.

Page 64

Horsing Around

Horses are beautiful and are very smart animals. They have excellent senses of smell, sight, and hearing.

Study this diagram of a horse. Write the names of its body parts shown by solving each puzzle.

- FL + [picture] – B *flank*
- [picture] – S – C + ERS *withers*
- CR + [picture] – S *croup*
- [picture] – TOR + K *dock*
- FET + [picture] *fetlock*
- EL + [picture] *elbow*
- H + [picture] – R *hoof*
- M + [picture] – PL *mane*
- FORE + [picture] – C *forelock*
- M + [picture] – P *muzzle*
- [picture] + ST – F *chest*
- K + [picture] – DLE *knee*
- [picture] + NON *cannon*

Page 65

Forgetful Fred

"I WAS GONNA DO MY HOMEWORK, BUT I SORTA KIND OF FORGOT TO REMEMBER TO DO IT!"

Each sentence tells about a problem. Think of a way to solve each one. Then write it on the lines.

Cathy is always late for school.
Answers will vary.

Brian forgets his eyeglasses every morning, and then his mother has to bring them to school.

Sara can't find her library book when she needs to return it to the school library.

Fred can't remember to do his homework.

Page 66

Think About It!

Arthur, the director of a play, had to handle many problems. Think about each problem and then write what you would have done to help each character solve it.

"Can you hear me!"

Sue Ellen didn't talk loudly enough.
Answers will vary.

"Huh?"

Buster could not remember what to say.

"whoops!"

Muffy kept dropping the basket filled with cranberries.

Page 67

Is That a Fact!

Read each sentence. If it states a fact, write the word **fact** on the line. If it states an opinion, write the word **opinion** on the line.

1. Eighth graders are too old to be rolling snowballs. *opinion*
2. A town square is part of a town. *fact*
3. Enough snow can fall in one night to become a foot deep. *fact*
4. Mr. Wetzel sells the best candy in the world. *opinion*
5. A fence is usually strong enough to stop a snowball. *fact*
6. Winter is the season after fall and before spring. *fact*
7. Everyone likes to play in the snow. *opinion*
8. Warm weather will make snow melt. *fact*
9. Emmett always makes the biggest and best snowballs. *opinion*
10. It is hard for wild animals to find food in the snow. *fact*

Page 68

Now Really!

Read each sentence. Draw and color an Easter egg on the line only if it tells something that could really happen.

1. Rabbits are good soccer players.
2. Chickens lay lots of eggs. [egg]
3. Farmers can lock rabbits in cages. [egg]
4. Children can decorate eggs. [egg]
5. Only one colony of rabbits decorates eggs for the Easter Bunny.
6. All rabbits learn how to decorate eggs in school.
7. A soccer player listens to the coach. [egg]
8. Chickens are good coaches.
9. Rabbits eat carrots. [egg]
10. Rabbits stuff baskets with eggs and jelly beans.

Page 69

A Penny for Your Thoughts

A **phrase** is an incomplete thought—it doesn't make sense all by itself. A **sentence**, on the other hand, is a complete thought.

Circle **phrase** or **sentence** to show whether each group of words below is an incomplete or a complete thought.

1. day of feasting in the village (**phrase**) sentence
2. it was a string of blue beads phrase (**sentence**)
3. the chief was pleased phrase (**sentence**)
4. played drums and danced (**phrase**) sentence
5. he looked at the ship phrase (**sentence**)
6. pointed to the north (**phrase**) sentence
7. rowed toward the ship (**phrase**) sentence
8. we will tell the chief phrase (**sentence**)
9. she is sad phrase (**sentence**)
10. going back to England (**phrase**) sentence

Copy each of the five sentences above using capital letters and periods.
It was a string of blue beads.
The chief was pleased.
He looked at the ship.
We will tell the chief.
She is sad.

Add words to the phrases above to make complete thoughts. Don't forget to begin each sentence with a capital letter and end it with a period!
It was a day of feasting in the village.
The Indians played drums and danced.
The compass pointed to the north.
He rowed toward the ship.
We are going back to England.
Sentences will vary.

Page 70

First Things First . . . But Not Always!

Below each sentence fill in the circle to show which event happened first. Remember that **sometimes** what happened first might be at the end of the sentence!

1. Henry walked straight to the diorama, then leaned over the counter.
   ● Henry walked straight to the diorama.
   ○ Henry leaned over the counter.

2. Henry opened one of the cabinets and took out a jar of peanut butter.
   ● Henry opened one of the cabinets.
   ○ Henry took out a jar of peanut butter.

3. Before eating his sandwich, Henry poured himself a glass of milk.
   ○ Henry ate his sandwich.
   ● Henry poured himself a glass of milk.

4. Tom and Lucy climbed into the jack-o'-lantern as soon as Henry closed the bathroom door.
   ○ Tom and Lucy climbed into the jack-o'-lantern.
   ● Henry closed the bathroom door.

5. After they had climbed to the top of the roof, Tom watched the yard, and Lucy watched the sky.
   ● They climbed to the top of the roof.
   ○ Tom watched the yard, and Lucy watched the sky.

6. Finally, the Littles gave up and went back to their apartment.
   ● The Littles gave up.
   ○ The Littles went back to their apartment.

7. Everyone noticed that things looked different because Uncle Nick had tidied up the living room.
   ○ Everyone noticed that things looked different.
   ● Uncle Nick tidied up the living room.

Page 71

Super Cookies!

Super Cookies
First mix
  1 cup sugar
  1 cup brown sugar
  1 cup butter
  2 teaspoons vanilla
Next add
  4 eggs
Mix in
  4 cups of flour
  3 teaspoons baking powder
  1 teaspoon salt
Stir in
  1½ cups milk
Then stir in
  1 cup chocolate pieces
  1 cup shredded coconut
  1 cup chopped cherries
  1 cup chopped nuts
Bake at 350° for 10 minutes.
Sprinkle on powdered sugar.

Number the directions in the correct order. Use the recipe to help you.

- 12 Bake the cookies for 10 minutes. Remove the pan from the oven.
- 9 Roll the dough into small balls.
- 14 When the cookies are cool, enjoy eating them.
- 1 Read the recipe first.
- 11 Put the pan in 350° oven and set the timer.
- 4 Mix the sugar, brown sugar, butter and vanilla until smooth.
- 7 Pour in the milk and stir carefully.
- 3 Take out all the ingredients and put them next to the utensils.
- 10 Place the balls of dough on a greased pan. Be sure there is a space between each ball.
- 8 Stir in the chocolate pieces, coconut, cherries and nuts. Mix well.
- 6 Then stir in the flour, baking powder and salt.
- 2 Get the measuring cups, spoons, bowls, mixer and pans ready.
- 13 Remove the cookies from the pan and sprinkle powdered sugar on top of them.
- 5 Add the eggs and mix well.
- Try the recipe!

Page 72

Waterworks

Use the diagram to help you number the sentences in the correct order to tell how water is purified.

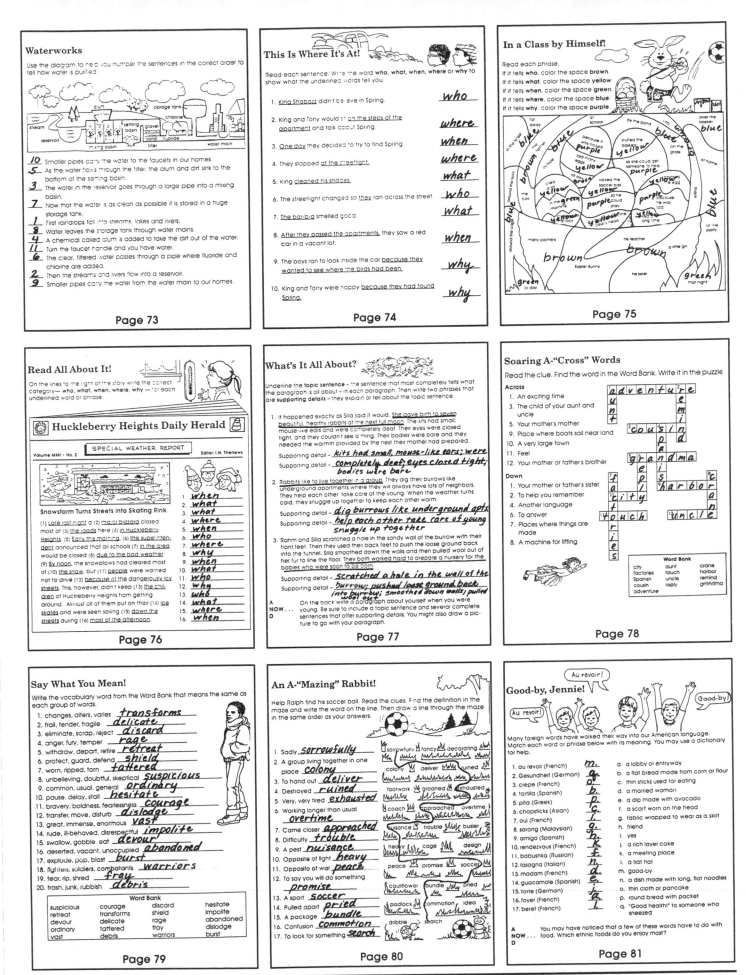

10 Smaller pipes carry the water to the faucets in our homes.

5 As the water flows through the filter, the alum and dirt sink to the bottom of the settling basin.

3 The water in the reservoir goes through a large pipe into a mixing basin.

7 Now that the water is as clean as possible it is stored in a huge storage tank.

1 First raindrops fall into streams, lakes and rivers.

8 Water leaves the storage tank through water mains.

4 A chemical called alum is added to take the dirt out of the water.

11 Turn the faucet handle and you have water.

6 The clear, filtered water passes through a pipe where fluoride and chlorine are added.

2 Then the streams and rivers flow into a reservoir.

9 Smaller pipes carry the water from the water main to our homes.

Page 73

This Is Where It's At!

Read each sentence. Write the word who, what, when, where or why to show what the underlined words tell you.

1. King Shapazz didn't believe in Spring. — *who*
2. King and Tony would sit on the steps of the apartment and talk about Spring. — *where*
3. One day they decided to try to find Spring. — *when*
4. They stopped at the streetlight. — *where*
5. King cleaned his shades. — *what*
6. The streetlight changed so they ran across the street. — *who*
7. The bar-b-q smelled good. — *what*
8. After they passed the apartments, they saw a red car in a vacant lot. — *when*
9. The boys ran to look inside the car because they wanted to see where the birds had been. — *why*
10. King and Tony were happy because they had found Spring. — *why*

Page 74

In a Class by Himself!

Read each phrase.
If it tells who, color the space brown.
If it tells what, color the space yellow.
If it tells when, color the space green.
If it tells where, color the space blue.
If it tells why, color the space purple.

Page 75

Read All About It!

On the lines to the right of the story write the correct category— who, what, when, where, why — for each underlined word or phrase.

Huckleberry Heights Daily Herald

Volume MMI • No. 2   Editor: I.N. Thenews

SPECIAL WEATHER REPORT

Snowstorm Turns Streets into Skating Rink

(1) Late last night a (2) major blizzard closed most of (3) the roads here (4) in Huckleberry Heights. (5) Early this morning, the superintendent announced that all schools (7) in the area would be closed (8) due to the bad weather. (9) By noon, the snowplows had cleared most of (10) the snow, but (11) people were warned not to drive (12) because of the dangerously icy streets. This, however, didn't keep (13) the children of Huckleberry Heights from getting around. Almost all of them had put on their (14) ice skates and were seen sailing (15) down the streets during (16) most of the afternoon.

1. *when*
2. *what*
3. *where*
4. *where*
5. *when*
6. *who*
7. *where*
8. *why*
9. *when*
10. *what*
11. *who*
12. *why*
13. *who*
14. *what*
15. *where*
16. *when*

Page 76

What's It All About?

Underline the topic sentence – the sentence that most completely tells what the paragraph is all about – in each paragraph. Then write two phrases that are supporting details – they explain or tell about the topic sentence.

1. It happened exactly as Silla said it would. She gave birth to seven beautiful, healthy rabbits at the next full moon. The kits had small, mouse-like ears and were completely deaf. Their eyes were closed tight, and they couldn't see a thing. Their bodies were bare and they needed the warmth provided by the nest their mother had prepared.

Supporting detail – *kits had small, mouse-like ears; were*
Supporting detail – *completely deaf; eyes closed tight; bodies were bare*

2. Rabbits like to live together in a group. They dig their burrows like underground apartments where they will always have lots of neighbors. They help each other take care of the young. When the weather turns cold, they snuggle up together to keep each other warm.

Supporting detail – *dig burrows like underground apts.*
Supporting detail – *help each other take care of young; snuggle up together*

3. Rahm and Silla scratched a hole in the sandy wall of the burrow with their front feet. Then they used their back feet to push the loose ground back into the tunnel. Silla smoothed down the walls and then pulled wool out of her fur to line the floor. They both worked hard to prepare a nursery for the babies who were soon to be born.

Supporting detail – *scratched a hole in the wall of the burrow; pushed loose ground back*
Supporting detail – *into burrow; smoothed down walls; pulled*

A NOW... D   On the back write a paragraph about yourself when you were young. Be sure to include a topic sentence and several complete sentences that offer supporting details. You might also draw a picture to go with your paragraph.

Page 77

Soaring A-"Cross" Words

Read the clue. Find the word in the Word Bank. Write it in the puzzle.

Across
1. An exciting time
3. The child of your aunt and uncle
5. Your mother's mother
9. Place where boats sail near land
10. A very large town
11. Feel
12. Your mother or father's brother

Down
1. Your mother or father's sister
2. To help you remember
4. Another language
6. To answer
7. Places where things are made
8. A machine for lifting

Across answers: adventure, cousin, grandma, harbor, city, touch, uncle
Down answers: aunt, remind, Spanish, reply, factories, crane

Word Bank
city	aunt	crane
factories	touch	harbor
Spanish	uncle	remind
cousin	reply	grandma
adventure		

Page 78

Say What You Mean!

Write the vocabulary word from the Word Bank that means the same as each group of words.

1. changes, alters, varies — *transforms*
2. frail, tender, fragile — *delicate*
3. eliminate, scrap, reject — *discard*
4. anger, fury, temper — *rage*
5. withdraw, depart, retire — *retreat*
6. protect, guard, defend — *shield*
7. worn, ripped, torn — *tattered*
8. unbelieving, doubtful, skeptical — *suspicious*
9. common, usual, general — *ordinary*
10. pause, delay, stall — *hesitate*
11. bravery, boldness, fearlessness — *courage*
12. transfer, move, disturb — *dislodge*
13. great, immense, enormous — *vast*
14. rude, ill-behaved, disrespectful — *impolite*
15. swallow, gobble, eat — *devour*
16. deserted, vacant, unoccupied — *abandoned*
17. explode, pop, blast — *burst*
18. fighters, soldiers, combatants — *warriors*
19. tear, rip, shred — *fray*
20. trash, junk, rubbish — *debris*

Word Bank
suspicious	courage	discard	hesitate
retreat	transforms	shield	impolite
devour	delicate	rage	abandoned
ordinary	tattered	fray	dislodge
vast	debris	warriors	burst

Page 79

An A-"Mazing" Rabbit!

Help Ralph find his soccer ball. Read the clues. Find the definition in the maze and write the word on the line. Then draw a line through the maze in the same order as your answers.

1. Sadly — *sorrowfully*
2. A group living together in one place — *colony*
3. To hand out — *deliver*
4. Destroyed — *ruined*
5. Very, very tired — *exhausted*
6. Working longer than usual — *overtime*
7. Came closer — *approached*
8. Difficulty — *trouble*
9. A pest — *nuisance*
10. Opposite of light — *heavy*
11. Opposite of war — *peace*
12. To say you will do something — *promise*
13. A sport — *soccer*
14. Pulled apart — *pried*
15. A package — *bundle*
16. Confusion — *commotion*
17. To look for something — *search*

Page 80

Good-by, Jennie!

Au revoir! Good-by! Au revoir!

Many foreign words have worked their way into our American language. Match each word or phrase below with its meaning. You may use a dictionary for help.

1. au revoir (French) — *m.*
2. Gesundheit (German) — *q.*
3. crepe (French) — *o.*
4. tortilla (Spanish) — *b.*
5. pita (Greek) — *p.*
6. chopsticks (Asian) — *c.*
7. oui (French) — *i.*
8. sarong (Malaysian) — *g.*
9. amigo (Spanish) — *h.*
10. rendezvous (French) — *k.*
11. babushka (Russian) — *f.*
12. lasagna (Italian) — *n.*
13. madam (French) — *d.*
14. guacamole (Spanish) — *e.*
15. torte (German) — *j.*
16. foyer (French) — *a.*
17. beret (French) — *l.*

a. a lobby or entryway
b. a flat bread made from corn or flour
c. thin sticks used for eating
d. a married woman
e. a dip made with avocado
f. a scarf worn on the head
g. fabric wrapped to wear as a skirt
h. friend
i. yes
j. a rich layer cake
k. a meeting place
l. a flat hat
m. good-by
n. a dish made with long, flat noodles
o. thin cloth or pancake
p. round bread with pocket
q. "Good health!" to someone who sneezed

A NOW... D   You may have noticed that a few of these words have to do with food. Which ethnic foods do you enjoy most?

Page 81

Fable-ology

Create your own fable about how an animal acquired a particular physical feature. Remember to have the animal learn a lesson. Illustrate your fable.

How the _____ Got Its _____

Long, long ago there lived a _____

Fables will vary.

_____
_____
_____
_____
_____
_____
_____

Moral: _____

Page 82

Mouse on the Moon

Stories are always more exciting when you can picture them happening in your mind. Descriptive words such as adverbs and adjectives help make the story more exciting. Imagine that the moon is really made of cheese, and that you are a mouse exploring it for the first time. With a partner, write two descriptive words for each category below. Then, use all of them in a story.

What I smell:
1. _____
2. _____

What I see:
1. _____
2. _____

What I hear:
1. _____
2. _____

What I feel:
1. _____
2. _____

What I taste:
1. _____
2. _____

_____
title

Stories will vary.

Page 83

Star Gazing

The Indians loved to watch the moon and the stars. Following the example, write a poem about the sun, moon, or stars.

Star Maiden
Beautiful, bright
Shining, glittering, sparkling
Came to live on earth
Water Lily

Line 1: a noun
Line 2: two adjectives that describe the noun
Line 3: three verbs with ing endings that tell what the noun does
Line 4: a phrase or sentence that tells something special about the noun
Line 5: a synonym for the noun. Repeat the noun if there is no synonym.

Poems will vary.

Page 84

Your Turn in the Poets Gallery

Fill in the blanks to make your own silly poems. The number at the end of each line tells the total number of syllables the line should have. Then draw a picture in each frame for the Poets Gallery.

Poems will vary.

There once was a _____ from _____ (8)
Who _____ (8)
With _____ (5)
And _____ (5)
Then _____ and cried _____ (8)

Twinkle, twinkle little _____ (7)
How I _____ what you _____ (7)
Way up _____ (7)
Like a _____ (7)
Twinkle, twinkle little _____ (7)
How I _____ (7)

I think _____ are rather _____ (7)
Their _____ are _____ (4)
Their _____ are _____ (4)
They haven't any _____ at all. (8)
They _____ things they shouldn't touch (8)
And no one seems to like them much. (8)
But I think _____ are _____ (6)

Page 85

Now Hiring

This is a job application to become a maid.
Please print neatly!

Answers will vary.

Name _____
        Last   First   Middle
Address _____
City, State, Zip Code _____
Previous experience that would make you a good maid:
_____
_____

Services you perform: _____
Hours you could work: _____
Vacation dates you prefer: _____
Salary required: _____

References (People who could tell us about you):
_____
_____
_____

Signature _____

Page 86

Dewey Decimal System

The Dewey Decimal System is used in most libraries to put books in order. This makes it easier for you to find the book you need.

Someone copied the system on a piece of scratch paper with the numbers in the wrong order. Number the system in order starting with 000-099.

Dewey Decimal		Types of Books
7	600-699	farming, medicine, building and cooking
4	300-399	jobs, education and customs
1	000-099	encyclopedias, almanacs and books of facts
10	900-999	people, places and events in history
5	400-499	dictionaries and languages
8	700-799	painting, music, dancing, sports and games
6	500-599	animals, math, stars and chemistry
3	200-299	religions
9	800-899	stories, poems and plays
2	100-199	great ideas and logical thinking

Read the titles. Write the Dewey Decimal numbers for each book.

700-799	Tap Dancing
500-599	Star Gazer
800-899	Poems about Animals
600-699	Cookie Cookbook Just for Kids
400-499	The Spanish Language Made Easy

Page 87

Skipping Through the Tens

Skip count by tens. Begin with the number on the first line. Write each number that follows.

0, 10, 20, 30, 40, 50, 60, 70, 80, 90, 100
3, 13, 23, 33, 43, 53, 63, 73, 83, 93, 103
1, 11, 21, 31, 41, 51, 61, 71, 81, 91, 101
8, 18, 28, 38, 48, 58, 68, 78, 88, 98, 108
6, 16, 26, 36, 46, 56, 66, 76, 86, 96, 106
4, 14, 24, 34, 44, 54, 64, 74, 84, 94, 104
2, 12, 22, 32, 42, 52, 62, 72, 82, 92, 102
5, 15, 25, 35, 45, 55, 65, 75, 85, 95, 105
7, 17, 27, 37, 47, 57, 67, 77, 87, 97, 107
9, 19, 29, 39, 49, 59, 69, 79, 89, 99, 109

What is ten more than ...

26	36	29	39
44	54	77	87
53	63	91	101
24	34	49	59
66	76	35	45
54	64	82	92

Page 88

Counting to 100

By twos:

2	4	6	8	10	12	14	16	18	20	22	24	26	28
30	32	34	36	38	40	42	44	46	48	50	52	54	56
58	60	62	64	66	68	70	72	74	76	78	80	82	84
86	88	90	92	94	96	98	100						

By threes:

3	6	9	12	15	18	21	24	27	30	33	36	39	42
45	48	51	54	57	60	63	66	69	72	75	78	81	84
87	90	93	96	99	102								

By fours:

4	8	12	16	20	24	28	32	36	40	44	48	52	56
60	64	68	72	76	80	84	88	92	96	100			

On the back, count by fives to 100. Can you count by sixes? Try it.

Page 89

Outstanding Elephant Math

Connect the dots in order.

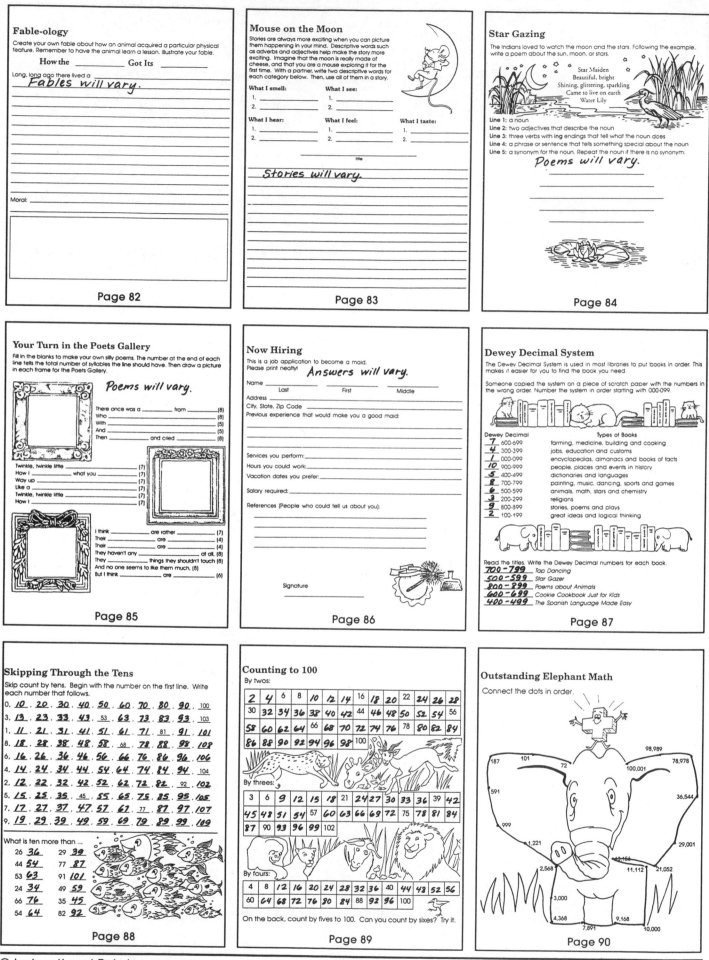

187, 101, 72, 98,989, 78,978, 591, 100,001, 36,544, 999, 1,221, 2,568, 29,001, 3,000, 12,166, 11,112, 21,052, 4,368, 9,168, 7,891, 10,000

Page 90

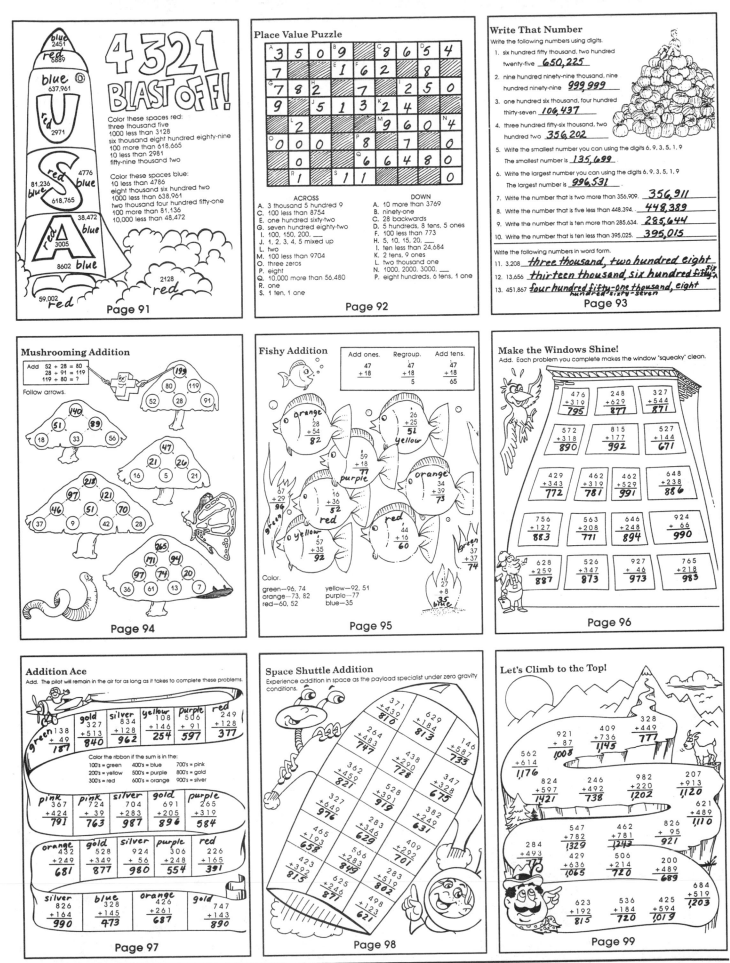

Page 91 — 4321 BLAST OFF!

Color these spaces red:
three thousand five
1000 less than 3128
six thousand eight hundred eighty-nine
100 more than 618,665
10 less than 2981
fifty-nine thousand two

Color these spaces blue:
10 less than 4786
eight thousand six hundred two
1000 less than 638,961
two thousand four hundred fifty-one
100 more than 81,136
10,000 less than 48,472

(rocket labels: blue 2451, red 6889, blue 637,961, red 2971, red 4776, blue, 81,236, blue 618,765, red 3005, 38,472 blue, 8602 blue, 2128 red, 59,002 red)

Page 92 — Place Value Puzzle

ACROSS
A. 3 thousand 5 hundred 9
C. 100 less than 8754
E. one hundred sixty-two
G. seven hundred eighty-two
I. 100, 150, 200, ___
J. 1, 2, 3, 4, 5 mixed up
L. two
M. 100 less than 9704
O. three zeros
P. eight
Q. 10,000 more than 56,480
R. one
S. 1 ten, 1 one

DOWN
A. 10 more than 3769
B. ninety-one
C. 28 backwards
D. 5 hundreds, 8 tens, 5 ones
F. 100 less than 773
H. 5, 10, 15, 20, ___
I. ten less than 24,684
K. 2 tens, 9 ones
L. two thousand one
N. 1000, 2000, 3000, ___
P. eight hundreds, 6 tens, 1 one

Page 93 — Write That Number

Write the following numbers using digits.

1. six hundred fifty thousand, two hundred twenty-five 650,225
2. nine hundred ninety-nine thousand, nine hundred ninety-nine 999,999
3. one hundred six thousand, four hundred thirty-seven 106,437
4. three hundred fifty-six thousand, two hundred two 356,202
5. Write the smallest number you can using the digits 6, 9, 3, 5, 1, 9. The smallest number is 135,699.
6. Write the largest number you can using the digits 6, 9, 3, 5, 1, 9. The largest number is 996,531.
7. Write the number that is two more than 356,909. 356,911
8. Write the number that is five less than 448,394. 448,389
9. Write the number that is ten more than 285,634. 285,644
10. Write the number that is ten less than 395,025. 395,015

Write the following numbers in word form.
11. 3,208 three thousand, two hundred eight
12. 13,656 thirteen thousand, six hundred fifty-six
13. 451,867 four hundred fifty-one thousand, eight hundred sixty-seven

Page 94 — Mushrooming Addition

Add. 52 + 28 = 80
28 + 91 = 119
119 + 80 = ?
Follow arrows.

Page 95 — Fishy Addition

Add ones.	Regroup.	Add tens.
47 +18	47 +18 5	47 +18 65

Color.
green—96, 74   yellow—92, 51
orange—73, 82   purple—77
red—60, 52   blue—35

Page 96 — Make the Windows Shine!

Add. Each problem you complete makes the window "squeaky" clean.

476 +319 = 795   248 +629 = 877   327 +544 = 871
572 +318 = 890   815 +177 = 992   527 +144 = 671
429 +343 = 772   462 +319 = 781   462 +529 = 991   648 +238 = 886
756 +127 = 883   563 +208 = 771   646 +248 = 894   924 +66 = 990
628 +259 = 887   526 +347 = 873   927 +46 = 973   765 +218 = 983

Page 97 — Addition Ace

Add. The pilot will remain in the air for as long as it takes to complete these problems.

Color the ribbon if the sum is in the:
100's = green   400's = blue   700's = pink
200's = yellow   500's = purple   800's = gold
300's = red   600's = orange   900's = silver

Page 98 — Space Shuttle Addition

Experience addition in space as the payload specialist under zero gravity conditions.

Page 99 — Let's Climb to the Top!

Picnic Problems

Help the ant find a path to the picnic. Work the problems. Shade the box if an answer has a 9 in it.

836 + 90 = 926	536 + 248 = 784	952 + 8 = 960	362 + 47 = 409	486 + 293 = 779	368 + 529 = 897
789 526 + 214 = 1,529	2846 + 6478 = 9,324	932 + 365 = 1,297	374 + 299 = 773	835 + 552 = 1,387	956 874 + 65 = 1,895
4768 + 2894 = 7,662	38 456 + 3894 = 4,388	4507 + 2743 = 7,250	404 + 289 = 693	1843 + 6752 = 8,595	4367 + 3571 = 7,938
639 + 77 = 716	587 342 + 679 = 1,608	5379 1865 + 2348 = 9,592	450 + 145 = 595	594 + 278 = 872	459 + 367 = 826
29 875 + 2341 = 3,245	387 29 + 5614 = 6,030	462 379 + 248 = 1,089			

Page 100

Bubble Math

Add the problems inside these bubbles.

9: 5642 + 1819 = 7461
3: 4629 + 1258 = 5887
4: 2647 + 3281 = 5928
6: 3426 + 2841 = 6267
5: 3690 + 2434 = 6124
7: 4625 + 1817 = 6442
17: 6843 + 2391 = 9234
14: 6241 + 2363 = 8604
10: 5942 + 1829 = 7771
13: 5642 + 2919 = 8561
1: 2648 + 1923 = 4571
8: 4826 + 2098 = 6924
15: 2641 + 6259 = 8900
18: 8465 + 1386 = 9851
16: 7205 + 1839 = 9044
19: 2643 + 7427 = 10,070
12: 5246 + 3187 = 8433
11: 4265 + 3827 = 8092
20: 9124 + 1348 = 10,472
2: 3142 + 2639 = 5781

These bubbles all popped in order from least to greatest. Number from 1 to 20 in the order in which they popped starting with the smallest sum.

Page 101

Yummy Additions

Add ones. Regroup.	Add tens. Regroup.	Add hundreds. Regroup.	Add thousands. Regroup.
7465 + 4978 = 3	7465 + 4978 = 43	7465 + 4978 = 443	7465 + 4978 = 12443

Do the problems. Color an answer containing a 3–brown, 4–red, 5–yellow.

6591 + 5569 = 12160
6843 + 7568 = 14,411 red
9224 + 7878 = 17,102
2549 + 9577 = 12,126
9853 + 8798 = 18,651 yellow
3849 + 7261 = 11,110
6456 + 4948 = 11,404 red
2698 + 8499 = 11,197
8796 + 8975 = 17,771
9764 + 7459 = 17,223 brown
7767 + 9899 = 17,666
5678 + 6984 = 12,662
9653 + 1568 = 11,221

Page 102

Mountaintop Getaway

Work all problems. Find a path to the cabin by shading in all answers that have a 3 in them.

		98 − 52 = 46	46 − 12 = 34	68 − 17 = 51
	79 − 53 = 26	65 − 23 = 42	63 − 31 = 32	86 − 32 = 54
59 − 45 = 14	75 − 64 = 11	67 − 24 = 43	97 − 54 = 43	55 − 43 = 12
87 − 65 = 22	44 − 32 = 12	57 − 24 = 33	88 − 25 = 63	75 − 61 = 14	48 − 26 = 22
69 − 25 = 44	95 − 24 = 71	48 − 13 = 35	58 − 16 = 42	35 − 13 = 22	39 − 17 = 22

SECRET PATHS

Page 103

Hats, Hats, Hats

Calculate the difference in each hat below.

736 − 629 = 107
466 − 327 = 139
837 − 529 = 308
742 − 428 = 314
784 − 565 = 219
673 − 458 = 215
648 − 426 = 222
982 − 665 = 317
947 − 729 = 218
543 − 426 = 117
928 − 619 = 309
847 − 628 = 219
427 − 318 = 109
524 − 318 = 206
245 − 126 = 119
852 − 328 = 524
545 − 221 = 324

Page 104

Soaring to the Stars

Connect the dots to form two stars. Begin one star with the subtraction problem whose difference is 100 and end with the problem whose difference is 109. Begin the other with 110 and end with 120. Color the pictures.

953 − 839 = 114
774 − 658 = 116
493 − 378 = 115
751 − 638 = 113
364 − 247 = 117
570 − 458 = 112
839 − 728 = 111
844 − 726 = 118
446 − 327 = 119
384 − 279 = 105
383 − 273 = 110
696 − 576 = 120
590 − 487 = 103
575 − 471 = 104
659 − 547 = 106
493 − 386 = 107
350 − 257 = 102
862 − 754 = 108
190 − 89 = 101
359 − 259 = 100
585 − 476 = 109

Page 105

Dino-Might

Whenever you're using "kid transportation," what is the best thing to do? To find out, work the problems. Then write the letters on the matching blanks.

A L W A Y S
195 92 265 195 185 45

W E A R A
265 171 195 183 195

H E L M E T !
181 171 92 93 171 191 74

A: 348 − 153 = 195
L: 765 − 673 = 92
S: 427 − 382 = 45
M: 568 − 475 = 93
T: 637 − 446 = 191
H: 878 − 697 = 181
Y: 548 − 363 = 185
W: 748 − 483 = 265
E: 824 − 653 = 171
R: 439 − 256 = 183
I: 447 − 373 = 74

Page 106

Find the Hidden Instrument

Solve each problem. Color each shape according to the key below.

purple: 529 − 373 = 156
blue: 484 − 364 = 120
red: 732 − 561 = 171
513 − 321 = 192
896 − 135 = 761
purple: 629 − 583 = 46
green
954 − 392 = 562
642 − 462 = 180 blue
705 − 443 = 262
548 − 283 = 265 yellow
635 − 573 = 62
926 − 564 = 362
blue: 664 − 482 = 182
orange: 529 − 364 = 165
439 − 275 = 164 yellow
853 − 522 = 331 orange
614 − 453 = 161
626 − 394 = 232
843 − 392 = 451 purple
green: 328 − 182 = 146

If the difference in the ten's column is:
1 = color red
2 = color blue
3 = color orange
4 = color green
5 = color purple
6 = color yellow
7 = color red
8 = color blue
9 = color purple

Page 107

Sailing Through Subtraction

Start at the bottom and work your way up the sails.

542 − 383 = 159
638 − 453 = 185
836 − 478 = 358
737 − 448 = 289
243 − 154 = 89
567 − 384 = 183
984 − 643 = 341
468 − 399 = 69
524 − 342 = 182
674 − 495 = 179
374 − 185 = 189
246 − 158 = 88
852 − 464 = 388
736 − 557 = 179
642 − 557 = 85
435 − 286 = 149

Page 108

© Instructional Fair, Inc.

300

IF8695 Super Book for Grade 3

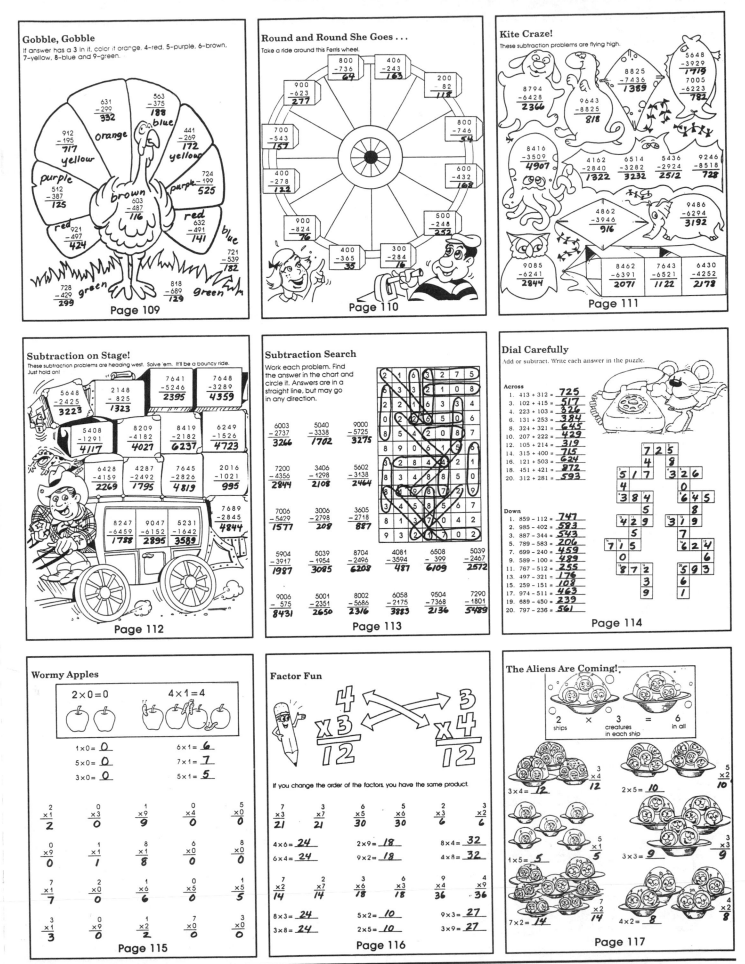

Gobble, Gobble
If answer has a 3 in it, color it orange. 4-red, 5-purple, 6-brown, 7-yellow, 8-blue and 9-green.

631−299=332
563−375=188 blue
912−195=717 yellow
441−269=172 yellow
orange
purple
724−199=525 purple
512−387=125
603−487=116 brown
red
632−491=141 blue
921−497=424 red
721−539=182 blue
728−429=299 green
818−689=129 green

Page 109

Round and Round She Goes . . .
Take a ride around this Ferris wheel.

800−736=64
406−243=163
900−623=277
200−82=118
800−746=54
700−543=157
600−432=168
400−278=122
900−824=76
500−248=252
400−365=35
300−284=16

Page 110

Kite Craze!
These subtraction problems are flying high.

5648−3929=1719
8825−7436=1389
7005−6223=782
8794−6428=2366
9643−8825=818
8416−3509=4907
4162−2840=1322
6514−3282=3232
5436−2924=2512
9246−8518=728
4862−3946=916
9486−6294=3192
9085−6241=2844
8462−6391=2071
7643−6521=1122
6430−4252=2178

Page 111

Subtraction on Stage!
These subtraction problems are heading west. Solve 'em. It'll be a bouncy ride. Just hold on!

5648−2425=3223
2148−825=1323
7641−5246=2395
7648−3289=4359
5408−1291=4117
8209−4182=4027
8419−2182=6237
6249−1526=4723
6428−4159=2269
4287−2492=1795
7645−2826=4819
2016−1021=995
8247−6459=1788
9047−6152=2895
5231−1642=3589
7689−2845=4844

Page 112

Subtraction Search
Work each problem. Find the answer in the chart and circle it. Answers are in a straight line, but may go in any direction.

6003−2737=3266
5040−3338=1702
9000−5725=3275
7200−4356=2844
3406−1298=2108
5602−3138=2464
7006−5429=1577
3006−2798=208
3605−2718=887
5904−3917=1987
5039−1954=3085
8704−2496=6208
4081−3594=487
6508−399=6109
5039−2467=2572
9006−575=8431
5001−2351=2650
8002−5686=2316
6058−2175=3883
9504−7368=2136
7290−1801=5489

Page 113

Dial Carefully
Add or subtract. Write each answer in the puzzle.

Across
1. 413 + 312 = 725
3. 102 + 415 = 517
4. 223 + 103 = 326
6. 131 + 253 = 384
8. 324 + 321 = 645
10. 207 + 222 = 429
12. = 319
14. 315 + 400 = 715
16. 121 + 503 = 624
18. 451 + 421 = 872
20. 312 + 281 = 593

Down
1. 859 − 112 = 747
2. 985 − 402 = 583
3. 887 − 344 = 543
5. 789 − 583 = 206
7. 699 − 240 = 459
9. 589 − 100 = 489
11. 767 − 512 = 255
13. 497 − 321 = 176
15. 121 − 13 = 108
17. 974 − 511 = 463
19. 689 − 450 = 239
20. 797 − 236 = 561

Page 114

Wormy Apples
2 × 0 = 0   4 × 1 = 4

1 × 0 = 0
5 × 0 = 0
3 × 0 = 0
6 × 1 = 6
7 × 1 = 7
5 × 1 = 5

2×1=2, 0×3=0, 1×9=9, 0×4=0, 5×0=0
0×9=0, 1×1=1, 8×1=8, 6×0=0, 8×0=0
7×1=7, 0×0=0, 1×6=6, 0×5=0, 1×5=5
3×1=3, 0×9=0, 1×2=2, 7×0=0, 3×0=0

Page 115

Factor Fun

4×3=12   3×4=12

If you change the order of the factors, you have the same product.

7×3=21, 3×7=21, 6×5=30, 5×6=30, 2×3=6, 3×2=6
4×6=24, 2×9=18, 8×4=32
6×4=24, 9×2=18, 4×8=32
7×2=14, 7×2=14, 6×3=18, 6×3=18, 9×4=36, 4×9=36
8×3=24, 5×2=10, 9×3=27
3×8=24, 2×5=10, 3×9=27

Page 116

The Aliens Are Coming!

2 ships × 3 creatures in each ship = 6 in all

3×4=12
2×5=10
1×5=5
3×3=9
7×2=14
4×2=8

Page 117

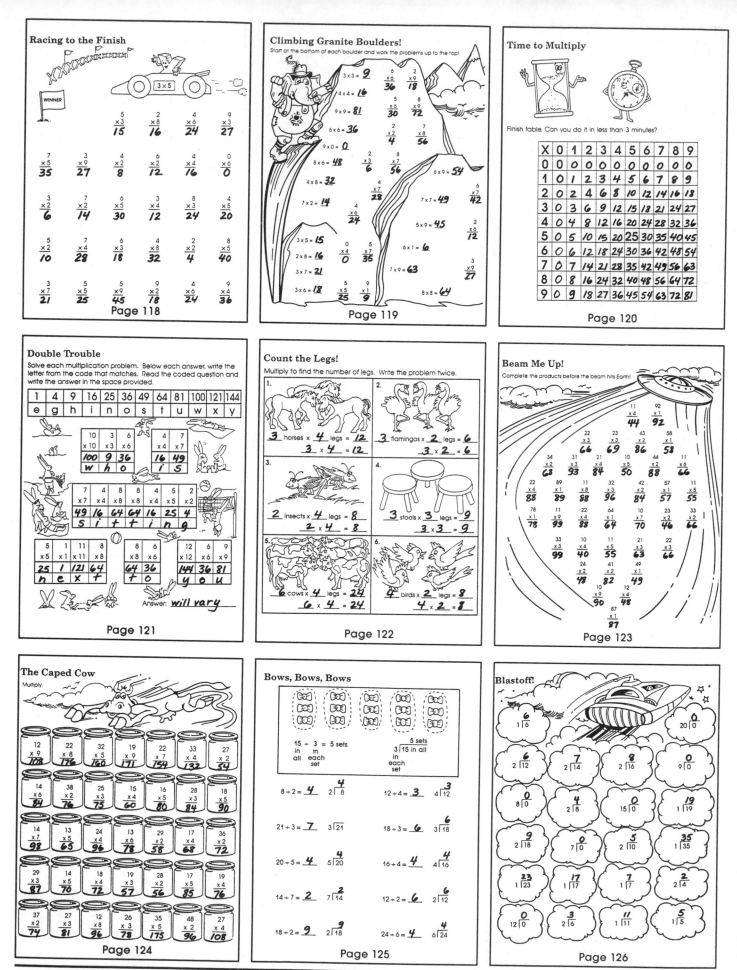

Racing to the Finish

3×5

5 ×3 = 15	2 ×8 = 16	4 ×6 = 24	9 ×3 = 27

| 7 ×5 = 35 | 3 ×9 = 27 | 4 ×2 = 8 | 6 ×2 = 12 | 4 ×4 = 16 | 0 ×6 = 0 |

| 3 ×2 = 6 | 7 ×2 = 14 | 6 ×5 = 30 | 3 ×4 = 12 | 8 ×3 = 24 | 4 ×5 = 20 |

| 5 ×2 = 10 | 7 ×4 = 28 | 6 ×3 = 18 | 4 ×8 = 32 | 2 ×2 = 4 | 8 ×5 = 40 |

| 3 ×7 = 21 | 5 ×5 = 25 | 5 ×9 = 45 | 9 ×2 = 18 | 4 ×6 = 24 | 9 ×4 = 36 |

Page 118

Climbing Granite Boulders!

Start at the bottom of each boulder and work the problems up to the top!

3×3 = 9
4×4 = 16
9×9 = 81
6×6 = 36
9×0 = 0
8×6 = 48
4×8 = 32
7×2 = 14
3×5 = 15
2×8 = 16
3×7 = 21
3×6 = 18

6 ×6 = 36, 9 ×2 = 18, 6 ×6 = 30, 9 ×8 = 72, 2 ×2 = 4, 8 ×7 = 56
3 ×5 = ... , 7 ×7 = ... 56
4 ×7 = 28, 4 ×6 = 24
0 ×4 = 0, 5 ×7 = 35

6×9 = 54
7×7 = 49, 6 ×7 = 42
5×9 = 45
6×1 = 6, 2 ×6 = 12
7×9 = 63, 3 ×9 = 27
5 ×5 = 25, 9 ×1 = 9
8×8 = 64

Page 119

Time to Multiply

Finish table. Can you do it in less than 3 minutes?

X	0	1	2	3	4	5	6	7	8	9
0	0	0	0	0	0	0	0	0	0	0
1	0	1	2	3	4	5	6	7	8	9
2	0	2	4	6	8	10	12	14	16	18
3	0	3	6	9	12	15	18	21	24	27
4	0	4	8	12	16	20	24	28	32	36
5	0	5	10	15	20	25	30	35	40	45
6	0	6	12	18	24	30	36	42	48	54
7	0	7	14	21	28	35	42	49	56	63
8	0	8	16	24	32	40	48	56	64	72
9	0	9	18	27	36	45	54	63	72	81

Page 120

Double Trouble

Solve each multiplication problem. Below each answer, write the letter from the code that matches. Read the coded question and write the answer in the space provided.

1	4	9	16	25	36	49	64	81	100	121	144
e	g	h	i	n	o	s	t	u	w	x	y

10 x 10 = 100 (w), 3 x 3 = 9 (h), 6 x 6 = 36 (o), 4 x 4 = 16 (i), 7 x 7 = 49 (s)
w h o   i s

7 x 7 = 49 (s), 4 x 4 = 16 (i), 8 x 8 = 64 (t), 8 x 8 = 64 (t), 4 x 4 = 16 (i), 5 x 5 = 25 (n), 4 x 1 = 4 (g)
s i t t i n g

5 x 5 = 25 (n), 1 x 1 = 1 (e), 11 x 11 = 121 (x), 8 x 8 = 64 (t)
n e x t
8 x 8 = 64 (t), 6 x 6 = 36 (o)
t o
12 x 12 = 144 (y), 6 x 6 = 36 (o), 9 x 9 = 81 (u)
y o u

Answer: will vary

Page 121

Count the Legs!

Multiply to find the number of legs. Write the problem twice.

1. 3 horses x 4 legs = 12 → 3 x 4 = 12
2. 3 flamingos x 2 legs = 6 → 3 x 2 = 6
3. 2 insects x 4 legs = 8 → 2 x 4 = 8
4. 3 stools x 3 legs = 9 → 3 x 3 = 9
5. 6 cows x 4 legs = 24 → 6 x 4 = 24
6. 4 birds x 2 legs = 8 → 4 x 2 = 8

Page 122

Beam Me Up!

Complete the products before the beam hits Earth!

11 ×4 = 44, 92 ×1 = 92
22 ×3 = 66, 23 ×3 = 69, 43 ×2 = 86, 58 ×1 = 58
34 ×2 = 63, 31 ×3 = 93, 21 ×4 = 84, 10 ×5 = 50, 44 ×2 = 88, 11 ×6 = 66
22 ×4 = 88, 89 ×1 = 89, 11 ×8 = 88, 32 ×3 = 96, 42 ×2 = 84, 57 ×1 = 57, 11 ×5 = 55
78 ×1 = 78, 11 ×9 = 99, 22 ×4 = 88, 64 ×1 = 64, 10 ×7 = 70, 23 ×2 = 46, 33 ×2 = 66
33 ×3 = 99, 10 ×4 = 40, 11 ×5 = 55, 21 ×3 = 63, 22 ×3 = 66
24 ×2 = 48, 41 ×2 = 82, 49 ×1 = 49
10 ×9 = 90, 12 ×4 = 48
87 ×1 = 87

Page 123

The Caped Cow

Multiply.

12 ×9 = 108	22 ×8 = 176	32 ×5 = 160	19 ×9 = 171	22 ×7 = 154	33 ×4 = 132	27 ×2 = 54
14 ×6 = 84	38 ×2 = 76	25 ×3 = 75	15 ×4 = 60	16 ×5 = 80	28 ×3 = 84	18 ×5 = 90
14 ×7 = 98	13 ×5 = 65	24 ×4 = 96	13 ×6 = 78	29 ×2 = 58	17 ×4 = 68	36 ×2 = 72
29 ×3 = 87	14 ×5 = 70	18 ×4 = 72	19 ×3 = 57	28 ×2 = 56	17 ×5 = 85	19 ×4 = 76
37 ×2 = 74	27 ×3 = 81	12 ×8 = 96	26 ×3 = 78	35 ×5 = 175	48 ×2 = 96	27 ×4 = 108

Page 124

Bows, Bows, Bows

15 ÷ 3 = 5 sets
in all ÷ in each set
5 sets, 3)15 in all, in each set

8 ÷ 2 = 4, 2)8 = 4
12 ÷ 4 = 3, 4)12 = 3
21 ÷ 3 = 7, 3)21
18 ÷ 3 = 6, 3)18 = 6
20 ÷ 5 = 4, 5)20 = 4
16 ÷ 4 = 4, 4)16 = 4
14 ÷ 7 = 2, 7)14 = 2
12 ÷ 2 = 6, 2)12 = 6
18 ÷ 2 = 9, 2)18 = 9
24 ÷ 6 = 4, 6)24 = 4

Page 125

Blastoff!

6, 1)6
20, 0)0
6, 2)12
7, 2)14
8, 2)16
0, 9)0
0, 8)0
4, 2)8
0, 15)0
19, 1)19
9, 2)18
0, 7)0
5, 2)10
35, 1)35
23, 1)23
17, 1)17
7, 1)7
2, 2)4
0, 12)0
3, 2)6
1, 1)11
1, 5)5

Page 126

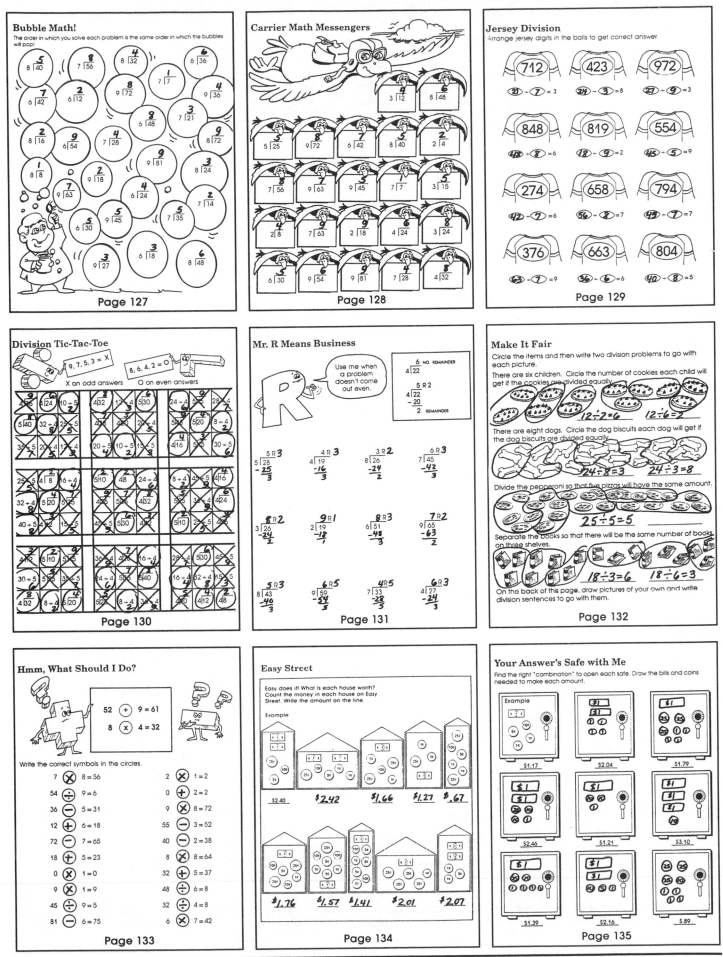

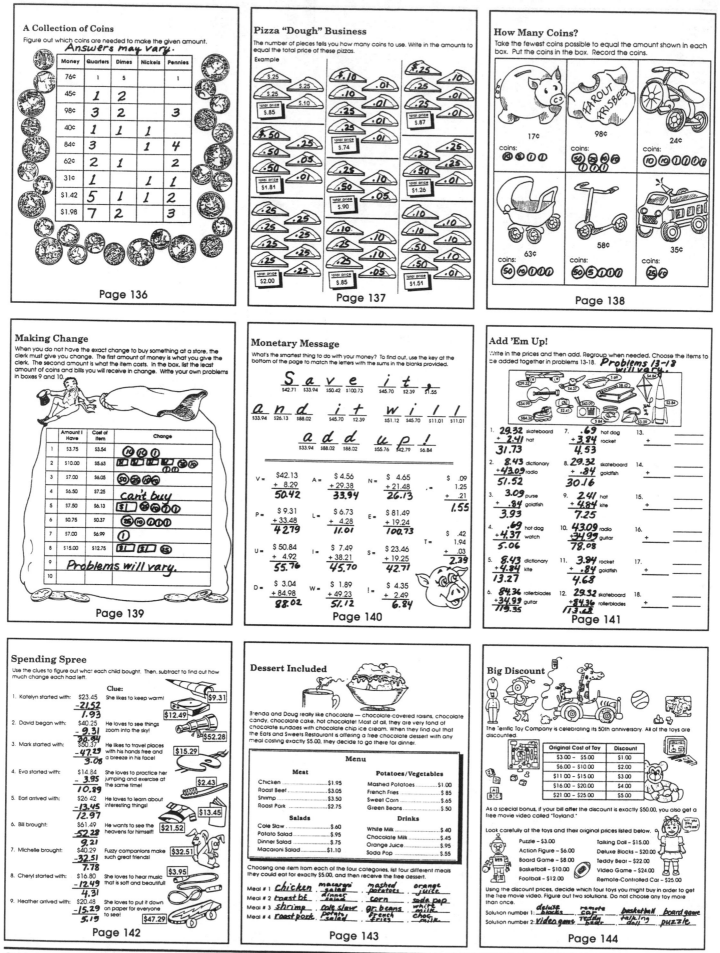

A Collection of Coins

Figure out which coins are needed to make the given amount.

Answers may vary.

Money	Quarters	Dimes	Nickels	Pennies
76¢	1		5	1
45¢	1	2		
98¢	3	2		3
40¢	1	1	1	
84¢	3		1	4
62¢	2	1		2
31¢	1		1	1
$1.42	5	1	1	2
$1.98	7	2		3

Page 136

Pizza "Dough" Business

The number of pieces tells you how many coins to use. Write in the amounts to equal the total price of these pizzas.

Example

total price $.85

total price $1.81

total price $2.00

total price $.74

total price $1.26

total price $.90

total price $.85

total price $.87

total price $1.51

Page 137

How Many Coins?

Take the fewest coins possible to equal the amount shown in each box. Put the coins in the box. Record the coins.

17¢ — coins:
98¢ — coins:
24¢ — coins:
63¢ — coins:
58¢ — coins:
35¢ — coins:

Page 138

Making Change

When you do not have the exact change to buy something at a store, the clerk must give you change. The first amount of money is what you give the clerk. The second amount is what the item costs. In the box, list the least amount of coins and bills you will receive in change. Write your own problems in boxes 9 and 10.

	Amount I Have	Cost of Item	Change
1	$3.75	$3.54	
2	$10.00	$5.63	
3	$7.00	$6.05	
4	$6.50	$7.25	can't buy
5	$7.50	$6.13	
6	$0.75	$0.37	
7	$7.00	$6.99	
8	$15.00	$12.75	
9			Problems will vary.
10			

Page 139

Monetary Message

What's the smartest thing to do with your money? To find out, use the key at the bottom of the page to match the letters with the sums in the blanks provided.

S a v e   i t ,
$42.71 $33.94 $50.42 $100.73 $45.70 $2.39 $1.55

a n d   i t   w i l l
$33.94 $26.13 $88.02 $45.70 $2.39 $51.12 $45.70 $11.01 $11.01

a d d   u p !
$33.94 $88.02 $88.02 $55.76 $42.79 $6.84

V = $42.13 + 8.29 = 50.42
A = $4.56 + 29.38 = 33.94
N = $4.65 + 21.48 = 26.13
, = $.09 + 1.25 + .21 = 1.55

P = $9.31 + 33.48 = 42.79
L = $6.73 + 4.28 = 11.01
E = $81.49 + 19.24 = 100.73
T = $.42 + 1.94 + .03 = 2.39

U = $50.84 + 4.92 = 55.76
I = $7.49 + 38.21 = 45.70
S = $23.46 + 19.25 = 42.71

D = $3.04 + 84.98 = 88.02
W = $1.89 + 49.23 = 51.12
I = $4.35 + 2.49 = 6.84

Page 140

Add 'Em Up!

Write in the prices and then add. Regroup when needed. Choose the items to be added together in problems 13–18. Problems 13–18 will vary.

1. 29.32 skateboard + 2.41 hat = 31.73
2. 8.43 dictionary + 43.09 radio = 51.52
3. 3.09 purse + .84 goldfish = 3.93
4. .69 hot dog + 4.37 watch = 5.06
5. 8.43 dictionary + 4.84 kite = 13.27
6. 84.36 rollerblades + 34.99 guitar = 119.35
7. .69 hot dog + 3.84 rocket = 4.53
8. 29.32 skateboard + .84 goldfish = 30.16
9. 2.41 hat + 4.84 kite = 7.25
10. 43.09 radio + 34.99 guitar = 78.08
11. 3.84 rocket + .84 goldfish = 4.68
12. 29.32 skateboard + 84.36 rollerblades = 113.68

13. +
14. +
15. +
16. +
17. +
18. +

Page 141

Spending Spree

Use the clues to figure out what each child bought. Then, subtract to find out how much change each had left.

		Clue:
1. Katelyn started with:	$23.45 −21.52 = 1.93	She likes to keep warm! ($21.52)
2. David began with:	$40.25 −9.31 = 30.94	He loves to see things zoom into the sky! ($9.31)
3. Mark started with:	$50.37 −47.29 = 3.08	He likes to travel places with his hands free and a breeze in his face! ($47.29)
4. Eva started with:	$14.84 −3.95 = 10.89	She loves to practice her jumping and exercise at the same time! ($3.95)
5. Earl arrived with:	$26.42 −13.45 = 12.97	He loves to learn about interesting things! ($13.45)
6. Bill brought:	$61.49 −52.28 = 9.21	He wants to see the heavens for himself! ($52.28)
7. Michelle brought:	$40.29 −32.51 = 7.78	Fuzzy companions make such great friends! ($32.51)
8. Cheryl started with:	$16.80 −12.49 = 4.31	She loves to hear music that is soft and beautiful! ($12.49)
9. Heather arrived with:	$20.48 −15.29 = 5.19	She loves to put it down on paper for everyone to see! ($15.29)

Page 142

Dessert Included

Brenda and Doug really like chocolate — chocolate-covered raisins, chocolate candy, chocolate cake, hot chocolate! Most of all, they are very fond of chocolate sundaes with chocolate chip ice cream. When they find out that the Eats and Sweets Restaurant is offering a free chocolate dessert with any meal costing exactly $5.00, they decide to go there for dinner.

Menu

Meat		Potatoes/Vegetables	
Chicken	$1.95	Mashed Potatoes	$1.00
Roast Beef	$3.05	French Fries	$.85
Shrimp	$3.50	Sweet Corn	$.65
Roast Pork	$2.75	Green Beans	$.50

Salads		Drinks	
Cole Slaw	$.60	White Milk	$.40
Potato Salad	$.95	Chocolate Milk	$.45
Dinner Salad	$.75	Orange Juice	$.95
Macaroni Salad	$1.10	Soda Pop	$.55

Choosing one item from each of the four categories, list four different meals they could eat for exactly $5.00, and then receive the free dessert.

Meal #1 chicken, macaroni salad, mashed potatoes, orange juice
Meal #2 roast bf, dinner salad, corn, soda pop
Meal #3 shrimp, cole slaw, gr. beans, white milk
Meal #4 roast pork, potato salad, french fries, choc. milk

Page 143

Big Discount

The Terrific Toy Company is celebrating its 50th anniversary. All of the toys are discounted.

Original Cost of Toy	Discount
$3.00 – $5.00	$1.00
$6.00 – $10.00	$2.00
$11.00 – $15.00	$3.00
$16.00 – $20.00	$4.00
$21.00 – $25.00	$5.00

As a special bonus, if your bill after the discount is exactly $50.00, you also get a free movie video called "Toyland."

Look carefully at the toys and their original prices listed below.

Puzzle – $3.00
Action Figure – $6.00
Board Game – $8.00
Basketball – $10.00
Football – $12.00
Talking Doll – $15.00
Deluxe Blocks – $20.00
Teddy Bear – $22.00
Video Game – $24.00
Remote-Controlled Car – $25.00

Using the discount prices, decide which four toys you might buy in order to get the free movie video. Figure out two solutions. Do not choose any toy more than once.

Solution number 1: deluxe blocks, remote car, basketball, board game
Solution number 2: video game, teddy bear, talking doll, puzzle

Page 144

Mind-Bogglers

These problems will boggle your mind. Don't give up. Try different problem-solving strategies to help you find the answers.

1. Marta receives an allowance of $2.25 a week. This week her mom pays her in nickels, dimes and quarters. She received more dimes than quarters. What coins did her mom use to pay her? **Answers will vary.**

2. You are asked to draw a picture of a dinosaur. You make the head 1/3 as long as the body. You draw the tail as long as the head and the body combined. The total length of the dinosaur is 56 inches. How long did you make each part of the dinosaur?
head **7"** tail **28"** body **21"**

Strategy I used: _____

3. Mr. Whitman takes his family on a trip to the amusement park. He brings $75 with him to buy the entrance tickets, food and souvenirs for the family. The tickets to get into the amusement park are $12.75 for adults and $8.45 for children. How much money will Mr. Whitman have for food and souvenirs after he buys entrance tickets for himself, Mrs. Whitman and their two children? **$32.60**

Strategy I used: _____

4. There are eight tables in the classroom. Normally, the teacher has two students sitting on each side. Today, she is going to do a special project so she pushes all eight tables in a long row. How many students can sit at the long table? **36**

5. Mr. Jonyou gives his three children a weekly allowance. He pays them in dollar bills. Tony is the first to get paid. He receives half the number of dollar bills his dad has. Joe gets his allowance second. He receives half of the remaining dollar bills plus one. Mr. Jonyou now has $2 left, which is Carmen's allowance. How much allowance do Tony and Joe receive?
Tony **$5** Joe **$3**

Strategy I used: _____

Page 145

Vote for Me!

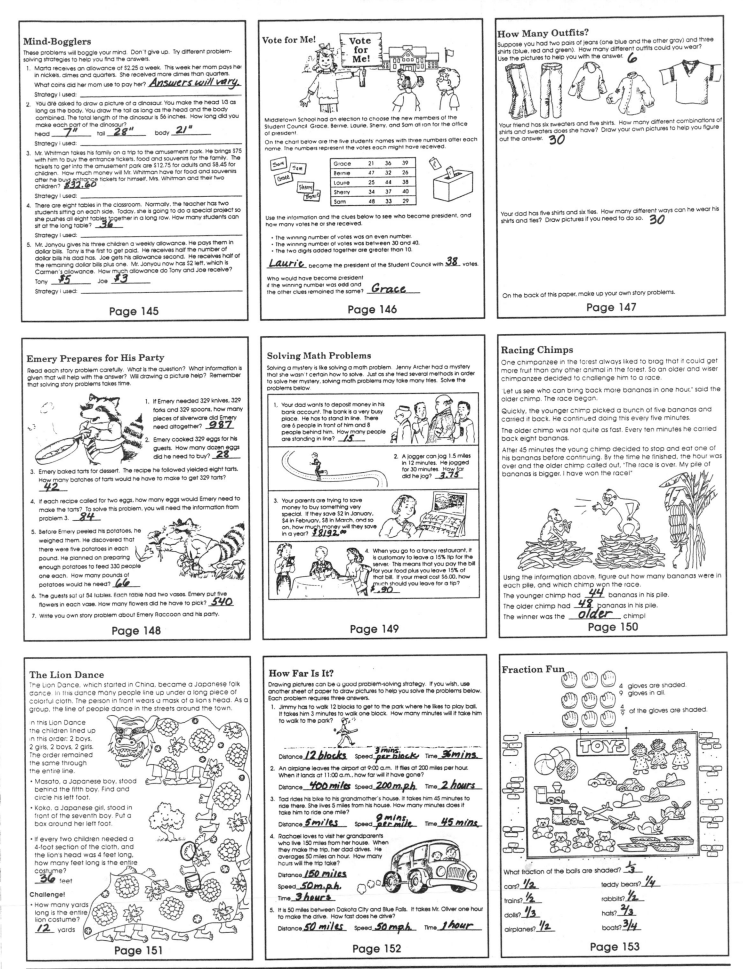

Middletown School had an election to choose the new members of the Student Council. Grace, Bernie, Laurie, Sherry, and Sam all ran for the office of president.

On the chart below are the five students' names with three numbers after each name. The numbers represent the votes each might have received.

Grace	21	36	39
Bernie	47	32	26
Laurie	25	44	38
Sherry	34	37	40
Sam	48	33	29

Use the information and the clues below to see who became president, and how many votes he or she received.

- The winning number of votes was an even number.
- The winning number of votes was between 30 and 40.
- The two digits added together were greater than 10.

Laurie became the president of the Student Council with **38** votes.

Who would have become president if the winning number was odd and the other clues remained the same? **Grace**

Page 146

How Many Outfits?

Suppose you had two pairs of jeans (one blue and the other gray) and three shirts (blue, red and green). How many different outfits could you wear? Use the pictures to help you with the answer. **6**

Your friend has six sweaters and five shirts. How many different combinations of shirts and sweaters does she have? Draw your own pictures to help you figure out the answer. **30**

Your dad has five shirts and six ties. How many different ways can he wear his shirts and ties? Draw pictures if you need to do so. **30**

On the back of this paper, make up your own story problems.

Page 147

Emery Prepares for His Party

Read each story problem carefully. What is the question? What information is given that will help with the answer? Will drawing a picture help? Remember that solving story problems takes time.

1. If Emery needed 329 knives, 329 forks and 329 spoons, how many pieces of silverware did Emery need altogether? **987**

2. Emery cooked 329 eggs for his guests. How many dozen eggs did he need to buy? **28**

3. Emery baked tarts for dessert. The recipe he followed yielded eight tarts. How many batches of tarts would he have to make to get 329 tarts? **42**

4. If each recipe called for two eggs, how many eggs would Emery need to make the tarts? To solve this problem, you will need the information from problem 3. **84**

5. Before Emery peeled his potatoes, he weighed them. He discovered that there were five potatoes in each pound. He planned on preparing enough potatoes to feed 330 people one each. How many pounds of potatoes would he need? **66**

6. The guests sat at 54 tables. Each table had two vases. Emery put five flowers in each vase. How many flowers did he have to pick? **540**

7. Write your own story problem about Emery Raccoon and his party.

Page 148

Solving Math Problems

Solving a mystery is like solving a math problem. Jenny Archer had a mystery that she wasn't certain how to solve. Just as she tried several methods in order to solve her mystery, solving math problems may take many tries. Solve the problems below.

1. Your dad wants to deposit money in his bank account. The bank is a very busy place. He has to stand in line. There are 6 people in front of him and 8 people standing in line behind him. How many people are standing in line? **15**

2. A jogger can jog 1.5 miles in 12 minutes. He jogged for 30 minutes. How far did he jog? **3.75**

3. Your parents are trying to save money to buy something very special. If they save $2 in January, $4 in February, $8 in March, and so on, how much money will they save in a year? **$8192.00**

4. When you go to a fancy restaurant, it is customary to leave a 15% tip for the server. This means that you pay the bill for your food plus you leave 15% of that bill. If your meal cost $6.00, how much should you leave for a tip? **.90**

Page 149

Racing Chimps

One chimpanzee in the forest always liked to brag that it could get more fruit than any other animal in the forest. So an older and wiser chimpanzee decided to challenge him to a race.

"Let us see who can bring back more bananas in one hour," said the older chimp. The race began.

Quickly, the younger chimp picked a bunch of five bananas and carried it back. He continued doing this every five minutes.

The older chimp was not quite as fast. Every ten minutes he carried back eight bananas.

After 45 minutes the young chimp decided to stop and eat one of his bananas before continuing. By the time he finished, the hour was over and the older chimp called out, "The race is over. My pile of bananas is bigger. I have won the race!"

Using the information above, figure out how many bananas were in each pile, and which chimp won the race.
The younger chimp had **44** bananas in his pile.
The older chimp had **48** bananas in his pile.
The winner was the **older** chimp!

Page 150

The Lion Dance

The Lion Dance, which started in China, became a Japanese folk dance. In this dance many people line up under a long piece of colorful cloth. The person in front wears a mask of a lion's head. As a group, the line of people dance in the streets around the town.

In this Lion Dance the children lined up in this order: 2 boys, 2 girls, 2 boys, 2 girls. The order remained the same through the entire line.

- Masato, a Japanese boy, stood behind the fifth boy. Find and circle his third boy.

- Koko, a Japanese girl, stood in front of the seventh boy. Put a box around her left foot.

- If every two children needed a 4-foot section of the cloth, and the lion's head was 4 feet long, how many feet long is the entire costume? **36** feet

Challenge:
- How many yards long is the entire lion costume? **12** yards

Page 151

How Far Is It?

Drawing pictures can be a good problem-solving strategy. If you wish, use another sheet of paper to draw pictures to help you solve the problems below. Each problem requires three answers.

1. Jimmy has to walk 12 blocks to get to the park where he likes to play ball. It takes him 3 minutes to walk one block. How many minutes will it take him to walk to the park?
Distance **12 blocks** Speed **3 mins. per block** Time **36 mins.**

2. An airplane leaves the airport at 9:00 a.m. It flies at 200 miles per hour. When it lands at 11:00 a.m., how far will it have gone?
Distance **400 miles** Speed **200 m.p.h.** Time **2 hours**

3. Tad rides his bike to his grandmother's house. It takes him 45 minutes to ride there. She lives 5 miles from his house. How many minutes does it take him to ride one mile?
Distance **5 miles** Speed **9 mins. per mile** Time **45 mins.**

4. Rachael loves to visit her grandparents who live 150 miles from her house. When they make the trip, it takes her dad 45 minutes. He averages 50 miles an hour. How many hours will the trip take?
Distance **150 miles** Speed **50 m.p.h.** Time **3 hours**

5. It is 50 miles between Dakota City and Blue Falls. It takes Mr. Oliver one hour to make the drive. How fast does he drive?
Distance **50 miles** Speed **50 mph** Time **1 hour**

Page 152

Fraction Fun

4 gloves are shaded.
9 gloves in all.
4/9 of the gloves are shaded.

What fraction of the balls are shaded? **1/3**
cars? **1/2** teddy bears? **1/4**
trains? **1/2** rabbits? **1/2**
dolls? **1/3** hats? **2/3**
airplanes? **1/2** boats? **3/4**

Page 153

IF8695 Super Book for Grade 3

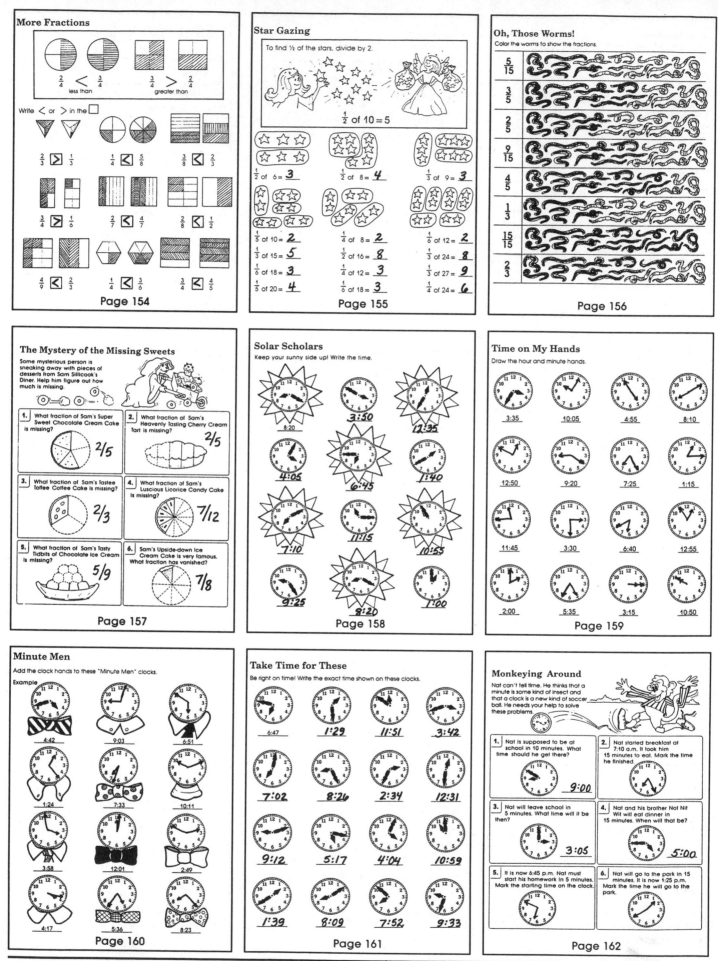

More Fractions

$\frac{2}{4}$ < $\frac{3}{4}$ less than $\frac{3}{4}$ > $\frac{2}{4}$ greater than

Write < or > in the □

$\frac{2}{3}$ > $\frac{1}{3}$ $\frac{1}{4}$ < $\frac{5}{8}$ $\frac{3}{8}$ < $\frac{2}{3}$

$\frac{3}{4}$ > $\frac{1}{6}$ $\frac{2}{7}$ < $\frac{4}{7}$ $\frac{2}{8}$ < $\frac{1}{2}$

$\frac{4}{9}$ < $\frac{2}{3}$ $\frac{1}{4}$ < $\frac{3}{6}$ $\frac{3}{4}$ < $\frac{4}{5}$

Page 154

Star Gazing

To find ½ of the stars, divide by 2.

½ of 10 = 5

½ of 6 = **3**   ½ of 8 = **4**   ⅓ of 9 = **3**

⅕ of 10 = **2**   ¼ of 8 = **2**   ⅙ of 12 = **2**

⅓ of 15 = **5**   ½ of 16 = **8**   ⅓ of 24 = **8**

⅙ of 18 = **3**   ¼ of 12 = **3**   ⅓ of 27 = **9**

⅕ of 20 = **4**   ⅙ of 18 = **3**   ¼ of 24 = **6**

Page 155

Oh, Those Worms!

Color the worms to show the fractions.

$\frac{5}{15}$

$\frac{3}{5}$

$\frac{2}{5}$

$\frac{9}{15}$

$\frac{4}{5}$

$\frac{1}{3}$

$\frac{15}{15}$

$\frac{2}{3}$

Page 156

The Mystery of the Missing Sweets

Some mysterious person is sneaking away with pieces of desserts from Sam Sillicook's Diner. Help him figure out how much is missing.

1. What fraction of Sam's Super Sweet Chocolate Cream Cake is missing? **2/5**

2. What fraction of Sam's Heavenly Tasting Cherry Cream Tart is missing? **2/5**

3. What fraction of Sam's Tastee Toffee Coffee Cake is missing? **2/3**

4. What fraction of Sam's Luscious Licorice Candy Cake is missing? **7/12**

5. What fraction of Sam's Tasty Tidbits of Chocolate Ice Cream is missing? **5/9**

6. Sam's Upside-down Ice Cream Cake is very famous. What fraction has vanished? **7/8**

Page 157

Solar Scholars

Keep your sunny side up! Write the time.

8:20   3:50   12:35

4:05   6:45   1:40

7:10   11:15   10:55

9:25   8:20   1:00

Page 158

Time on My Hands

Draw the hour and minute hands.

3:35   10:05   4:55   8:10

12:50   9:20   7:25   1:15

11:45   3:30   6:40   12:55

2:00   5:35   3:15   10:50

Page 159

Minute Men

Add the clock hands to these "Minute Men" clocks.

Example

4:42   9:03   6:51

1:24   7:33   10:11

3:58   12:01   2:49

4:17   5:36   8:23

Page 160

Take Time for These

Be right on time! Write the exact time shown on these clocks.

6:47   1:29   11:51   3:42

7:02   8:26   2:34   12:31

9:12   5:17   4:04   10:59

1:39   8:09   7:52   9:33

Page 161

Monkeying Around

Nat can't tell time. He thinks that a minute is some kind of insect and that a clock is a new kind of soccer ball. He needs your help to solve these problems.

1. Nat is supposed to be at school in 10 minutes. What time should he get there? **9:00**

2. Nat started breakfast at 7:10 a.m. It took him 15 minutes to eat. Mark the time he finished.

3. Nat will leave school in 5 minutes. What time will it be then? **3:05**

4. Nat and his brother Not Nit Wit will eat dinner in 15 minutes. When will that be? **5:00**

5. It is now 6:45 p.m. Nat must start his homework in 5 minutes. Mark the starting time on the clock.

6. Nat will go to the park in 15 minutes. It is now 1:25 p.m. Mark the time he will go to the park.

Page 162

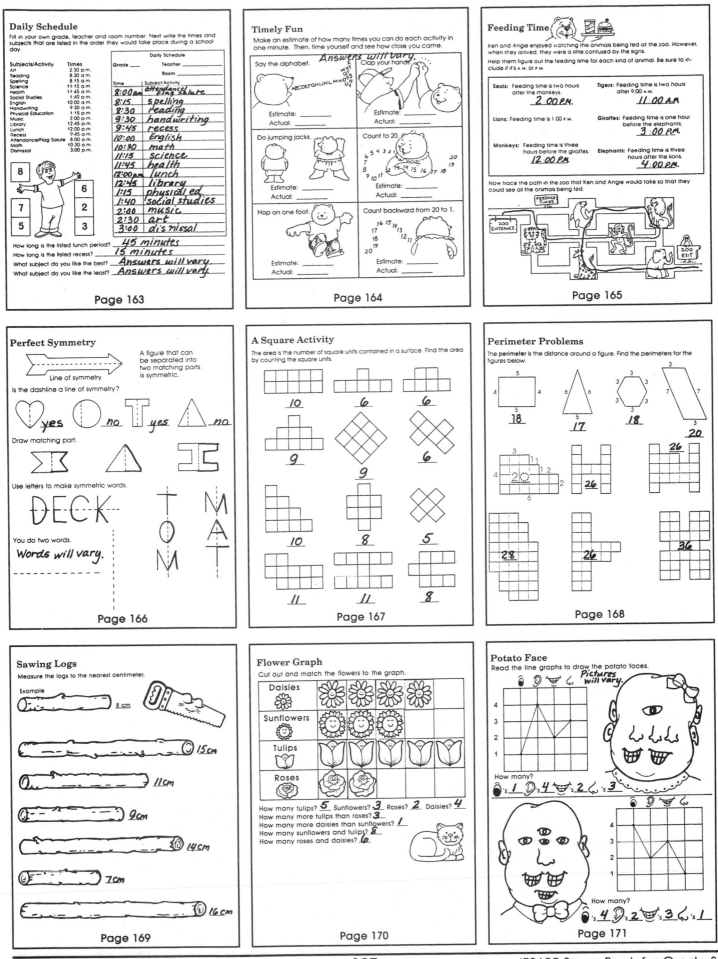

Daily Schedule

Page 163

Fill in your own grade, teacher and room number. Next write the times and subjects that are listed in the order they would take place during a school day

Subjects/Activity	Times
Art	2:30 p.m.
Reading	8:30 a.m.
Spelling	8:15 a.m.
Science	11:15 a.m.
Health	11:45 a.m.
Social Studies	1:40 p.m.
English	10:00 a.m.
Handwriting	9:30 a.m.
Physical Education	1:15 p.m.
Music	2:00 p.m.
Library	12:45 p.m.
Lunch	12:00 p.m.
Recess	9:45 a.m.
Attendance/Flag Salute	8:00 a.m.
Math	10:30 a.m.
Dismissal	3:00 p.m.

Daily Schedule
Grade _____ Teacher _____ Room _____

Time	Subject/Activity
8:00 am	attendance/flag salute
8:15	spelling
8:30	reading
9:30	handwriting
9:45	recess
10:00	English
10:30	math
11:15	science
11:45	health
12:00 pm	lunch
12:45	library
1:15	physical ed.
1:40	social studies
2:00	music
2:30	art
3:00	dismissal

How long is the listed lunch period? 45 minutes
How long is the listed recess? 15 minutes
What subject do you like the best? Answers will vary.
What subject do you like the least? Answers will vary.

Timely Fun

Page 164

Make an estimate of how many times you can do each activity in one minute. Then, time yourself and see how close you came.

Answers will vary.

Say the alphabet. ABCDEFGHIJKLMNOPQRSTUVWXYZ
Estimate: _____ Actual: _____

Clap your hands.
Estimate: _____ Actual: _____

Do jumping jacks.
Estimate: _____ Actual: _____

Count to 20.
Estimate: _____ Actual: _____

Hop on one foot.
Estimate: _____ Actual: _____

Count backward from 20 to 1.
Estimate: _____ Actual: _____

Feeding Time

Page 165

Ken and Angie enjoyed watching the animals being fed at the zoo. However, when they arrived, they were a little confused by the signs.

Help them figure out the feeding time for each kind of animal. Be sure to include if it's A.M. or P.M.

Seals: Feeding time is two hours after the monkeys. **2:00 P.M.**

Tigers: Feeding time is two hours after 9:00 A.M. **11:00 A.M.**

Lions: Feeding time is 1:00 P.M.

Giraffes: Feeding time is one hour before the elephants. **3:00 P.M.**

Monkeys: Feeding time is three hours before the giraffes. **12:00 P.M.**

Elephants: Feeding time is three hours after the lions. **4:00 P.M.**

Now trace the path in the zoo that Ken and Angie would take so that they could see all the animals being fed.

Perfect Symmetry

Page 166

A figure that can be separated into two matching parts is symmetric.

Line of symmetry

Is the dashline a line of symmetry?
yes   no   yes   no

Draw matching part.

Use letters to make symmetric words.
DECK   TOM   MAT

You do two words.
Words will vary.

A Square Activity

Page 167

The area is the number of square units contained in a surface. Find the area by counting the square units.

10   6   6
9   9   6
10   8   5
11   11   8

Perimeter Problems

Page 168

The perimeter is the distance around a figure. Find the perimeters for the figures below.

18   17   18   20
20   26   26
28   26   36

Sawing Logs

Page 169

Measure the logs to the nearest centimeter.

Example — 8 cm
15 cm
11 cm
9 cm
14 cm
7 cm
16 cm

Flower Graph

Page 170

Cut out and match the flowers to the graph.

Daisies				
Sunflowers				
Tulips				
Roses				

How many tulips? 5   Sunflowers? 3   Roses? 2   Daisies? 4
How many more tulips than roses? 3
How many more daisies than sunflowers? 1
How many sunflowers and tulips? 8
How many roses and daisies? 6

Potato Face

Page 171

Read the line graphs to draw the potato faces.

Pictures will vary.

How many? 👂's 1 👃 4 😁 2 👁's 3

How many? 👂's 4 👃 2 😁 3 👁 1

Frog Bubbles

Color the picture.

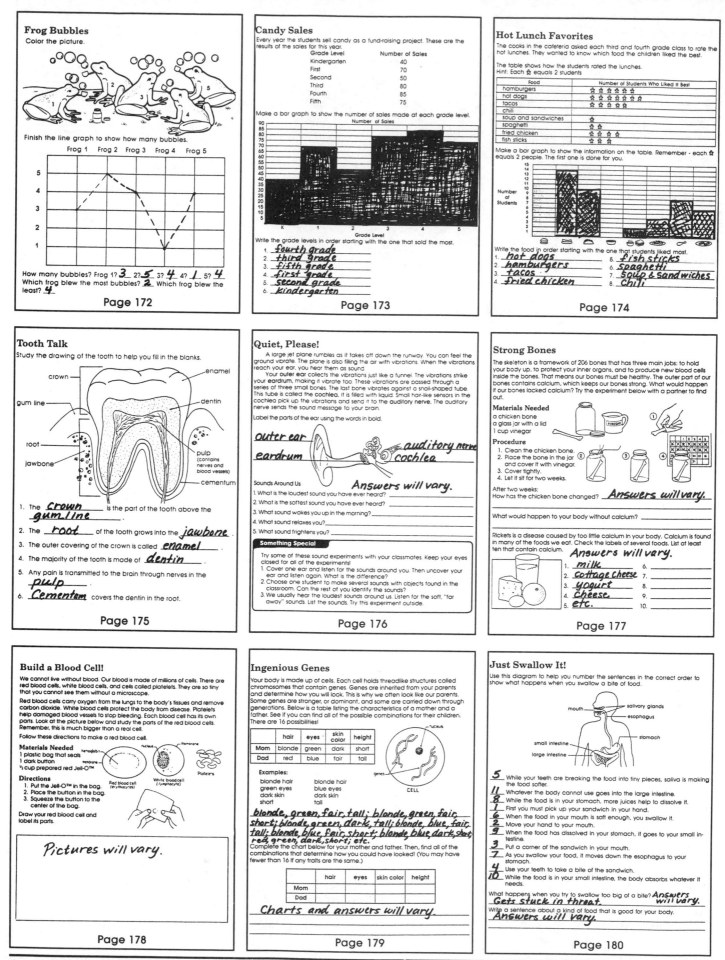

Finish the line graph to show how many bubbles.

Frog 1 Frog 2 Frog 3 Frog 4 Frog 5

How many bubbles? Frog 1? **3** 2? **5** 3? **4** 4? **1** 5? **4**
Which frog blew the most bubbles? **2** Which frog blew the least? **4**

Page 172

Candy Sales

Every year the students sell candy as a fund-raising project. These are the results of the sales for this year.

Grade Level	Number of Sales
Kindergarten	40
First	70
Second	50
Third	80
Fourth	85
Fifth	75

Make a bar graph to show the number of sales made at each grade level.

Write the grade levels in order starting with the one that sold the most.

1. **fourth grade**
2. **third grade**
3. **fifth grade**
4. **first grade**
5. **second grade**
6. **kindergarten**

Page 173

Hot Lunch Favorites

The cooks in the cafeteria asked each third and fourth grade class to rate the hot lunches. They wanted to know which food the children liked the best.

The table shows how the students rated the lunches.
Hint: Each ☆ equals 2 students

Food	Number of Students Who Liked It Best
hamburgers	☆☆☆☆☆
hot dogs	☆☆☆☆☆☆
tacos	☆☆☆☆
chili	
soup and sandwiches	☆
spaghetti	☆☆
fried chicken	☆☆☆
fish sticks	☆☆☆

Make a bar graph to show the information on the table. Remember - each ☆ equals 2 people. The first one is done for you.

Write the food in order starting with the one that students liked most.

1. **hot dogs**   5. **fish sticks**
2. **hamburgers**   6. **spaghetti**
3. **tacos**   7. **soup & sandwiches**
4. **fried chicken**   8. **chili**

Page 174

Tooth Talk

Study the drawing of the tooth to help you fill in the blanks.

1. The **crown** is the part of the tooth above the **gum line**
2. The **root** of the tooth grows into the **jawbone**
3. The outer covering of the crown is called **enamel**
4. The majority of the tooth is made of **dentin**
5. Any pain is transmitted to the brain through nerves in the **pulp**
6. **Cementum** covers the dentin in the root.

Page 175

Quiet, Please!

A large jet plane rumbles as it takes off down the runway. You can feel the ground vibrate. The plane is also filling the air with vibrations. When the vibrations reach your ear, you hear them as sound.

Your outer ear collects the vibrations just like a funnel. The vibrations strike your eardrum, making it vibrate too. These vibrations are passed through a series of three small bones. The last bone vibrates against a snail-shaped tube. This tube is called the cochlea. It is filled with liquid. Small hair-like sensors in the cochlea pick up the vibrations and send it to the auditory nerve. The auditory nerve sends the sound message to your brain.

Label the parts of the ear using the words in bold.

outer ear   **auditory nerve**
eardrum   **cochlea**

Sounds Around Us   **Answers will vary.**
1. What is the loudest sound you have ever heard? _____
2. What is the softest sound you have ever heard? _____
3. What sound wakes you up in the morning? _____
4. What sound relaxes you? _____
5. What sound frightens you? _____

Something Special

Try some of these sound experiments with your classmates. Keep your eyes closed for all of the experiments!
1. Cover one ear and listen for the sounds around you. Then uncover your ear and listen again. What is the difference?
2. Choose one student to make several sounds with objects found in the classroom. Can the rest of you identify the sounds?
3. We usually hear the loudest sounds around us. Listen for the soft, "far away" sounds. List the sounds. Try this experiment outside.

Page 176

Strong Bones

The skeleton is a framework of 206 bones that has three main jobs: to hold your body up, to protect your inner organs, and to produce new blood cells inside the bones. That means our bones must be healthy. The outer part of our bones contains calcium, which keeps our bones strong. What would happen if our bones lacked calcium? Try the experiment below with a partner to find out.

Materials Needed
a chicken bone
a glass jar with a lid
1 cup vinegar

Procedure
1. Clean the chicken bone.
2. Place the bone in the jar and cover it with vinegar.
3. Cover tightly.
4. Let it sit for two weeks.

After two weeks:
How has the chicken bone changed? **Answers will vary.**

What would happen to your body without calcium? _____

Rickets is a disease caused by too little calcium in your body. Calcium is found in many of the foods we eat. Check the labels of several foods. List at least ten that contain calcium. **Answers will vary.**

1. **milk**   6. _____
2. **cottage cheese**   7. _____
3. **yogurt**   8. _____
4. **cheese**   9. _____
5. **etc.**   10. _____

Page 177

Build a Blood Cell!

We cannot live without blood. Our blood is made of millions of cells. There are red blood cells, white blood cells, and cells called platelets. They are so tiny that you cannot see them without a microscope.

Red blood cells carry oxygen from the lungs to the body's tissues and remove carbon dioxide. White blood cells protect the body from disease. Platelets help damaged blood vessels to stop bleeding. Each blood cell has its own parts. Look at the picture below and study the parts of the red blood cells. Remember, this is much bigger than a real cell.

Follow these directions to make a red blood cell.

Materials Needed
1 plastic bag that seals
1 dark button
½ cup prepared red Jell-O™

Directions
1. Put the Jell-O™ in the bag.
2. Place the button in the bag.
3. Squeeze the button to the center of the bag.

Draw your red blood cell and label its parts.

Pictures will vary.

Page 178

Ingenious Genes

Your body is made up of cells. Each cell holds threadlike structures called chromosomes that contain genes. Genes are inherited from your parents and determine how you will look. This is why we look like our parents. Some genes are stronger, or dominant, and some are carried down through generations. Below is a table listing the characteristics of a mother and a father. See if you can find all of the possible combinations for their children. There are 16 possibilities!

	hair	eyes	skin color	height
Mom	blonde	green	dark	short
Dad	red	blue	fair	tall

Examples:

blonde hair   blonde hair
green eyes   blue eyes
dark skin   dark skin
short   tall

blonde, green, fair, tall; blonde, green, fair, short; blonde, green, dark, tall; blonde, blue, fair, tall; blonde, blue, fair, short; red, green, dark, short; etc.

Complete the chart below for your mother and father. Then, find all of the combinations that determine how you could have looked! (You may have fewer than 16 if any traits are the same.)

	hair	eyes	skin color	height
Mom				
Dad				

Charts and answers will vary.

Page 179

Just Swallow It!

Use this diagram to help you number the sentences in the correct order to show what happens when you swallow a bite of food.

5 While your teeth are breaking the food into tiny pieces, saliva is making the food softer.
11 Whatever the body cannot use goes into the large intestine.
8 While the food is in your stomach, more juices help to dissolve it.
1 First you must pick up your sandwich in your hand.
6 When the food in your mouth is soft enough, you swallow it.
2 Move your hand to your mouth.
9 When the food has dissolved in your stomach, it goes to your small intestine.
3 Put a corner of the sandwich in your mouth.
7 As you swallow your food, it moves down the esophagus to your stomach.
4 Use your teeth to take a bite of the sandwich.
10 While the food is in your small intestine, the body absorbs whatever it needs.

What happens when you try to swallow too big of a bite? **Answers will vary.**
Gets stuck in throat.

Write a sentence about a kind of food that is good for your body.
Answers will vary.

Page 180

Going Around in Circles!

The circulatory system is responsible for moving blood throughout your body. It is blood that carries food and oxygen to your body's cells and carries away carbon dioxide and other wastes. This system also carries disease-fighting substances that help prevent you from getting sick.

The main components of your body's circulatory system are: the heart, blood vessels, blood, and the lymphatic system. Your heart controls this system.

The heart is responsible for sending blood mixed with oxygen to the rest of your body through blood vessels called arteries. Blood vessels called veins return blood to your heart. Your veins look blue because the blood in them has no oxygen. Back toward the heart, the blood gathers more oxygen as it passes through your lungs and becomes red. This cycle occurs about one time every minute. It is your heart's constant pumping that keeps your blood circulating.

Use the information above to solve the puzzle.

Across
2. The **heart** controls the circulatory system.
4. Blood without oxygen is **blue**.
6. Arteries carry blood mixed with **oxygen** from the heart to the rest of your body.
7. **Veins** carry blood to the heart.

Down
1. **Arteries** carry blood away from the heart.
3. Blood is **red** when it contains oxygen.
5. Blood gets oxygen from your **lungs**.

Page 181

Backbone or No Backbone?

Which part of your body helps you stand tall or sit up straight? It is your backbone. You are a member of a large group of animals that all have backbones. Animals with backbones are called vertebrates. Birds, fish, reptiles, amphibians, and mammals are all vertebrates.

Some animals do not have backbones. These animals are called invertebrates. Worms, centipedes, and insects are all invertebrates.

Classifying
Find the five vertebrates and five invertebrates hidden in the wordsearch. Then write them in the correct group.

Invertebrates
1. beetle
2. worm
3. spider
4. fly
5. moth

Vertebrates
1. lion
2. giraffe
3. whale
4. rabbit
5. frog

Your neighborhood has many animals in or near it. Add their names to the lists.

Invertebrates / **Vertebrates**
6. Answers will vary.
7.
8.
9.
10.

Find Out
There are many more invertebrates than vertebrates. Nine out of ten animals is an invertebrate. Which group has the largest animals? Which group has the smallest animals?

Page 182

Insects in Winter

In the summertime, insects can be seen buzzing and fluttering around us. But as winter's cold weather begins, suddenly the insects seem to disappear. Do you know where they go?

Many insects, such as flies and mosquitoes, find a warm place to spend the winter. They live in cellars, barns, attics, caves and tree holes.

Beetles and ants try to dig deep into the ground. Some beetles stack up in piles under rocks or dead leaves.

In the fall, female grasshoppers and crickets lay their eggs and die. The eggs hatch in the spring.

Bees also try to protect themselves from the winter cold. Honeybees gather in a ball in the middle of their hive. The bees stay in this tight ball trying to stay warm.

Winter is very hard for insects, but each spring the survivors come out and the buzzing and fluttering begins again.

Write.
When cold weather begins, **insects** seem to disappear.

Unscramble and check.
Mosquitoes and **flies** find a warm place in:
☐ beds ☑ barns ☑ caves ☑ cellars ☑ attics ☐ sweaters

Circle Yes or No.
In the winter, insects look for a warm place to live. **Yes** No
Noise, such as buzzing, can be heard all winter long. Yes **No**
Some beetles and ants dig deep into the ground. **Yes** No
Every insect finds a warm home for the winter. Yes **No**
Crickets and grasshoppers lay their eggs and die. **Yes** No
The honeybees gather in a ball in their hive. **Yes** No
Survivors of the cold weather come out each spring. **Yes** No

Page 183

Six-Legged Friends

The largest group of animals belongs to the group called invertebrates—or animals without backbones. This large group is the insect group.

Insects are easy to tell apart from other animals. Adult insects have three body parts and six legs. The first body part is the head. On the head are the mouth, eyes, and antennae. The second body part is the thorax. On it are the legs and wings. The third part is the abdomen. On it are small openings for breathing.

Color the body parts of the insect above.
head-red, thorax-yellow, abdomen-blue

Draw an insect below. Make your insect a one-of-a-kind. Be sure it has the correct number of body parts, legs, wings, and antennae. Fill in the information.

Pictures and answers will vary.

Insect's name _____
Length _____
Where found _____
Food _____
Warning: _____

Find Out
Many people think that spiders are insects. Spiders and insects are alike in many ways, but spiders are not insects. Find out how the two are different.

Page 184

Go Bats for Bats

Bats live all over the world. The bats found in the rainforest play an important role because they control insects and pollinate and disperse seeds for avocados, bananas, cashews, figs, peaches and other fruits. However, the bats that live in the rainforest are in danger due to the increasing destruction of their habitat. This could mean that our supply of fruits, nuts and spices could decrease and possibly vanish if the destruction continues. Read the description of each bat below. Notice how each one is different and has special features to suit its survive. Put the letter of each description next to the bat it describes and the bat's food.

A. Notice the long nose and tongue this bat uses to dip into the durian blossom.
B. This bat's large ears and nose flap enable it to locate insects at night.
C. With its long feet and claws, this bat captures certain small prey.
D. The long snout on this bat helps it eat fruit like figs.

Once you have matched up the bats and their food, cut all the pictures apart. Glue each bat to a piece of construction paper. Glue the food it eats to the back. Punch a hole in each piece of construction paper. Put a piece of string through each piece of paper and tie the bats to a hanger. Now, you have a bat mobile to hang from the ceiling.

Page 185

A Sampling of Snakes

The Snake House is a very popular place to visit at the zoo. There are many different types and sizes of snakes. Some snakes are poisonous while others are not. Some snakes are harmless to most creatures, and some are very dangerous.

The five snakes described here are held in the cages below.

Decide which snake belongs in each cage by using the clues given here and beneath the boxes. Then write each name in the correct cage.

The King Cobra is the longest poisonous snake in the world. One of these snakes measured almost 19 feet long. It comes from southeast Asia and the Philippines.

The Gaboon Viper, a very poisonous snake, has the longest fangs of all snakes (nearly 2 inches). It comes from tropical Africa.

The Reticulated Python is the longest snake of all. One specimen measured 32 feet 9½ inches. It comes from southeast Asia, Indonesia, and the Philippines. It crushes its prey to death.

The Black Mamba, the fastest-moving land snake, can move at speeds of 10-12 m.p.h. It lives in the eastern part of tropical Africa.

The Anaconda is almost twice as heavy as a reticulated python of the same length. One anaconda that was almost 28 feet long weighed nearly 500 pounds.

#1 Anaconda #2 King Cobra #3 Ret. Python #4 Gaboon Viper #5 Black Mamba

Clues:
- The snake in cage #5 moves the fastest on land.
- The longest snake of all is between the snake that comes from tropical Africa and the longest poisonous snake.
- The very heavy snake is to the left of the longest poisonous snake.

Page 186

From Egg to Tadpole to Frog

The poem below tells about the changes that occur in frogs during their life cycles. In every line, there is one word that doesn't make sense. Find the correct word in the Word Bank and write it in the puzzle. Hint: The correct word rhymes with it.

The Life Cycle of a Frog

There is jelly on the legs (13)
To protect the entire match. (11)
It takes tree to twenty-five days (7↓)
Until they're ready to catch. (5)

Out comes a polliwog (18)
When the time is just bright. (8)
It breathes using hills (14)
And its size is very light. (4)

It loses its long scale (9)
After pegs begin to grow. (1)
Digestion and breathing strange (12)
In a process fast and glow. (2)

What helps a frog to seethe (3)
Is its thin and moist chin. (6↓)
It also uses rungs (15)
To let the hair in. (10)

Some frogs can skim like a duck (6→)
And some can mop like a rabbit. (16)
Others climb bees like a squirrel (7→)
Which may seem a bunny habit. (17)

Word Bank
lungs, eggs, right, hatch, funny, tail, slow, change, legs, trees, slight, breathe, gills, skin, hop, three, swim, polliwog, batch

Page 187

The Mighty Bear

Bears are large and powerful animals. Depending on the type of bear, they can weigh from 60 to 2,000 pounds.

Listed below are four different kinds of bears. The lengths of these bears are 3 feet, 5 feet, 8 feet, and 9 feet. Use the clues to match each bear to its length. Write the answers in the blanks.

Clues:

Alaskan brown bear + American black bear = 14 feet

Polar bear + Alaskan brown bear = 17 feet

American black bear + Sun bear = 8 feet

The Alaskan brown bear is **9** feet in length.
The American black bear is **5** feet in length.
The polar bear is **8** feet in length.
The sun bear is **3** feet in length.

Page 188

Toadly Froggin' Around

Harry and Song Lee loved frogs and similar creatures. Read the information about frogs and toads. Then write true or false in front of each statement.

Frogs and Toads

Both frogs and toads are amphibians. Amphibians spend part of their lives as water animals and part as land animals. In the early stages of their lives, amphibians breathe through gills, while as adults they develop lungs. Most amphibians lay eggs near water. Newly hatched frogs and toads both have tails that they later lose. Both often have poison glands in their skin to protect them from their enemies.

Frogs and toads are different in several ways. Most toads are broader, darker, and flatter. Their skin is drier. Toads are usually covered with warts while frogs have smooth skin. Most toads live on land while most frogs prefer being in or near the water.

true 1. Both frogs and toads usually lay eggs near water.
false 2. Most frogs have drier skin than toads.
false 3. Very young amphibians breathe with lungs.
true 4. Frogs tend to be lighter in color.
false 5. An adult frog's tail helps support him while sitting.
true 6. Poison glands often protect frogs from an enemy.
true 7. A toad's skin is often bumpy.
true 8. Frogs and toads are both amphibians.

Page 189

A Re-Appearing Act

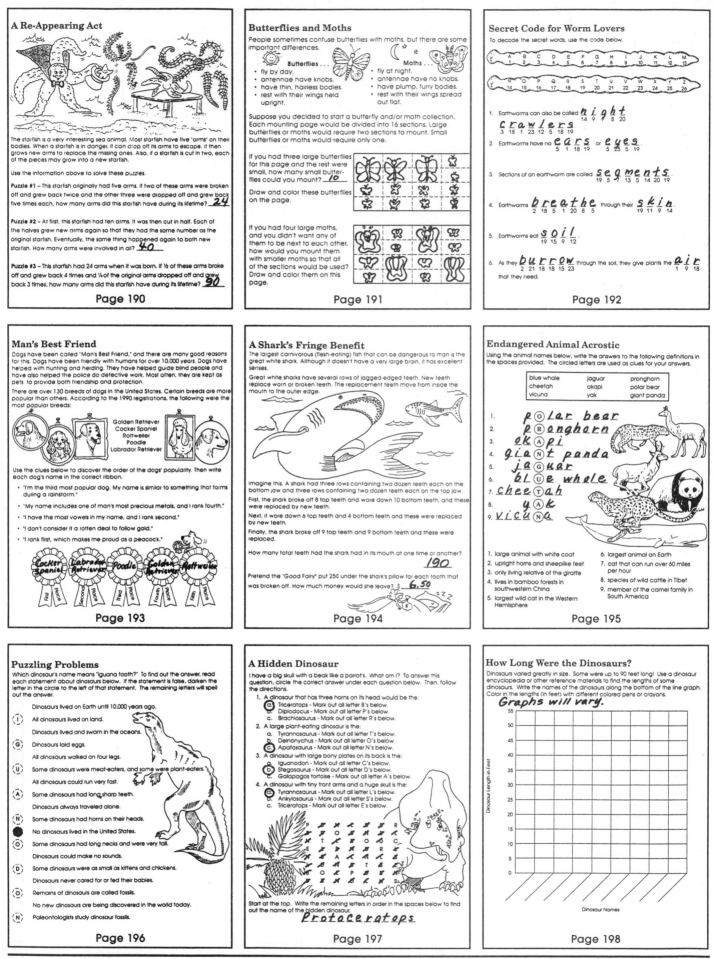

The starfish is a very interesting sea animal. Most starfish have five "arms" on their bodies. When a starfish is in danger, it can drop off its arms to escape. It then grows new arms to replace the missing ones. Also, if a starfish is cut in two, each of the pieces may grow into a new starfish.

Use the information above to solve these puzzles.

Puzzle #1 – This starfish originally had five arms. If two of these arms were broken off and grew back twice and the other three were dropped off and grew back five times each, how many arms did this starfish have during its lifetime? __24__

Puzzle #2 – At first, this starfish had ten arms. It was then cut in half. Each of the halves grew new arms again so that they had the same number as the original starfish. Eventually, the same thing happened again to both new starfish. How many arms were involved in all? __40__

Puzzle #3 – This starfish had 24 arms when it was born. If ½ of these arms broke off and grew back 4 times and ¼ of the original arms dropped off and grew back 3 times, how many arms did this starfish have during its lifetime? __90__

Page 190

Butterflies and Moths

People sometimes confuse butterflies with moths, but there are some important differences.

Butterflies . . .
- fly by day.
- antennae have knobs.
- have thin, hairless bodies.
- rest with their wings held upright.

Moths . . .
- fly at night.
- antennae have no knobs.
- have plump, furry bodies.
- rest with their wings spread out flat.

Suppose you decided to start a butterfly and/or moth collection. Each mounting page would be divided into 16 sections. Large butterflies or moths would require two sections to mount. Small butterflies or moths would require only one.

If you had three large butterflies for this page and the rest were small, how many small butterflies could you mount? __10__

Draw and color these butterflies on the page.

If you had four large moths, and you didn't want any of them to be next to each other, how would you mount them with smaller moths so that all of the sections would be used? Draw and color them on this page.

Page 191

Secret Code for Worm Lovers

To decode the secret words, use the code below.

A	B	C	D	E	F	G	H	I	J	K	L	M
1	2	3	4	5	6	7	8	9	10	11	12	13

N	O	P	Q	R	S	T	U	V	W	X	Y	Z
14	15	16	17	18	19	20	21	22	23	24	25	26

1. Earthworms can also be called __n i g h t__ (14 9 7 8 20) __c r a w l e r s__ (3 18 1 23 12 5 18 19)

2. Earthworms have no __e a r s__ (5 1 18 19) or __e y e s__ (5 25 5 19)

3. Sections of an earthworm are called __s e g m e n t s__ (19 5 7 13 5 14 20 19)

4. Earthworms __b r e a t h e__ (2 18 5 1 20 8 5) through their __s k i n__ (19 11 9 14)

5. Earthworms eat __s o i l__ (19 15 9 12)

6. As they __b u r r o w__ (2 21 18 18 15 23) through the soil, they give plants the __a i r__ (1 9 18) that they need.

Page 192

Man's Best Friend

Dogs have been called "Man's Best Friend," and there are many good reasons for this. Dogs have been friendly with humans for over 10,000 years. Dogs have helped with hunting and herding. They have helped guide blind people and have also helped the police do detective work. Most often, they are kept as pets to provide both friendship and protection.

There are over 130 breeds of dogs in the United States. Certain breeds are more popular than others. According to the 1990 registrations, the following were the most popular breeds:

Golden Retriever
Cocker Spaniel
Rottweiler
Poodle
Labrador Retriever

Use the clues below to discover the order of the dogs' popularity. Then write each dog's name in the correct ribbon.

- "I'm the third most popular dog. My name is similar to something that forms during a rainstorm."
- "My name includes one of man's most precious metals, and I rank fourth."
- "I have the most vowels in my name, and I rank second."
- "I don't consider it a rotten deal to follow gold."
- "I rank first, which makes me proud as a peacock."

Cocker Spaniel (First) Labrador Retriever (Second) Poodle (Third) Golden Retriever (Fourth) Rottweiler (Fifth)

Page 193

A Shark's Fringe Benefit

The largest carnivorous (flesh-eating) fish that can be dangerous to man is the great white shark. Although it doesn't have a very large brain, it has excellent senses.

Great white sharks have several rows of jagged-edged teeth. New teeth replace worn or broken teeth. The replacement teeth move from inside the mouth to the outer edge.

Imagine this. A shark had three rows containing two dozen teeth each on the bottom jaw and three rows containing two dozen teeth each on the top jaw.

First, the shark broke off 8 top teeth and wore down 10 bottom teeth, and these were replaced by new teeth.

Next, he wore down 6 top teeth and 4 bottom teeth and these were replaced by new teeth.

Finally, the shark broke off 9 top teeth and 9 bottom teeth and these were replaced.

How many total teeth had the shark had in its mouth at one time or another? __190__

Pretend the "Good Fairy" put 25¢ under the shark's pillow for each tooth that was broken off. How much money would she leave? $ __6.50__

Page 194

Endangered Animal Acrostic

Using the animal names below, write the answers to the following definitions in the spaces provided. The circled letters are used as clues for your answers.

blue whale	jaguar	pronghorn
cheetah	okapi	polar bear
vicuna	yak	giant panda

1. p(o)lar bear
2. p(r)onghorn
3. ok(a)pi
4. gian(t) panda
5. (j)aguar
6. bl(u)e whale
7. chee(t)ah
8. (y)ak
9. vicu(n)a

1. large animal with white coat
2. upright horns and sheeplike feet
3. only living relative of the giraffe
4. lives in bamboo forests in southwestern China
5. largest wild cat in the Western Hemisphere
6. largest animal on Earth
7. cat that can run over 60 miles per hour
8. species of wild cattle in Tibet
9. member of the camel family in South America

Page 195

Puzzling Problems

Which dinosaur's name means "iguana tooth?" To find out the answer, read each statement about dinosaurs below. If the statement is false, darken the letter in the circle to the left of that statement. The remaining letters will spell out the answer.

Dinosaurs lived on Earth until 10,000 years ago.

(I) All dinosaurs lived on land.

(G) Dinosaurs lived and swam in the oceans.

Dinosaurs laid eggs.

(U) All dinosaurs walked on four legs.

Some dinosaurs were meat-eaters, and some were plant-eaters.

(A) All dinosaurs could run very fast.

Some dinosaurs had long, sharp teeth.

Dinosaurs always traveled alone.

(N) Some dinosaurs had horns on their heads.

● No dinosaurs lived in the United States.

(O) Some dinosaurs had long necks and were very tall.

Dinosaurs could make no sounds.

(D) Some dinosaurs were as small as kittens and chickens.

Dinosaurs never cared for or fed their babies.

(O) Remains of dinosaurs are called fossils.

No new dinosaurs are being discovered in the world today.

(N) Paleontologists study dinosaur fossils.

Page 196

A Hidden Dinosaur

I have a big skull with a beak like a parrot's. What am I? To answer this question, circle the correct answer under each question below. Then, follow the directions.

1. A dinosaur that has three horns on its head would be the:
   a. Triceratops - Mark out all letter B's below.
   b. Diplodocus - Mark out all letter P's below.
   c. Brachiosaurus - Mark out all letter R's below.

2. A large plant-eating dinosaur is the:
   a. Tyrannosaurus - Mark out all letter T's below.
   b. Deinonychus - Mark out all letter O's below.
   c. Apatosaurus - Mark out all letter N's below.

3. A dinosaur with large bony plates on its back is the:
   a. Iguanodon - Mark out all letter C's below.
   b. Stegosaurus - Mark out all letter D's below.
   c. Galapagos tortoise - Mark out all letter A's below.

4. A dinosaur with tiny front arms and a huge skull is the:
   a. Tyrannosaurus - Mark out all letter L's below.
   b. Ankylosaurus - Mark out all letter S's below.
   c. Triceratops - Mark out all letter E's below.

Start at the top. Write the remaining letters in order in the spaces below to find out the name of the hidden dinosaur.

__Protoceratops__

Page 197

How Long Were the Dinosaurs?

Dinosaurs varied greatly in size. Some were up to 90 feet long! Use a dinosaur encyclopedia or other reference materials to find the lengths of some dinosaurs. Write the names of the dinosaurs along the bottom of the line graph. Color in the lengths (in feet) with different colored pens or crayons.

Graphs will vary.

(Vertical axis: Dinosaur Length in Feet — 5, 10, 15, 20, 25, 30, 35, 40, 45, 50, 55)

Dinosaur Names

Page 198

Dinosaur Diagram

A Venn diagram is a great tool to use to compare things. Use the one below to compare two dinosaurs. Fill in the Iguanodon with characteristics common only to it. Fill in the Triceratops with characteristics common only to the Triceratops. Above Same, write characteristics that both dinosaurs share. Write a story about your findings on the lines below.

Answers will vary.
about 30 ft. long
lived during period Cretaceous
plant-eater
no horns
walked on 2 legs
3 horns
walked on 4 legs

Different   Same   Different

Stories will vary

Page 199

A Dinosaur Tale

Study the dinosaurs illustrated below. Then complete each category with words that you associate with these animals. A few examples are already written under each heading. Use the words to compose a poem or short story about these dinosaurs. You can write your own composition or poem or you can share your ideas with other students and write a group composition or poem. Read your work aloud. *Words will vary.*

Nouns	Verbs	Adjectives
tail	walk	huge
teeth	run	spiked
head	eat	sharp

Title: _____

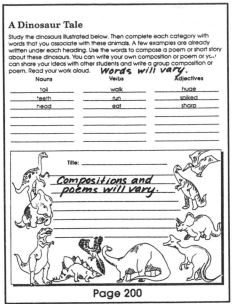

Compositions and poems will vary.

Page 200

Get a Clue!

Get a Clue! is a fun way to gain information about dinosaurs. To play, read the 16 clues below about a certain dinosaur. Use your science book or other resource materials and your own logical thinking to guess the name of the dinosaur. When you are finished, write your own clues about another dinosaur. Give it to another student to see if he/she can guess the answer.

I am a dinosaur.
1. My name means "three-horned face."
2. My skull is 7 or 8 feet long.
3. I have a beaked mouth like a parrot.
4. I eat plants.
5. I walk on all four legs.
6. I am 30 feet long.
7. I weigh up to 10 tons.
8. I am one of the last dinosaurs to live.
9. I have 3 claws on my front feet.
10. I live in Canada and the U.S.
11. I have a thick neck frill.
12. I have 3 horns on my skull.
13. I am the best-known horned dinosaur.
14. I use my horns for protection.
15. I have a small hoof on each toe.
16. I was named by O. C. Marsh in 1889.

I am a *triceratops*.

Clues will vary.
I am a dinosaur.
1. _____   6. _____
2. _____   7. _____
3. _____   8. _____
4. _____   9. _____
5. _____   10. _____
I am a _____.

Page 201

The End of the Dinosaurs

What could have killed all the dinosaurs? Scientists are not really sure. They have many different theories, or explanations, for why the dinosaurs died out.

Several theories are listed below. Each theory has a cause and an effect. A cause is "a change that happened on earth" and an effect is "what resulted from the change on earth." Draw a line from each cause to its effect.

Cause
- A huge meteor hit the earth, starting fires and making a thick cloud of dust and smoke that covered the earth.
- Small, fast mammals that liked to eat eggs quickly spread around the world.
- New kinds of flowering plants started to grow on the earth. These plants had poison in them that the dinosaurs could not taste.
- When dinosaurs were living, the earth was warm all year long. Suddenly the earth became cooler with cold winter months.

Effect
- Dinosaurs were cold-blooded and they couldn't find places to hibernate. They had no fur or feathers to keep them warm. They froze to death.
- The sunlight was blocked and plants couldn't grow. The dinosaurs starved to death.
- Fewer and fewer baby dinosaurs were born.
- The dinosaurs ate poison without even knowing it and they died.

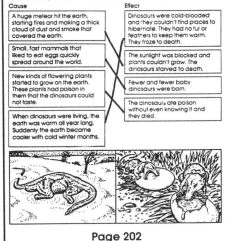

Page 202

Animal Mysteries

As long as people have studied animals, there have been mysteries about why animals act in certain ways.

One mystery has to do with some animals' strange behavior **before** earthquakes. Horse and cattle stampedes, screeching seabirds, howling dogs, even animals coming out of hibernation early, are examples of this mysterious behavior.

Another mystery involves birds and ants. No one can explain why a bird will pick up an ant in its beak and rub the ant over its feathers again and again. This is called "anting," and birds have been known to do this for an hour without stopping.

One animal mystery is very sad. For hundreds of years, some whales have mysteriously swam from the ocean onto a beach where they would die. Reports of "beached whales" occur about five times a year somewhere in the world.

There are hundreds of other animal mysteries—such as how and why animals hibernate—that scientists have not solved. Can you think of another animal mystery?

3 Animal Mysteries

Write.
1. Some animals act strangely before an *earthquake*.
Check.
This strange behavior includes: ☐ laughing birds ☑ howling dogs
☑ horse and cattle stampedes ☐ barking whales
☑ leaving hibernation early ☑ screeching seabirds
Write.
2. This mystery is about *birds* rubbing *ants* over their feathers.
Write.
3. A sad mystery is about *whales* swimming onto a *beach* and dying.
• Write a solution to one of the animal mysteries.

Page 203

Hibernation

Have you ever wondered why some animals hibernate? Hibernation is a long sleep that some animals go into for the winter.

Animals get their warmth and energy from food. Some animals cannot find enough food in the winter. They must eat large amounts of food in the fall. Their bodies store this food as fat. Then in winter, they sleep in hibernation. Their bodies live on the stored fat. Since their bodies need much less food during hibernation, they can stay alive without eating new food during the winter.

Some animals that hibernate are: bats, chipmunks, bears, snakes and turtles.

Underline.
Hibernation ___ is a sleep that some animals go into for the winter.
___ is the time of year to gather food for the winter.

Yes or No.
Animals get their warmth and energy from food.   Yes No
Animals cannot find enough food in the winter.   Yes No
Animals hibernate because they are lazy.   Yes No
Animals need less food while they are hibernating.   Yes No

Match.
Animals that hibernate . . .
eat and store food   in the winter.
go to sleep   in the fall.

Color the animals that hibernate.

Page 204

Rain in the Rainforest

At least 80 inches of rain falls and thundershowers may occur for 200 or more days each year in a rainforest. Rainforests need a lot of rain so that the plants native to them do not dry out. Fill in the precipitation graph below with the average rainfall of a typical tropical rainforest. The amounts are listed beneath the graph.

Month	0 2 4 6 8 10 12 14 16 18 20 22 24 26 28 30
JANUARY	
FEBRUARY	
MARCH	
APRIL	
MAY	
JUNE	
JULY	
AUGUST	
SEPTEMBER	
OCTOBER	
NOVEMBER	
DECEMBER	

J F M A M J J A S O N D
24" 20" 13" 11" 10" 7" 8" 9" 9" 11" 14" 18"

What was the total rainfall for the year in this rainforest? *154"*
What is the total rainfall for a year in your area? _____

Page 205

Lightning

Lightning is a flash of light caused by electricity in the sky. Clouds are made of many water droplets. All of these droplets together contain a large electrical charge. Sometimes these clouds set off a huge spark of electricity called lightning. Lightning travels very fast. As it cuts through the air, it can cause thunder.

Lightning takes various forms. Some lightning looks like a zigzag in the sky. Sheet lightning spreads and lights the sky. Ball lightning looks like a ball of fire.

1 - ball
2 - sheet
3 - zigzag

Underline.
Lightning is a flash of light caused by sunshine.
caused by electricity in the sky.

Yes or No
Sometimes clouds set off a huge spark of electricity.   Yes No
Lightning is caused by dry weather.   Yes No
Lightning travels very fast.   Yes No
Lightning can cause thunder.   Yes No

Unscramble and write in the puzzle above.

1 - *ball*   2 - *sheet*   3 - *zigzag*
   labl   tehse   gglzaq
   3214   53214   352104

• Draw a picture of a sky with the three kinds of lightning.

Page 206

A Funnel Cloud—Danger!

Did you know that a tornado is the most violent windstorm on Earth? A tornado is a whirling, twisting storm that is shaped like a funnel.

A tornado usually occurs in the spring on a hot day. It begins with thunderclouds and thunder. A cloud becomes very dark. The bottom of the cloud begins to twist and form a funnel. Rain and lightning begin. The funnel cloud drops from the dark storm clouds. It moves down toward the ground.

A tornado is very dangerous. It can destroy almost everything in its path.

Circle.
A (tornado) is the most violent windstorm on Earth.

Check.
Which words describe a tornado?
☑ whirling ☑ twisting ☐ icy ☑ funnel-shaped ☑ dangerous

Underline.
A funnel shape is: ◯ ▢ ⬭ ▽ ⤬

Write and Circle.
A tornado usually occurs in the *spring* on a (cool/hot) day.

Write 1-2-3 below and in the picture above.
3 The funnel cloud drops down to the ground.
1 A tornado begins with dark thunderclouds.
2 The dark clouds begin to twist and form a funnel.

Page 207

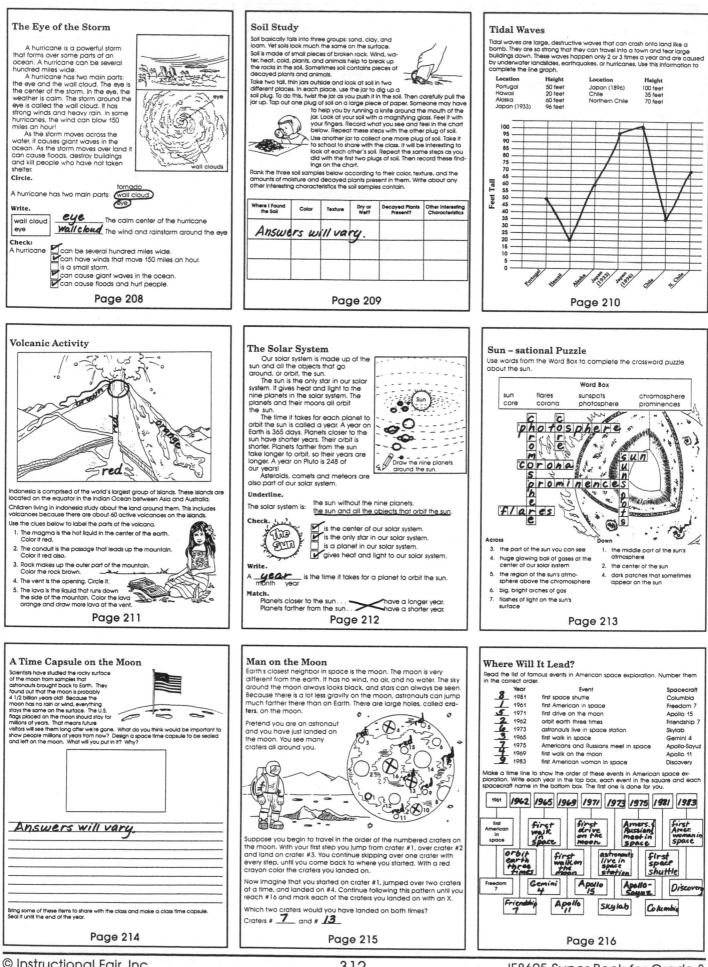

The Eye of the Storm

A hurricane is a powerful storm that forms over some parts of an ocean. A hurricane can be several hundred miles wide.

A hurricane has two main parts: the eye and the wall cloud. The eye is the center of the storm. In the eye, the weather is calm. The storm around the eye is called the wall cloud. It has strong winds and heavy rain. In some hurricanes, the wind can blow 150 miles an hour!

As the storm moves across the water, it causes giant waves in the ocean. As the storm moves over land it can cause floods, destroy buildings and kill people who have not taken shelter.

Circle.

A hurricane has two main parts: tornado (wall cloud) (eye)

Write.

wall cloud / eye

eye The calm center of the hurricane
wall cloud The wind and rainstorm around the eye

Check:

A hurricane

☑ can be several hundred miles wide.
☑ can have winds that move 150 miles an hour.
☐ is a small storm.
☑ can cause giant waves in the ocean.
☑ can cause floods and hurt people.

Page 208

Soil Study

Soil basically falls into three groups: sand, clay, and loam. Yet soils look much the same on the surface.
Soil is made of small pieces of broken rock. Wind, water, heat, cold, plants, and animals help to break up the rocks in the soil. Sometimes soil contains pieces of decayed plants and animals.
Take two tall, thin jars outside and look at soil in two different places. In each place, use the jar to dig up a soil plug. To do this, twist the jar as you push it in the soil. Then carefully pull the jar up. Tap out one plug of soil on a large piece of paper. Someone may have to help you by running a knife around the mouth of the jar. Look at your soil with a magnifying glass. Feel it with your fingers. Record what you see and feel in the chart below. Repeat these steps with the other plug of soil.
Use another jar to collect one more plug of soil. Take it to school to share with the class. It will be interesting to look at each other's soil. Repeat the same steps as you did with the first two plugs of soil. Then record these findings on the chart.
Rank the three soil samples below according to their color, texture, and the amounts of moisture and decayed plants present in them. Write about any other interesting characteristics the soil samples contain.

Where I Found the Soil	Color	Texture	Dry or Wet?	Decayed Plants Present?	Other Interesting Characteristics
Answers will vary.					

Page 209

Tidal Waves

Tidal waves are large, destructive waves that can crash onto land like a bomb. They are so strong that they can travel into a town and tear large buildings down. These waves happen only 2 or 3 times a year and are caused by underwater landslides, earthquakes, or hurricanes. Use this information to complete the line graph.

Location	Height	Location	Height
Portugal	50 feet	Japan (1896)	100 feet
Hawaii	20 feet	Chile	35 feet
Alaska	60 feet	Northern Chile	70 feet
Japan (1933)	96 feet		

Page 210

Volcanic Activity

Indonesia is comprised of the world's largest group of islands. These islands are located on the equator in the Indian Ocean between Asia and Australia.

Children living in Indonesia study about the land around them. This includes volcanoes because there are about 60 active volcanoes on the islands.

Use the clues below to label the parts of the volcano.

1. The magma is the hot liquid in the center of the earth. Color it red.
2. The conduit is the passage that leads up the mountain. Color it red also.
3. Rock makes up the outer part of the mountain. Color the rock brown.
4. The vent is the opening. Circle it.
5. The lava is the liquid that runs down the side of the mountain. Color the lava orange and draw more lava at the vent.

Page 211

The Solar System

Our solar system is made up of the sun and all the objects that go around, or orbit, the sun.

The sun is the only star in our solar system. It gives heat and light to the nine planets in the solar system. The planets and their moons all orbit the sun.

The time it takes for each planet to orbit the sun is called a year. A year on Earth is 365 days. Planets closer to the sun have shorter years. Their orbit is shorter. Planets farther from the sun take longer to orbit, so their years are longer. A year on Pluto is 248 of our years!

Asteroids, comets and meteors are also part of our solar system.

Draw the nine planets around the sun.

Underline.

The solar system is: the sun without the nine planets.
<u>the sun and all the objects that orbit the sun.</u>

Check.

☑ is the center of our solar system.
☑ is the only star in our solar system.
☐ is a planet in our solar system.
☑ gives heat and light to our solar system.

Write.

A *year* is the time it takes for a planet to orbit the sun.
month / year

Match.

Planets closer to the sun . . . have a longer year.
Planets farther from the sun . . . have a shorter year.

Page 212

Sun – sational Puzzle

Use words from the Word Box to complete the crossword puzzle about the sun.

Word Box

sun	flares	sunspots	chromosphere
core	corona	photosphere	prominences

Answers (filled in grid): photosphere, corona, sun, sunspots, prominences, flares, chromosphere, core

Across

3. the part of the sun you can see
4. huge glowing ball of gases at the center of our solar system
5. the region of the sun's atmosphere above the chromosphere
6. big, bright arches of gas
7. flashes of light on the sun's surface

Down

1. the middle part of the sun's atmosphere
2. the center of the sun
4. dark patches that sometimes appear on the sun

Page 213

A Time Capsule on the Moon

Scientists have studied the rocky surface of the moon from samples that astronauts brought back to Earth. They found out that the moon is probably 4 1/2 billion years old. Because the moon has no rain or wind, everything stays the same on the surface. The U.S. flags placed on the moon should stay for millions of years. That means future visitors will see them long after we're gone. What do you think would be important to show people millions of years from now? Design a space time capsule to be sealed and left on the moon. What will you put in it? Why?

Answers will vary.

Bring some of these items to share with the class and make a class time capsule. Seal it until the end of the year.

Page 214

Man on the Moon

Earth's closest neighbor in space is the moon. The moon is very different from the earth. It has no wind, no air, and no water. The sky around the moon always looks black, and stars can always be seen. Because there is a lot less gravity on the moon, astronauts can jump much farther there than on Earth. There are large holes, called craters, on the moon.

Pretend you are an astronaut and you have just landed on the moon. You see many craters all around you.

Suppose you begin to travel in the order of the numbered craters on the moon. With your first step you jump from crater #1, over crater #2 and land on crater #3. You continue skipping over one crater with every step, until you come back to where you started. With a red crayon color the craters you landed on.

Now imagine that you started on crater #1, jumped over two craters at a time, and landed on #4. Continue following this pattern until you reach #16 and mark each of the craters you landed on with an X.

Which two craters would you have landed on both times?

Craters # _7_ and # _13_

Page 215

Where Will It Lead?

Read the list of famous events in American space exploration. Number them in the correct order.

	Year	Event	Spacecraft
8	1981	first space shuttle	Columbia
1	1961	first American in space	Freedom 7
5	1971	first drive on the moon	Apollo 15
2	1962	orbit earth three times	Friendship 7
6	1973	astronauts live in space station	Skylab
3	1965	first walk in space	Gemini 4
7	1975	Americans and Russians meet in space	Apollo-Soyuz
4	1969	first walk on the moon	Apollo 11
9	1983	first American woman in space	Discovery

Make a time line to show the order of these events in American space exploration. Write each year in the top box, each event in the square and each spacecraft name in the bottom box. The first one is done for you.

1961	1962	1965	1969	1971	1973	1975	1981	1983
first American in space	orbit earth three times	first walk in space	first walk on the moon	first drive on the moon	astronauts live in space station	Amers. & Russians meet in space	first space shuttle	first Amer. woman in space
Freedom 7	Friendship 7	Gemini 4	Apollo 11	Apollo 15	Skylab	Apollo-Soyuz	Columbia	Discovery

Page 216

IF8695 Super Book for Grade 3

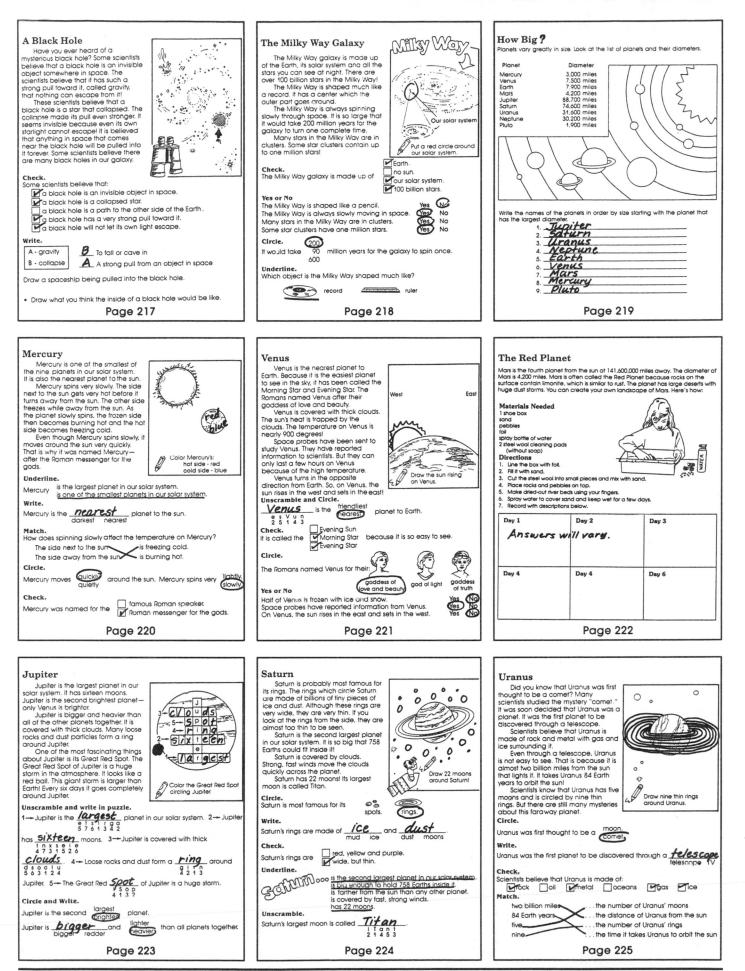

A Black Hole

Have you ever heard of a mysterious black hole? Some scientists believe that a black hole is an invisible object somewhere in space. The scientists believe that it has such a strong pull toward it, called gravity, that nothing can escape from it!

These scientists believe that a black hole is a star that collapsed. The collapse made its pull even stronger. It seems invisible because even its own starlight cannot escape! It is believed that anything that comes near the black hole will be pulled into it forever. Some scientists believe there are many black holes in our galaxy.

Check.
Some scientists believe that:
- ☑ a black hole is an invisible object in space.
- ☑ a black hole is a collapsed star.
- ☐ a black hole is a path to the other side of the Earth.
- ☑ a black hole has a very strong pull toward it.
- ☑ a black hole will not let its own light escape.

Write.

| A - gravity | **B** To fall or cave in |
| B - collapse | **A** A strong pull from an object in space |

Draw a spaceship being pulled into the black hole.

• Draw what you think the inside of a black hole would be like.

Page 217

The Milky Way Galaxy

The Milky Way galaxy is made up of the Earth, its solar system and all the stars you can see at night. There are over 100 billion stars in the Milky Way!

The Milky Way is shaped much like a record. It has a center which the outer part goes around.

The Milky Way is always spinning slowly through space. It is so large that it would take 200 million years for the galaxy to turn one complete time.

Many stars in the Milky Way are in clusters. Some star clusters contain up to one million stars!

Check.
The Milky Way galaxy is made up of
- ☑ Earth.
- ☐ no sun.
- ☑ our solar system.
- ☑ 100 billion stars.

Yes or No
The Milky Way is shaped like a pencil. Yes (No)
The Milky Way is always slowly moving in space. (Yes) No
Many stars in the Milky Way are in clusters. (Yes) No
Some star clusters have one million stars. (Yes) No

Circle.
It would take (200) / 600 million years for the galaxy to spin once.

Underline.
Which object is the Milky Way shaped much like?
record ~~ruler~~

Put a red circle around our solar system.

Page 218

How Big ?

Planets vary greatly in size. Look at the list of planets and their diameters.

Planet	Diameter
Mercury	3,000 miles
Venus	7,500 miles
Earth	7,900 miles
Mars	4,200 miles
Jupiter	88,700 miles
Saturn	74,600 miles
Uranus	31,600 miles
Neptune	30,200 miles
Pluto	1,900 miles

Write the names of the planets in order by size starting with the planet that has the largest diameter.

1. Jupiter
2. Saturn
3. Uranus
4. Neptune
5. Earth
6. Venus
7. Mars
8. Mercury
9. Pluto

Page 219

Mercury

Mercury is one of the smallest of the nine planets in our solar system. It is also the nearest planet to the sun. Mercury spins very slowly. The side next to the sun gets very hot before it turns away from the sun. The other side freezes while away from the sun. As the planet slowly spins, the frozen side then becomes burning hot and the hot side becomes freezing cold.

Even though Mercury spins slowly, it moves around the sun very quickly. That is why it was named Mercury— after the Roman messenger for the gods.

Color Mercury's:
hot side - red
cold side - blue

Underline.
Mercury ~~is the largest planet in our solar system.~~
is one of the smallest planets in our solar system.

Write.
Mercury is the **nearest** planet to the sun.
darkest / nearest

Match.
How does spinning slowly affect the temperature on Mercury?
The side next to the sun —— is freezing cold.
The side away from the sun —— is burning hot.

Circle.
Mercury moves (quickly) / quietly around the sun. Mercury spins very lightly / (slowly).

Check.
Mercury was named for the
- ☐ famous Roman speaker.
- ☑ Roman messenger for the gods.

Page 220

Venus

Venus is the nearest planet to Earth. It is the easiest planet to see in the sky. It has been called the Morning Star and Evening Star. The Romans named Venus after their goddess of love and beauty.

Venus is covered with thick clouds. The sun's heat is trapped by the clouds. The temperature on Venus is nearly 900 degrees!

Space probes have been sent to study Venus. They have reported information to scientists. But they can only last a few hours on Venus because of the high temperature.

Venus turns in the opposite direction from Earth. So, on Venus, the sun rises in the west and sets in the east!

Draw the sun rising on Venus.

Unscramble and Circle.
Venus is the friendliest / (nearest) planet to Earth.
e s V u n
2 5 1 4 3

Check.
It is called the
- ☐ Evening Sun
- ☑ Morning Star — because it is so easy to see.
- ☑ Evening Star

Circle.
The Romans named Venus for their:
(goddess of love and beauty) / god of light / goddess of truth

Yes or No
Half of Venus is frozen with ice and snow. Yes (No)
Space probes have reported information from Venus. (Yes) No
On Venus, the sun rises in the east and sets in the west. Yes (No)

Page 221

The Red Planet

Mars is the fourth planet from the sun at 141,600,000 miles away. The diameter of Mars is 4,200 miles. Mars is often called the Red Planet because rocks on the surface contain limonite, which is similar to rust. The planet has large deserts with huge dust storms. You can create your own landscape of Mars. Here's how:

Materials Needed
1 shoe box
sand
pebbles
foil
spray bottle of water
2 steel wool cleaning pads
(without soap)

Directions
1. Line the box with foil.
2. Fill it with sand.
3. Cut the steel wool into small pieces and mix with sand.
4. Place rocks and pebbles on top.
5. Make dried-out river beds using your fingers.
6. Spray water to cover sand and keep wet for a few days.
7. Record with descriptions below.

Day 1	Day 2	Day 3
Answers will vary.		

Day 4	Day 4	Day 6

Page 222

Jupiter

Jupiter is the largest planet in our solar system. It has sixteen moons. Jupiter is the second brightest planet— only Venus is brighter.

Jupiter is bigger and heavier than all of the other planets together. It is covered with thick clouds. Many loose rocks and dust particles form a ring around Jupiter.

One of the most fascinating things about Jupiter is its Great Red Spot. The Great Red Spot of Jupiter is a huge storm in the atmosphere. It looks like a red ball. This giant storm is larger than Earth! Every six days it goes completely around the sun.

Color the Great Red Spot circling Jupiter.

Unscramble and write in puzzle.
1→ Jupiter is the **largest** planet in our solar system.
e t s i r g a
5 7 6 1 3 4 2

2→ Jupiter has **sixteen** moons.
t n x s e i e
4 7 3 1 5 2 6

3→ Jupiter is covered with thick **clouds**.
d s o c l u
5 6 3 1 2 4

4→ Loose rocks and dust form a **ring** around Jupiter.
g i n r
4 2 1 3

5→ The Great Red **Spot** of Jupiter is a huge storm.
y s o p
4 1 3 2

Circle and Write.
Jupiter is the second largest / (brightest) planet.
Jupiter is **bigger** and (heavier) / lighter than all planets together.
bigger / redder

Page 223

Saturn

Saturn is probably most famous for its rings. The rings which circle Saturn are made of billions of tiny pieces of ice and dust. Although these rings are very wide, they are very thin. If you look at the rings from the side, they are almost too thin to be seen.

Saturn is the second largest planet in our solar system. It is so big that 758 Earths could fit inside it!

Saturn is covered by clouds. Strong, fast winds move the clouds quickly across the planet.

Saturn has 22 moons! Its largest moon is called Titan.

Draw 22 moons around Saturn.

Circle.
Saturn is most famous for its spots / (rings).

Write.
Saturn's rings are made of **ice** and **dust**.
mud / ice   dust / moons

Check.
Saturn's rings are
- ☐ red, yellow and purple.
- ☑ wide, but thin.

Underline.
Saturn is the second largest planet in our solar system.
is big enough to hold 758 Earths inside it.
is farther from the sun than any other planet.
is covered by fast, strong winds.
has 22 moons.

Unscramble.
Saturn's largest moon is called **Titan**.
i T a n t
2 1 4 5 3

Page 224

Uranus

Did you know that Uranus was first thought to be a comet? Many scientists studied the mystery "comet." It was soon decided that Uranus was a planet. It was the first planet to be discovered through a telescope.

Scientists believe that Uranus is made of rock and metal with gas and ice surrounding it.

Even through a telescope, Uranus is not easy to see. That is because it is almost two billion miles from the sun that lights it. It takes Uranus 84 Earth years to orbit the sun!

Scientists know that Uranus has five moons and is circled by nine thin rings. But there are still many mysteries about this faraway planet.

Draw nine thin rings around Uranus.

Circle.
Uranus was first thought to be a moon / (comet).

Write.
Uranus was the first planet to be discovered through a **telescope**.
telescope / TV

Check.
Scientists believe that Uranus is made of:
- ☑ rock
- ☐ oil
- ☑ metal
- ☐ oceans
- ☑ gas
- ☑ ice

Match.
two billion miles —— ...the number of Uranus' moons
84 Earth years —— ...the distance of Uranus from the sun
five —— ...the number of Uranus' rings
nine —— ...the time it takes Uranus to orbit the sun

Page 225

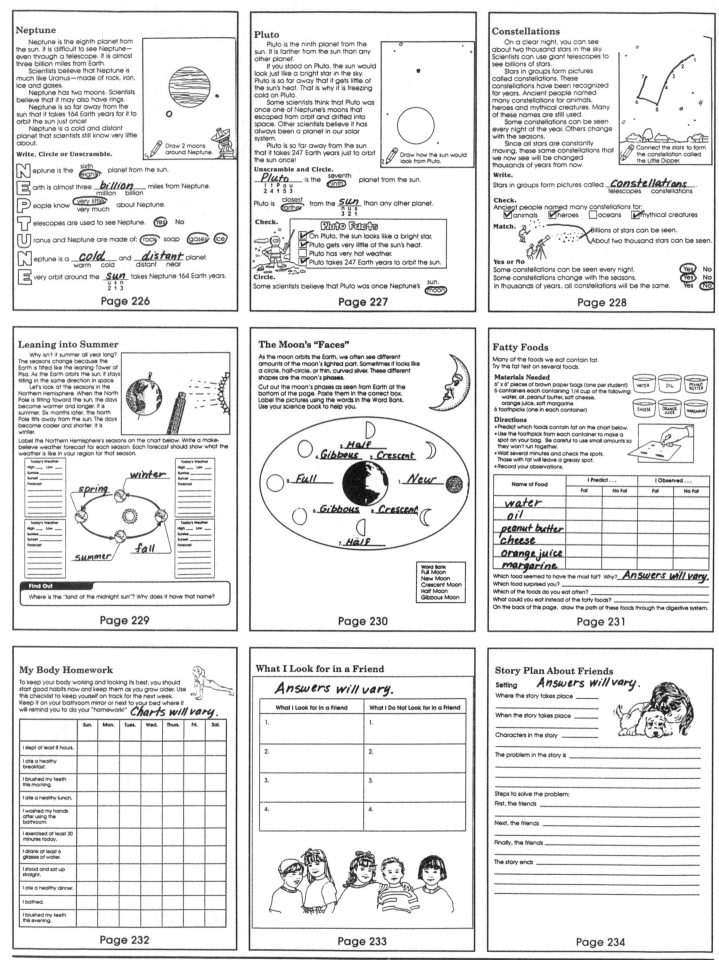

Neptune

Neptune is the eighth planet from the sun. It is difficult to see Neptune—even through a telescope. It is almost three billion miles from Earth.

Scientists believe that Neptune is much like Uranus—made of rock, iron, ice and gases.

Neptune has two moons. Scientists believe that it may also have rings.

Neptune is so far away from the sun that it takes 164 Earth years for it to orbit the sun just once!

Neptune is a cold and distant planet that scientists still know very little about.

Draw 2 moons around Neptune.

Write, Circle or Unscramble.

N eptune is the ~~sixth~~ (eighth) planet from the sun.

E arth is almost three _billion_ miles from Neptune. (million / billion)

P eople know (very little) about Neptune. (very little / very much)

T elescopes are used to see Neptune. (Yes) No

U ranus and Neptune are made of: (rock) soap (gases) (ice)

N eptune is a _cold_ and _distant_ planet. (warm / cold) (distant / near)

E very orbit around the _sun_ takes Neptune 164 Earth years. (u s n / 2 1 3)

Page 226

Pluto

Pluto is the ninth planet from the sun. It is farther from the sun than any other planet.

If you stood on Pluto, the sun would look just like a bright star in the sky. Pluto is so far away that it gets little of the sun's heat. That is why it is freezing cold on Pluto.

Some scientists think that Pluto was once one of Neptune's moons that escaped from orbit and drifted into space. Other scientists believe it has always been a planet in our solar system.

Pluto is so far away from the sun that it takes 247 Earth years just to orbit the sun once!

Draw how the sun would look from Pluto.

Unscramble and Circle.

Pluto is the ~~seventh~~ (ninth) planet from the sun. (l t P o u / 2 4 1 5 3)

Pluto is _closest_ from the _sun_ than any other planet. (closest / farther) (n u s / 3 2 1)

Check.

Pluto Facts

✓ On Pluto, the sun looks like a bright star.
✓ Pluto gets very little of the sun's heat.
☐ Pluto has very hot weather.
✓ Pluto takes 247 Earth years to orbit the sun.

Circle.

Some scientists believe that Pluto was once Neptune's sun. (moon)

Page 227

Constellations

On a clear night, you can see about two thousand stars in the sky. Scientists can use giant telescopes to see billions of stars.

Stars in groups form pictures called constellations. These constellations have been recognized for years. Ancient people named many constellations for animals, heroes and mythical creatures. Many of these names are still used.

Some constellations can be seen every night of the year. Others change with the seasons.

Since all stars are constantly moving, these same constellations that we now see will be changed thousands of years from now.

Connect the stars to form the constellation called the Little Dipper.

Write.

Stars in groups form pictures called _Constellations_ (telescopes / constellations)

Check.

Ancient people named many constellations for:
✓ animals ✓ heroes ☐ oceans ✓ mythical creatures

Match.

Billions of stars can be seen.
About two thousand stars can be seen.

Yes or No

Some constellations can be seen every night. (Yes) No
Some constellations change with the seasons. (Yes) No
In thousands of years, all constellations will be the same. Yes (No)

Page 228

Leaning into Summer

Why isn't it summer all year long? The seasons change because the Earth is tilted like the leaning Tower of Pisa. As the Earth orbits the sun it stays tilting in the same direction in space.

Let's look at the seasons in the Northern Hemisphere. When the North Pole is tilting toward the sun, the days become warmer and longer. It is summer. Six months later, the North Pole tilts away from the sun. The days become cooler and shorter. It is winter.

Label the Northern Hemisphere's seasons on the chart below. Write a make-believe weather forecast for each season. Each forecast should show what the weather is like in your region for that season.

winter
spring
summer
fall

Find Out

Where is the "land of the midnight sun"? Why does it have that name?

Page 229

The Moon's "Faces"

As the moon orbits the Earth, we often see different amounts of the moon's lighted part. Sometimes it looks like a circle, half-circle, or thin, curved silver. These different shapes are the moon's **phases.**

Cut out the moon's phases as seen from Earth at the bottom of the page. Paste them in the correct box. Label the pictures using the words in the Word Bank. Use your science book to help you.

3. Half
2. Gibbous   4. Crescent
1. Full   5. New
8. Gibbous   6. Crescent
7. Half

Word Bank
Full Moon
New Moon
Crescent Moon
Half Moon
Gibbous Moon

Page 230

Fatty Foods

Many of the foods we eat contain fat. Try this fat test on several foods.

Materials Needed
6" x 6" pieces of brown paper bags (one per student)
6 containers each containing 1/4 cup of the following:
   water, oil, peanut butter, soft cheese,
   orange juice, soft margarine
6 toothpicks (one in each container)

Directions
• Predict which foods contain fat on the chart below.
• Use the toothpick from each container to make a spot on your bag. Be careful to use small amounts so they won't run together.
• Wait several minutes and check the spots. Those with fat will leave a greasy spot.
• Record your observations.

Name of Food	I Predict . . .		I Observed . . .	
	Fat	No Fat	Fat	No Fat
water				
oil				
peanut butter				
cheese				
orange juice				
margarine				

Which food seemed to have the most fat? Why? _Answers will vary._
Which food surprised you? ___
Which of the foods do you eat often? ___
What could you eat instead of the fatty foods? ___
On the back of this page, draw the path of these foods through the digestive system.

Page 231

My Body Homework

To keep your body working and looking its best, you should start good habits now and keep them as you grow older. Use this checklist to keep yourself on track for the next week. Keep it on your bathroom mirror or next to your bed where it will remind you to do your "homework!" _Charts will vary._

	Sun.	Mon.	Tues.	Wed.	Thurs.	Fri.	Sat.
I slept at least 8 hours.							
I ate a healthy breakfast.							
I brushed my teeth this morning.							
I ate a healthy lunch.							
I washed my hands after using the bathroom.							
I exercised at least 30 minutes today.							
I drank at least 6 glasses of water.							
I stood and sat up straight.							
I ate a healthy dinner.							
I bathed.							
I brushed my teeth this evening.							

Page 232

What I Look for in a Friend

Answers will vary.

What I Look for in a Friend	What I Do Not Look for in a Friend
1.	1.
2.	2.
3.	3.
4.	4.

Page 233

Story Plan About Friends

Setting   _Answers will vary._

Where the story takes place ___

When the story takes place ___

Characters in the story ___

The problem in the story is ___

Steps to solve the problem:
First, the friends ___

Next, the friends ___

Finally, the friends ___

The story ends ___

Page 234

Your Family

1. What is a family? *Answers will vary.*

2. What is the purpose of a family? _____

3. Who in your family do you go to . . .
   when you are sick? _____
   for help with homework? _____
   for advice? _____
   when you are afraid? _____
   when you want something? _____
   when you are unhappy? _____
   when you have had a bad day? _____
   Have you always gone to the same person in each situation or do you go to different people in the family at different times? _____
   Explain your answer. _____

4. What does your family do for recreation? _____

5. Compare your family with others. How is it the same? How is it different? _____

6. Do you think families around the world are like families you know? Explain your answer. _____

Page 235

What Do You See?

Look at the pictures below. Write three sentences about each one concerning (1) the appearance of the person(s), (2) the means of transportation and (3) the landscape.

Answers will vary.

Draw a picture in the box of you going somewhere. Write three sentences describing yourself.

Page 236

The Secret Message

One morning in late June, Sally, Jim, and Lee Cruise found a very strange note on the breakfast table. It looked like a secret code. Suddenly, Lee realized that it was a rebus. Each line contained one word in the message. Help the Cruise children read the rebus.

L + (🕊 – j) + 's = *Let's*

s + (🐝 – b) = *see*

(👟 – rap) + (🐔 – n) = *the*

(🦄 – 🐄) + t + (🐑 – b) = *United*

(🛳 – pler) + (⚙ – ir) + s = *States.*

Then Mom and Dad yelled, "Surprise! Do you want to go?"
The excited children answered their parents' question with a rebus of their own. Fill in the missing blanks.

Y + (♟ – CH – S) = *Yes* !

Page 237

The Best Way to Tell It

There are many vehicles that can be used to convey a message, such as a telephone, a fax machine, a radio, etc. Tell by which vehicle you think the information below would best be delivered. In some instances, there may be more than one choice. *Answers will vary.*

You will be late coming home from school. *Telephone, note*

How you looked when you were a baby *Photo albums, parents*

An urgent need for help *Telephone*

How the world looked 5,000,000 years ago *science book*

The first Thanksgiving *history book*

National news *radio, TV, newspaper*

A make-believe story *book*

Asking someone to visit your home on their vacation *letter, telephone*

A garage sale *ad, poster*

Something that happened "once upon a time" *book*

A funny experience *person-to-person, comedian on TV*

What you saw *person-to-person, story*

A baseball game *attend in person, TV*

An adventure in space *TV, book*

A series of strange events and their solutions *book*

Tell someone you missed them. *letter*

Your dog ran away. *poster, ad*

A true story *another person*

Page 238

It Says the Same Thing Differently

Translate and write the rebus message. Then do what it tells you to do on this line:

W + ▽ – P + △ – NT   *Write*

☉ – YO + ◯ – N   *your*

🔨 + 👥 – ILN   *name*

🏃 + 〰 – TE + 📞 – OOR   *backward.*

Use the Code Key below to translate the message under it.

A	B	C	D	E	F	G	H	I	J	K	L	M	N	O	P	Q	R	S	T	U	V	W	X	Y	Z

LETTERS IN SOME ALPHABETS

LOOK LIKE LETTERS WE KNOW

IN OTHER ALPHABETS.

Make a code of your own. Fill in the Code Key below with a symbol to represent each letter. Write a direction using your code.

A	B	C	D	E	F	G	H	I	J	K	L	M	N	O	P	Q	R	S	T	U	V	W	X	Y	Z

Codes will vary.

Page 239

Symbol-Sign Communication

Here are some familiar symbol-signs:

Handicapped   Hospital   No Parking   Railroad Crossing

Design, draw and color symbol-signs for the following:

Pictures will vary.

Children's Playground | Watch Your Step | Monkey House | Bicycle Path

Blind Corner | Narrow Bridge | Library | Picnic Area

Protect Earth – Recycle | Fishing Only From 6:00-7:00 p.m. | Wildflower Sanctuary | Dogs Must Be On Leash

Page 240

Land Ho!

Read each clue. Find the matching word in the Word Bank. Write it in the puzzle.

Across
1. Opposite of south
4. Raised land smaller than mountain
5. Opposite of east
6. A very high hill
10. Water with land all around it
11. Water on three sides of this landform
12. Opposite of west
14. A very large piece of land

Down
2. Large body of salt water
3. Flat land that is higher than the land around it
7. Water is all around this land
8. Very dry, sandy land
9. A large stream of water
11. Flat land
13. Opposite of north

Word Bank
continent, desert, east, hill, island, lake, mountain, north, ocean, peninsula, plain, plateau, river, south, west

Page 241

The Long Climb

Mom, Dad, Sally, Lee, and Jim started their vacation by visiting some places in the state of New York.

They decided to visit the Statue of Liberty. Two sets of parallel stairways rise from the statue's base to its crown. First Dad gave the children clues so they could find out how many steps are in each stairway.

Clue 1: The number is between 160 and 170.
Clue 2: It is an even number.
Clue 3: If you add the 3 digits in the number, the answer is 15. How many steps are in each stairway? *168*

Next, Dad asked them to figure out the statue's height in inches from its base to its torch.

Clue 1: The number is less than 1,820 and more than 1,800.
Clue 2: It is an odd number.
Clue 3: The sum of the digits is 13. The Statue of Liberty is *1,813* inches tall.

Finally, Dad had them compute the statue's weight in tons.

Clue 1: The number is between 200 and 250.
Clue 2: It is divisible by 5.
Clue 3: The sum of the digits is 9. The Statue of Liberty weighs *225* tons.

Extra: The Statue of Liberty weighs *450,000* pounds.

Page 242

Music in the Air

While in New York City, the Cruise family saw a famous play on Broadway. Both Sally and Lee thought it was funny, and Jim really enjoyed the music.

To find out the name of the musical, read the sentence hidden in the chart below. Look up, down and sideways, connecting all the letters into words as you go.

End

Start

Write the sentence here: *The name of the New York play is "Annie."*

Page 243

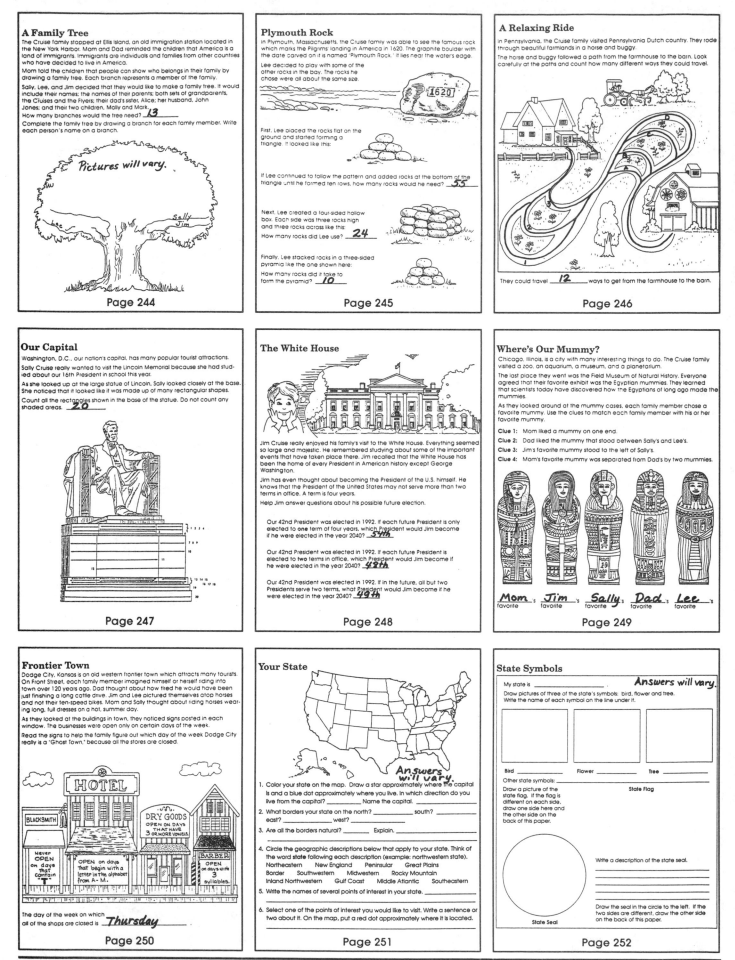

A Family Tree

The Cruise family stopped at Ellis Island, an old immigration station located in the New York Harbor. Mom and Dad reminded the children that America is a land of immigrants. Immigrants are individuals and families from other countries who have decided to live in America.

Mom told the children that people can show who belongs in their family by drawing a family tree. Each branch represents a member of the family.

Sally, Lee, and Jim decided that they would like to make a family tree. It would include their names; the names of their parents; both sets of grandparents, the Cruises and the Flyers; their dad's sister, Alice; her husband, John Jones; and their two children, Molly and Mark.
How many branches would the tree need? __13__

Complete the family tree by drawing a branch for each family member. Write each person's name on a branch.

Pictures will vary.

Page 244

Plymouth Rock

In Plymouth, Massachusetts, the Cruise family was able to see the famous rock which marks the Pilgrims' landing in America in 1620. The graphite boulder with the date carved on it is named "Plymouth Rock." It lies near the water's edge.

Lee decided to play with some of the other rocks in the bay. The rocks he chose were all about the same size.

First, Lee placed the rocks flat on the ground and started forming a triangle. It looked like this:

If Lee continued to follow the pattern and added rocks at the bottom of the triangle until he formed ten rows, how many rocks would he need? __55__

Next, Lee created a four-sided hollow box. Each side was three rocks high and three rocks across like this:
How many rocks did Lee use? __24__

Finally, Lee stacked rocks in a three-sided pyramid like the one shown here:
How many rocks did it take to form the pyramid? __10__

Page 245

A Relaxing Ride

In Pennsylvania, the Cruise family visited Pennsylvania Dutch country. They rode through beautiful farmlands in a horse and buggy.

The horse and buggy followed a path from the farmhouse to the barn. Look carefully at the paths and count how many different ways they could travel.

They could travel __12__ ways to get from the farmhouse to the barn.

Page 246

Our Capital

Washington, D.C., our nation's capital, has many popular tourist attractions.

Sally Cruise really wanted to visit the Lincoln Memorial because she had studied about our 16th President in school this year.

As she looked up at the large statue of Lincoln, Sally looked closely at the base. She noticed that it looked like it was made up of many rectangular shapes. Count all the rectangles shown in the base of the statue. Do not count any shaded areas. __20__

Page 247

The White House

Jim Cruise really enjoyed his family's visit to the White House. Everything seemed so large and majestic. He remembered studying about some of the important events that have taken place there. Jim recalled that the White House has been the home of every President in American history except George Washington.

Jim has even thought about becoming the President of the U.S. himself. He knows that the President of the United States may not serve more than two terms in office. A term is four years.

Help Jim answer questions about his possible future election.

Our 42nd President was elected in 1992. If each future President is only elected to one term of four years, which President would Jim become if he were elected in the year 2040? __54th__

Our 42nd President was elected in 1992. If each future President is elected to two terms in office, which President would Jim become if he were elected in the year 2040? __48th__

Our 42nd President was elected in 1992. If in the future, all but two Presidents serve two terms, what President would Jim become if he were elected in the year 2040? __49th__

Page 248

Where's Our Mummy?

Chicago, Illinois, is a city with many interesting things to do. The Cruise family visited a zoo, an aquarium, a museum, and a planetarium.

The last place they went was the Field Museum of Natural History. Everyone agreed that their favorite exhibit was the Egyptian mummies. They learned that scientists today have discovered how the Egyptians of long ago made the mummies.

As they looked around at the mummy cases, each family member chose a favorite mummy. Use the clues to match each family member with his or her favorite mummy.

Clue 1: Mom liked a mummy on one end.
Clue 2: Dad liked the mummy that stood between Sally's and Lee's.
Clue 3: Jim's favorite mummy stood to the left of Sally's.
Clue 4: Mom's favorite mummy was separated from Dad's by two mummies.

__Mom__'s favorite   __Jim__'s favorite   __Sally__'s favorite   __Dad__'s favorite   __Lee__'s favorite

Page 249

Frontier Town

Dodge City, Kansas is an old western frontier town which attracts many tourists. On Front Street, each family member imagined himself or herself riding into town over 120 years ago. Dad thought about how tired he would have been just finishing a long cattle drive. Jim and Lee pictured themselves atop horses and not their ten-speed bikes. Mom and Sally thought about riding horses wearing long, full dresses on a hot, summer day.

As they looked at the buildings in town, they noticed signs posted in each window. The businesses were open only on certain days of the week.

Read the signs to help the family figure out which day of the week Dodge City really is a "Ghost Town," because all the stores are closed.

The day of the week on which all of the shops are closed is __Thursday__

Page 250

Your State

Answers will vary.

1. Color your state on the map. Draw a star approximately where the capital is and a blue dot approximately where you live. In which direction do you live from the capital? _____ Name the capital. _____

2. What borders your state on the north? _____ south? _____ east? _____ west? _____

3. Are all the borders natural? _____ Explain. _____

4. Circle the geographic descriptions below that apply to your state. Think of the word state following each description (example: northwestern state).
Northeastern   New England   Peninsular   Great Plains
Border   Southwestern   Midwestern   Rocky Mountain
Inland Northwestern   Gulf Coast   Middle Atlantic   Southeastern

5. Write the names of several points of interest in your state.

6. Select one of the points of interest you would like to visit. Write a sentence or two about it. On the map, put a red dot approximately where it is located.

Page 251

State Symbols

My state is _____   Answers will vary.

Draw pictures of three of the state's symbols: bird, flower and tree.
Write the name of each symbol on the line under it.

Bird _____   Flower _____   Tree _____

Other state symbols: _____

State Flag

Draw a picture of the state flag. If the flag is different on each side, draw one side here and the other side on the back of this paper.

Write a description of the state seal. _____

State Seal

Draw the seal in the circle to the left. If the two sides are different, draw the other side on the back of this paper.

Page 252

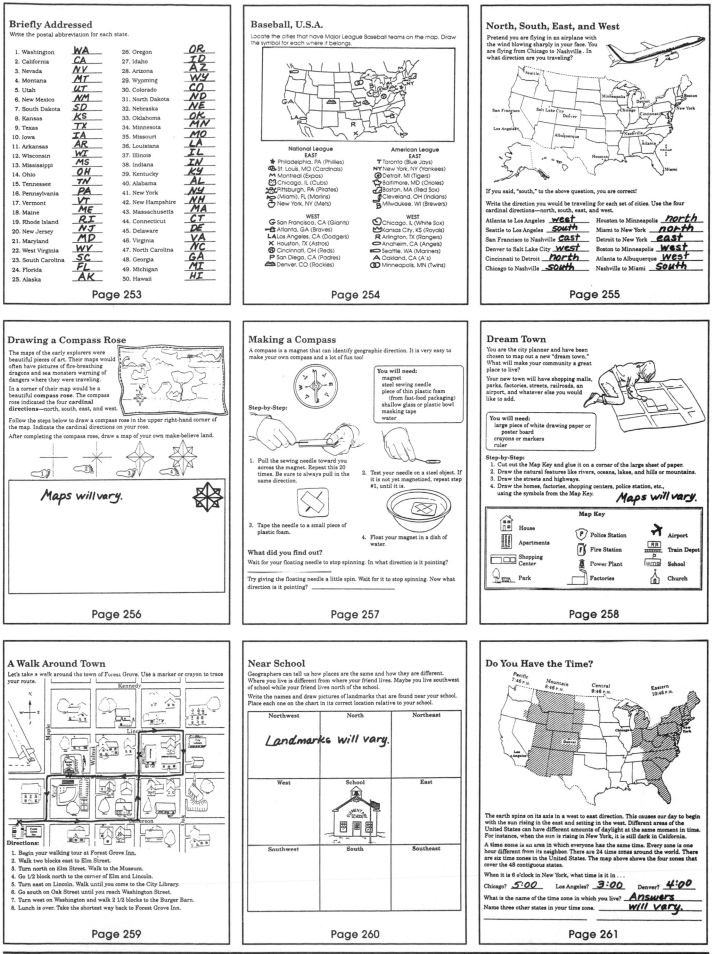

Briefly Addressed

Write the postal abbreviation for each state.

1. Washington	WA	26. Oregon	OR
2. California	CA	27. Idaho	ID
3. Nevada	NV	28. Arizona	AZ
4. Montana	MT	29. Wyoming	WY
5. Utah	UT	30. Colorado	CO
6. New Mexico	NM	31. North Dakota	ND
7. South Dakota	SD	32. Nebraska	NE
8. Kansas	KS	33. Oklahoma	OK
9. Texas	TX	34. Minnesota	MN
10. Iowa	IA	35. Missouri	MO
11. Arkansas	AR	36. Louisiana	LA
12. Wisconsin	WI	37. Illinois	IL
13. Mississippi	MS	38. Indiana	IN
14. Ohio	OH	39. Kentucky	KY
15. Tennessee	TN	40. Alabama	AL
16. Pennsylvania	PA	41. New York	NY
17. Vermont	VT	42. New Hampshire	NH
18. Maine	ME	43. Massachusetts	MA
19. Rhode Island	RI	44. Connecticut	CT
20. New Jersey	NJ	45. Delaware	DE
21. Maryland	MD	46. Virginia	VA
22. West Virginia	WV	47. North Carolina	NC
23. South Carolina	SC	48. Georgia	GA
24. Florida	FL	49. Michigan	MI
25. Alaska	AK	50. Hawaii	HI

Page 253

Baseball, U.S.A.

Locate the cities that have Major League Baseball teams on the map. Draw the symbol for each where it belongs.

National League
EAST
- ★ Philadelphia, PA (Phillies)
- St. Louis, MO (Cardinals)
- Montreal (Expos)
- Chicago, IL (Cubs)
- Pittsburgh, PA (Pirates)
- (Miami), FL (Marlins)
- New York, NY (Mets)

WEST
- G San Francisco, CA (Giants)
- Atlanta, GA (Braves)
- LA Los Angeles, CA (Dodgers)
- ✕ Houston, TX (Astros)
- Cincinnati, OH (Reds)
- P San Diego, CA (Padres)
- Denver, CO (Rockies)

American League
EAST
- T Toronto (Blue Jays)
- NY New York, NY (Yankees)
- Detroit, MI (Tigers)
- Baltimore, MD (Orioles)
- Boston, MA (Red Sox)
- Cleveland, OH (Indians)
- B Milwaukee, WI (Brewers)

WEST
- Chicago, IL (White Sox)
- Kansas City, KS (Royals)
- R Arlington, TX (Rangers)
- Anaheim, CA (Angels)
- Seattle, WA (Mariners)
- Oakland, CA (A's)
- Minneapolis, MN (Twins)

Page 254

North, South, East, and West

Pretend you are flying in an airplane with the wind blowing sharply in your face. You are flying from Chicago to Nashville. In what direction are you traveling?

If you said, "south," to the above question, you are correct!

Write the direction you would be traveling for each set of cities. Use the four cardinal directions—north, south, east, and west.

Atlanta to Los Angeles	west
Seattle to Los Angeles	south
San Francisco to Nashville	east
Denver to Salt Lake City	west
Cincinnati to Detroit	north
Chicago to Nashville	south
Houston to Minneapolis	north
Miami to New York	north
Detroit to New York	east
Boston to Minneapolis	west
Atlanta to Albuquerque	west
Nashville to Miami	south

Page 255

Drawing a Compass Rose

The maps of the early explorers were beautiful pieces of art. Their maps would often have pictures of fire-breathing dragons and sea monsters warning of dangers where they were traveling.

In a corner of their map would be a beautiful **compass rose**. The compass rose indicated the four **cardinal directions**—north, south, east, and west.

Follow the steps below to draw a compass rose in the upper right-hand corner of the map. Indicate the cardinal directions on your rose.

After completing the compass rose, draw a map of your own make-believe land.

Maps will vary.

Page 256

Making a Compass

A compass is a magnet that can identify geographic direction. It is very easy to make your own compass and a lot of fun too!

You will need:
magnet
steel sewing needle
piece of thin plastic foam
  (from fast-food packaging)
shallow glass or plastic bowl
masking tape
water

Step-by-Step:

1. Pull the sewing needle toward you across the magnet. Repeat this 20 times. Be sure to always pull in the same direction.

2. Test your needle on a steel object. If it is not yet magnetized, repeat step #1, until it is.

3. Tape the needle to a small piece of plastic foam.

4. Float your magnet in a dish of water.

What did you find out?

Wait for your floating needle to stop spinning. In what direction is it pointing? _____

Try giving the floating needle a little spin. Wait for it to stop spinning. Now what direction is it pointing? _____

Page 257

Dream Town

You are the city planner and have been chosen to map out a new "dream town." What will make your community a great place to live?

Your new town will have shopping malls, parks, factories, streets, railroads, an airport, and whatever else you would like to add.

You will need:
large piece of white drawing paper or
  poster board
crayons or markers
ruler

Step-by-Step:
1. Cut out the Map Key and glue it on a corner of the large sheet of paper.
2. Draw the natural features like rivers, oceans, lakes, and hills or mountains.
3. Draw the streets and highways.
4. Draw the homes, factories, shopping centers, police station, etc., using the symbols from the Map Key.

Maps will vary.

Map Key
- House
- Apartments
- Shopping Center
- Park
- P Police Station
- F Fire Station
- Power Plant
- Factories
- Airport
- RR Train Depot
- School
- Church

Page 258

A Walk Around Town

Let's take a walk around the town of Forest Grove. Use a marker or crayon to trace your route.

Directions:
1. Begin your walking tour at Forest Grove Inn.
2. Walk two blocks east to Elm Street.
3. Turn north on Elm Street. Walk to the Museum.
4. Go 1/2 block north to the corner of Elm and Lincoln.
5. Turn east on Lincoln. Walk until you come to the City Library.
6. Go south on Oak Street until you reach Washington Street.
7. Turn west on Washington and walk 2 1/2 blocks to the Burger Barn.
8. Lunch is over. Take the shortest way back to Forest Grove Inn.

Page 259

Near School

Geographers can tell us how places are the same and how they are different. Where you live is different from where your friend lives. Maybe you live southwest of school while your friend lives north of the school.

Write the names and draw pictures of landmarks that are found near your school. Place each one on the chart in its correct location relative to your school.

Northwest	North	Northeast
	Landmarks will vary.	
West	School	East
Southwest	South	Southeast

Page 260

Do You Have the Time?

Pacific 7:46 P.M. Mountain 8:46 P.M. Central 9:46 P.M. Eastern 10:46 P.M.

The earth spins on its axis in a west to east direction. This causes our day to begin with the sun rising in the east and setting in the west. Different areas of the United States can have different amounts of daylight at the same moment in time. For instance, when the sun is rising in New York, it is still dark in California.

A time zone is an area in which everyone has the same time. Each time zone is one hour different from its neighbor. There are 24 time zones around the world. There are six time zones in the United States. The map above shows the four zones that cover the 48 contiguous states.

When it is 6 o'clock in New York, what time is it in . . .

Chicago? 5:00   Los Angeles? 3:00   Denver? 4:00

What is the name of the time zone in which you live? _Answers will vary._
Name three other states in your time zone. _____

Page 261

© Instructional Fair, Inc.   317   IF8695 Super Book for Grade 3

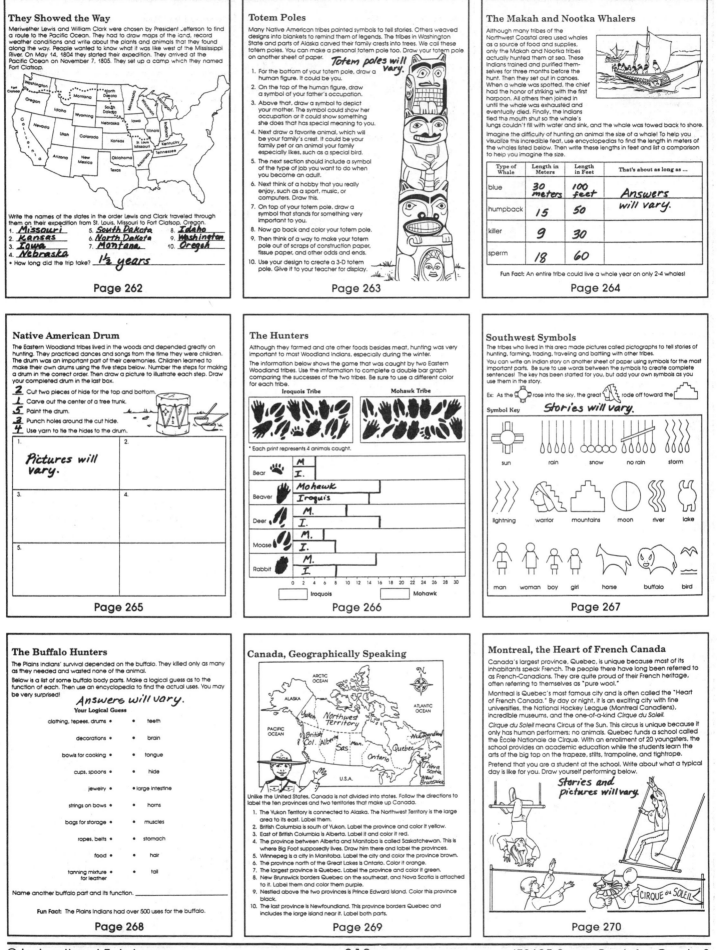

They Showed the Way

Meriwether Lewis and William Clark were chosen by President Jefferson to find a route to the Pacific Ocean. They had to draw maps of the land, record weather conditions and write about the plants and animals that they found along the way. People wanted to know what it was like west of the Mississippi River. On May 14, 1804 they started their expedition. They arrived at the Pacific Ocean on November 7, 1805. They set up a camp which they named Fort Clatsop.

Write the names of the states in the order Lewis and Clark traveled through them on their expedition from St. Louis, Missouri to Fort Clatsop, Oregon.

1. Missouri
2. Kansas
3. Iowa
4. Nebraska
5. South Dakota
6. North Dakota
7. Montana
8. Idaho
9. Washington
10. Oregon

• How long did the trip take? 1½ years

Page 262

Totem Poles

Many Native American tribes painted symbols to tell stories. Others weaved designs into blankets to remind them of legends. The tribes in Washington State and parts of Alaska carved their family crests into trees. We call these totem poles. You can make a personal totem pole too. Draw your totem pole on another sheet of paper.

Totem poles will vary.

1. For the bottom of your totem pole, draw a human figure. It could be you.
2. On the top of the human figure, draw a symbol of your father's occupation.
3. Above that, draw a symbol to depict your mother. The symbol could show her occupation or it could show something she does that has special meaning to you.
4. Next draw a favorite animal, which will be your family's crest. It could be your family pet or an animal your family especially likes, such as a special bird.
5. The next section should include a symbol of the type of job you want to do when you become an adult.
6. Next think of a hobby that you really enjoy, such as a sport, music, or computers. Draw this.
7. On top of your totem pole, draw a symbol that stands for something very important to you.
8. Now go back and color your totem pole.
9. Then think of a way to make your totem pole out of scraps of construction paper, tissue paper, and other odds and ends.
10. Use your design to create a 3-D totem pole. Give it to your teacher for display.

Page 263

The Makah and Nootka Whalers

Although many tribes of the Northwest Coastal area used whales as a source of food and supplies, only the Makah and Nootka tribes actually hunted them at sea. These Indians trained and purified themselves for three months before the hunt. Then they set out in canoes. When a whale was spotted, the chief had the honor of striking with the first harpoon. All others then joined in until the whale was exhausted and eventually died. Finally, the Indians tied the mouth shut so the whale's lungs couldn't fill with water and sink, and the whale was towed back to shore.

Imagine the difficulty of hunting an animal the size of a whale! To help you visualize this incredible feat, use encyclopedias to find the length in meters of the whales listed below. Then write these lengths in feet and list a comparison to help you imagine the size.

Type of Whale	Length in Meters	Length in Feet	That's about as long as ...
blue	30 meters	100 feet	Answers will vary.
humpback	15	50	
killer	9	30	
sperm	18	60	

Fun Fact: An entire tribe could live a whole year on only 2-4 whales!

Page 264

Native American Drum

The Eastern Woodland tribes lived in the woods and depended greatly on hunting. They practiced dances and songs from the time they were children. The drum was an important part of their ceremonies. Children learned to make their own drums using the five steps below. Number the steps for making a drum in the correct order. Then draw a picture to illustrate each step. Draw your completed drum in the last box.

2 Cut two pieces of hide for the top and bottom.
1 Carve out the center of a tree trunk.
5 Paint the drum.
3 Punch holes around the cut hide.
4 Use yarn to tie the hides to the drum.

1.	2.
Pictures will vary.	
3.	4.
5.	

Page 265

The Hunters

Although they farmed and ate other foods besides meat, hunting was very important to most Woodland Indians, especially during the winter.

The information below shows the game that was caught by two Eastern Woodland tribes. Use the information to complete a double bar graph comparing the successes of the two tribes. Be sure to use a different color for each tribe.

Iroquois Tribe   **Mohawk Tribe**

* Each print represents 4 animals caught.

Bear — M / I.
Beaver — Mohawk / Iroquis
Deer — M. / I.
Moose — M. / I.
Rabbit — M. / I.

0 2 4 6 8 10 12 14 16 18 20 22 24 26 28 30

☐ Iroquois   ☐ Mohawk

Page 266

Southwest Symbols

The tribes who lived in this area made pictures called pictographs to tell stories of hunting, farming, trading, traveling and battling with other tribes.

You can write an Indian story on another sheet of paper using symbols for the most important parts. Be sure to use words between the symbols to create complete sentences! The key has been started for you, but add your own symbols as you use them in the story.

Ex: As the ☐ rose into the sky, the great ☐ rode off toward the ☐.

Symbol Key   Stories will vary.

sun   rain   snow   no rain   storm

lightning   warrior   mountains   moon   river   lake

man   woman   boy   girl   horse   buffalo   bird

Page 267

The Buffalo Hunters

The Plains Indians' survival depended on the buffalo. They killed only as many as they needed and wasted none of the animal.

Below is a list of some buffalo body parts. Make a logical guess as to the function of each. Then use an encyclopedia to find the actual uses. You may be very surprised!

Answers will vary.

Your Logical Guess

clothing, tepees, drums • • teeth
decorations • • brain
bowls for cooking • • tongue
cups, spoons • • hide
jewelry • • large intestine
strings on bows • • horns
bags for storage • • muscles
ropes, belts • • stomach
food • • hair
tanning mixture for leather • • tail

Name another buffalo part and its function. _____

Fun Fact: The Plains Indians had over 500 uses for the buffalo.

Page 268

Canada, Geographically Speaking

Unlike the United States, Canada is not divided into states. Follow the directions to label the ten provinces and two territories that make up Canada.

1. The Yukon Territory is connected to Alaska. The Northwest Territory is the large area to its east. Label them.
2. British Columbia is south of Yukon. Label the province and color it yellow.
3. East of British Columbia is Alberta. Label it and color it red.
4. The province between Alberta and Manitoba is called Saskatchewan. This is where Big Foot supposedly lives. Draw him there and label the provinces.
5. Winnipeg is in Manitoba. Label the city and color the province brown.
6. The province north of the Great Lakes is Ontario. Color it orange.
7. The largest province is Quebec. Label the province and color it green.
8. New Brunswick borders Quebec on the southeast, and Nova Scotia is attached to it. Label them and color them purple.
9. Nestled above the two provinces is Prince Edward Island. Color this province black.
10. The last province is Newfoundland. This province borders Quebec and includes the large island near it. Label both parts.

Page 269

Montreal, the Heart of French Canada

Canada's largest province, Quebec, is unique because most of its inhabitants speak French. The people there have long been referred to as French-Canadians. They are quite proud of their French heritage, often referring to themselves as "pure wool."

Montreal is Quebec's most famous city and is often called the "Heart of French Canada." By day or night, it is an exciting city with fine universities, the National Hockey League (Montreal Canadiens), incredible museums, and the one-of-a-kind Cirque du Soleil.

Cirque du Soleil means Circus of the Sun. This circus is unique because it only has human performers; no animals. Quebec funds a school called the École Nationale de Cirque. With an enrollment of 20 youngsters, the school provides an academic education while the students learn the arts of the big top on the trapeze, stilts, trampoline, and tightrope.

Pretend that you are a student at the school. Write about what a typical day is like for you. Draw yourself performing below.

Stories and pictures will vary.

CIRQUE du SOLEIL

Page 270

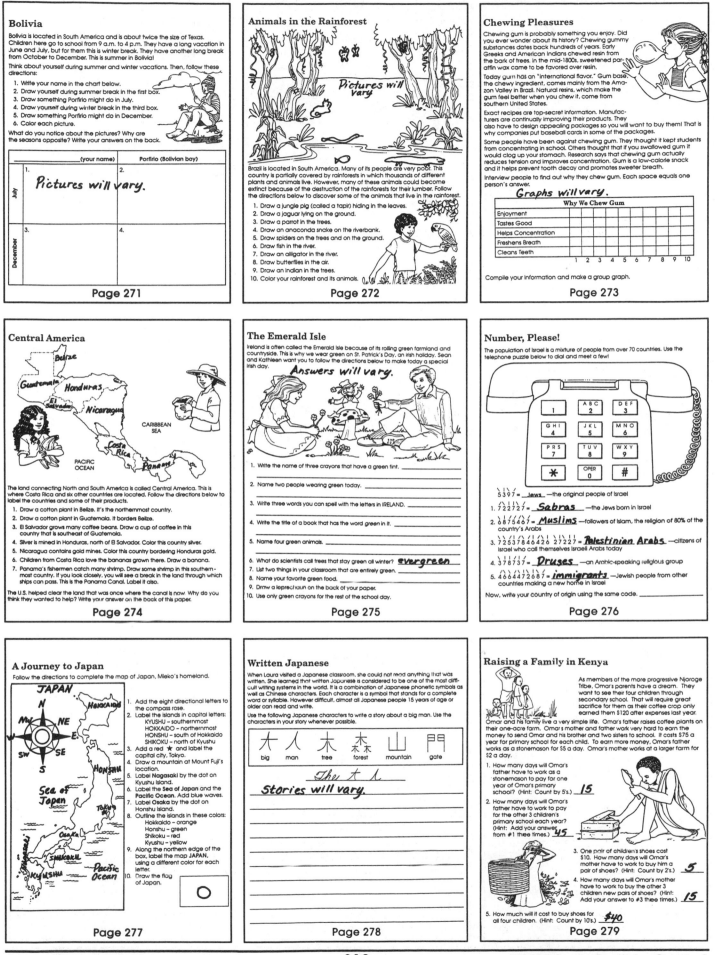

Bolivia

Bolivia is located in South America and is about twice the size of Texas. Children here go to school from 9 a.m. to 4 p.m. They have a long vacation in June and July, but for them this is winter break. They have another long break from October to December. This is summer in Bolivia!

Think about yourself during summer and winter vacations. Then, follow these directions:

1. Write your name in the chart below.
2. Draw yourself during summer break in the first box.
3. Draw something Porfirio might do in July.
4. Draw yourself during winter break in the third box.
5. Draw something Porfirio might do in December.
6. Color each picture.

What do you notice about the pictures? Why are the seasons opposite? Write your answers on the back.

	_____(your name)	Porfirio (Bolivian boy)
July	1. *Pictures will vary.*	2.
December	3.	4.

Page 271

Animals in the Rainforest

Pictures will vary

Brazil is located in South America. Many of its people are very poor. This country is partially covered by rainforests in which thousands of different plants and animals live. However, many of these animals could become extinct because of the destruction of the rainforests for their lumber. Follow the directions below to discover some of the animals that live in the rainforest.

1. Draw a jungle pig (called a tapir) hiding in the leaves.
2. Draw a jaguar lying on the ground.
3. Draw a parrot in the trees.
4. Draw an anaconda snake on the riverbank.
5. Draw spiders on the trees and on the ground.
6. Draw fish in the river.
7. Draw an alligator in the river.
8. Draw butterflies in the air.
9. Draw an Indian in the trees.
10. Color your rainforest and its animals.

Page 272

Chewing Pleasures

Chewing gum is probably something you enjoy. Did you ever wonder about its history? Chewing gummy substances dates back hundreds of years. Early Greeks and American Indians chewed resin from the bark of trees. In the mid-1800s, sweetened paraffin wax came to be favored over resin.

Today gum has an "international flavor." Gum base, the chewy ingredient, comes mainly from the Amazon Valley in Brazil. Natural resins, which make the gum feel better when you chew it, come from southern United States.

Exact recipes are top-secret information. Manufacturers are continually improving their products. They also have to design appealing packages so you will want to buy them! That is why companies put baseball cards in some of the packages.

Some people have been against chewing gum. They thought it kept students from concentrating in school. Others thought that if you swallowed gum it would clog up your stomach. Research says that chewing gum actually reduces tension and improves concentration. Gum is a low-calorie snack and it helps prevent tooth decay and promotes sweeter breath.

Interview people to find out why they chew gum. Each space equals one person's answer.

Graphs will vary.

Why We Chew Gum										
Enjoyment										
Tastes Good										
Helps Concentration										
Freshens Breath										
Cleans Teeth										
	1	2	3	4	5	6	7	8	9	10

Compile your information and make a group graph.

Page 273

Central America

The land connecting North and South America is called Central America. This is where Costa Rica and six other countries are located. Follow the directions below to label the countries and some of their products.

1. Draw a cotton plant in Belize. It's the northernmost country.
2. Draw a cotton plant in Guatemala. It borders Belize.
3. El Salvador grows many coffee beans. Draw a cup of coffee in this country that is southeast of Guatemala.
4. Silver is mined in Honduras, north of El Salvador. Color this country silver.
5. Nicaragua contains gold mines. Color this country bordering Honduras gold.
6. Children from Costa Rica love the bananas grown there. Draw a banana.
7. Panama's fishermen catch many shrimp. Draw some shrimp in this southernmost country. If you look closely, you will see a break in the land through which ships can pass. This is the Panama Canal. Label it also.

The U.S. helped clear the land that was once where the canal is now. Why do you think they wanted to help? Write your answer on the back of this paper.

Page 274

The Emerald Isle

Ireland is often called the Emerald Isle because of its rolling green farmland and countryside. This is why we wear green on St. Patrick's Day, an Irish holiday. Sean and Kathleen want you to follow the directions below to make today a special Irish day.

Answers will vary.

1. Write the name of three crayons that have a green tint. _____
2. Name two people wearing green today. _____
3. Write three words you can spell with the letters in IRELAND. _____
4. Write the title of a book that has the word *green* in it. _____
5. Name four green animals. _____
6. What do scientists call trees that stay green all winter? *evergreen*
7. List two things in your classroom that are entirely green.
8. Name your favorite green food.
9. Draw a leprechaun on the back of your paper.
10. Use only green crayons for the rest of the school day.

Page 275

Number, Please!

The population of Israel is a mixture of people from over 70 countries. Use the telephone puzzle below to dial and meet a few!

5397 = _Jews_ —the original people of Israel

1. 722727 = _Sabras_ —the Jews born in Israel
2. 6875467 = _Muslims_ —followers of Islam, the religion of 80% of the country's Arabs
3. 7253846426 27227 = _Palestinian Arabs_ —citizens of Israel who call themselves Israeli Arabs today
4. 378737 = _Druses_ —an Arabic-speaking religious group
5. 4664472687 = _immigrants_ —Jewish people from other countries making a new home in Israel

Now, write your country of origin using the same code. _____

Page 276

A Journey to Japan

Follow the directions to complete the map of Japan, Mieko's homeland.

1. Add the eight directional letters to the compass rose.
2. Label the islands in capital letters:
   KYUSHU – southernmost
   HOKKAIDO – northernmost
   HONSHU – south of Hokkaido
   SHIKOKU – north of Kyushu
3. Add a red ★ and label the capital city, Tokyo.
4. Draw a mountain at Mount Fuji's location.
5. Label Nagasaki by the dot on Kyushu Island.
6. Label the Sea of Japan and the Pacific Ocean. Add blue waves.
7. Label Osaka by the dot on Honshu Island.
8. Outline the islands in these colors:
   Hokkaido – orange
   Honshu – green
   Shikoku – red
   Kyushu – yellow
9. Along the northern edge of the box, label the map JAPAN, using a different color for each letter.
10. Draw the flag of Japan.

Page 277

Written Japanese

When Laura visited a Japanese classroom, she could not read anything that was written. She learned that written Japanese is considered to be one of the most difficult writing systems in the world. It is a combination of Japanese phonetic symbols as well as Chinese characters. Each character is a symbol that stands for a complete word or syllable. However difficult, almost all Japanese people 15 years of age or older can read and write.

Use the following Japanese characters to write a story about a big man. Use the characters in your story whenever possible.

大	人	木	森	山	門
big	man	tree	forest	mountain	gate

The 大 人

Stories will vary.

Page 278

Raising a Family in Kenya

As members of the more progressive Njoroge Tribe, Omar's parents have a dream. They want to see their four children through secondary school. That will require great sacrifice for them. Omar's coffee crop only earned them $120 after expenses last year.

Omar and his family live a very simple life. Omar's father raises coffee plants on their one-acre farm. Omar's mother and father work very hard to earn the money to send Omar and his brother and two sisters to school. It costs $75 a year for primary school for each child. To earn more money, Omar's father works as a stonemason for $5 a day. Omar's mother works at a larger farm for $2 a day.

1. How many days will Omar's father have to work as a stonemason to pay for one year of one child's primary school? (Hint: Count by 5's.) _15_
2. How many days will Omar's father have to work to pay for the other 3 children's primary school each year? (Hint: Add your answer from #1 three times.) _45_
3. One pair of children's shoes cost $10. How many days does Omar's mother have to work to buy him a pair of shoes? (Hint: Count by 2's.) _5_
4. How many days will Omar's mother have to work to buy the other 3 children new pairs of shoes? (Hint: Add your answer to #3 three times.) _15_
5. How much will it cost to buy shoes for all four children. (Hint: Count by 10's.) _$40_

Page 279

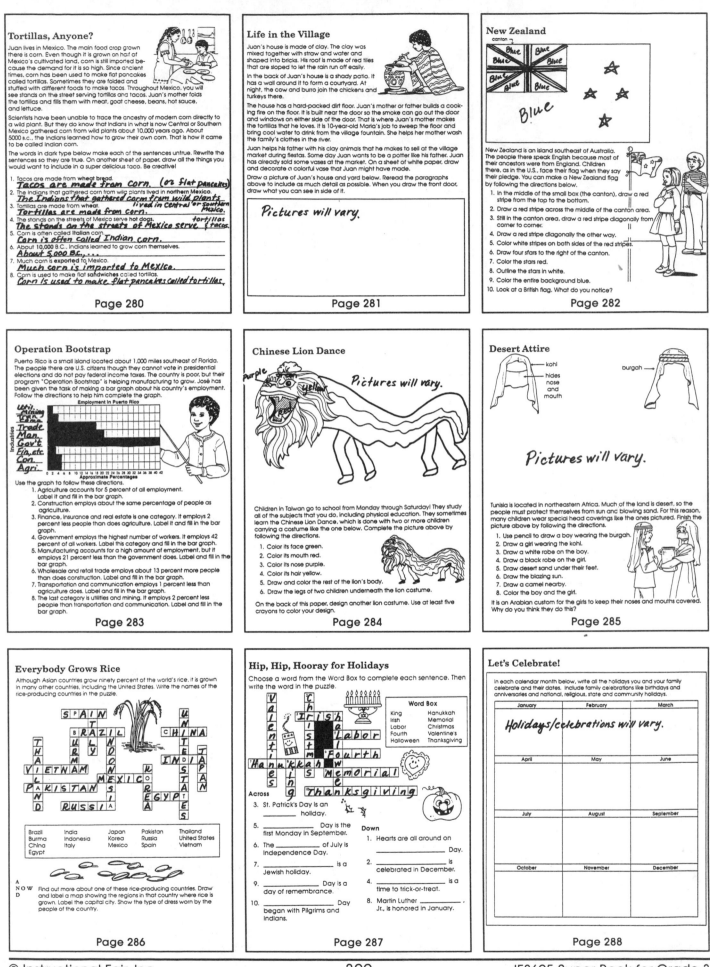

Tortillas, Anyone?

Juan lives in Mexico. The main food crop grown there is corn. Even though it is grown on half of Mexico's cultivated land, corn is still imported because the demand for it is so high. Since ancient times, corn has been used to make flat pancakes called tortillas. Sometimes they are folded and stuffed with different foods to make tacos. Throughout Mexico, you will see stands on the street serving tortillas and tacos. Juan's mother folds the tortillas and fills them with meat, goat cheese, beans, hot sauce, and lettuce.

Scientists have been unable to trace the ancestry of modern corn directly to a wild plant. But they do know that Indians in what is now Central or Southern Mexico gathered corn from wild plants about 10,000 years ago. About 5000 B.C., the Indians learned how to grow their own corn. That is how it came to be called Indian corn.

The words in dark type below make each of the sentences untrue. Rewrite the sentences so they are true. On another sheet of paper, draw all the things you would want to include in a super delicious taco. Be creative!

1. Tacos are made from **wheat bread**.
   Tacos are made from corn. (or flat pancakes)
2. The Indians that gathered corn from wild plants lived in **northern Mexico**.
   The Indians that gathered corn from wild plants lived in Central or Southern Mexico.
3. Tortillas are made from **wheat**.
   Tortillas are made from corn.
4. The stands on the streets of Mexico serve **hot dogs**.
   The stands on the streets of Mexico serve tortillas & tacos.
5. Corn is often called **Italian** corn.
   Corn is often called Indian corn.
6. About **10,000 B.C.**, Indians learned to grow corn themselves.
   About 5,000 B.C.,...
7. Much corn is **exported** to Mexico.
   Much corn is imported to Mexico.
8. Corn is used to make flat **sandwiches** called tortillas.
   Corn is used to make flat pancakes called tortillas.

Page 280

Life in the Village

Juan's house is made of clay. The clay was mixed together with straw and water and shaped into bricks. His roof is made of red tiles that are sloped to let the rain run off easily.

In the back of Juan's house is a shady patio. It has a wall around it to form a courtyard. At night, the cow and burro join the chickens and turkeys there.

The house has a hard-packed dirt floor. Juan's mother or father builds a cooking fire on the floor. It is built near the door so the smoke can go out the door and windows on either side of the door. That is where Juan's mother makes the tortillas that he loves. It is 10-year-old Maria's job to sweep the floor and bring cool water to drink from the village fountain. She helps her mother wash the family's clothes in the river.

Juan helps his father with his clay animals that he makes to sell at the village market during fiestas. Some day Juan wants to be a potter like his father. Juan has already sold some vases at the market. On a sheet of white paper, draw and decorate a colorful vase that Juan might have made.

Draw a picture of Juan's house and yard below. Reread the paragraphs above to include as much detail as possible. When you draw the front door, draw what you can see in side of it.

Pictures will vary.

Page 281

New Zealand

Blue (labels)

New Zealand is an island southeast of Australia. The people there speak English because most of their ancestors were from England. Children there, as in the U.S., face their flag when they say their pledge. You can make a New Zealand flag by following the directions below.

1. In the middle of the small box (the canton), draw a red stripe from the top to the bottom.
2. Draw a red stripe across the middle of the canton area.
3. Still in the canton area, draw a red stripe diagonally from corner to corner.
4. Draw a red stripe diagonally the other way.
5. Color white stripes on both sides of the red stripes.
6. Draw four red stars to the right of the canton.
7. Color the stars red.
8. Outline the stars in white.
9. Color the entire background blue.
10. Look at a British flag. What do you notice?

Page 282

Operation Bootstrap

Puerto Rico is a small island located about 1,000 miles southeast of Florida. The people there are U.S. citizens though they cannot vote in presidential elections and do not pay federal income taxes. The country is poor, but their program "Operation Bootstrap" is helping manufacturing to grow. José has been given the task of making a bar graph about his country's employment. Follow the directions to help him complete the graph.

Employment in Puerto Rico

Use the graph to follow these directions.

1. Agriculture accounts for 5 percent of all employment. Label it and fill in the bar graph.
2. Construction employs about the same percentage of people as agriculture.
3. Finance, insurance and real estate is one category. It employs 2 percent less people than does agriculture. Label it and fill in the bar graph.
4. Government employs the highest number of workers. It employs 42 percent of all workers. Label this category and fill in the bar graph.
5. Manufacturing accounts for a high amount of employment, but it employs 21 percent less than the government does. Label and fill in the bar graph.
6. Wholesale and retail trade employs about 13 percent more people than does construction. Label and fill in the bar graph.
7. Transportation and communication employs 1 percent less than agriculture. Label and fill in the bar graph.
8. The last category is utilities and mining. It employs 2 percent less people than transportation and communication. Label and fill in the bar graph.

Page 283

Chinese Lion Dance

Pictures will vary.

Children in Taiwan go to school from Monday through Saturday! They study all of the subjects that you do, including physical education. They sometimes learn the Chinese Lion Dance, which is done with two or more children carrying a costume like the one below. Complete the picture above by following the directions.

1. Color its face green.
2. Color its mouth red.
3. Color its nose purple.
4. Color its hair yellow.
5. Draw and color the rest of the lion's body.
6. Draw the legs of two children underneath the lion costume.

On the back of this paper, design another lion costume. Use at least five crayons to color your design.

Page 284

Desert Attire

kohl / hides nose and mouth / burgah (labels)

Pictures will vary.

Tunisia is located in northeastern Africa. Much of the land is desert, so the people must protect themselves from sun and blowing sand. For this reason, many children wear special head coverings like the ones pictured. Finish the picture above by following the directions.

1. Use pencil to draw a boy wearing the burgah.
2. Draw a girl wearing the kohl.
3. Draw a white robe on the boy.
4. Draw a black robe on the girl.
5. Draw desert sand under their feet.
6. Draw the blazing sun.
7. Draw a camel nearby.
8. Color the boy and the girl.

It is an Arabian custom for the girls to keep their noses and mouths covered. Why do you think they do this?

Page 285

Everybody Grows Rice

Although Asian countries grow ninety percent of the world's rice, it is grown in many other countries, including the United States. Write the names of the rice-producing countries in the puzzle.

SPAIN / BRAZIL / CHINA / ITALY / INDONESIA / JAPAN / THAILAND / VIETNAM / MEXICO / INDIA / KOREA / PAKISTAN / EGYPT / BURMA / RUSSIA

Brazil	India	Japan	Pakistan	Thailand
Burma	Indonesia	Korea	Russia	United States
China	Italy	Mexico	Spain	Vietnam
Egypt				

A NOW D Find out more about one of these rice-producing countries. Draw and label a map showing the regions in that country where rice is grown. Label the capital city. Show the type of dress worn by the people of the country.

Page 286

Hip, Hip, Hooray for Holidays

Choose a word from the Word Box to complete each sentence. Then write the word in the puzzle.

Word Box
King / Hanukkah / Irish / Memorial / Labor / Christmas / Fourth / Valentine's / Halloween / Thanksgiving

Valentine's / Irish / Christmas / Labor / Fourth / Hanukkah / Memorial / Thanksgiving (puzzle answers)

Across
3. St. Patrick's Day is an _____ holiday.
5. _____ Day is the first Monday in September.
6. The _____ of July is Independence Day.
7. _____ is a Jewish holiday.
9. _____ Day is a day of remembrance.
10. _____ Day began with Pilgrims and Indians.

Down
1. Hearts are all around on _____ Day.
2. _____ is celebrated in December.
4. _____ is a time to trick-or-treat.
8. Martin Luther _____ Jr., is honored in January.

Page 287

Let's Celebrate!

In each calendar month below, write all the holidays you and your family celebrate and their dates. Include family celebrations like birthdays and anniversaries and national, religious, state and community holidays.

Holidays/celebrations will vary.

January	February	March
April	May	June
July	August	September
October	November	December

Page 288